Social Transformations

Social Transformations

A General Theory
of Historical Development

Expanded Edition

Stephen K. Sanderson

ROWMAN & LITTLEFIELD PUBLISHERS, INC.
Lanham • Boulder • New York • Oxford

ROWMAN & LITTLEFIELD PUBLISHERS, INC.

Published in the United States of America
by Rowman & Littlefield Publishers, Inc.
4720 Boston Way, Lanham, Maryland 20706

12 Hid's Copse Road
Cumnor Hill, Oxford OX2 9JJ, England

British Library Cataloguing in Publication Information Available

Library of Congress Cataloging-in-Publication Data

Sanderson, Stephen K.
    Social transformations : a general theory of historical
development, expanded edition / Stephen K. Sanderson.
        p.   cm.
    "Expanded ed."
    Includes bibliographical references.
    ISBN 0-8476-9187-X (cloth : alk. paper). — ISBN 0-8476-9188-8
(paper : alk. paper)
    1. Social evolution.   2. Economic anthropology.   3. Capitalism.
I. Title.
GN360.S2652   1999
303.4—dc21   99-11557
                                                                 CIP

Printed in the United States of America

♾ ™ The paper used in this publication meets the minimum requirements of
American National Standard for Information Sciences—Permanence of Paper for
Printed Library Materials, ANSI Z39.48–1992.

For Gerhard Lenski, Marvin Harris,
and Immanuel Wallerstein

Contents

Preface

This book is intended to finish the task begun in my *Social Evolutionism* (Blackwell, 1990). In that book, one of my main aims was to clear away a great deal of theoretical debris concerning theories of social evolution. In sketching and critically analyzing the historical development of evolutionary theories I hoped to show that many myths and misconceptions had accumulated in regard to them. I attacked these myths and misconceptions and tried to show that an evolutionary interpretation of world history was both possible and desirable. *Social Transformations* formulates such an interpretation, which I refer to by the name of evolutionary materialism, and applies it to what I regard as the world's most important historical transformations: the Neolithic Revolution, the origin of civilization and the state, and the transformation that ushered in the modern world, the transition from feudalism to capitalism in western Europe and Japan. Since this book's aim is that of articulating and empirically testing a general theory of social evolution, I have had to read extensively in the various literatures of the leading historically minded social sciences, mainly archaeology, history, and historical sociology. Unless one plans to spend the better part of a lifetime on such a project, one can attempt to cope with only so many historical details. Therefore, I hope that specialists in these fields and their many subfields will be tolerant of the inevitable limits of my knowledge of their particular specialty, judging the book in terms of the aim of producing a coherent picture of the general lines of world history rather than subtle and nuanced accounts of specific historical and prehistorical events.

The subtitle of the book, "A General Theory of Historical Development," was chosen in preference to the subtitle considered first

("A General Theory of Social Evolution") because I wish to emphasize that the book is concerned only with the broad outlines of social evolution (parallel and convergent evolution) rather than with divergent evolutionary processes. Nonetheless, the theory developed here may properly be regarded as a general theory of evolution that has applicability to all evolutionary processes.

I am grateful to many individuals who read and commented on various portions of the manuscript and who made helpful suggestions for improving it: Christopher Chase-Dunn, Randall Collins, Ray Scupin, Thomas Conelly, Victor Garcia, Christopher DeCorse, Peter Peregrine, Gary Leupp, Jonathan Turner, Immanuel Wallerstein, Walter Goldfrank, Thomas Hall, Larry Miller, and Dick Betlem. I express my thanks to my university, Indiana University of Pennsylvania, for granting me a sabbatical leave during the Spring 1994 semester so that I could devote myself full-time to finishing this book. I also wish to acknowledge Mary Sampson and the staff of the Interlibrary Loan Office at IUP. They acquired for me many books and articles necessary to the completion of this book, and they did so cheerfully and expeditiously. Finally, I am grateful to John Davey for agreeing to have another of my books published by Blackwell.

I have dedicated this book to Gerhard Lenski, Marvin Harris, and Immanuel Wallerstein, because they are the scholars who have influenced my thinking the most. Lenski first pointed me in the direction of doing sociology in comparative, evolutionary, and materialist terms. Harris then showed how such an approach could be developed in a very elaborate and detailed way. Finally, Wallerstein added a critically important dimension necessary to understanding the development of the modern world, that of the world-system as a single evolving unit.

Some of the materials in this book have been previously published. Most of chapter 1 appeared as "Evolutionary materialism: a theoretical strategy for the study of social evolution," in *Sociological Perspectives*, vol. 37, no. 1, 1994. Portions of chapter 4 appeared as "Expanding world commercialization: the link between world-systems and civilizations," in *Comparative Civilizations Review*, no. 30, 1994. Portions of chapters 4 and 5 appeared as "The transition from feudalism to capitalism: the theoretical significance of the Japanese case," in *Review*, vol. XVII, no. 1, 1994. I am grateful to the editors of these journals for granting permission to use the contents of those articles in this book.

Figure 7.1 is reprinted from "The world-economy and the institutionalization of science in seventeenth-century Europe," by Robert Wuthnow, which appeared in *Studies of the Modern World-System*, copyright © 1980 edited by Albert Bergesen, with permission from Robert Wuthnow and Academic Press, San Diego, California.

Figures 9.1 and 9.2 are reprinted from *Beyond the Limits*, copyright © 1992 by Meadows, Meadows, and Randers, with permission from Chelsea Publishing Co., White River Junction, Vermont.

A note on chronologies: The expressions "BP," "BC," and "AD" are all used in this book. BP, which stands for "Before the Present," has become standard usage among archaeologists and is used to represent prehistoric dates. BC is most commonly used by historians and historical sociologists and is used when historical rather than prehistoric dates are being referred to. BC dates can be converted to BP dates by adding 2000, BP dates converted to BC dates by subtracting 2000.

Preface to the Expanded Edition

In 1977 I began the study of long-term social evolution in earnest, and by 1995 I had formulated a general theory of social evolution—evolutionary materialism—which is the focus of this book. However, I had always hoped to be able to bring biological evolution, in particular sociobiology, into the picture and formulate an even more general theory of human society. My first attempts at this were unsuccessful, but in recent years my ideas along this line have come together and gelled. The result is a new theory, which I call *synthetic materialism*, that includes evolutionary materialism as a special case. A full-scale book presenting this theory along with detailed supporting empirical evidence will eventually be published, but at this point the theory exists only in the form of conference papers. The willingness of Rowman and Littlefield to reprint *Social Transformations* gives me a greatly desired opportunity to present an abbreviated version of synthetic materialism and to make explicit the links between it and evolutionary materialism. Therefore this expanded edition of *Social Transformations* contains an afterword that attempts to accomplish these things.

1

Evolutionary Materialism: A General Theory of Historical Development

Numerous theoretical approaches to social evolution have been developed within the social sciences over the past century and a half. These approaches vary greatly in terms of their underlying assumptions, explanatory logic, and many other dimensions, and all have strengths and weaknesses (Sanderson, 1990). But even the best of these approaches, which I believe to be Marvin Harris's (1968, 1977, 1979) cultural materialist version of social evolutionism, suffers to some extent from a failure to apply adequately to the full range of world historical phenomena. Harris's materialist evolutionism is exceptionally well suited to deal with the kinds of evolutionary phenomena of most concern to anthropologists and archaeologists: for example, the origins of agriculture, the emergence of social stratification, and the evolution of chiefdoms and states. However, it is somewhat less capable of coming to grips with those evolutionary events that most interest historians and sociologists, which generally concern evolutionary events that occur within complex agrarian civilizations and modern world capitalism and industrialism: the rise and fall of dynasties, the commercialization of agrarian states, the rise of Europe to world dominance after the sixteenth century, or the evolution of the contemporary world economic system. Cultural materialism's principles are perhaps overly general when it comes to more complex societies. Although historians and sociologists have often done a better job of explaining these kinds of phenomena, they have unfortunately not done very well with just those things at which Harris and other anthropologists have succeeded. What is needed, I believe, is a comprehensive theoretical model that can successfully explain all of the important evolutionary events revealed by world history.

This book is intended to fill this need. In this chapter I set forth a formalized version of such a model, which I call by the name of *evolutionary materialism*, and in the remaining chapters I apply it to the most crucial evolutionary events in world history: the worldwide origin of agriculture after 10,000 years ago, the worldwide transition to civilization and the state after some 5,000 years ago, the evolutionary dynamics of agrarian civilizations, the rise of modern capitalism in western Europe and Japan after approximately 500 years ago, the evolution of the modern world-system in which most of the world's societies now participate, and the emergence of the basic institutional features of modernity. The main parent theoretical tradition of evolutionary materialism is Harris's cultural materialism. However, evolutionary materialism also borrows extensively from various currents of contemporary Marxism, especially world-system theory, and blends in certain features of Weberian historical sociology, interpreted as a version of conflict theory à la Randall Collins (1975, 1986a, 1986b). A few other theoretical notions also go into the attempted synthesis. Evolutionary materialism is highly compatible with cultural materialism and in no way is intended as any sort of refutation, or even partial rejection, of it. Evolutionary materialism is essentially an extension of cultural materialism's theoretical logic, especially with respect to the analysis of complex agrarian and industrial societies.

Evolutionary materialism is an example of what I prefer to call a *theoretical strategy*, which is very similar to what others have variously called a *paradigm* (Kuhn, 1970), a *research tradition* (Laudan, 1977), or a *research strategy* (Harris, 1979). A theoretical strategy is a highly abstract set of assumptions, concepts, and principles designed to serve as a broad theoretical guide to explaining empirical reality. It functions as an orienting device for the formulation and empirical assessment of theories. As such, it contains numerous theories, which are limited and specific propositions (or sets of propositions) designed to explain specific phenomena. All of the theories within a given theoretical strategy are similar in that they spring from the same underlying foundations. However, these theories may be and sometimes are mutually contradictory. Commitment to a theoretical tradition does not imply commitment to any particular theory within that tradition. It is the theories that really count intellectually in the end, because it is they that are focused on the particular content of what we want to explain, and it is they that are directly subjected to empirical test. The theoretical strategies are tested, but only indirectly through the testing of their constituent theories. A good theoretical strategy is one that has generated many empirically successful theories and that is capable of being extended to larger and larger bodies of empirical phenomena. It should also be parsimonious – simple and economical in its employment of assumptions, concepts, and principles – and provide a coherent picture of the world in the sense that it brings into sharp relief the interconnectedness among the phenomena it studies. It should perhaps be stressed that, as I develop and apply it, evolutionary materialism is conceived to be primarily oriented to the study of long-term sociohistorical development, rather than to the myriad evolutionary events that form all of the many details of social evolution. I do believe that this strategy does have considerable applicability to the great variety of evolutionary events, at least in a general sort of way; but to be truly useful in this way various aspects of the approach would have to be worked out in more detail. As applied to long-term sociohistorical development, however, I think that evolutionary materialism is a remarkably comprehensive and useful guide. Or at least that is what I hope this book will ultimately be able to show.

The remainder of this chapter lays out evolutionary materialism as a theoretical strategy and outlines the world-historical phenomena to which this approach is then applied. In presenting the theory I mix in as needed various discussions that provide important background information for understanding parts of the theory. (In my *Social Evolutionism* [1990] extensive background discussions necessarily shortened dramatically here can be found. The relevant page numbers where the most pertinent discussions are located are indicated in brackets along with some of the theoretical propositions.)

THE THEORETICAL STRATEGY OF EVOLUTIONARY MATERIALISM

I THE NATURE OF WORLD HISTORY

A major bone of contention between sociologists and historians for most of the present century has been the degree to which human history reveals basic regularities. Sociologists have usually lined up on the nomothetic side of the matter, holding that history reveals many regularities that can be understood in terms of general theories, whereas historians have generally opted for an idiographic or particularist stance in which few historical regularities are seen and general theories are strongly eschewed. Social evolutionists have, even more than most sociologists, subscribed to the view of regularized developmental trends in history. In recent years there has been an idiographic turn even in sociology (especially in historical sociology) and such well-known sociologists as Robert Nisbet (1969) and Michael Mann (1986) have argued against evolutionary interpretations. In contrast to thcm, I am led to assert Proposition I.1:

> I.1 *World history reveals social transformations and directional trends of sufficient generality such that typologies of social forms can be fruitfully constructed. These directional sequences of change constitute the bulk of what is known as social evolution. Social evolutionists concentrate on general and repeatable patterns of social evolution, i.e., on parallel and convergent evolution. (Parallel evolution involves directional sequences in which two or more societies evolve along similar lines and at similar rates; convergent evolution occurs when two or more societies that are initially dissimilar evolve in a manner so as to become increasingly similar.) However, good social evolutionists show due respect for the unique and nonrecurrent in world history. The unique and nonrecurrent may legitimately be called social evolution (i.e., divergent evolution) so long as they mark out a directional sequence. Divergent evolution should be explained by using the same general explanatory principles designed to explain parallel and convergent evolution. [Social Evolutionism (SE), pp. 216–19, and passim.]*

It is frequently charged that evolutionary theories are falsified by the fact that social stasis or continuity is a more common phenomenon than evolutionary change (Nisbet, 1969), or by the existence of various forms of sociocultural regression or extinction (cf. Tainter, 1988). However, in contrast to such arguments, I present Proposition I.2:

> I.2 *Social stasis, devolution, and extinction are basic facts of world history that should not be ignored by evolutionary theory. Stasis involves the preservation of the basic social patterns of a social system; devolution involves a retrogression to an earlier historical state or evolutionary stage; extinction involves the elimin-*

ation of the basic patterns of a social system, either through the death of its members or its absorption into another social system. Stasis, devolution, and extinction do not undermine an evolutionary interpretation of world history, and themselves should be explained in terms of the same general evolutionary principles that explain parallel, convergent, and divergent evolution.

A great deal of discussion in regard to evolutionary theories has concerned whether these theories are teleological or developmentalist in nature, that is, whether they assume that directional patterns of social change represent the automatic unfolding of inherent tendencies toward some preordained goal or endpoint. The philosopher of history Maurice Mandelbaum (1971), for example, has asserted that evolutionary theories are by their very nature teleological or developmentalist, and the sociologists Robert Nisbet (1969) and Anthony Giddens (1981, 1984), along with numerous others, have made similar claims. However, such a view is, when not downright wrong, a clear exaggeration, virtually a caricature. Most recent social evolutionists have not been developmentalists or teleologists, and certainly social evolution is not a teleological process. This leads to Proposition I.3:

I.3 World-historical transformations, whether parallel, convergent, or divergent evolution, are not the unfolding of predetermined patterns; that is, they are not developmentalist or teleological processes. Instead, they represent the grand aggregation and multiplication of the actions of individuals and groups in concrete historical circumstances as these individuals are responding to a multiplicity of biological, psychological, and social needs (see Section III). Social evolution is to be accounted for by using the sorts of ordinary causal explanations that are basic to science as a mode of inquiry. [SE, pp. 16–27, 54–9, 64–8, 113–16, and 124–6]

II THE SUBSTANCE OF SOCIAL EVOLUTION

The nature of social evolution and the types of units within which it occurs is specified in Proposition II.1:

II.1 Social evolution involves processes that occur within social systems of all levels, e.g., dyads, age sets, kinship groups, social classes, complex organizations, societies, any of the institutional sectors of societies, and various types of intersocietal networks. Although it is studied mostly at a macrosociological *level, evolutionary events occur also at the simplest microsociological levels. Macrolevel social evolution represents the temporal and spatial aggregation of microlevel evolutionary events.*

Recent evolutionists within the functionalist tradition (especially Talcott Parsons [1966, 1971]), and even evolutionists outside that tradition (especially Robert Carneiro [1972]), frequently claim that the evolutionary process is essentially one of increasing social complexity or differentiation. However, not all evolutionary theories focus on differentiation as the great evolutionary trend, nor is increasing differentiation necessarily the most important component of the evolutionary process. Accordingly, Proposition II.2 reads:

II.2   *Increasing social complexity or differentiation is a basic evolutionary process. However, much social evolution involves transformations that have little or nothing to do with differentiation, and dedifferentiation is an important evolutionary (actually, devolutionary) phenomenon. Differentiation is only one of many important evolutionary processes. [SE, pp. 119–20 and 190–5]*

A great deal of attention has been devoted over many years to discussing social evolution by means of an analogy with biological evolution. In a textbook discussion of social evolutionism, for example, Randall Collins (1988) seems to suggest that biological evolutionism ought to serve as some sort of model for social evolutionists. In view of these considerations, I offer Propositions II.3 through II.6:

II.3   *Social evolution is both analogous and disanalogous to biological evolution. The major similarities between social and biological evolution concern the fact that both are adaptational processes (see Section IV), as well as the fact that both exhibit both general (parallel and convergent) and specific (divergent) sequences of change. [SE, pp. 169–208]*

II.4   *The basic differences between social and biological evolution are [SE, pp. 169–208]:*

(a)   *Biological evolution consists mainly of divergent evolution (cladogenesis), whereas social evolution is more frequently parallel and convergent evolution.*

(b) *The genetic variations that provide the basis for biological evolution arise randomly, but the variations in human thought and action on which social evolutionary selection operates arise primarily in a deliberate and purposive manner (there is no strict equivalent of genetic mutation in social evolution).*

(c) *As a consequence of (a) and (b), if we started biological evolution all over again we would get very different results; however, if we started social evolution all over again we would get very similar results (social evolution therefore has a predictive quality that is lacking in biological evolution).*

(d) *Social evolution is extremely rapid compared to biological evolution (even allowing for "punctuationalist" bioevolutionary changes).*

(e) *The social evolutionary process of diffusion has no counterpart in the organic world.*

(f) *Natural selection operates to a substantial extent in social evolution, but as such is only a process, not an actual cause of evolution; social evolutionists cannot stop their analyses with the identification of social evolution as a process of natural selection, but must go on to identify the specific causal factors that operate within the context of the process of natural selection.*

II.5 *The differences between social and biological evolution are great enough to require that social evolution be studied as a process in its own right, and not merely along the lines of an analogy with biological evolution.* [SE, pp. 170–4]

II.6 *Coevolution, or the simultaneous evolution of genes and social patterns, must be acknowledged as a process of some significance. However, most social evolution neither produces nor results from significant changes in gene frequencies, and therefore is independent of biological evolution.* [SE, pp. 174–80]

In nineteenth-century evolutionary theories, and in some evolutionary theories developed earlier in the twentieth century, social evolution was often seen as a process closely akin to, and in fact intertwined with, the psychological development of the individual. In the twentieth century Lucien Lévy-Bruhl (1923) has been the foremost proponent of this idea. However, in contrast Proposition II.7 states:

II.7 *Social evolution is a process entirely separate from the psychological development of individuals. Any analogies that might be drawn between social evolution and individual psychological development are artificial and cannot imply any causal connection between the two kinds of processes.* [SE, pp. 215–16]

III   THE PRINCIPAL CAUSAL FACTORS IN SOCIAL EVOLUTION

Evolutionary theories have differed greatly in terms of the basic causal mechanisms they espouse. The nineteenth-century theories of Lewis Henry Morgan (1974[1877]) and Edward Burnett Tylor (1871, 1916) were somewhat eclectic, but with a strong tendency toward theoretical idealism. Herbert Spencer (Peel, ed., 1972) was a materialist who emphasized population growth, warfare, and economic factors. In the twentieth century there is also a considerable mixture of theories. Of the two best-known twentieth-century theories developed by sociologists, one (that of Talcott Parsons [1966, 1971]) is strongly idealist, while the other (that of Gerhard Lenski [1966, 1970]) is decidedly materialist. By and large, in the twentieth century materialist theories have dominated. The revivers of evolutionism after the long period of Boasian antievolutionism between the 1890s and the 1940s – V. Gordon Childe (1936, 1951, 1954), Leslie White (1943, 1959), and Julian Steward (1949, 1955) – were strong materialists, with Childe and White emphasizing the causal role of technological advance and Steward emphasizing the role of ecology. Students and followers of these thinkers – in particular Robert Carneiro (1970, 1981), Marshall Sahlins (1958, 1960), and Marvin Harris (1968, 1977, 1979) – have also been materialists. Harris has been the most vigorous champion of materialism, emphasizing the combined or individual effect of four kinds of material conditions: technology, economics, ecology, and demography. My theory follows in the evolutionary tradition of Harris. It sets forth as its chief causal arguments Propositions III.1 through III.5:

III.1   *The principal causal factors in social evolution are the material conditions of human existence, i.e., the demographic, ecological, technological, and economic forces at work in social life. Demographic factors basically concern variations in human population, especially the growth and pressure of population on vital resources. Ecological factors involve all aspects of the natural or physical environment, especially as these interact with technology and demography. Technological factors are those related to the inventory of knowledge, tools, and techniques available to the members of a society or other sociocultural system. Economic factors relate to the modes of social organization whereby people produce, distribute, and exchange goods and services; an especially important dimension of economics is the nature of the ownership of the basic means of production.* [SE, pp. 153–66]

III.2 *These causal factors operate probabilistically – in the long run and over the majority of cases – and allowance is made for "superstructural feedback." No claim is being made that the material conditions of human existence totally determine the trajectories of social evolution. Nonmaterial factors play a role in evolutionary processes, even if ordinarily in a highly secondary way.*

III.3 *The material conditions of human existence have the causal significance they do because they relate to basic human needs concerning the production of subsistence and the reproduction of human life. Human needs relating to production and reproduction have an "ontological priority" that translates into a causal priority.*

III.4 *Which of the material conditions of human existence, or which combination of these conditions, is most causally important varies from one historical period and evolutionary stage to another, and therefore cannot be stated on a priori grounds. The precise identification of the causal significance of the material conditions of human existence, alone or in particular combinations, is a matter for empirical study.*

III.5 *Different types of social systems in different historical epochs and at different evolutionary stages embody different "evolutionary logics." The driving engines of social evolution differ from one social-systemic type (historical epoch, evolutionary stage) to another. There is no such thing as a universal cause of social evolution. The causes of social evolution are themselves evolving phenomena.*

IV   THE ADAPTATIONAL CHARACTER OF SOCIAL EVOLUTION

At the very heart of debates about social evolutionary theories has been the concept of adaptation. Irving Zeitlin (1973) and Anthony Giddens (1981, 1984) have correctly pointed out that this concept usually figures prominently in theories of social evolution, even those that may otherwise be quite disparate. Zeitlin and Giddens, as do other social theorists, link the concept of adaptation with functionalism, and, since they are antifunctionalists, recommend the abandonment of this concept. My own view is that the concept, while often problematic, can be reformulated so as to rid it of functionalist baggage; it can be rehabilitated and made into an extremely useful point of departure for theories of social evolution. With respect to the concept of adaptation, I submit Propositions IV.1 through IV.10. [I would strongly recommend the reader consult my discussions of this concept in SE, pp. 97–8, 108–9, 120–1, and 180–90. It might also be desirable to go back to some of the original sources cited in these discussions.]

IV.1   *Much of social evolution results from adaptational processes. The concept of adaptation is therefore a useful starting point for evolutionary analyses. Even when evolutionary events are not adaptational, the concept retains a heuristic significance because it helps us gain more insight into evolutionary phenomena than would otherwise be possible.*

IV.2   *Adaptation must be sharply distinguished from adaptedness. Adaptation is the process whereby individuals originate (inherit, borrow) social patterns that are devoted to meeting various of their needs and wants (it refers to the origin or persistence of a social pattern). Adaptedness involves the extent to which a social pattern actually benefits the individuals who originated (inherited, borrowed) it. That is, it refers to the consequences of a social pattern, whether that pattern is an adaptation or not).*

IV.3   *Although adaptations frequently lead to adaptedness, there are numerous instances in which this is not the case. Although adaptations must logically create adaptedness (or at least the perception of adaptedness) in the short run (otherwise they could not exist as adaptations), in the longer run this adaptedness may disappear and even lapse into maladaptedness.*

IV.4   *The extent to which adaptations lead to adaptedness varies greatly from one set of individuals and from one time to another. The more complex and unequal a society, the more this rule of thumb applies. Adaptations that are adaptive for the members of dominant groups may be nonadaptive or maladaptive for the members of subordinate groups. A social pattern that is adaptive for the members of one group at one time may become nonadaptive or maladaptive for the members of that same group at another time, and vice versa.*

IV.5   *Adaptation is a process pertaining to individuals and never* to any social unit larger than the individual. Social groups and societies cannot be adaptational units because they are only abstractions. Only concrete, flesh-and-blood individuals can be adaptational units because only they have needs and wants. Any social pattern that might be said to be adaptive for a group or society as a whole is so only because it is adaptive for all (or nearly all) of the individuals within that group or society. Patterns that are adaptive for groups or societies are but statistical aggregations of individual adaptedness.

IV.6   Adaptations may arise in response to either the physical environment, the social environment, or both. Many adaptations arise in response to any number of features of the total social environment. The total social environment exerts powerful constraints on the nature of the adaptations that are likely to arise. The total social environment makes some adaptations possible or likely and renders others impossible or unlikely.

IV.7   When identifying a social unit as an adaptation, it is incumbent upon the social scientist to specify the sense in which it is an adaptation. That is, the social scientist must specify the particular needs or combination of needs that provide the basis for the origin of an alleged adaptation.

IV.8   Individuals who originate (inherit, borrow) adaptations are not necessarily engaging in a process of attempted optimization. Individuals are frequently content with a satisfactory, rather than an optimal, way of meeting their needs and wants. In other words, adaptations are often (probably most often) the products of satisficing rather than optimizing behaviors.

IV.9   The concept of adaptation implies no universal tendency toward human mastery that is the driving engine of social evolution. This drive is absent in many preindustrial societies, where a "technological inertia" commonly prevails. When a drive for mastery exists in a human social system, it is a culturally conditioned motive rather than a universal human biopsychological drive. If such a culturally conditioned motive exists in a social system, it will constitute a powerful adaptational mechanism driving social evolution at that particular time and place. A drive for mastery establishes a goal or set of goals to which the adaptational behaviors of particular persons are strongly directed.

IV.10   *Given no transcendent human drive for mastery involved in social evolution, new social forms cannot be regarded as higher on some proposed scale of adaptedness. Adaptedness is not a quality that necessarily increases or improves throughout social evolution. New social forms are adaptations to local conditions and lead to adaptedness only relative to those immediate conditions (rather than in some general or absolute sense). Social evolution is not to be taken as equivalent to, or necessarily even indicative of, social progress. Social evolution produces outcomes that may be evaluatively progressive, regressive, or neutral. Some criteria exist for the objective assessment of social progress or regression, but to a large extent assessments of progress can be made only in evaluative (rather than theoretical or empirical) terms.*

V   AGENCY AND STRUCTURE IN SOCIAL EVOLUTION

The debate over the role of structure and agency in human society has been at the forefront of discussions among social theorists in recent years, and it cannot be denied that the issue is a vital one. Perhaps no one has contributed more than Anthony Giddens (1984) to bringing this issue to our attention. Giddens argues that good social theory recognizes the continuous interplay between structure and agency, and properly so. However, he seems to go overboard in characterizing some social theories as heavily biased in the direction of structure. He considers Marxism, as well as evolutionism, as giving virtually all the weight to structure and none to the role of humans as active creators of their world. I would argue that this presents a distorted picture. While evolutionary theories on the surface may seem to be biased toward structure, and while some of them (such as Leslie White's) actually are biased in this way, a closer look will reveal that most contemporary evolutionary theories give due weight to agency – perhaps not enough for Giddens's taste, but there is a conception of agency nonetheless. I think the claim can be supported that two of the most successful recent theories, those of Lenski and Harris, are in fact operating with a conception of the continuous dialectical interplay of structure and agency. This leads to four basic propositions, V.1 through V.4 [SE, pp. 212–15]:

V.1   *Human individuals are egoistic beings who are highly moti-vated to satisfy their own needs and wants. They seek to behave adaptively by maximizing the benefits and minimizing the costs of any course of action (or at least generating more benefits than costs). This egoistic and adaptive behavior must be a central focus of evolutionary analysis. (It is crucial that a distinction be drawn between what might be called "phenotypic" and "genotypic" forms of both egoism and altruism [Durham, 1991]. Much human behavior is phenotypically altruistic or cooperative in the sense that other individuals benefit from this behavior. However, my argument is that the very behavior that is phenotypically altruistic is almost always genotypically selfish, that is, it is driven by motives that are purely egoistic. Human behavior includes large amounts of both phenotypic egoism and phenotypic altruism, but virtually all human behavior is egoistic at the genotypic level.)*

V.2 Nevertheless, individuals acting in their own interests create social structures and systems that are the sum total and product of these socially oriented individual actions. These social structures and systems are frequently constituted in ways that individuals never intended, and thus individually purposive human action leads to many unintended consequences. Social evolution is driven by purposive or intended human actions, but it is to a large extent not itself a purposive or intended phenomenon.

V.3 The social structures and systems that individuals create through their purposive action reflect back on these and other individuals in the sense that they create new sets of constraints within which individually purposive action must operate. Social evolution represents the long-term consequences of the dialectical interplay between human agency and social structure.

V.4 Human agency is never something that occurs "freely"; all purposive human action is constrained by both the biopsychological nature of human organisms and by the social structures that previous generations of individual actors created through their agency. Agency is therefore never to be taken as action that is "free" or "voluntary."

VI THE UNITS OF SOCIAL EVOLUTION

Evolutionary biologists are currently debating whether the basic unit of natural selection is the organism, the gene, the population, the species, or even some higher-order phenomenon. Most have come out in favor of selection operating either at the level of the organism or the gene. I myself regard selection at any level above the organism as incomprehensible within any natural selectionist framework that regards the intensely selfish struggle for survival as the driving force of evolution. Correlatively, I argue that there is no such thing as "group selection" in human societies. Nevertheless, it is groups and societies that do the actual evolving, even if only by virtue of selection and adaptation taking place at the level of individuals. It should be stressed that this position does not amount to methodological individualism in its most narrow sense because, as stated in Propositions V.2 and V.3, individuals pursuing courses of action inevitably create structures that further constrain action. It is those structures that evolve. Thus we have Proposition VI.1:

> VI.1 *Although individuals are the units of adaptation, they are not the units of actual evolution. The units of evolution are necessarily social groups, structures, and systems at all levels of size and complexity. It is they that evolve, even though they do so only through the purposive action of individuals.*

Sociologists have long debated the extent to which social change results from endogenous (internal) or exogenous (external) processes, and a frequent criticism of evolutionary theories is that they give far too much emphasis to endogenous mechanisms and processes, perhaps even ignoring exogenous processes altogether. This was, for example, a central argument in Nisbet's (1969) famous attempted demolition of evolutionary theories. The alleged endogenous nature of social evolutionism, though, is really a caricature, and there is no reason in principle why evolutionary theories cannot emphasize exogenous factors as much as, or even more than, endogenous ones. Indeed, the question arises, endogenous or exogenous *to what?* Followers of the work of Immanuel Wallerstein (1974a,b, 1979, 1980a, 1989) on world-system theory stress exogenous variables over endogenous ones, and some of these thinkers are trying to extend this kind of argument back into ancient history and prehistory, and thus to the study of long-term social evolution (cf. Chase-Dunn and Hall, eds, 1991). Accordingly, I offer Proposition VI.2, which stresses both endogenous and exogenous dimensions of social evolution:

> VI.2 *Much social evolution is endogenous to societies as politically and geographically bounded systems. However, societies are*

seldom closed off to interactions with, and influences from, other societies. Societies are frequently integrated into larger "world-networks" or "world-systems" that greatly affect their evolutionary dynamics. The possible existence of these intersocietal networks must always be taken into consideration in evolutionary analysis. Social evolution occurs both endogenously (as the result of forces within a society) and exogenously (as the result of intersocietal relations), and neither of these can be causally privileged on a priori grounds. Determining the balance of endogenous and exogenous evolutionary forces occurring at any given time and place is an empirical matter that must be pursued case by case. In some cases it is the intersocietal network that is the basic unit of social evolution, within which societies evolve only as parts of the whole. [SE, pp. 210–11]

VII THE PACE OF SOCIAL EVOLUTION

The recent debate over "gradualism" versus "punctuationalism" in biological evolutionism has had some spillover effect on discussions of social evolution. Randall Collins (1988), for instance, although not particularly sympathetic to evolutionism, nonetheless holds that if theories of social evolution are appropriate then they must be formulated in "punctuationalist" terms. However, punctuated equilibrium theory is still a minority view among evolutionary biologists, and its applicability to social evolution is very questionable. Clearly much social evolution is best characterized in gradualist terms. Taking a pluralistic position on this issue, I offer Propositions VII.1 and VII.2 [SE, pp. 207–8]:

VII.1 *Both "gradualist" and "punctuationalist" forms of change characterize social evolution. The pace of social evolution varies from one historical epoch and evolutionary stage to another, and is a matter for empirical study.*

VII.2 *Nonetheless, it is likely that social evolution at earlier historical periods and evolutionary stages is considerably slower and more gradualist than social evolution in more recent times and at later evolutionary stages. Social evolution is itself a process that evolves.*

VIII METHODS OF STUDYING SOCIAL EVOLUTION

A standard criticism of social evolutionism, made by Franz Boas (1940[1896]) and his fellow antievolutionists in the late nineteenth and early twentieth centuries, and repeated today by such contemporary antievolutionists as Nisbet (1969), is that it is invalidated by reliance upon an inappropriate methodology. This is the comparative method, which relies upon the ordering of synchronic data so as to make diachronic (evolutionary) inferences. However, this method has been defended by such recent evolutionists as Elman Service (1971) and Marvin Harris (1968), and is a perfectly legitimate method so long as certain precautions are taken. Moreover, in recent years the enormous growth of archaeological data has made the comparative method less necessary, and evolutionary reconstructions can be tested against detailed prehistoric sequences known archaeologically. Accordingly, the theory of evolutionary materialism sets forth four basic methodological claims [SE, pp. 37–41 and 211–12]:

VIII.1   *The comparative method is an important, and sometimes necessary, tool of evolutionary analysis. This method involves ordering synchronic data into typologies that are assumed to reflect an actual historical transition from one evolutionary stage to another. It is justified to the extent that an evolutionary typology can be independently corroborated by historical and prehistorical data.*

VIII.2   *For evolutionary analyses, diachronic (historical and prehistorical) data acquired by historians and archaeologists are generally to be preferred to synchronic data. The historical method is a more suitable method for evolutionary analysis when it can be employed.*

VIII.3   *Evolutionary analysis is not something separate and distinct from historical analysis. On the contrary, it is a form of historical analysis. Just as much as archaeologists and historians, social evolutionists must spend time analyzing concrete historical and prehistorical cases in detail.*

VIII.4   *In the end, proper evolutionary analysis requires the extended acquisition and synthesis of data from ethnographic, archaeological, historical, and sociological sources. Each of these contributes vitally to the development of evolutionary theories about world history over the very long term.*

EVOLUTIONARY MATERIALISM AND WORLD HISTORY

The remainder of this book represents an extensive application and empirical evaluation of the strategy of evolutionary materialism using a large mass of data from world history and prehistory. I start with the period immediately preceding 10,000 BP and end right at the present. Although some use of the comparative method is made, emphasis is placed on data from archaeology and history. It is hoped that this will provide the most rigorous test of the theory possible by disarming antievolutionists who see evolutionary theories as resting on static comparisons.

Chapter 2 takes up the first great evolutionary transformation in world history, the Neolithic Revolution, which ushered in agriculture and settled village life. This was the first great instance of parallel evolution in world history. The Neolithic Revolution occurred independently in at least eight major regions of the world, and also in many different subregions within each of these regions.

In due time most of those regions of the world that went through the transition from nomadic hunting and gathering to settled village life based on agriculture began to evolve those much more complex and elaborate forms of social life that we know as civilization and the state. Tracing out and attempting to explain the nature of this second great evolutionary transformation is the subject of chapter 3. Once again we have a major example of parallel evolutionary trends from many different world regions and subregions. The evolution of civilization and the state is a critical problem for any self-respecting evolutionary theory.

The agrarian civilizations that evolved after 5000 BP became the dominant form of social life of their time. After the evolution of this kind of society, social evolution essentially slowed its pace, and no fundamental evolutionary transformations out of the agrarian stage occurred until just the last few centuries. Thus most of the agrarian civilizations seemed to have had very little "evolutionary potential." Chapter 4 explores the basic "evolutionary logic" of agrarian civilizations. Did they all tend toward a kind of "stagnation" characterized by a cyclical process of dynastic rise and fall, and, if so, why was this so? The strong tendency of agrarian civilizations to massive devolutionary collapse will be an important concern as well. The chapter will also take up and evaluate the argument now being made by a number of scholars that world-systems with core-periphery hierarchies existed during this stage of social evolution and significantly affected the evolutionary dynamics of these societies.

Chapter 5 looks at what I regard as the third great evolutionary transformation in world history, the rise of modern capitalism after the sixteenth century. It is usually assumed that this was an occurrence unique to Europe. To some degree, of course, that is true; however, a remarkably parallel transition to capitalism occurred as well at approximately the same time in Japan. This chapter will look in detail at both the European and the Japanese cases, searching out their similarities and differences and asking what these cases reveal about the evolutionary dynamics of human social life. Why were the agrarian civilizations of western Europe and Japan the ones to make the fateful transition to modern capitalism, and why did it take so many thousands of years after the initial appearance of civilization and the state for this to occur?

Many sociologists argue that the real transition out of the agrarian stage of social evolution occurred only with the Industrial Revolution of the eighteenth century, and that that revolution represents the great evolutionary transition of recent centuries. The argument of chapter 5, of course, is that it was the earlier sixteenth-century transition to capitalism that represented the critical break. Chapters 6 and 7 explore the further evolutionary consequences of the capitalist revolution. Chapter 6 looks at the evolution of the modern world as it has been driven by the evolutionary logic inherent in capitalism as a large-scale world-system. It explores the major evolutionary trends characteristic of that world-system over the past few centuries, and takes an especially close look at the markedly unequal levels of economic development historically and currently found among the various societies within the world-system. However, the argument is also made that we cannot understand the nature of societies in the present day as simply the outcome of world-system processes. Other kinds of factors primarily internal to modernizing societies played a significant role as well, and thus it is necessary to see the evolution of contemporary societies as the outcome of the interaction between their internal features and their mode of participation within the capitalist world-system. With this assumption in mind, chapter 7 explores the evolution of the most important institutional features of modernity, which exist not only in the advanced capitalist societies, but in "socialist" ones as well: industrialism, class stratification with substantial mobility rates, the nation-state, parliamentary democracy (although totalitarianism for awhile in socialist states), mass education, and advanced science and technology.

Chapter 8 looks back at the past 10,000 years and tries to assess the extent to which social evolution over that period has been progressive or regressive, drawing on the very few criteria available for the objective assessment of the extent of social progress or regression. Chapter 9 attempts to use the understanding of the evolutionary dynamics of the modern world to project the short- to medium-term future of humankind. The chapter looks in particular at the implications of current rates of population growth and ecological degradation, as well as at the implications of the capitalist inter-state system for possible nuclear annihilation. The chapter also goes on to inquire into such questions as whether the future will be characterized by capitalism, socialism, or barbarism, whether a world state is possible, and whether such an institution would worsen or improve humankind's current predicament.

Chapter 10 concludes the book by reflecting upon the major evolutionary dynamics of world history as they bear on the theoretical strategy of evolutionary materialism. The chapter thus provides an opportunity for assessing evolutionary materialism's capability of serving as a valuable guide to human sociohistorical development over the past 10,000 years.

2

The Neolithic Revolution

For most of the more than three million years of their existence,
humans lived entirely as members of hunting and gathering groups.
Then, beginning some 10,000 years ago, the first steps toward settled
village life based on agriculture were made. These first steps were
to culminate in what would turn out to be a dramatic transformation
of human social life, known generally as the Neolithic Revolution.
This chapter tells the story of this first great evolutionary transformation in world history. After sketching out the nature of the transition
to agriculture in the various regions of the world in which it
occurred, I embark upon a detailed analysis of some of the most
important theories that have been offered to explain this transition.
Before doing either of these things, however, we first need to take a
look at what hunter-gatherer societies prior to the Neolithic were
like.

HUNTER-GATHERER SOCIETIES BEFORE 10,000 BP

In the last three decades hunter-gatherer societies have been an
intense object of anthropological research, with a great deal having
been learned about them. Most of this research has been ethnographic rather than archaeological, the basic assumption being that
contemporary surviving hunter-gatherers are a reasonable reflection
of their prehistoric counterparts. Ethnographies of such hunter-
gatherers as the !Kung San of southern Africa (Lee, 1978, 1979,
1984), the Hadza of Tanzania (Woodburn, 1968), and the Mbuti of
the central rainforest of Zaire (Turnbull, 1961), along with numerous

other groups, have given us a picture of hunter-gatherer social organization that has become highly familiar. Hunter-gatherer societies are composed of very small bands (usually less than 25 members) that are highly mobile and that move frequently in search of food. The primary hunters of wild game are men, whereas the primary gatherers of wild plant foods are usually women. Such groups are altogether lacking in true private property, the ownership of crucial productive resources either being communal or, perhaps more accurately, essentially absent. While people may own personal objects individually, and while some productive resources (such as waterholes) may be owned by families, no individual has the right or capability of depriving any other individual of access to essential productive resources. There being no private property, there is thus no social class or stratification system, and powerful social norms emphasizing social and economic equality pervade social life. These norms are reinforced by strong sanctions for failure to live up to the ideas of sharing and generosity. This economic and social equality is accompanied by a fundamental democracy in political life. No elite groups capable of compelling others to do their bidding exist, and persons of leadership have only the capacity to advise and persuade, not to rule coercively.

It used to be thought that living by hunting and gathering was a bad way to live. Life was a constant struggle for survival in which people had to work long and hard just to make any sort of living at all. But beginning in the 1960s a number of anthropologists began to challenge this notion, the most important of whom was Marshall Sahlins. Sahlins (1972) argued that hunter-gatherers were actually much better off than had been imagined, and that in fact they constituted a kind of "original affluent society." They lived in surprisingly abundant environments that provided all of the basic calories, nutrients, and proteins they needed, and they worked relatively few hours in order to enjoy these things. This left them plenty of free time for visiting relatives, playing games, or just relaxing. This newer viewpoint was by no means accepted by everyone, but it has been widely influential, and there are good reasons for thinking it reasonably accurate (Sanderson, 1991a:69–71).

Anthropologists have always been aware of the possible dangers of generalizing about prehistoric hunting and gathering societies on the basis of what is known about contemporary groups, but they have done it anyway, and probably with considerable justification.

Much of what we know about prehistoric foragers suggests that they must have been very similar in important ways to surviving groups, and in many cases even more affluent in Sahlins's sense. However, in recent years evidence has emerged to show that at least some prehistoric hunter-gatherers departed significantly from the usual image of them as highly egalitarian democracies. It has long been known that the various hunter-gatherer groups of the Northwest Coast of North America, which were organized into stratified chiefdoms, departed from this image, but it was assumed that they were a rare exception. It turns out that they are not so rare. A number of ancient hunter-gatherer societies have been similarly organized. Such groups, known generally as complex hunter-gatherers, had large populations, sedentism, facilities for food storage, social hierarchies controlled by chiefs or "big men," demands for luxury goods, occupational specialization, and long-distance trade networks (Price and Brown, 1985; M. Cohen, 1985).

We cannot really say just how common such groups were archaeologically. Although Douglas Price and James Brown suggest "that at one time [they] may have been more typical of past human societies" (1985:4), it is not clear just how typical this is. Mark Cohen (1985) suggests that the model of hunter-gatherers as simple and egalitarian is probably correct for most of the archaeological record, and that complex hunter-gatherers were clustered in fairly late pre-Neolithic times (cf. Mellars, 1985). And what accounts for complexity among ancient hunter-gatherers? Although a number of scholars have seen it as rooted in affluence (resource abundance), Cohen offers an interpretation that emphasizes population pressure and resource stress. As he puts it (1985:106):

I suggest that the largely irreversible appearance of complex institutions late in the Pleistocene reflects the increasing and largely irreversible requirement for large aggregates to remain permanently in the vicinity of the relatively few resources plentiful and storable enough to provide for the growing population. The special features of complex society can then be explained in part as means of reducing the stresses of permanent aggregation. A review of aspects of crowding stress and their relation to social complexity serves to amplify this point.

Paul Mellars has suggested that, paradoxically, both affluence and economic stress may have operated to produce complex forms of prehistoric hunter-gatherer society (1985:292):

The main point to be emphasized is that these arguments in favor of a general "stress" model for the emergence of social complexity are only convincing where the elements of stress can be seen to be acting on communities that are living in relatively high population densities, and living for at least part of the annual cycle in relatively large, semisedentary settlements. If this is true, then we would need to invoke not only the stress model to account for the rise of complexity, but also at least some elements of a more general "affluence" model to explain how these social aggregations could be supported in basic economic terms. . . . When conceived in these terms, the simultaneous use of both "stress" and "affluence" models to account for the emergence of social complexity in hunter-gatherer societies need not be contradictory in more than a narrow semantic sense.

Cohen's interpretation of complexity among prehistoric hunter-gatherers is an evolutionary one that dovetails with his general theoretical model of the origins of agriculture, which we shall examine later in this chapter. But I am in danger of running slightly ahead of my argument. At this point, what is important is to keep in front of us the image of a typical prehistoric hunting and gathering society as small, simple, highly mobile, egalitarian, and democratic, as well as one that probably conformed fairly well to Sahlins's notion of an "original affluent society." It was this kind of society that was transformed, and ultimately radically so, by the events of the late Pleistocene and early Holocene, that is, during late Upper Paleolithic, Mesolithic, and early Neolithic times.

THE WORLDWIDE TRANSITION TO AGRICULTURE

One of the most striking features of the Neolithic Revolution was that it was a worldwide phenomenon. It used to be thought that there was simply one Neolithic, that of the Middle East, which in due time spread to many other regions of the world. This old idea is now emphatically rejected in favor of the view that there were many Neolithic Revolutions, most of which occurred entirely independently in at least eight world regions: southwest Asia, China, southeast Asia, Europe, Africa, Mesoamerica, South America, and North America. We need to look at the nature of the Neolithic in each of these regions. In doing so, it is important to keep in mind that the earliest agriculture was really what is more appropriately called horticulture – the cultivation of small garden plots with hand tools, such as digging sticks or hoes. What some people call "true" agriculture – intensive cultivation of large fields, usually with the plow and draft animals – followed the Neolithic by several thousand years.

The Neolithic in the Old World

Archaeologists are generally agreed that the world's first transition to agriculture was made in southwest Asia, beginning probably a little over 10,000 years ago. The most important domesticated plants were emmer and einkorn wheat and barley, but lentils and peas were also domesticated. Sheep and goats were the most important domesticated animals, and they made the full-scale development of permanent villages possible. By 8000 BP domesticated sheep and goats were to be found throughout southwest Asia. Cattle and pigs also became important domesticated animals. Domesticated cattle were widespread throughout southwest Asia, as pigs seemingly were too. Pig bones have constituted as much as 30 percent of all mammal remains at numerous large sites (Fagan, 1989; Wenke, 1990).

There were three primary centers of domestication throughout southwest Asia (A.M.T. Moore, 1989), and the transition to agriculture was more or less an independent occurrence in each of these regions (Fagan, 1989). In the Levant the Neolithic can be dated to about 10,500 BP. Some 140 Neolithic sites have been identified there, among the most important of which are those at Jericho and Abu Hureyra. A variety of Neolithic cultures also arose in the Zagros foothills and Mesopotamia from about 10,000 BP. Among the best preserved of the Neolithic settlements in this area are Zawi Chemi Shanidar, Jarmo, and Ali Kosh. Anatolia (modern-day Turkey) was also an important center of agricultural developments. The earliest good evidence for plant and animal domestication in this region is dated at around 9500 BP, but farming may have developed somewhat earlier. The best-known site in this region is Çatal Hüyük, which is known from as early as 8000 BP. Çatal Hüyük was a town of many houses built out of sun-dried brick that covered some 32 acres.

Brian Fagan has stressed that the southwest Asian Neolithic was a process marked by gradual change over a relatively long period of time (1989:289):

The development of the new food-producing economies took place in two stages. The first saw some agriculture and control of animals, but most of the diet came from game and wild vegetable foods. Then, about 8,000 years ago, more productive cereal grains and cattle, sheep, goats, and pigs were completely domesticated, creating the fully agricultural and stock-raising economy that was to persist into historic times, albeit in elaborated forms.

This drawn-out and gradual nature of the southwest Asian Neolithic is, as we will see, the very same kind of process that occurred in the other regions of the Neolithic.

China was another major world center of agricultural development. Agriculture emerged here entirely independent of Neolithic developments in southwest Asia. Like southwest Asia, China was home to several regional Neolithics, each of which was largely a separate process (Fagan, 1989). It is important to distinguish the specific character of agriculture in north China from that in south China (Fagan, 1989; Chang, 1986; Zhimin, 1989). In north China agriculture began at least 7,000 years ago, and quite possibly as early as 8000–8500 BP, in a number of different areas (Crawford, 1992). Probably the best known of the north Chinese Neolithic regions is that of Yang-shao. Here, as elsewhere in north China, the principal domesticated plants were foxtail and broom-corn millet, although the soybean was also important. Dogs and pigs were the most important domesticated animals; cattle, sheep, and goats were also domesticated, but they were much less common than dogs and pigs. Yang-shao cultivators lived in villages and apparently practiced a kind of shifting cultivation, probably using the slash-and-burn technique (Chang, 1986). The remains of such cultivating instruments as hoes, spades, and digging sticks have been found. The early Yang-shao culture was, however, not involved in full-time agriculture, as hunting, fishing, and wild grain collecting were still being carried on (Chang, 1986). Kwang-chih Chang (1986) suggests that the Yang-shao people were constructing houses of a fairly permanent nature, and that within a village the houses were arranged in a circular manner facing a kind of plaza. He also suggests that the segmentation of these houses, plus the layout of cemeteries, suggests that village members were organized into unilineal lineages and clans.

In south China agriculture began at least as early as in north China, and Chang speculates that it might have begun much earlier. Here rice was the principal plant domesticate, and taro and yams were also grown. Such animals as dogs, pigs, and water buffalo were domesticated. Many farming sites dating to between 7000 and 5000 BP have been identified in the Lake T'ai-hu region of south China, but only some of these have so far been excavated. At the earliest Lake T'ai-hu sites the people lived in rectangular houses and cultivated the soil with hoes made of animal shoulder blades (Fagan, 1989; Zhimin, 1989).

Southeast Asia may also have been the site of an indigenous Neolithic Revolution. Much archaeological research in southeast Asia has focused on Spirit Cave in Thailand, in which a number of botanical remains dating to about 9000 BP have been found (M. Cohen, 1977). Fagan notes that there has been speculation concerning rice cultivation at this time (1989:326–7): "The material culture of the Spirit Cave people shows a distinct change after about 9,000 years ago. From then on until approximately 7,600 years ago, the inhabitants began to use adzes, pottery, and slate knives. The knives strongly resemble later artifacts used for rice cultivation in parts of Indonesia and could be interpreted as a suggestion that cereals were cultivated near the site." However, there is clear evidence that the domestication of rice, and possibly also of taro and yams, had begun in other regions of southeast Asia by no later than 5000 BP and possibly as early as 9000 BP, although whether this was an indigenous development remains to be determined (M. Cohen, 1977). The site of Khok Phanom Di in Thailand has revealed rice specimens and other indications of agriculture dating as far back as 7000 BP (Fagan, 1989). Mark Cohen (1977) argues that the site of Non Nok Tha in Thailand reveals clear evidence of domesticated rice as early as the sixth millennium BP, and that implements typically connected with rice cultivation have been found at this site dating to as early as 9000 BP. Agriculture could thus be quite old in this region of the world.

Discussion of the European Neolithic has been marked by the delineation of an archaeological stage, the Mesolithic, often said to be unique to Europe. However, although the name may be uniquely applied to Europe, as we will see some of the evolutionary developments during this stage transpired prior to the Neolithic in all of the major regions of the world where agriculture originated (in the New World the stage comparable to the Mesolithic is known as the Archaic). During the Mesolithic, hunter-gatherers began to exploit a wider range of plant and animal resources and live in larger, more permanent, and more complex social groups. These were prominent examples of the complex hunter-gatherers discussed in the last section.

The European Mesolithic dates from about 10,000 BP to about 5500 BP. It comes to an end in Greece and other parts of southeastern Europe by 8000 BP, the time at which agriculture begins there. The earliest Neolithic Europeans cultivated the land with digging sticks and hoes and planted wheat, barley, millet, lentils, and legumes (Milisauskas, 1978). Of these, wheat was the most important crop. Cattle were the most important domesticated animal (Milisauskas, 1978), although sheep and pigs were also raised (Fagan, 1989). Until recently it was thought that agriculture developed in Europe as the result of diffusion from southwest Asia, but it is now recognized that European agriculture was a largely independent development (Fagan, 1989; cf. Zvelebil, 1986).

Between about 7000 and 5000 BP, agriculture gradually spread throughout temperate Europe, arriving last in such regions of northern Europe as the British Isles and Scandinavia. The early farmers of temperate Europe, known collectively as the Bandkeramik people, cultivated wheat and barley and raised cattle, sheep, goats, and dogs. Their farming was based on a system of crop rotation and fallowing that allowed them to occupy the same plots of land for long periods (rather than practice shifting cultivation). This enabled them to build large permanent houses constructed of timber, an activity that would have been an impractical use of time and energy for shifting cultivators (Fagan, 1989).

In the other Old World region in which significant archaeological research has been done, Africa, our knowledge of agricultural developments is still very sketchy. David Phillipson (1985) has provided one of the best analyses of the African Neolithic. He suggests that agriculture did not become widely developed throughout the northern parts of Africa until after the beginning of the eighth millennium BP, and much later in Africa south of the Equator. He also believes that much African agriculture was independently evolved rather than derivative, a conclusion that is supported by the fact that most African domesticates have been indigenous. These plants include certain types of yams, African rice, sorghum, finger millet, bulrush millet, and the Ethiopian plants ensete and noog. Domesticated animals, however, appear to have been derived from elsewhere, probably southwest Asia. There were no African prototypes for sheep and goats, cattle could be descended from wild ancestors in southwest Asia, and none of the primary domesticated animals of sub-Saharan Africa were derived from species that were native to that part of Africa.

In the Sudanese Nile Valley agriculture began around 6000 BP at the earliest. Sorghum, finger millet, and panicum were grown, and sheep, goats, and cattle were raised. In the Egyptian Nile Valley agriculture began as early as 7000 BP, or perhaps slightly earlier. Here barley, emmer wheat, and flax were cultivated, and cattle, sheep, goats, and pigs were raised. In west and central Africa agriculture may have developed as early as 6500 BP. Pottery and ground stone tools have been dated this early, as have implements with so-called sickle-sheen. These artifacts suggest that agriculture was being practiced, although they could have been used by semisedentary hunter-gatherers. In Ghana the earliest possible evidence for agriculture occurs about 3800 BP. Much of agriculture in west Africa may have been derived from contacts with areas farther to the north.

Ethiopia may have played an especially important role in the development of African agriculture. Several domesticates, such as teff, ensete, and noog, have been cultivated there and only there, which strongly suggests an independent evolutionary sequence of agricultural development. Phillipson (1985) suggests that there might have been two basic agricultural sequences in Ethiopia beginning after 6000 BP, a northerly one based on the cultivation of cereals, and one in the southwest founded on ensete. In east Africa there is evidence of domesticated cattle, sheep, and goats from about 4500 BP in northern Kenya. Farther south in southern Kenya and northern Tanzania food-producing industries have been discovered that date to somewhat earlier than 3000 BP. It is important to note that, by and large, the farther south one goes in Africa the more recent agriculture seems to have originated. Indeed, in most of Africa below the Equator there is no reliable evidence for agriculture before AD 1. After that time agriculture spread throughout sub-Saharan Africa.

The Neolithic in the New World

In the New World agriculture arose in different regions of Mesoamerica, South America, and North America. It was once thought that New World agriculture originated as a result of contacts with the Old World, but this notion is now firmly rejected. The New World Neolithic occurred entirely independent of that in the Old World; moreover, it is now assumed that agricultural development in South America constituted an evolutionary sequence largely independent from the agricultural sequence in Mesoamerica, even though the principal Mesoamerican domesticate, maize, diffused from there into South America. North American agricultural development may also have been largely separate from the agricultural sequences in Mesoamerica and South America.

Knowledge of the origins of agriculture in Mesoamerica rests heavily on archaeological research done in the Tehuacán Valley and the northeastern Mexican state of Tamaulipas. This research shows a slow and gradual shift away from hunting and gathering toward increased reliance on domesticates (cf. MacNeish, 1978), and with sedentary village life appearing long after domestication had occurred (Stark, 1986). Richard MacNeish's (1970, 1978) painstaking research in the Tehuacán Valley shows that the wild ancestor of maize, the most important Mesoamerican domesticate, was probably first cultivated around 7000 BP. MacNeish has demonstrated to the satisfaction of most archaeologists that the likely wild ancestor of maize was a plant known as *teosinte*. In addition to maize, communities in the Tehuacán Valley were cultivating such plants as beans, squash, gourds, amaranths, and chili peppers (Fiedel, 1987).

In Tamaulipas there is evidence that gourds, chili peppers, and pumpkins might have been under cultivation as early as 7000 BP, or perhaps somewhat earlier. The beginnings of agriculture in Tamaulipas may therefore have been earlier than its beginnings in the Tehuacán Valley; moreover, there has been speculation that some of the domesticates found in Tehuacán may have originally come from Tamaulipas (Fiedel, 1987). A third center of Mesoamerican plant domestication was the Valley of Oaxaca, which is close to the Tehuacán Valley. In some of the shallow caves of Oaxaca, remains of black beans, bottle gourd rinds, and the seeds of either squash or pumpkins have been found dating to as early as 9000 BP. These plants were probably under cultivation by this time (Fiedel, 1987).

A striking feature of Mesoamerican agriculture is the absence of any large domesticated animals (although dogs, turkeys, and ducks were domesticated), as well as the fact that settled village life did not begin until perhaps 3700 BP in Oaxaca and 3500 BP in Tehuacán (Fiedel, 1987). Marvin Harris (1977) views these two phenomena as being closely related. The lack of large domesticated animals, he argues, is explained by the simple absence of any large species suitable for domestication, and this absence is the reason for the gap of several thousand years between the first steps toward domestication and the appearance of permanent villages. Harris claims that settled village life could not begin in the early stages of plant cultivation because the early cultivators still had to follow wild game around in order to acquire their supply of animal protein. Permanent villages were not developed until they were necessitated by a strong commitment to and dependence on plant domesticates. This contrasts with the situation in the Old World, where sedentism and the origins of agriculture occurred together (or, indeed, where sedentism sometimes preceded agriculture).

In South America there were also several regions where agriculture originated. In Ecuador, maize may have been cultivated by 5000 BP. This conclusion is reached on the basis of grain processing implements found at various sites, as well as pottery designs interpreted as portraying maize (Fiedel, 1987). Ancient Ecuadorians may also have been cultivating a root crop, beans, and cotton.

In Peru, agriculture arose in a variety of highland, lowland, and coastal regions. Maize and such plants as potatoes, squash, gourds, beans, lucuma, and quinoa were the principal cultivated plants, and guinea pigs and llamas were the main animal domesticates. Although some archaeologists have seen agriculture beginning at an even earlier date, the earliest reliable evidence for domestication comes from Guitarrero Cave by about 8000 BP and somewhat later (probably around 7000 BP) at Ayacucho (Stark, 1986). After about 6000 BP the peoples of Ayacucho were becoming increasingly dependent on agriculture. They were using hoes to cultivate potatoes, maize, squash, and beans (Fagan, 1989). The Ayacucho agricultural sequence demonstrates what is true for the rest of Peru, South America, the New World, and, indeed, the world as a whole: that the transition from hunting and gathering to agriculture was a slow and gradual process that often took thousands of years to complete (Fagan, 1989). This point will loom large in our consideration of theories of the Neolithic Revolution.

Early agriculture in the Amazon Basin, which may have been independent of agricultural development elsewhere in South America, was heavily characterized by manioc. Griddles presumably used for the toasting of manioc flour have been dated to at least

3000 BP, and possibly to 4000 BP or even earlier (Fiedel, 1987).

Maize was carried to North America from Mesoamerica as early as 5500 BP, as were common beans by about 3000–2500 BP (Fiedel, 1987; Fagan, 1991). These domesticates eventually became an important part of the diets of societies throughout North America. In what is now the American Southwest, several early agricultural traditions are well known to archaeologists. After about 2300 BP the Hohokam tradition appeared rather suddenly. The Hohokam lived in villages and practiced irrigation agriculture in which maize, beans, and squash were the principal crops. Perhaps because of intrusions by the Hohokam, the Mogollon tradition was formed after about AD 250. The Mogollon lived in villages characterized by pit-houses, which were normally situated on mesas that overlooked the valleys where their crops were grown. Also in the Southwest, the Anasazi tradition evolved around AD 1. By this date the Anasazi were incipient agriculturalists who were gradually making cultivated crops an increasing part of their diet. After AD 450, domesticated beans and turkeys were added to Anasazi diets, and thus their dependence on agriculture grew (Fiedel, 1987).

In eastern North America agriculture was based on both borrowed and indigenous plants (Stark, 1986). After 4000 BP the sunflower, sumpweed, and goosefoot were domesticated. Sunflowers were grown for edible seeds and oil, and sumpweed was cultivated throughout the midwest after 3000 BP. According to Patty Jo Watson (1989:559), "by 500 BC a full-fledged horticultural complex is evident at several sites." However, it was still to be some time – probably not until around AD 400 – before agriculture based on maize and beans was to become a regular part of the subsistence strategies of eastern North American societies (Fagan, 1989, 1991; Stark, 1986).

The principal characteristics of the Neolithic

Before turning to examine the array of arguments that have been used to explain the Neolithic Revolution, it is crucial that we have a clear understanding of just what the most important characteristics of this evolutionary transformation were. At least five such characteristics can be identified.

First, the Neolithic Revolution led to essentially the same social consequences for the cultures and societies that underwent it. Before the Neolithic most hunter-gatherers lived in small, highly mobile, and highly egalitarian and democratic bands. After the Neolithic, they began to live in larger permanent or semipermanent villages. At first these early Neolithic societies were able to retain the same basic economic and social equality and political democracy that characterized most pre-Neolithic hunting and gathering groups. In due time, however, the egalitarian and democratic character of these agricultural societies gave way to social ranking, and then to class stratification and along with it the emergence of political elites that undermined the democratic character of political decision-making. We shall explore these phenomena in detail when we consider the rise of civilization and the state in the next chapter.

It is true, of course, that a number of late Upper Paleolithic or Mesolithic populations had already evolved ranked or stratified societies characterized by "big men" or chiefs. Therefore, since these things could develop without agriculture, the Neolithic was not absolutely essential in bringing them about. Nevertheless, it did bring them about in many instances. Moreover, even when these traits of social complexity had evolved prior to the adoption of agriculture, the same basic kinds of factors seem to explain their evolution regardless of whether they occurred within an agricultural or a preagricultural context. In other words, explaining the Neolithic is essentially the same intellectual problem as explaining the sociopolitical and technoeconomic changes that preceded it by several millennia. The late Upper Paleolithic, the Mesolithic, and the Neolithic really form together into one long and continuous evolutionary sequence.

A second characteristic of the Neolithic Revolution was its worldwide character.[1] Not only did it develop all over the world, but it did so at remarkably similar times. Mark Cohen sees this as one of the crucial features of the Neolithic. As he says (1977:5; emphasis Cohen's):

The most striking fact about agriculture . . . is precisely that it is such a universal event. Slightly more than 10,000 years ago, virtually all men lived on wild foods. By 2,000 years ago the overwhelming majority of people lived by farming. In the four million year history of *Homo sapiens,* the spread of agriculture was accomplished in about 8,000 years.

And not only was the Neolithic a worldwide phenomenon, but it was an independent evolutionary occurrence in most of the major world regions and subregions in which agriculture appeared over the past ten millennia. If we add together all of the subregions where agriculture appeared independently, we can probably locate several dozen independent instances of agricultural development, a striking situation of worldwide parallel evolution. Actually, the parallel evolution may be far more extensive than we might immediately imagine, for as Cohen has said (1977:24):

In fact, if we look at the botanical evidence concerning the precise point of origin of our various cultigens, the number of separate centers of domestication becomes almost infinite, even if we confine ourselves to the major recognized crop plants. Unfortunately, in most of these areas, the archaeological evidence is not yet adequate to establish whether cultivation was achieved independent of stimuli from other regions or was dependent on stimulus diffusion. I believe however that as our archaeological knowledge of poorly studied regions and obscure cultigens becomes more complete, the number of apparently independent hearths of domestication will grow rapidly.

Cohen's prediction has been more than adequately fulfilled in the years since he made it, and I suspect it will continue to be confirmed in the years ahead. Before the 1960s archaeologists depicted agriculture as having originated once and then diffused outward to the rest of the world. This idea bit the dust long ago, and the Neolithic as a multiple evolutionary occurrence has long been well established. The more research that is done, the greater the number of independent centers of agricultural origins archaeologists discover. It is likely that this number will grow considerably in the years ahead, from several dozen to perhaps even a hundred or more, at least if we can extrapolate from the trends of the past three decades.

The transition to agriculture was also a remarkably gradual occurrence. Despite the name, the Neolithic Revolution was not revolutionary at all in a temporal sense. It was evolutionary in perhaps the best-known common-sense meaning of that term. It is now well established that the Neolithic was really just the culmination of trends that had been in play for thousands of years. As Cohen (1977) has demonstrated, in the late Upper Paleolithic hunting and gathering societies that had been concentrating their subsistence efforts on big game animals gradually began to shift toward a "broad-spectrum" foraging pattern. They made smaller game an increasing part of their diet and began to pay more attention to plant foods and to a range of aquatic resources. This occurred all over the world in the millennia preceding the Neolithic. Furthermore, when hunter-gatherers began to adopt agriculture they did not do so all at once and immediately abandon foraging. Quite the contrary: they started by supplementing their foraging activities with domesticates, very gradually making them a larger and larger part of their diet until they had eventually, over a period of perhaps several thousand years, made a complete transition to dependence on agriculture.[2] The Neolithic Revolution was certainly revolutionary in its social consequences, but how misnamed it is in terms of time.

Two other characteristics of the Neolithic are important to note. One of these concerns the now reasonably well-established notion that ancient hunter-gatherers would have had considerable knowledge concerning how plants and animals could be domesticated. As Cohen (1977) has argued, it is inconceivable that such knowledge could have escaped them, living as they did in such extensive contact with the flora and fauna of their environments, and dependent as they were on intimate knowledge of these flora and fauna. The Neolithic Revolution was not a revolution in knowledge, therefore, but a revolutionary application of knowledge that already existed. In other words, it was a technological revolution but not a conceptual one. Finally, ethnographic evidence from contemporary hunting and gathering societies strongly suggests that ancient foragers must have greatly resisted taking up agriculture, mainly because they would have seen it as involving too great an expenditure of time and energy for too little gain. This resistance would only have been overcome when the greater investment of time and energy would have come to be seen as an economic necessity. The implications of this statement will become clear in due course.

EXPLAINING THE WORLDWIDE TRANSITION
TO AGRICULTURE

Numerous theories of the origins of agriculture have been developed by anthropologists and archaeologists in recent years. Most of these are materialist theories that emphasize demographic or ecological causes, or some combination of these. We need to examine several of these theories in detail, but before doing that it will be helpful to look at the explanation for agricultural origins that was the most widely accepted one before the mid-1960s.

The origin of agriculture as automatic technological growth

Until about three decades ago, the dominant explanation for the emergence of agriculture viewed it as simply one part of a long-term, automatic trend in the evolution of human technology. Although this theory appears at first sight to be a materialist theory since it is technology that is the focus of attention, it is really idealist in nature because it sees technological growth as stemming from the expansion in the store of human ideas. According to this theory, the human mind is inherently self-expanding and such expansion is the underlying foundation of most social progress. Technological change in general, and the development of agriculture in particular, are in the end really self-evident processes that need no real explanation. Harlan, de Wet, and Stemler (1976:3) have elegantly described the nature of this theory, which can be traced not only to V. Gordon Childe in the 1930s, but as far back as the nineteenth-century evolutionists Morgan and Tylor:

The idea of an agricultural revolution as elaborated by V. Gordon Childe for the Near East was basically applied to the social and cultural consequences of food-producing economies. Food production, as opposed to hunting and gathering, was considered to be so superior that, once invented, no one would dream of returning to the old ways. The new system would spread rapidly at the expense of the more "savage" tribes. Civilization could arise only from agricultural societies because everyone else was too busy eking out a living by hunting and gathering to have the time to develop the cultural traits of "civilization," such as writing, metallurgy, specialized crafts, standing armies, priestly castes, professional classes, and so on. It was the food-producing economy that lifted man from "barbarism."

Revolutionary attributes were also applied to domesticated plants. The idea of growing food plants on purpose was thought of as having been "discovered" by some prehistoric genius, and the idea had such obvious merit that it would be adopted readily and diffused widely from its center of origin. Indeed, it seemed to be widely accepted that the concept of food production versus food harvesting required such brilliant insight and superior knowledge that it could only have been thought of once or at most a few times.

This theory gradually came to be rejected by the vast majority of anthropologists and archaeologists after the 1960s, and it is now known to be incompatible with several crucial facts. We now know that agriculture was independently evolved by many different hunter-gatherer communities all over the world; that ancient hunter-gatherers undoubtedly had basic knowledge of agriculture tens of thousands of years ago; that there is often great resistance on the part of hunter-gatherers to the adoption of agriculture, who obviously see no self-evident benefits to it at all; and that ancient hunter-gatherers were probably better nourished and worked less than the agriculturalists of later times. As a result, the traditional explanation of the emergence of agriculture has been abandoned by almost everyone, and in recent years a great deal of energy has been devoted to developing new theories.

Population pressure theories

As Robert Wenke (1990) has noted, population pressure has been the most popular recent explanation of agricultural origins, and most current theories incorporate it in some way. Population pressure has been central to the theories of Smith and Young (1972), Wilkinson (1973), Binford (1983), and Johnson and Earle (1987), and it has played an important role in the arguments of Marvin Harris (1977), David Harris (1977), Pryor (1986), Redding (1988), and Henry (1989). By far the most elaborate and extensive development of a population pressure model of agricultural origins has come from the archaeologist Mark Cohen (1977). His model, and the sophisticated and impressive arguments he makes in its behalf, need to be examined in some detail.

Like other current population pressure arguments, Cohen's model is rooted in Ester Boserup's argument in her classic *The Conditions of Agricultural Growth* (1965) that the main factor impelling the intensification of agricultural technologies was population growth and subsequent population pressure. Boserup assumed that people operated in accordance with a "Law of Least Effort" that led them to attempt to minimize the amount of time and energy spent in gaining subsistence. Since more intensive modes of agricultural technology required greater time and energy, people would avoid them unless compelled by rising numbers to intensify their efforts in order to keep their standard of living from falling, or at least from falling too drastically. Thus a kind of technological inertia governed human subsistence practices, and this inertia could only be counteracted by population pressure.

Although in *The Conditions of Agricultural Growth* Boserup did not address the transition from hunting and gathering to agriculture (she did, however, in a later work [Boserup, 1981]), Cohen believes that her argument applies well to that transition. The basic cause of the emergence of agriculture is population pressure. But what, exactly, is population pressure? As Cohen notes, this critical issue has been muddied by a strong tendency among anthropologists and archaeologists to consider population pressure to exist only when the *carrying capacity* of an environment has been reached or exceeded. However, for Cohen this is not what population pressure consists in. He observes that the concept of carrying capacity is difficult to apply to human populations, and he seeks to avoid its use. For Cohen, population pressure exists when it is necessary for people to shift from the foods they prefer to ones they find increasingly less desirable, regardless of the extent to which they have reached the presumed carrying capacity of their environment. More formally, he defines population pressure as *"nothing more than an imbalance between a population, its choice of foods, and its work standards, which forces the population either to change its eating habits or to work harder (or which, if no adjustment is made, can lead to the exhaustion of certain resources)"* (Cohen, 1977:50; emphasis Cohen's). As Cohen remarks, this definition of population pressure is more realistic and workable, because population pressure "can be seen to motivate technological change in the food quest without ever threatening carrying capacity in the absolute sense, without ever reducing the human population to starvation, and without threatening to break down the ecosystem" (1977:50).

Cohen's argument rests on a number of basic facts that have been learned about the development of agriculture in recent years, some of which we have already noted. First, the transition to agriculture was a long, very gradual process that was preceded by a substantial period in which hunter-gatherers were intensifying their subsistence efforts within the context of a hunting and gathering mode of production. Second, agriculture originated on a worldwide basis during a relatively short period of time, and it did so independently in many different world regions and subregions. Third, all ancient hunter-gatherers probably had a basic understanding of how to practice agriculture but delayed for tens of thousands of years in putting such knowledge to use. Moreover, there is considerable evidence from contemporary hunting and gathering groups that they have a strong resistance to the practice of agriculture because they see few benefits (and several costs) in it. This is closely related to Cohen's fourth notion, which is that agriculture is now known to be neither easier nor more capable of providing a secure existence than hunting and gathering.[3] As Cohen notes, agriculture has only one real advantage over foraging: it can produce more calories per unit of land. This is obviously an advantage only when so many calories need to be produced in order to provide the standard of living that the members of a population desire.

Cohen's argument also rests upon a number of important assumptions about the demography of pre-Neolithic populations. First, he assumes that human populations have tended to grow fairly continuously throughout history. Despite the various ways in which pre-Neolithic populations have attempted to regulate their populations (e.g., abortion, infanticide, prolonged lactation), these checks have served to reduce but not to prevent population growth. Second, Cohen argues that, although the rate of population growth throughout the Pleistocene was very slow (estimates vary between about .0011 percent and .0030 percent per year [Cohen, 1977:52]), such a slow rate does not undermine a population pressure argument. The rate of population growth throughout the Pleistocene was still sufficient for population pressure, in Cohen's sense, to have built up not only by the later stages of the Upper Paleolithic, but throughout prehistory. Finally, Cohen assumes that Paleolithic hunting and gathering bands had well-developed structures designed to assess population density over wide areas and thus to equalize population pressure over these areas. Such structures may actually have operated over huge geographical spaces.[4] This assumption helps to explain the similar timing of agriculture in so many different areas of the world. As Cohen says, "Such a system of population flux might be theoretically capable of distributing population pressure evenly enough so that groups throughout the world would be forced to adopt agriculture within a few thousand years of one another" (1977:65).

It is also important to mention the wide variety of ways in which Cohen infers the existence of population pressure in the archaeological record. He lists no fewer than 14 indicators of population pressure that can be extracted from the data of prehistory. Population pressure can be assumed to exist when (1977:78–82):

1 people are traveling longer distances for food;
2 groups are expanding into new ecological zones and territories, especially if this expansion is into areas that pose new adaptive difficulties;
3 groups become more eclectic in their exploitation of microniches, thus using areas of their environment that had previously been ignored;
4 populations shift toward more eclectic food gathering patterns as shown by decreasing selectivity in foods eaten;
5 groups increase their use of aquatic relative to land-based resources;
6 people shift from eating large land mammals to consuming smaller mammals, birds, reptiles, and land molluscs; smaller fauna are less desirable and yield fewer calories per unit of effort expended;
7 populations make plant foods a greater part of their diets;
8 there is a shift to foods that require greater amounts of preparation, i.e., more cooking, grinding, pounding, or leaching of poisons;
9 there is evidence of environmental degradation, especially through using fire and clearing land so as to maintain subclimax vegetation;
10 skeletal evidence of malnutrition increases over time;
11 the size or quality of organisms exploited from a given species declines over time;
12 an exploited species disappears from the archaeological and fossil record;
13 there is increased regional specialization of artifacts (this assumes a breakdown in the system of population flux as the result of increasing jealousy and guarding of resources);
14 there is the emergence of (or an increase in) sedentism and food storage (sedentism implies high labor costs in much food acquisition as well as reduced dietary variety).

Cohen argues that the archaeological record reveals that many if not most (in some cases even all) of these important trends can be observed throughout the world in the Upper Paleolithic (or even tens of thousands of years earlier in the case of some trends), Mesolithic, and early Neolithic. Both individually and, more especially, in combination they point strongly to population pressure as the driving engine of subsistence change during this period of prehistory.

Despite its well thought-out, elaborate, and sometimes elegant nature, Cohen's population pressure argument has been subjected to persistent criticism. Some of the criticisms are based more on misunderstandings of the specifics of Cohen's arguments than on disagreements about empirical matters. Some of the most important leading critics have been Bennet Bronson (1972, 1975), George Cowgill (1975), Fekri Hassan (1981), Brian Hayden (1981), and Benjamin White (1982). A persistent theme in the arguments of these and other critics is that the population pressure argument assumes some sort of automatic tendency for prehistoric populations to grow, a tendency that does not exist. Human populations, it is charged, whether contemporary or prehistoric, do not grow automatically. Whether they grow or not, and the rate at which they grow, is determined by a range of social and cultural factors. George Cowgill, for instance, says, "Rather than seeing population growth as an inherent tendency of human population which is *permitted* by technological innovations, I see population growth as a human possibility which is *encouraged* by certain institutional, as well as technological or environmental circumstances, but equally may be *discouraged* by other circumstances" (1975:516; emphasis Cowgill's). Proponents of this line of argument usually like to stress that prehistoric populations have ordinarily made use of a number of techniques of population control – such as infanticide, abortion, prolonged lactation, or various taboos on intercourse – that have allowed them to keep their populations from growing. However, Cohen insists that human populations throughout the Pleistocene have in fact grown continuously, and that despite the efforts that prehistoric peoples do make to regulate these numbers, such efforts only serve to slow down the rate of growth rather than to prevent it entirely. William Sanders (1984) takes an even stronger position, holding that most population-regulation techniques employed by prehistoric peoples have done little even to slow the rate of growth. He concludes that population growth is not extraordinary and does not even need to be explained. On the contrary, he asserts, it is the failure of prehistoric populations to grow that cries out for explanation.

Another persistent theme of many critics is the notion that, empirically speaking, population levels in various world regions and subregions have often been well below the carrying capacity of the environment, and therefore population pressure could not exist as a cause of the intensification of subsistence and the eventual transition to agriculture. As we have seen, however, Cohen's argument dispenses with the notion of carrying capacity, which he regards as a troublesome concept that is very difficult to apply to human populations. Cohen's argument does not assume that population pressure exists only when the carrying capacity of the environment has been reached or exceeded, and thus that people only innovate technologically when they are near starvation. On the contrary, he sees population pressure as existing whenever people must make adjustments in their subsistence strategies in order to maintain a living standard or to prevent that standard from dropping too low. For him, then, population pressure can exist at much lower levels of population density than others often assume. Frederic Pryor (1983) has caught exceptionally well the essence of Cohen's notion of population pressure and how its logic in relation to subsistence change is worked out over long periods of time. I quote at length from Pryor's illuminating exegesis (1983:105–6; emphasis added):

Although it is certainly possible for gatherers and hunters to limit their numbers to some fraction of the alleged carrying capacity of the land, such a mechanism might not be invoked for two reasons. First, *the population may be changing imperceptibly.* Second, the carrying capacity of the land is not fixed but changes with the intensity of the gathering and hunting activities; and the very slow changes in population can be accommodated by very slow changes in food gathering and hunting methods.

The force of *such imperceptible population changes* can be seen in some simple calculations. Let us accept the estimate . . . that the theoretical maximum land density to support a gathering-and-hunting society is 1 person per square mile. If one-fifth of the land mass of the world excluding Antarctica is suitable for such hunting and gathering (i.e., roughly 10 million square miles), how long would it take an initial population of 10,000 people to populate this area at that maximum density? If the population were growing at 0.01 percent per year, it would take roughly 69,000 years; at 0.05 percent per year, roughly 14,000 years; and 0.1 percent per year, roughly 6900 years. These calculations suggest a world population considerably higher than the common estimate of 3 million in 10,000 BC . . ., but their purpose is not to estimate population but merely to show that *we are talking about a long time span where slow rates of population have a relentless force. Paralleling such slow population changes would be imperceptible adaptations of techniques of obtaining food* so that the population would always lie below the "carrying capacity"; in this way, population limitation techniques would not need to be invoked.

. . . *Such imperceptible population increases would eventually result in diminishing returns in gathering and hunting activities.*

Fekri Hassan has proposed a number of additional criticisms of population pressure arguments. Some of these criticisms (and my responses to them) are (Hassan, 1981:161–3):

1 Population pressure is often a vague and ill-defined concept (*response*: this may be true in the formulations of some, but it is certainly not true in Cohen's case; he makes very clear what population pressure means in his theory).

2 Rates of population growth are related to various social and cultural factors and are not completely independent variables (*response*: population pressure theorists do not assume that population growth is entirely an independent variable and recognize that it is affected by social and cultural conditions; however, because human populations cannot achieve zero population growth, it is a variable that is significantly independent).

3   Population pressure models are monocausal and therefore not in line with the multicausal and frequently nondemographic nature of culture change (*response*: population pressure models do not deny that much of culture change is multicausal and nondemographic, nor do they make population pressure the only variable producing subsistence intensification and agricultural origins; if population pressure is the primary cause of the origin of agriculture, it does not act alone but in concert with environmental and technological factors).

4   Population pressure models assume that carrying capacity is infinitely elastic (*response*: actually, as we have clearly seen, Cohen's model makes no use at all of the notion of carrying capacity).

5   Technological innovations may not always be available when a food imbalance occurs, and the probability of the right innovation at the right time is very low (*response*: this would only be true under the assumption that technological change, including the emergence of agriculture, has occurred in rapid and sudden bursts; however, technological change leading up to the emergence of agriculture has been an extremely slow and gradual process, thus allowing plenty of time for the right technological innovations to develop).

6   The concept of population pressure places too much emphasis on population size (*response*: this is simply untrue; it is not the size of a population alone that is critical, but its size in relation to a whole range of environmental characteristics; groups with less dense populations may experience greater population pressure than groups with more dense populations if the former exist in much less bountiful environments).

In the final analysis, the criticisms of Cohen's population pressure theory of the emergence of agriculture do no real damage to it. It is my view that this theory is the very best of all current theories of agricultural origins. However, in order to see why this is the case, we need to look at the other major theories that currently compete with it.

Theories emphasizing climate change

Theories of the Neolithic Revolution focusing on climate change have been presented by Donald Henry (1989), Joy McCorriston and Frank Hole (1991), and Fekri Hassan (1981:213–19). Since the latter two theories are quite similar to Henry's, I shall concentrate on it.

Henry's argument is limited to the emergence of agriculture in the Levant and views agriculture as emerging from foraging in two distinct phases. The first phase began as the result of the global warming trend that followed the retreat of the glaciers at the end of the last ice age about 13,000 years ago. According to Henry, this warming in the Levant favored the expansion of stands of wild grasses, and foraging populations were attracted to these stands as a principal food source. As they began to depend on the wild grasses, simple foragers were transformed into sedentary, complex foragers with large populations. These were the famous Natufians. The Natufian adaptation, though, was inherently unstable, because it was more susceptible to the pressures of newly arisen population pressure and to resource variation. When resources became more scarce with the onset of much drier conditions after about 11,000 BP, this, combined with population pressure, created severe food stresses that necessitated the beginnings of the adoption of agriculture.[5]

Although thoughtfully argued, Henry's theory suffers from a fatal flaw: it is addressed to only one specific center of agricultural development and completely ignores the rest of the world. One of the virtues of Cohen's population pressure theory is that it is fully intended to explain the worldwide transition to agriculture. Henry's theory, though, is exactly the opposite: it denies the possibility of any theory that can explain the origin of agriculture in all the different world regions. Indeed, Henry makes a virtue of his particularistic explanation, claiming that "there was no single factor or set of factors that prompted the emergence of food-production worldwide" (1989:236). Henry's theoretical ambitions are limited in scope, and he doesn't want to think nomothetically. Astoundingly, he goes on to add that an "examination of . . . incipient agriculture in various regions of the world reveals few parallels" (1989:236). It is hard to understand just what would count as a parallel for Henry, but for many other scholars one of the most important dimensions of the transition to agriculture worldwide is the striking set of parallels it reveals.

McCorriston and Hole (1991), whose theory is similar to Henry's, have a similar particularistic outlook, holding that the emergence of agriculture in the Levant was "the outcome of historical accident rather than components of a sweeping global process" (1991:47). Their theory emphasizes that the Levant had certain preconditions that paved the way for agriculture once resource shortages began to become critical. These preconditions included sedentism and a seed-grinding technology. But why should these preconditions, which were prevalent all over the world (at least in the case of the grinding technology, less so in the case of sedentism), have been there in the first place? Were they not the result of earlier forms of subsistence intensification, and could not such intensification be explained in terms of population pressure? McCorriston and Hole do not address such questions, quite possibly because of their particularistic bias.

Resource stress theories

Ecologically based theories emphasizing resource stress have been presented by Marvin Harris (1977), David Harris (1977), and Brian Hayden (1981). These theories have some similarities to the climate-based theories, but they do not invoke climate *per se* as a causal factor and they are meant to be general, nomothetic models.

Marvin Harris's and David Harris's theories are broadly similar, so let us look simply at the former. This theory emphasizes the ecological effects of the retreat of the glaciers at the end of the last ice age about 13,000 years ago. Harris holds that the retreat of the glaciers gradually turned grasslands into forests, which decreased the availability of the big game animals on which Upper Paleolithic hunter-gatherers throughout the world had been relying heavily for their food supply. These animals were eventually hunted to extinction, thus making it necessary for hunter-gatherers to turn toward smaller game, aquatic resources, and eventually domesticated plants for their food supply. In this theory, population pressure is a part of the picture, but it is the result of ecological change rather than a driving force in its own right.

There are two difficulties with this kind of argument. In addition to the fact that it ignores the general, long-term significance of population pressure, it is, at best, applicable to only some parts of the world. It cannot be used to explain agricultural developments in southwest Asia, China, or southeast Asia (Fiedel, 1987). As Stuart Fiedel notes, for example, "In the Near East [southwest Asia], the earliest cultivators continued to hunt gazelle, deer, and wild cattle, as their ancestors had done for thousands of years before" (1987:164). Donald Henry (1989) makes the same point.

Brian Hayden's theory works from the assumption that prehistoric populations were frequently confronted with periods of resource stress because of natural fluctuations in resource availability. People were thus motivated to reduce the unreliability of their resources, and throughout most of prehistory they have done this by attempting to increase the diversity of their resource base by technological innovation and environmental manipulation. The most prominent trend in this regard has been the gradual shift from the pursuit of *K*-selected species (large animals that reproduce slowly and leave few offspring) to the pursuit of *r*-selected species (small animals that reproduce rapidly and leave many offspring, such as small mammals, fish and shellfish, insects, and grasses). Increased reliance on *r*-selected species has meant the need to expand technology and to invent complicated processing or storage procedures in order to make the pursuit of such species worthwhile. Also, because *r*-selected species are almost inexhaustible and because they are so much more productive than *K*-selected species, the resource base gradually became more stable and secure, and this greater stability led to important social and cultural changes, such as sedentism, increased population density, and the emergence of social complexity. By very late prehistory, the stage was finally set for the development of agriculture, which was just an extension of earlier attempts to increase resource stability. The technological development that had occurred throughout the Pleistocene by the early Holocene had made the transition to agriculture possible. As Hayden puts it, "domestication resulted from attempts to increase resource reliability by increasing resource diversity in areas that were not well endowed with *r*-selected resources but in which some use and manipulation of such resources was possible" (1981:529).

Hayden's argument is full of problems. To limit ourselves just to the most serious, it is difficult to see first of all how his resource stress model is capable of accounting for the particular directionality of the long-term social evolution leading up to and through the emergence of agriculture. If the reason people change their subsistence practices is because of periodic resource stress, then why don't they revert to previous practices when that stress subsides? The existence of a *linear* direction to subsistence change implies the existence of some other *linear* process that is involved in pushing it along. But this second process cannot be Hayden's concept of resource stress as he has formulated it, because he refers to this stress as involving the *cyclical fluctuation* of resources. Population growth and ensuing population pressure are, however, logical candidates for the linear process that is pushing subsistence change.[6]

In addition, Hayden seems to hold a very distorted view of what population pressure theorists like Cohen are arguing. Hayden perpetuates several of the misunderstandings about these theories that we reviewed earlier, and he makes the curious statement that "an entire school of prehistorians would have us believe that neither 'population pressure' nor stress existed – or at least that they were not significant for cultural evolution – for over 2,000,000 years. They argue that . . . real 'population pressure' only came to exist at the end of the Pleistocene. I maintain that this is untenable and does not accord with the data at hand" (1981:529). Hayden is absolutely right. Such a notion is untenable and does not fit the archaeological data. But who makes such an argument? Certainly not Cohen. As we have seen, he explicitly makes population pressure a continuous process throughout prehistory. Indeed, one must almost wonder whether Hayden is actually a population pressure theorist in spite of himself. Such a notion might help us understand Cohen's (1981a) otherwise puzzling statement that Hayden's theory is really a refinement and extension of his own population pressure model rather than a refutation of it.[7]

A cultural selectionist theory

A fascinating and very unusual theory of agricultural origins has been presented by David Rindos (1980, 1984, 1989). Rindos's theory is formulated as an explicitly Darwinian evolutionary theory that he believes is sharply at variance with social evolutionary (non-Darwinian) interpretations. According to Rindos, domestication evolved as an entirely unintentional, nondeliberate process having nothing to do with human choice. The evolution of domestication was a mechanistic process governed entirely by objective evolutionary forces. Rindos refers to his theory as a type of *cultural selectionism.*

Rindos argues that all theories of the origin of agriculture have erred in looking at plant–human relationships entirely from the standpoint of humans and suggests that we need to refocus the analysis so as to give much more attention to the plant side of these relationships. It is Rindos's contention that agriculture ultimately arose as the result of a series of plant–human symbioses that benefitted both plants and humans. Plants and humans have interacted in ways that have increased the fitness of both, and it is this enhanced fitness of both parties, Rindos claims, that has driven the evolution of domestication.

Rindos distinguishes among three types of domestication, each of which marks a type of evolutionary level. *Incidental domestication*, the simplest and earliest form of domestication, occurs when there is a change in certain morphological characteristics of a plant as a result of its relationship with humans. Humans act as opportunistic agents for the plant, by protecting it in some way for example, and thus produce changes in the plant that increase its fitness.[8] Since humans feed on the plant, an increase in its fitness increases their fitness as well. The next level of domestication is *specialized domestication*, which involves an intensification and elaboration of tendencies present in incidental domestication. Humans act as dispersal agents for particular plants, and thus these plants become more common (and hence more fit in the Darwinian sense). Since the plants are being dispersed throughout the areas of human habitation, humans are feeding on them more and becoming increasingly dependent on them. The stage is eventually set for *agricultural domestication*, which occurs when humans are actively involved in planting, tending, and harvesting plants – that is, they are practicing agriculture as we commonly understand it. Rindos specifies just how this entire evolutionary process actually works in the following terms (1984:192–3):

Early domesticatory interactions indirectly increase the total potential yield obtainable from an environment. . . . the early evolution of domesticated plants proceeds very slowly. The major effect of domestication during these early periods comes from the increases in wild yield that it encourages. Increase in total available yield permits human population growth. Population growth, however, brings with it increased environmental disturbance and therefore increased potential for the initiation of specialized domestication. . . .

In moving from incidental to agricultural domestication, humans experience a radical shift in feeding strategy. Rather than construct diets from the most highly valued foods in the environment, humans begin to feed on all resources in direct proportion to their perceived abundance; all available resources as perceived by the culture are utilized, or diet breadth is increased. The interaction of shift toward higher levels of utilization of resources and the increasing abundance and yield of domesticates provides the positive feedback system that brings about the transition to full agricultural subsistence. This transition is rapid relative to the processes occurring during incidental and specialized domestication.

Rindos emphasizes that population growth and population pressure make important contributions to this process, but not in the way suggested by Cohen and other population pressure theorists. They are not direct causes of the process, but simply covariants of it. As he says, "Population 'pressures' exist, but they are only a partial expression of a fundamental dynamic" (1984:247).

Rindos's model of the evolution of domestication throughout prehistory is intriguing and elaborately argued, but it does not stand up well to careful inspection. One of the most obvious problems with it is its uncompromising Darwinian nature. Rindos insists that the evolution of domestication is an entirely mechanistic process devoid of any human intent needed to make it work. He rejects the idea that it is any sort of adaptive process because he sees the concept of adaptation as tied up inextricably with human intentionality and choice. But the general theory guiding this book insists that social evolution is indeed an adaptational process resting on human intent and choice, and *Social Evolutionism* argued at length for such a notion. Purging human choice from a theory of social evolution is a very unwise move. Theories thought to be "mechanistic" or "objectivistic" are widely suspect in the social sciences (indeed, the word "mechanistic" is usually a term of abuse), and the widespread (but erroneous) belief that most social evolutionary theories are such has been one reason for the rejection of social evolutionism.

Moreover, Rindos's claim that the variation that is selected for in the process of domestication is undirected is a fatal trap into which most Darwinian theorists of social evolution fall. In *Social Evolutionism* I showed the unreasonableness of this notion. Most of the variation that is selected for in social evolution is highly purposive and deliberate rather than random and undirected, a fact that makes social evolution sharply distinct from biological evolution.

An additional problem with Rindos's theory concerns the specifics of the worldwide transition to agriculture. It is extremely difficult to see how the process described by Rindos – a mechanical process devoid of human intent and resting on undirected variation – could have produced such striking parallels all over the world in the nature of the shift to agriculture and the extraordinary similarity in the timing of this shift in so many world regions and subregions. The remarkable parallel evolution that the agricultural transition represents would seem to implicate human intent and choice in the deepest way (Redding, 1988; Rosenberg, 1990).

CONCLUSIONS

Research over the past 30 years has decisively disproved the old idealist theory that the emergence of agriculture was really a conceptual revolution – that agriculture was a difficult discovery that, once made, had self-evident virtues that caused it to spread all over the world. The evidence is now overwhelmingly against this interpretation, which was more or less the prevailing argument from at least the late nineteenth century to the 1960s. We now have a good understanding of what will not work, and that has helped give us a much better understanding of what does seem to work in explaining the first great evolutionary transition in human history.

Most current theories of the Neolithic Revolution are materialist theories of one sort or another. I have argued in favor of Cohen's population pressure theory as the best of all these theories, not least because of its capacity to explain the fully worldwide character of the agricultural transition and its extraordinary simultaneity throughout the world. More research is certainly needed to build on and solidify the kind of argument Cohen presents, as well as to show the ways in which this argument will undoubtedly need to be qualified or modified in the years ahead. Critics of the population pressure argument are forced to recognize that most current theories give population pressure at least some role in prehistoric subsistence intensification and the rise of agriculture, even if they do not give it the major role. The major competitors of the population pressure theory, the climatological and resource stress theories, give it a role, as does even Rindos's cultural selectionist theory. There can be little doubt that population pressure has played a significant role in the evolutionary events of the Upper Paleolithic, Mesolithic, and Neolithic. Had Paleolithic hunter-gatherers been able to keep their populations from growing, the whole world would likely still be surviving entirely by hunting and gathering, and it would have been neither possible nor necessary for me to have written this book.

Before closing this chapter, a final note about the specific evolutionary character of the agricultural transition. Earlier I emphasized that the concept of the Neolithic Revolution was really a misnomer in terms of time. The Neolithic Revolution was not something that occurred suddenly, as used to be thought. Once humans began to make use of domesticated plants and animals, they did so only gradually, and it usually took thousands of years for them to move from complete reliance on foraging to complete (or at least primary) dependence on agriculture. Moreover, the Neolithic was basically just the continuation of a process that had begun among hunting and gathering groups thousands, even tens of thousands, of years earlier. Upper Paleolithic big game hunting populations, which dominated the Earth at 20,000 BP and earlier, gradually intensified their subsistence by pursuing smaller animals; by fishing, collecting shellfish, and exploiting other forms of aquatic life; and by making plants of many types an ever larger part of their diet. Agriculture came to be practiced once the declining returns and food stresses of the foraging life made the extra work of agriculture worth the effort, or perhaps even necessary.

So the Neolithic Revolution was not temporally a revolution at all. To this it must be added that some anthropologists think of it as not especially revolutionary even in a social sense. The French anthropologist Alain Testart (1982, 1988) and the archaeologist Stuart Fiedel (1987) question the fundamental distinction that has traditionally been made between hunter-gatherers and agricultural-ists as different types of society. Speaking for his generation, Fiedel notes that (1987:162) "the consensus among archaeologists today is that the dichotomy between hunting and gathering and agriculture was too sharply drawn by past theorists." For his part, Testart notes that hunter-gatherers often differ significantly among themselves. He distinguishes between hunter-gatherers who store food and those who do not, noting that the latter tend to be nomadic, have low population densities, and be highly egalitarian, whereas the former tend to be sedentary or semisedentary, have high population densi-ties, and have significant social differentiation and inequality. Testart is referring to recent hunter-gatherers known ethnographically, but we saw early in this chapter how his point applies very well to the complex prehistoric hunter-gatherers of Mesolithic times and perhaps earlier. Testart concludes that storing hunter-gatherers have an economy much more like that of agriculturalists than like that of nonstoring hunter-gatherers. What sense does it make, then, he asks, to oppose hunter-gatherers as a category to agriculturalists as a category (1982:530):

The adoption of an agricultural way of life is currently considered a turning point in history comparable in importance to the Industrial Revolution: hence, the notion of a "Neolithic Revolution" .... This conception has its roots in the idea that there is a neat opposition between hunter-gatherers and agriculturalist-pastoralists . . . . Now, storing hunter-gatherer societies exhibit . . . characteristics . . . which have been considered typical of agricultural societies and possible only with an agricultural way of life. . . . Agriculturalists and storing hunter-gatherers together are [in the final analysis] neatly in opposition to nonstoring hunter-gatherers.

Testart does make an important point. Is there any remaining sense, then, in which we are entitled to think of the Neolithic Revolution as revolutionary? The answer is yes, for the Neolithic Revolution was truly revolutionary in its eventual *consequences*. Hunter-gatherers who store food, have dense populations, and live sedentary lives are able to create some of the dimensions of social complexity and inequality typical of many agriculturalists, but they can go only so far in this direction on a hunting and gathering base. Once societies made the transition to an agricultural economy, they not only began to be characterized by social inequalities, but the way was paved for the emergence of complexities and inequalities on a scale unimaginable in any hunter-gatherer society. For within a few thousand years after the Neolithic Revolution there occurred a second great evolutionary transformation, the rise of civilization and the state. The pace of social evolution was accelerating, and the second revolution was far greater in its impact on human life than the first. The next chapter is devoted to exploring the nature of this second revolution.

NOTES

1 By use of the word "worldwide" I do not literally mean in every single nook and cranny of the globe. I mean simply throughout a large portion of the world.

2 This is nowhere more clearly shown than in some recent quantitative research on the transition to agriculture in the Tehuacán Valley of Mesoamerica (Christenson, 1980). At the very beginning of the practice of agriculture it is estimated that domesticates provided no more than about 4 percent of subsistence. After 7800 BP this had increased to only about 14 percent, and to only about 22 percent after 6150 BP. It was not until approximately 3000 BP that people were gaining more than half of their subsistence from domesticates.

3 Indeed, detailed paleopathological studies surveyed by Cohen (Cohen and Armelagos, 1984; Cohen, 1989) consistently show prehistoric hunter-gatherer populations to be better nourished and freer of disease than later agricultural populations. This evidence constitutes very strong support for Sahlins's "original affluent society" thesis, and provides another excellent reason for comprehending the resistance of hunter-gatherers to the adoption of agriculture.

4 The ability of hunter-gatherers to assess population densities over wide areas and shift individuals from areas of higher density to areas of lower density was probably rooted in their extremely flexible group boundaries. The frequent movement of people from one local band to another would have meant that a great deal of information about the relationship between numbers and resources would have been produced. Through a complex chain of interacting bands, information could be obtained about the state of affairs of groups hundreds or even thousands of miles away.

5 We see that Henry's theory does give a role to population pressure. However, as he would be the first to point out, its role is quite different from its role in Cohen's theory. In Cohen's theory it is a "prime mover," whereas in Henry's it is a specific result of climatic, ecological, and subsistence changes.

6 Hayden's probable reply would be that once people have developed a new technology in response to resource unreliability they will be motivated to retain it because of the advantages it has brought them and can continue to bring them. Further instances of resource stress then bring about further episodes of technological innovation, until the level of agricultural technology is finally reached. However, the argument that a floor is always being placed on technological development – that, once acquired, a given level of technology will always be retained – is known to be false. Ester Boserup (1965) mentions a number of instances in which people have regressed in their level of technology under certain circumstances. The main circumstance in which this occurs appears to be a reduction in population pressure. It seems logical to assume that technological regression would also result from a reduction in resource stress.

7 In a more recent work, Hayden (1990) has made a significant alteration in his argument. He suggests that technological advances allowed Upper Paleolithic hunter-gatherers living in resource-rich/environments to concentrate on *r*-selected resources, which are virtually impossible to overexploit. This resource abundance led to the rise of status competition similar to that observed among "big men" in contemporary horticultural societies. As status competition intensified and became more elaborate, agriculture was developed as a further means for high-status individuals to maintain and enhance their status. This argument seems to me no more successful, and perhaps even less successful, than Hayden's original resource stress theory. The only evidence Hayden presents to support it is highly circumstantial and unconvincing. A similar argument has been presented by Barbara Bender (1978, 1985), but it is even less convincing, for, unlike Hayden, Bender sees the rise of status competition as a self-levitating process that appears out of nowhere.

8 Rindos gives as an example of incidental domestication one of the subsistence habits of the Chukchi, hunter-gatherers in northeast Asia. They gather large supplies of plant foods for the winter far away from their tents. As a result of bringing these plants to their tents, their seeds are dispersed and they end up growing in the refuse right around their tents. One of these plants, the cineraria, has come to be found only around the tents.

3

The Origin of Civilization and the State

In the previous chapter the argument was made that the Neolithic Revolution was truly revolutionary not in a temporal sense, but in the extraordinary evolutionary consequences it engendered. In the millennia after about 10,000 BP, societies all over the world evolved along remarkably parallel lines. These societies became much larger and more complex, evolved stratified systems of social organization, and developed political systems in which power and control were increasingly concentrated in the hands of small elites and increasingly used by these elites for purposes of self-aggrandizement. In this chapter I trace this momentous process of evolutionary transformation by relying exclusively upon archaeological evidence. At the end of the chapter I try to show that a very similar evolutionary process can be inferred through several typological orderings of ethnographic data.

A TYPOLOGY OF SOCIOPOLITICAL EVOLUTION

Archaeological reconstructions of evolutionary sequences of sociopolitical change have been greatly aided in the past two or three decades by evolutionary typologies generated from ethnographic data. The typology that has been used most frequently is that of Elman Service (1962, 1971), who distinguishes four major stages of sociopolitical evolution: bands, tribes, chiefdoms, and states. Although Service's typology has been criticized in various ways and slightly different ones proposed, to my mind it still represents the best typology we have, or at least one that is as good as any other.

Bands are small groups ordinarily containing a few dozen people who move continuously in the search for food. They are associated only with a hunting and gathering form of subsistence economy. These groups are markedly egalitarian, and so much so that they frequently maintain ritualized forms of social interaction designed to put an end to any economic selfishness and hoarding before it gets much of a start. Bands contain informal leaders who may suggest and give guidance, but these leaders have no power or authority if by power we mean the capacity to control others even despite their resistance and by authority the legitimate right to control others.

Tribes are similar in many respects to bands. They contain only informal leaders, and no person acquires real power or authority over anyone else. Like bands, they are highly democratic in their decision-making roles and processes. Unlike bands, however, they are normally associated with societies devoted to horticulture or pastoralism rather than hunting and gathering. Politically, tribes are what have sometimes been called *segmentary societies*, or societies composed of autonomous villages. Linkages between villages are limited to kinship or ceremonial relations, and there is no overarching political structure uniting the villages into a single functioning whole. Tribes are also highly egalitarian; some, however, especially the so-called "big man systems" widely found throughout Melanesia in contemporary times, are characterized by highly competitive relations in which men vigorously compete for social status. These systems have a form of what Morton Fried (1967) has called "social ranking."

With the *chiefdom* we encounter a radically new kind of sociopolitical system. Robert Carneiro (1981:45) defines a chiefdom as "an autonomous political unit comprising a number of villages or communities under the permanent control of a paramount chief." A slightly more specific definition is offered by Claessen and Skalnik (1978a:22): "Chiefdoms are socio-political organizations with a centralized government, hereditary hierarchical status arrangements with an aristocratic ethos but no formal, legal apparatus of forceful repression, and without the capacity to prevent fission." It is clear that chiefdoms are hierarchical societies, although they do vary significantly among themselves in terms of size and scale of integration; some are a good deal more hierarchical than others (Carneiro, 1981; Earle, 1987). Earle (1987:288) notes that chiefdoms may "vary in size from simple chiefdoms integrating populations of perhaps a thousand to complex chiefdoms with populations in the tens of thousands." In recent times chiefdoms have been found in several parts of the world, especially in Polynesia and Africa.

The relationship between chiefdoms and social stratification is an important issue that has unfortunately been muddied in recent years. Following Fried's (1967) distinction between "ranking" and "stratification," numerous scholars have tended to equate chiefdoms with "rank societies." Rank societies are those with elaborate status distinctions – social ranking – but without corresponding inequalities in social power and material privilege – without class stratification, in other words. Unfortunately, Fried used the term "rank society" to cover more evolutionary territory than Service's concept of chiefdom (Carneiro, 1981, 1991). Some of Fried's examples of rank societies were chiefdoms, but some were also more simply organized "big man systems." Although Fried has usually been interpreted as equating rank societies and chiefdoms, as Carneiro notes many chiefdoms have gone beyond ranking and developed stratification. In fact, it is likely that most chiefdoms are stratified, with only the simplest chiefdoms having ranking without stratification. Rank societies are characteristic of the simplest chiefdoms or, more likely, certain forms of tribal society ("big man systems").

I follow those who see the chiefdom in a decidedly evolutionary sense, that is, as a form of sociopolitical organization intermediate between tribes and states, and as an organizational form that is an essential precursor of the state (Carneiro, 1981, 1991; Earle, 1987).[1] Some scholars have seen chiefdoms as evolutionary dead ends, or as an evolutionary alternative to the state rather than a precursor to it (Webb, 1973; Sanders and Webster, 1978). There are two problems with this latter idea. For one thing, it is much too large an evolutionary leap from tribal society to the state without some intermediate form of organization (Carneiro, 1981). It is implausible to assume that societies can evolve from autonomous villages to the complexity and scale of organization represented by the state without first going through less drastic changes. Moreover, Earle has commented that "since archaeological evidence now suggests that chiefdoms temporally precede states in many areas, a good argument may be made for the evolutionary development from chiefdom to state" (Earle, 1978:2; cited in Carneiro, 1981:52).

We now come to the *state*. There has been far from complete consensus in defining this term. Here are two definitions from well-known scholars of the state: "A state is an autonomous political unit, encompassing many communities within its territory and having a centralized government with the power to draft men for war or work, levy and collect taxes, and decree and enforce laws" (Carneiro, 1970:733). "The . . . state is a centralized socio-political organization for the regulation of social relations in a complex, stratified society divided into at least two basic strata, or emergent social classes – viz., the rulers and the ruled – whose relations are characterized by political dominance of the former and tributary obligations of the latter, legitimized by a common ideology of which reciprocity is the basic principle" (Claessen and Skalnik, 1978b:640). The problem with these definitions is that they do not make clear just how one can distinguish between chiefdoms and states, inasmuch as all of the characteristics listed in these definitions can be found in at least some chiefdoms. From these definitions it appears that the distinction between chiefdoms and states is simply a quantitative one – states have what chiefdoms have, but more of it.

I propose that the distinction between chiefdoms and states should be made on qualitative rather than quantitative grounds. I would define a state as *a form of sociopolitical organization that has achieved a monopoly over the means of violence within a specified territory.* The key phrase here is "monopoly over the means of violence." This is precisely what a state has that a chiefdom lacks. Using this definition, we would call aboriginal Hawaii at the time of European contact a chiefdom because the Hawaiian leaders lacked the capacity to extend their realm of power beyond a certain point. Successful rebellions against the Hawaiian chiefs were common, especially when they "ate the powers of government too much" (Sahlins, 1963). The Aztec of central Mexico at the time of European contact, on the other hand, had achieved what the Hawaiians had not – a monopoly of force – and this allowed them a leeway of political action much greater than what prevailed in aboriginal Hawaii.

The emphasis on monopolistic control of force as the criterion of statehood is perhaps the most common ingredient in definitions of the state, but it has been objected to by Carneiro (1981) and Anthony Giddens (1985), who claim that there are societies that are widely considered states in which a complete monopoly over the use of force did not exist. While this is undoubtedly true, it is not a *complete* monopoly over the use of force that I am emphasizing. A monopoly of force exists not when it is complete or total, but when it is sufficient to crush rebellions against state power. Moreover, to claim that a state maintains a capacity to crush rebellions does not mean that it can successfully do so 100 percent of the time. There are weak and strong states, and weak states do sometimes encounter successful rebellions. The point is, however, that states are generally successful in crushing rebellion, whereas chiefdoms are generally unsuccessful at doing so.

Sanders and Webster (1978) have identified some of the typical characteristics of societies having the state. In addition to a monopoly over the use of force, these include large, dense populations based on agriculture; highly centralized organizational foci; centralized and highly specialized political institutions; unequal access to basic subsistence resources; complex economic specialization focused on both subsistence and nonsubsistence goods; and a social class structure that is at least partially hereditary. Ronald Cohen (1978) has also produced a list of some of the most basic features of state-level societies. He identifies the following: a ruling class under a wealthy monarch, the wealth of which is extracted from the rest of the population; urbanism and the architectural expression of class differences between an urban upper class and the rest of the society; occupational differentiation into such groups as peasants, craftsmen, traders, priests, diviners, and entertainers; a complex system of trade and markets; and a complex set of judicial procedures developed to mediate disputes. States do not necessarily have all of these characteristics, but they do tend to have most of them. (And I would add, of course, that they must have a monopoly over the means of violence.)

Sanders and Webster's point that states have highly specialized institutions perhaps deserves some elaboration. Johnson and Earle (1987) make the same point, noting that the political institutions of chiefdoms tend to be highly generalized. In states the "military is responsible for conquest, for defense, and often for internal peace; the bureaucracy is responsible for mobilizing the state's income, for meeting many local managerial responsibilities, and more generally for handling and monitoring information flow; the state religion serves both to organize production and to sanctify state rule" (Johnson and Earle, 1987:246). The specialized institutions of the state are at least partially independent of the kinship system, whereas the political institutions of the chiefdom are still strongly rooted in kinship connections.

Many scholars have used the term *civilization* in addition to, or instead of, the term state. For the most part, the two terms have been used interchangeably. Brian Fagan (1989) lists as the leading characteristics of a civilization urbanism and city life; economies devoted to capital accumulation through tribute and taxation and which are capable of supporting many non-food producers; long-distance trade; craft specialization; public buildings and other forms of monumental architecture; advances in the areas of record keeping, science, and mathematics; and some type of writing. This is very similar to the lists of state characteristics provided by Sanders and Webster and by Cohen. It is probably fair to say that the term civilization is the more inclusive one and that, technically speaking, the term state might be reserved for the particular form of political organization normally characteristic of a civilization. (I say "normally" because civilizations have not necessarily always had states. Some of the earliest civilizations may have been based on very advanced chiefdoms.) However, it seems best to avoid putting ourselves into a conceptual straitjacket. Henceforth we shall employ the terms civilization, state, and state-level society virtually interchangeably. Context will make it clear just what we are talking about. In the rare instance in which a civilization may be associated with a chiefdom instead of a state, this will be made apparent.[2]

THE ORIGIN OF CIVILIZATION AND THE STATE AS A PROCESS OF PARALLEL EVOLUTION

The very first states and civilizations – what Morton Fried (1967) has called "pristine" states – began to arise in several parts of the Old World after about 5,000 years ago. The same process of sociopolitical evolution also took place somewhat later in various regions of the New World. It is extraordinary that several of the regions of state formation were the same regions that witnessed the Neolithic Revolution several millennia earlier. Like the Neolithic Revolution, the process of state formation was also one in which the state evolved independently in each major world region. We once again encounter a remarkable process of parallel evolution, a process that we now need to trace region by region.

State formation in Mesopotamia

The world's very first states arose in Mesopotamia around 5100 BP. The first Mesopotamian state was centered around the city of Uruk. This settlement contained upwards of 10,000 people and several large temples, one of which was built on a ziggurat, or stepped pyramid. The civilization that developed in this area has come to be known as the Sumerian civilization. It consisted of some 13 city-states that were politically autonomous. Despite their autonomy, however, these city-states belonged to the same basic cultural tradition and "had collectively developed many of the classical elements of southwest Asian civilization, including ziggurats, brick platforms, the potter's wheel, wheeled carts, metalworking, sailboats, and writing" (Wenke, 1990). There is wide agreement that Sumerian civilization was highly stratified (Lamberg-Karlovsky and Sabloff, 1979; R.M. Adams, 1966). At the very top of the social hierarchy was a god-king, below which was a class of nobles or princely families. As Mesopotamian civilization was heavily involved in trade, there was a class of wealthy merchants, and of course artisans of many types. The bulk of the population consisted of peasants, and at the very bottom of the social order was a class of slaves. That there was considerable occupational specialization within the economy is indicated by the different kinds of palace entertainers and servants: gatekeepers, cooks, stewards, cup-bearers, messengers, and concubines, for example. Different kinds of craftsmen included masons, potters, reed-weavers, clothworkers, leatherworkers, carpenters, smiths, stonecutters, millers, and brewers (R.M. Adams, 1966; Wenke, 1990).

Politically, early Mesopotamian civilization was theocratic, but over the centuries there was a gradual shift in a more secular direction, with the power of kings increasing at the expense of priests. Rulers eventually came to have imperialistic ambitions, and warfare became almost constant. One of the most imperialistic of the Mesopotamian rulers was Sargon of Akkad, who came to power in about 4350 BP. Sargon and some of his successors launched military expeditions in all directions, conquering numerous city-states (Wenke, 1990).

Mesopotamian society was complex and depended on an intensive form of agriculture based on the plow. Peasants produced large economic surpluses that were essential for the maintenance of a complex urban economy. This urban economy was integrated into a vast system of trade, and trade routes developed along the delta waterways. Raw materials were obtained from distant areas and used in the manufacture of numerous finished products, such as ornaments and weapons. As the demand for raw materials increased over time, market networks spread into increasingly remote areas (Fagan, 1989). Because of the importance of trade, individual merchants and "capitalists" became an important part of the urban economy (Wenke, 1990).

Civilization and the state in Egypt and the rest of Africa

Egyptian civilization developed at about the same time as Mesopotamia, 5100 BP. Many scholars have paid close attention to the contrasts between Mesopotamia and Egypt. Politically, there is a very important contrast. Whereas Mesopotamia was characterized by a highly decentralized city-state system, Egypt had a highly centralized, bureaucratic state (Janssen, 1978; Trigger, 1982). In this context, Egyptian civilization was centered much more around a royal court, royal mortuary complexes, and, in general, on the person of the king (Trigger, 1982). Along economic lines, in contrast to Mesopotamia Egyptian civilization during its early centuries had no significant economic slavery, and there were no independent merchants as there were in Mesopotamia (Wenke, 1990).

Like Mesopotamia, though, Egypt had extremely powerful political leaders and a well-developed class system. The Egyptian kings – the pharaohs – claimed divine status (Janssen, 1978; Trigger, 1982). The pharaoh's person was taboo, and it was he who "guaranteed and maintained the cosmic order as well as its counterpart, law and order on earth" (Janssen, 1978:219). At the top of the class hierarchy was, of course, the pharaoh. Below him were great nobles, lesser nobles, wealthy farmers, craftsmen and retainers, soldiers, and peasants (Wenke, 1990; Trigger, 1982).

Egypt also had two of the other leading characteristics of civilization, writing and monumental architecture. Their system of hieroglyphic writing is, of course, famous, as is the leading feature of their monumental architecture, the pyramids. The first of these pyramids was constructed by Djoser around 4680 BP. This pyramid and the others that were built later are generally understood as grand symbols of the power of the state. As Brian Fagan (1989:421) has commented, "There is something megalomaniacal about the pyramids, built as they were with an enormous expenditure of labor and energy. They reflect the culmination of centuries of gradual evolution of the Egyptian state, during which the complexity of the state and the authority of the bureaucracy grew hand in hand."

The emergence of the state in the rest of Africa came later. Until recently it had been thought that African states arose as a result of external influences, especially trade. But the rise of states in Africa is now viewed as the result of both external and internal influences. It is recognized that trade was undoubtedly important, but much of African state formation is now seen to have been a process of independent evolution (McIntosh and McIntosh, 1988; Connah, 1987).

The best analysis of the origin of states in Africa is that of Connah (1987), who points out that the earliest African states outside of Egypt arose along the middle Nile. The Nubian kingdom of Kerma achieved the peak of its development about 3600 BP. Kerma might have been a chiefdom rather than a true state, but at any rate it was followed by Napata around 2900 BP, which in turn was succeeded by Meroë around 2400 BP. As Connah (1987) notes, archaeological evidence strongly indicates both urbanization and true statehood for Meroë. This evidence includes the remains of towns and cities, monumental architecture (including palaces and temples), and sculptures depicting gods, rulers, and defeated enemies. Meroë was a stratified society that contained a high level of occupational specialization, and it was greatly involved in a network of external trade.

In the Ethiopian highlands, the state of Axum arose sometime after about 2500 BP. Axum had writing, urban centers, multistoreyed buildings, palaces, and large stelae. It seemed to be a stratified society containing both peasants and slaves, and the economy contained substantial occupational differentiation. Axum was located at the center of a complex web of trade routes, and there can be little doubt that trade significantly influenced its development.

In the west African savanna, there is some evidence for a state at the site of Jenne after around AD 200. In the west African forest, there are indicators of state formation and urbanization around the beginning of the second millennium AD. The main states here were Ife and Benin, which seemed to be based on a conception of divine kingship. As for the east African coast, the archaeological evidence is inconclusive, but Connah thinks that some cities, especially Moga-dishu, Pate, Malindi, Mombasa, and Kilwa, may have functioned as small city-states sometime after AD 1000, and that some of these city-states may have come to dominate others.

In southern Africa, the most important site is what is now known as Great Zimbabwe. During the second quarter of the present millennium, a small elite seemed to have gained power over the rest of the population, and thus Great Zimbabwe may have been the center of a state. Great Zimbabwe was undergoing urbanization, and there are a number of indicators of social stratification.

The state and civilization in China

Another of the great transitions to civilization and the state in the Old World occurred in China. As Kwang-chih Chang (1986:314) has noted, archaeological excavations of the so-called Erh-li-t'ou Culture, dated to around 4100–3800 BP, have

yielded a whole range of remains indicative of a stage of cultural and social development qualitatively different from the Lung-shan Culture [the previous culture], a stage that is characterized by palatial architecture, tombs of royal proportions . . . furnished with scarce goods, bronze ritual vessels and weapons, sets of specialized wine vessels, possible human sacrifice at rituals, and a hint of writing. These new features point to the existence in Erh-li-t'ou society of a powerful and wealthy elite that was decidedly a level higher than the chiefly aristocracy of the Lung-shan Culture sites.

In other words, civilization and the state were emerging. At or slightly after this time all of the major social and cultural correlates of the state and civilization were present or in the process of emerging: monumental architecture; large population concentrations; occupa-tional specialization; written records; dramatic differences in wealth, power, and prestige; and major public works projects (Wenke, 1990).

As Robert Wenke (1990) has said, during this time China was in the process of really becoming China. And Chinese civilization was clearly on a par with Mesopotamia and Egypt. As Wenke notes (1990:442), "The Shang ceremonial and administrative structures are perhaps not as impressive in size or cost as the ziggurats and temples of Mesopotamia, but the level of occupational specialization, the immense wealth of the burials, and the intensity of organization of the agricultural and economic systems remind one of the Mesopo-

tamian city-states of the late fourth millennium BC."
Early Chinese civilization was highly stratified and was headed
by a king who was assisted by a hierarchically-arranged nobility.
Around the end of the Shang period, about 3100 BP, many nobles
had achieved a certain autonomous control over their own domains.
About this same time there were many walled towns throughout
China, undoubtedly an indicator of the frequency of warfare. After
3100 BP with the end of the Shang dynasty and the emergence of
the Chou dynasty, the political economy of China resembled a feudal
system (Wenke, 1990).

Chinese civilization was based upon a highly intensive system of
agriculture, but after about 2500 BP this system was further intensified. The irrigation systems for which China has long been famous
were developed. Irrigation agriculture permitted very intensive cultivation of wet-rice species and helped to support huge population
densities. Also introduced were the ox-drawn plow and systems of
crop rotation (Wenke, 1990).

The Indus valley civilization

Perhaps the least known of the early civilizations is the one that
arose in the Indus River valley in what is now Pakistan around 4600
BP. Our understanding of this civilization, which has come to be
known as the Harappan civilization, is very general and sketchy. Not
only are the archaeological data very limited but, as Possehl (1990)
notes, there is no really useful historical record that could help to
fill in the gaps left by archaeological research.

The Harappan civilization contained a number of cities, the largest
of which, Mohenjo-daro, contained an estimated 40,000 people at
its peak around 4000 BP. Harappan civilization as a whole may have
contained around 200,000 people at that time. Archaeological work
reveals considerable occupational specialization at Mohenjo-daro:
farmers, herdsmen, goldsmiths, potters, weavers, brickmasons, and
architects, for example (Wenke, 1990). Whether the Harappan civilization was stratified or not is disputed. Miller (1985) claims that
there is no evidence for classes of wealthy and impoverished individuals. Possehl (1990) disputes this, claiming that the existence of
sumptuous items of personal adornment and a growth in the use
of precious metals and beads indicates a stratified society. And not

only is the stratified character of Harappan society in dispute, but it has even been claimed that it was a chiefdom rather than a true state (cf. Possehl, 1990). Although Possehl and others think of it as a genuine state, the limited archaeological and historical data do not yet allow a firm conclusion. As Lamberg-Karlovsky and Sabloff (1979:203) note, "To date, not a single temple or palace has been uncovered, not a single royal tomb excavated."

Early European states

For a long time the first states in Europe were regarded as secondary states, but it is now recognized that the emergence of many of these states was due just as much to indigenous developments as to external influences (Champion et al., 1984). States developed first in Mediterranean Europe, especially in Greece. Fagan (1989) regards the complex Minoan and Mycenaean societies that emerged after about 4000 BP as states, as does Milisauskas (1978). Champion et al. (1984), on the other hand, see these societies as chiefdoms rather than states; they view the state as emerging only after about 2700 BP. After this time there were societies that "possessed centralized institutions of political and military authority, a monopoly over the exercise of force within the community and a permanent class of specialized rulers and administrators" (Champion et al., 1984:259). The disagreement between Fagan and Milisauskas on the one hand and Champion et al. on the other may be due largely to how the state is to be defined. Milisauskas's definition of the state is a loose one that makes no reference to a monopoly of force, whereas Champion et al., as the quote above makes clear, consider a mono-poly of force fundamental to the state. At any rate, we can safely say that states in Mediterranean Europe arose no later than 2700 BP and perhaps as early as 4000 BP.

With respect to temperate Europe there seems to be more agree-ment. Milisauskas sees simple chiefdoms emerging in this region after about 5000 BP, and he argues that the Bronze Age (beginning around 3900 BP in central Europe, around 3500 BP in Scandinavia) witnessed "a spectacular flowering of complex chiefdoms." Appar-ently even the late Bronze Age was still an age of chiefdoms rather than states (Champion et al., 1984). Champion et al. see the first states of temperate Europe emerging by the second century BC among the Celts. The Celtic kingdoms, they say, "were a form of state, with centralized authority, a hierarchical structure and a specialized ruling elite. This elite comprised the king himself and his immediate retinue of companions; supreme power rested with the king, and the companions were his political and military lieutenants, in a relationship not unlike clientage" (Champion et al., 1984:316). These early states were associated with growing populations, increasingly complex forms of social and economic organization, agricultural expansion and intensification, and craft specialization (Champion et al., 1984).

Civilization and the state in Mesoamerica

In the New World states developed entirely independently from Old World states. The main areas of New World state formation were Mesoamerica and Peru. Much more is known about state formation in the New World, especially in Mesoamerica, because much more archaeological research has been conducted there (cf. R.E.W. Adams, 1991). We can therefore say more, and speak with more certainty, about state formation in this part of the world than we could for the Old World regions of state formation, especially the Indus Valley.

There have been three major regions of the development of civilization in Mesoamerica: the lowlands, the Valley of Oaxaca, and the Valley of Mexico. The two major civilizations to emerge in the lowlands were the Olmec and the Maya (R.E.W. Adams, 1991). Olmec civilization arose along the Gulf Coast of Mexico sometime after about 3200 BP. Many sites have been explored archaeologically, but the most important are those at San Lorenzo, Tres Zapotes, and, especially, La Venta. At each of these sites large ceremonial centers were built. The center at La Venta was a complex of mounds, platforms, pyramids, and plazas (Fiedel, 1987). The Olmec have perhaps become most known for the large stone heads that they built. These heads, which were nine feet tall and appear to be wearing some sort of helmet, were probably intended to represent chiefs. It is not likely that the Olmec had evolved politically beyond the chiefdom level. Although they had many of the characteristics of a civilization, they were probably not a true state (Blanton et al., 1981).

The pinnacle of socioeconomic and political evolution in the lowlands was achieved by the Maya, who extended from the northern Gulf Coast region of Mexico all the way down into what is now Guatemala, Belize, and Honduras (R.E.W. Adams, 1991). Mayan chiefdoms arose as early as 2300 BP. Within several centuries these had evolved into states. The Maya achieved the peak of their development between AD 300 and 900. Stuart Fiedel (1987) places the Mayan transition from chiefdom to state in the sixth century AD. During this time, he contends, "where formerly there had been a two-level hierarchy of sites, there were now four levels, presumably indicative of a more complex administrative structure" (Fiedel, 1987:287). Like the Olmec, the Maya constructed ceremonial centers, but the Mayan ones were considerably larger and more elaborate than those of the Olmec. As Blanton et al. (1981:195–6) note, the Maya centers "had formal arrangements of plaza groups and causeways, 'acropolises' or mazelike complexes of palaces and courtyards, towering temple pyramids, ball courts, stelae, and altars." The greatest ceremonial center was the one at Tikal, which may have contained as many as 80,000 inhabitants. Mayan society had achieved elaborate occupational specialization, with flint and obsidian workers, potters, woodworkers, stoneworkers, textile weavers, human carriers, leatherworkers, musicians, manuscript painters, merchants, basket makers, and barkcloth makers (Blanton et al., 1981).

In the Valley of Oaxaca civilization was focused around the city of Monte Albán, which was founded around 2500 BP. By 2200 BP Monte Albán had essentially achieved statehood; its peak was achieved between AD 200 and 700, when it may have had as many as 30,000 inhabitants (Fiedel, 1987). Monte Albán contained an enclosed plaza area, along the sides of which were a ball court, several residences, and a number of buildings of unknown function. At the south end of the plaza was a palace complex that consisted of colonnaded halls, a sunken patio surrounded by pyramids, and the residence of Monte Albán's ruling family (Blanton et al., 1981).

In the Valley of Mexico civilization and the state had emerged by AD 1. Here there was established one of the greatest cities in all of pre-Hispanic Mesoamerica, Teotihuacán (R.E.W. Adams, 1991). Teotihuacán unified the entire Valley of Mexico and controlled it for hundreds of years. At its peak, Teotihuacán contained at least 125,000 inhabitants, and perhaps as many as 200,000. The city was planned with great care, containing two large pyramids, the Pyramid of the Sun and the Pyramid of the Moon, which were laid along the central avenue known as the Street of the Dead. This street also contained many temple complexes. Most of the political, commercial, and religious activity of the Valley of Mexico was concentrated in this great center (Blanton et al., 1981). After the collapse of Teotihuacán around AD 700, the Toltecs, with their capital at Tula, gradually came to power, although this capital was never the equal of Teotihuacán (Blanton et al., 1981). The most complex and elaborate civilization in all of pre-Hispanic Mesoamerica was that established by the Aztec, who achieved their peak between AD 1400 and 1520 (R.E.W. Adams, 1991). The Aztec established their capital at Tenochtitlán, on an island in the middle of a lake. Tenochtitlán covered some five square miles and had a population of 150,000 to 200,000. The city was linked by canals and causeways to outlying regions or suburbs, which together with the city itself may have totalled 400,000 inhabitants (Fiedel, 1987).

The Aztec developed a highly intensive agricultural system in order to feed the population. They are famed for their *chinampas* ("floating gardens"), which were constructed in Lake Texcoco by piling up mud in the lake and then planting crops in it. The Aztec were also a highly stratified society. At the top was the king, and below him were nobles with their own estates. Most of the population consisted of commoners, who belonged to clans (known as *calpulli*) that jointly farmed the land. Below the commoners were conquered and displaced farmers who, because they had no land, had to make their living by working the estates of the nobles. The lowest social classes consisted of porters and slaves (Fiedel, 1987).

The Aztec were a highly militaristic and imperialistic society constantly involved in extending their range of political control and famed for extensive human sacrifice and cannibalism. Countless numbers of prisoners of war were ritually sacrificed on Aztec temples and consumed in dishes made of peppers and indigenous spices (M. Harris, 1977). In 1521 they were conquered and subordinated by Cortes and his band of Spaniards.

Civilization and the state in Peru

Civilization and the state began in South America in the Andes sometime during the early part of the first millennium AD. One of the first states in this region was the Mochica civilization, which flourished between AD 200 and 700 (Fiedel, 1987). The capital city of this civilization was Moche, which contained two huge adobe structures, an extensive plaza, and a large residential zone. One of the adobe structures, the Huaca del Sol, was a terraced platform that stood 135 feet high (Fiedel, 1987). It is apparent that Mochica society was also highly stratified. As Fiedel (1987:326) has pointed out,

distinctive modes of dress denoted . . . specialized positions in Mochica society: rulers, nobles, priests, warriors, slaves, messengers, servants, hunters, fishermen and farmers. Marked differences in the wealth of grave goods that accompanied burials suggest that Mochica society was stratified, and scenes on the painted pots offer clear proof of hierarchical organization. Rulers are shown being carried about in sedan chairs, sitting on canopied thrones, receiving tribute and presiding at the executions of war captives.

Another important Andean state was the Chimu Empire, whose capital, Chan Chan, was founded around AD 800. The Chimu were a highly imperialistic, multivalley conquest state that at its peak came to control valleys over a distance of some 625 miles (Fiedel, 1987). The Chimu, though, were themselves conquered and incorporated into the Inca Empire, clearly the apex of sociopolitical evolution in pre-Hispanic South America. Like the Aztec, the Inca achieved their peak in the fifteenth and sixteenth centuries AD. At the top of the Inca political hierarchy was Sapa Inca, the emperor who claimed to be descended from Inti, the Sun God (Fiedel, 1987). The Inca Empire was geographically vast, stretching all the way from Colombia in the north to central Chile in the south. The various parts of the Empire were connected by a large network of paved roads. The Inca did not build cities, proving that urbanism is not a *sine qua non* of civilization and the state. Only the Sapa Inca's court and priests occupied the Inca capital, Cuzco, and most people lived in small towns or villages (Fiedel, 1987).

EXPLAINING THE ORIGIN OF CIVILIZATION AND THE STATE

The single most important feature of the rise of civilization and the state, it may be argued, is the striking parallelism in the evolutionary trajectories of numerous societies spaced widely throughout the globe. Not only did these societies evolve along remarkably parallel lines, but they did so within a period of only some 3,000 years, a fleeting moment in time, really, as archaeologists measure it. Years ago Marvin Harris (1968) called attention to the way in which the state societies of the New World constituted a kind of "second earth" for the comparison of evolutionary sequences and the testing of nomothetic theories of human sociocultural life. Harris singled out Robert Adams's (1966) comparison of the striking similarities between Mesopotamia and Mesoamerica in their transition to statehood, noting that it was a major contribution to the revival of nomothetic theories of human history and prehistory. But what was relatively novel in the 1960s has now become old hat, and archaeologists comment on the evolutionary parallelism in the rise of the state with frequency.

That civilization and the state arose in largely independent fashion in all of the major world centers of state formation is now widely accepted by archaeologists. Even African states, which had long been thought to be secondary results of external trade, are now being viewed as substantially independent occurrences. In this chapter we have identified eight major centers of independent state formation: Mesopotamia, Egypt, Africa outside of Egypt, China, the Indus Valley, Europe, Mesoamerica, and Peru.[3] But the state did not evolve only once in each of these regions, for in many of them there were several independent subcenters of state formation. We may add to this list the instances of political evolution in North America, South America outside of Peru, and Polynesia. Although true statehood was never achieved in any of these zones, advanced chiefdoms did develop, and there are striking parallels in sociopolitical evolution between these regions and the eight regions of state formation that we have considered (cf. Fiedel, 1987; Kirch, 1984).

What all of this means, I believe, is that the worldwide parallelism in the rise of civilization and the state is the single most important thing that must be explained by any theory of the origin of the state. While the differences among the early states and the evolutionary trajectories that led to them are also worthy of consideration and must also ultimately be explained, priority must be given to those theories that account in the most comprehensive way for state development as a worldwide process. Many theories of the rise of the state have been developed, and numerous factors have been proposed as major causes (cf. Athens, 1977). My survey of current theories of state formation suggests that there are basically five kinds of theories: theories emphasizing trade or economic exchange, Marxian theories, theories emphasizing population growth, theories emphasizing irrigation agriculture, and the well-known circumscription theory developed by Robert Carneiro. I want to discuss in turn the basic arguments of each of these theories and assess their adequacy as general theories of the origin of the state. Numerous scholars (e.g., Claessen and Skalnik, 1978b,c; Claessen and van de Velde, 1985; R. Cohen, 1978) have favored eclectic explanations in which many factors – a "whole wagonload" according to Carneiro (1987b) – are seen as combining to produce the state, but I shall leave these theories aside. To my mind, eclectic explanations are objectionable in principle because they unnecessarily confuse and complicate the search for workable theories and violate the time-honored scientific aim of parsimonious explanation.[4] One might also consider theories with an idealist cast, but there are few of these, and such theories as do exist (e.g., Coe, 1981; Freidel, 1981) often combine ideational factors with others, including material ones, and thus end up being eclectic.

Theories emphasizing trade or economic exchange

Theories emphasizing trade as the crucial factor in the origin of the state have been developed by Rathje (1971, 1972) and by Wright and Johnson (1975). The basic idea behind these theories is that the management of the economic apparatus of trade requires a complex political administration of the type that we call the state. Rathje's theory focuses on the emergence of the state in the Mesoamerican lowlands. From the point of view of their involvement in trade with the Mesoamerican highlands, Rathje sees the lowlands as having two different zones, a buffer zone and a core zone. The buffer zone is nearer to the highlands, and as a result it is easier for this zone to trade with the highlands than it is for the core zone. The advantageous position of the buffer zone puts pressure on the core zone to organize itself economically so as to be able to compete successfully with the buffer zone. As Jonathan Haas (1982:141) has pointed out, the occupants of the core zone "not only have to organize long-distance trade networks to obtain the resources, but since the buffer zone already supplies foodstuffs, they also must find other goods or services to offer in exchange. It is this set of circumstances that

Rathje sees as conducive to the development of state societies in the lowland core areas."

Wright and Johnson's theory is designed to explain the emergence of the state in Mesopotamia, specifically in southwest Iran. Other scholars have attempted to generalize the theory to state formation in Mesoamerica and Peru (Marcus, 1975; Isbell and Schreiber, 1978). The basic argument of this theory is quite similar to that of Rathje, although Wright and Johnson's theory focuses on intraregional rather than interregional trade. Wright and Johnson claim that increased demands for various resources led to increasing economic (especially labor) specialization, and this increasing specialization required increasing administrative specialization. A hierarchy of administrative units developed, and when there was at least a three-level hierarchy the state had emerged.

More recent theories with a similar emphasis have been developed by Richard Blanton and Gary Feinman and their colleagues (Blanton et al., 1981; Feinman, 1991). These archaeologists have been attempting to apply a model similar to Immanuel Wallerstein's (1974a, 1974b, 1979) world-system model of modern capitalism to the evolution of chiefdoms and states in Mesoamerica, especially to the Valley of Oaxaca. They insist that sociopolitical evolution at this level cannot be understood by looking only at the internal features of societies. It is necessary to engage in regional-level analyses in which different societies are seen as embedded in a larger whole and as functioning only as a part of that whole (rather than autonomously). Economic exchange is apparently the critical process that occurs within regional systems, and it is the key to sociopolitical evolution. Particular emphasis is given to the production and exchange of prestige goods among different societies within a region. As Feinman (1991:256–7) has noted,

the emergence of a greater degree of politico-ritual differentiation by the end of the Early Formative is cross-regionally tied both to the differential participation of households in that exchange sphere, as well as to the agglomeration of population around those communities that were more actively involved in exchange and had distinctive civic-ceremonial construction. In such instances, an emerging chief has both increased spatial access to potential surplus production, as well as a means to realize that surplus through exotic goods used either ritually and/or in local exchanges.

Blanton, Feinman, and others not only emphasize the importance of exchange networks involving prestige or exotic goods, but actually see elite control over the exchange of such goods as more important than their control over basic or more utilitarian goods (cf. Helms, 1979). The ability of elites to provide exotic goods for their followers is seen as vital to the legitimation and maintenance of elite power. This is one of the things that separates these more recent theories from the earlier trade theories.

These theories do not seem to me to be very satisfactory. The trade theories are not intended as general explanations of the world-wide emergence of the state, but focus instead on the rise of the state in a specific region. As Haas has pointed out (1982:145), "They are confined to particular circumstances . . . which are not found in all areas of initial state formation." To me, the more recent theories emphasizing elite exchange of prestige goods seem even more dubious. If the regional exchange of basic goods is not to be regarded as vital to state formation, it is even more difficult to see how the exchange of exotic items can be of more than minor significance. Graham Connah (1987) has suggested that trade with external regions may have operated as an *intensifier* of state development in Africa, but he believes that it usually did not play a major role in the original rise of African states. I would argue that his point can be extended to the problem of the worldwide formation of states.

Marxian theories

Marx and Engels regarded the state as an instrument of a society's dominant economic class (Engels, 1970[1884]). Once a society had come to be divided into dominant and subordinate classes, the struggle between them made the state essential if the dominant group was to protect its favored position. Subordinate groups could not be expected to accept their fate willingly and would be highly motivated to rebel against the dominant group, expropriate its wealth, and reallocate this wealth so as to gain a greater share of it for themselves. The ruling class recognized the need to protect themselves from this otherwise virtually inevitable eventuality. This led them to create an administrative apparatus that would have the power to prevent the threat posed by subordinate classes to the ruling class's economic position, which would be an apparatus holding a monopoly over the means of violence.

The most vigorous contemporary advocate of this theory is

Morton Fried (1967, 1978). As a cultural anthropologist, Fried has articulated and defended his theory on the basis of ethnographic rather than archaeological data. He argues that the emergence of social stratification is the key to the formation of the state. As we have seen, he distinguishes between stratification and social ranking. Social ranking exists when a society elaborates prestige differences among individuals that carry no corresponding differences in material wealth. In a rank society, some individuals command more respect and deference than others, but these high-status individuals do not control material resources so as to be able to carve out more material privilege than others. In many societies ranking has given way to stratification, which exists when there emerges what Fried has termed "differential access to resources." With stratification rather than ranking, the differential access of some groups to resources puts them in a position to use this access to acquire wealth. Hereditary strata form in which individuals are differentiated not only by social ranking, but by privilege and power as well.

According to Fried, a stratified society is unstable for exactly the reason identified by Marx and Engels: subordinate classes resent the wealth of others that has been achieved as the result of exploitation and domination of the subordinate classes, and thus are likely to rebel against any such arrangement. Therefore they must create an organization linked to them and holding the administrative and military capacity to protect them from below – in a word, the state. Fried goes on to say that once a stratified society has emerged, one of two things must happen. Because of the unstable situation stratification produces, a stratified society must either devolve back to an unstratified level, or go on to establish a state. There can therefore never be, except only very temporarily, a stratified society without a state.

It is hard to dismiss this argument, at least in its more general form. As we have seen, all of the early states were stratified, and thus there is certainly a connection between stratification and the state. However, two difficulties may be identified. First, it is unfortunate that Fried mars his otherwise cogent analysis by insisting that when a society becomes stratified it must develop a state or devolve to the tribal level. In fact there are many societies that are stratified but that lack a state. Most chiefdoms are stratified, some of them (such as aboriginal Hawaii) elaborately so, and thus a condition of stratification does not require a state (cf. Carneiro, 1991). Where

Fried has gone wrong is not in his conception of the state, but in his ability to identify stratified societies in the ethnographic litera- ture, since some of the societies that he says have only ranking obviously are stratified. Stratification is therefore not a sufficient condition for the formation of the state. However, it is still possible to argue that it is a *necessary* condition for the emergence of the state.

This last point can be developed further with respect to the Marxian argument more generally. We have seen that we do find stratified societies without states. However, the reverse is never true: there are no examples of state-level societies without stratification. This would suggest a high probability that stratification in itself is a necessary but not sufficient condition for the rise of the state. We might go on to say that it is not the mere existence of stratification, but the existence of *a certain level* of stratification that is critical. This seems highly plausible when we recognize that the stratification systems of nonstate societies are generally less harsh in their impact on subordinate classes than the stratification systems of state-level societies. In Polynesian and African chiefdoms, for example, the ruling class is still tied to commoners by kinship, and the differences in the standard of living between dominant and subordinate classes is usually not great. Moreover, as Gerhard Lenski (1966) has pointed out, in these kinds of societies there usually remains what he calls a "redistributive ethic." Chiefs are expected to be generous and to redistribute at least some of the surplus they extract to commoners. Definite limits are placed on the power of chiefs, and successful rebellions are not uncommon. As Marshall Sahlins (1963) has put it, aboriginal Polynesian chiefs were usually deposed if they "ate the powers of government too much."

It seems reasonable to conclude, then, that stratification can exist without the state, but once a reasonably intense level of stratification has emerged the state may well be necessary to protect *that*. Yet this still leaves a difficulty, which is the second difficulty that I referred to above: if a sufficient level of stratification produces the state, then what leads a society to develop a sufficient level of stratification? To put it slightly differently, are there other factors involved in the rise of the state besides a high level of stratification? The answer to this question is, I believe, an affirmative one. In order to see what these other factors might be, we need to examine some other well-known theories of the rise of the state.

Population pressure theories

Just as population pressure theories have been widely proposed for the Neolithic Revolution, so have they been widely proposed for the origin of civilization and the state. Patrick Kirch (1984) has made population pressure a key factor in his explanation of sociopolitical evolution in Polynesia (although here, of course, complex chiefdoms were the most advanced forms of political organization), and Graham Connah (1987) sees population pressure as a very important factor in the emergence of African states. Population pressure theories intended as general explanations of the worldwide emergence of the state have been presented by, *inter alia*, Dumond (1972), Santley (1980), Mark Cohen (1981b), and Johnson and Earle (1987). Dumond sees population pressure as increasing the scarcity of and the demand for land, which leads to increasing efforts to control it privately. This ultimately produces class stratification, which leads in its turn to increasing political centralization. (To be fair to Fried, he presents the same sort of demographic argument to explain the development of stratification.) Dumond stresses that population pressure by itself is not a sufficient condition for the rise of stratification and the state, but that it is nonetheless a necessary condition.

Robert Santley (1980) sees population pressure contributing to the formation of the state through its influence on agricultural intensification and competition. His argument has been formulated for Mesoamerica, specifically the Monte Albán state in the Valley of Oaxaca, but there is little doubt that he would intend his argument to apply much more generally. As he puts it (1980:141):

The process of agricultural intensification, itself engendered by rising demographic pressures, contributes heavily to competitive behavior within sociopolitical groupings, and this selects for greater centralized controls in decision making, the by-product to a large degree of viable dispute arbitration. . . . Success in dispute arbitration within local sociopolitical systems in turn fosters an increase in competition between whole social systems as land scarcities become prominent: this competition in turn leads to larger and larger communities, themselves made possible by continuing population growth and agricultural intensification. In areas where agricultural productivity varies dramatically, one competing social system attains paramount status due to its success in dominating neighboring political units.

Allen Johnson and Timothy Earle (1987) make essentially the same argument. They consider population growth the main engine of sociocultural evolution, including sociopolitical development over its full course. Population pressure leads directly to subsistence intensification, which at a certain point produces social stratification, which in its turn leads to higher levels of sociopolitical development – chiefdoms and states.

Population pressure theories of the origin of the state have been subjected to many of the same criticisms that we encountered in regard to demographic explanations of the Neolithic Revolution. Perhaps the two most important of these criticisms with respect to state formation are that there is no natural tendency for populations to grow, and that empirical evidence shows that many areas of pristine state formation were well below the carrying capacity of their environments when states first arose. The first criticism has been made especially by Marxist or Marxist-inspired social scientists, who assert that population growth is only a dependent variable that varies according to prevailing social relations. But as we saw in chapter 2, the notion that there is no natural tendency for human populations to grow is completely unfounded (Sanders, 1984; Santley, 1980; Lee, 1990). All human communities make use of various forms of birth and population control, and population growth is significantly influenced by varying social relations (Harris and Ross, 1987), but no preindustrial society has been able to achieve zero population growth. As Richard Lee, himself a Marxist, has noted (1990:236), "Population growth has to be regarded as a starting-point in the analysis of directional social change. Human numbers tend to grow, however slowly, and the growth of humankind has been a constant push over the millennia."

Richard Blanton (1980; Blanton et al., 1981) has argued that, at least for Mesoamerica, available evidence suggests that its population was well below carrying capacity before it developed complex regional political institutions, and that rapid population growth did not seem to occur until after the development of chiefdoms and states. Here again is the old bugaboo of "carrying capacity." As we noted in chapter 2, Cohen's population pressure theory of the Neolithic Revolution depends in no way on this concept. As he points out, population pressure can begin long before carrying capacity is reached. People do not have to wait until carrying capacity is achieved before they begin to feel stresses and the need to respond to them. There is no reason why this argument for the Neolithic Revolution cannot be applied in principle to the evolution of chiefdoms and states. As Santley (1980:141) has said in this connection, "Evolutionary development can occur . . . before regional carrying capacity is reached, as prime lands become fully utilized. In consequence, considerable pressure selects very rapidly for an economically stratified society based on differential access to low-risk crop land."

It is my view that population pressure has been a crucial factor in the evolution of chiefdoms and states, but that it is a necessary but not sufficient cause. This requires us to consider what other important factor or factors might be missing from consideration.

The irrigation hypothesis

Not long after Karl Wittfogel first began to develop his famous theory of Oriental despotism in the 1930s (Wittfogel, 1957), anthropologists and archaeologists became eager to apply it to the rise of civilization and the state. Unfortunately, these social scientists misunderstood Wittfogel. My reading of Wittfogel is that he was trying to explain why a particularly despotic type of state, which he called a hydraulic state or an Oriental despotism, came to prevail in ancient history at certain points around the globe. Wittfogel claimed that such regions as ancient China and India, as well as even earlier Egypt and Mesopotamia, developed this type of state because of their dependence on large-scale irrigation agriculture. The complex irrigation works in these civilizations required an elaborate bureaucracy to manage them, and such bureaucratic organization led in short order to an enormous concentration of power – to an Oriental despotism. Wittfogel went on to argue that areas that depended on rainfall farming rather than irrigation agriculture, such as Europe during the Middle Ages, developed decentralized feudal states that were much weaker and much less oppressive of the general population.

Unfortunately, since many anthropologists and archaeologists have erroneously interpreted Wittfogel as offering a general theory of state formation (cf. Harris, 1977), their application of his idea to state formation is therefore no test at all of what he was arguing. Nevertheless, since the hydraulic theory of state formation has been widely promoted and discussed, it can be assessed on its own terms by leaving Wittfogel out of the matter. One of the earliest proponents of an irrigation theory of state formation was the social evolutionist Julian Steward (1949), but this idea has perhaps been most closely associated with the work of William Sanders and his colleagues (Sanders, 1972; Sanders and Price, 1968; Sanders, Parsons, and Santley, 1979; Sanders and Nichols, 1988). The work of these scholars has been focused on Mesoamerica, but it can be regarded as highly generalizable. Like numerous others, Sanders regards population pressure as a critical driving force in the emergence of civilization and the state, but by itself he thinks it is insufficient. For him the other critical factor is irrigation agriculture. The basic argument is nicely stated in the following passage (Sanders, 1972:152–3):

One of the more interesting aspects of Mesoamerican history is the close relationship between the appearance of large urban centers like Teotihuacán, Cholula, Tenochtitlán, and Monte Albán and hydraulic agriculture. . . . Hydraulic agriculture provides first of all a new dimension of power – control of water as well as the control of land. The maintenance of an irrigation system also requires coordinated organization of labor in a way that other agricultural systems do not. Furthermore, irrigated land is universally private land because of the heavy investment of capital labor . . . and this stimulates class distinctions based on land ownership. Irrigated land also is permanently cropped land, and the demographic capacity of permanently cropped land of this type is considerably greater than any other system of farming. This permits a greater regional population density and the establishment of larger agrarian communities. Communities of this type with continued population growth and pressure may easily evolve into urban centers. A close juxtaposition of areas of hydraulic agriculture with their strikingly higher productive potential and nonhydraulic areas in the Mexican highlands furthermore is a powerful stimulus to competition. Thus it was no accident that the politically dominant communities became those with the control of hydraulic resources.

This kind of argument was once fairly favorably endorsed, but in the past two or three decades it has fallen on hard times. One of the main lines of critical attack against the irrigation theory has been the claim that irrigation agriculture cannot have been instrumental in the initial rise of the state, because in several world regions complex irrigation works appeared only *after* the state's emergence (Carneiro, 1970; Haas, 1982). This argument has been made, for instance, for Mesopotamia by Adams (1966), for Egypt by Butzer (1976), and for China by Kwang-chih Chang (1986). Marvin Harris (1977) has defended a more strictly Wittfogelian version of the irrigation theory by claiming that in several world regions there was a step-by-step increase in the power and complexity of the state that corresponded to a step-by-step increase in the size of irrigation works. This more original version of the theory is likely to be more workable than the usual version. In other words, while it is doubtful that irrigation agriculture was a general factor in the *genesis* of the state, it may have played an important role in intensifying the power and complexity of the state in some instances.

The circumscription theory

Perhaps the best-known general theory of the origin of the state is Robert Carneiro's (1970, 1981, 1987a) circumscription theory. In addition to its other strong points, this theory has the merit of being deliberately formulated as a theory of the worldwide parallel evolution of the state. Carneiro's theory makes use of three basic factors: population pressure, warfare, and environmental circumscription. For Carneiro, population pressure is a basic driving engine of sociocultural evolution. However, it must be combined with the two other factors in order for evolution, rather than what is best called expansion, to occur. Carneiro illustrates this point with respect to the Amazon Basin of South America, an area today characterized by political units no more evolutionarily advanced than the tribe. This region of the world has long been characterized by very low population densities, and there are still large unoccupied areas. Population pressure has repeatedly led to warfare among many tribes, as the famous case of the Yanomama shows (Chagnon, 1983; Harris, 1977). But where land is still relatively plentiful, people can respond to population pressure and warfare by simply picking up and moving into unoccupied or lightly populated zones. In other words, they can expand geographically to cope ' with growing numbers.

What happens, though, when land is not widely available? This is where Carneiro establishes the critical factor in his theory. According to him, the major regions of worldwide state formation were all characterized by *environmental circumscription*, or geographical obstacles to the further expansion of growing populations. Environmental circumscription exists when people have been living in relatively fertile areas surrounded by natural obstacles to movement, such as inhospitable deserts, mountain ranges, or large bodies of water. In such an area, population growth and warfare eventually cause the area to be "filled up." At some point people can no longer move away, and when this point is reached groups turn on and attempt to conquer each other. In doing so, they evolve politically, first by tribes conquering other tribes and forming chiefdoms, then by chiefdoms conquering other chiefdoms and eventually forming states, and ultimately by states conquering each other to form multistate empires. The state thus arises as a response to population pressure and warfare in highly circumscribed environments.

Circumscription is a geographical phenomenon, but Carneiro argues that another form of it, what he calls *social* circumscription, also exists. This occurs when concentrations of people rather than natural barriers constitute the barriers to movement. Like geographical circumscription, social circumscription can be an important factor in the formation of chiefdoms and states. Another wrinkle added to the theory by Carneiro is the factor of *resource concentration*. This may be an additional complicating factor in state formation, and it may also explain the formation of chiefdoms in regions that are neither geographically nor socially circumscribed. Resource concentration exists when an area is unusually abundant in resources, a phenomenon that allows it to attract large numbers of people and stimulate population growth. What results is in essence a kind of social circumscription that, in combination with warfare, leads to political evolution. Carneiro believes that it was resource concentration that led to the formation of chiefdoms in some parts of Amazonia in the sixteenth century, and that resource concentration played a significant role in all of the regions of the world where pristine states originated. The early states then, evolved under the impact of two conditions, geographical circumscription and resource concentration.

This theory has been one of the most, if not the most, thoroughly discussed and extensively tested theories of the formation of the state. Although it has had its critics (e.g., Haas, 1982:135–6), my own view is that the evidence fairly consistently supports it (cf. Carneiro, 1988). I agree with Robert Schacht (1988:446) when he says that "Carneiro has come very close to perceiving the essence of the causal nexus involved in the evolution of the state." A careful test of the circumscription theory has been carried out by Patrick Kirch (1984, 1988) with respect to Polynesia. Here is an area of the world consisting of island societies that inhabit some of the world's most circumscribed environments. Although indigenous states never developed in Polynesia, complex chiefdoms nearly at the state level existed in Hawaii and Tonga. Kirch has shown that at the time of European contact these especially tightly circumscribed regions contained the highest population densities throughout Polynesia. Moreover, Kirch (1988:423) notes that, within Hawaii itself, "the region in which political evolution was most intense was the eastern islands of Hawai'i and Maui, where the absence of prime irrigable land meant that pressure on and competition for arable land was much more acute than in the western islands of Molaka'i, O'ahu, and Kaua'i."

It might be wondered why, given circumscription and intense population pressure, the most politically advanced parts of Polynesia never developed states. Kirch's answer, and it is Carneiro's (1988) as well, is that an insufficient amount of time had passed for this to occur. Given enough time, they say, Polynesia would eventually have witnessed the emergence of states. They make the same line of argument for the failure of even chiefdoms to develop in densely occupied parts of contemporary New Guinea. Obviously the evolution of complex political systems takes time; it is not an overnight occurrence.

I believe that Carneiro's theory is probably our best theory of the evolution of the state. However, it is not without flaw. As I see it, the one serious inadequacy in the theory is its failure to deal with the *socioeconomic* dimension of the evolution of civilization and the state. The theory focuses too much on warfare and political conquest and not enough on emerging patterns of *economic ownership* and *class stratification*. Malcolm Webb (1975) and Robert Schacht (1988) see it this way too. Webb has argued that where there is severe competition between and among societies for scarce resources, the war leaders are placed in a situation in which they can gain control over these resources. Such a situation is ripe for the generation of social stratification and the eventual emergence of the coercive power of the state. Schacht puts it this way (1988:445): "Rather than focusing only on warfare as a major variable in state formation, we ought to be looking for evidence of all kinds of competition, especially economic, and of the systemic structures that evolve as a result." Schacht goes on to say that warfare is a part of the process of state formation but it is only one way in which competition for resources can manifest itself. We also need to be looking at the emergence of economic hierarchies and social stratification, he suggests, for they are a major part of the highly competitive process by which the state is formed.

In effect, what Webb and Schacht are suggesting is something of a marriage of Carneiro and Marx. Population pressure and circumscription contribute to the evolution of the state, but not just through warfare and political conquest; population pressure and warfare create severe inequities in economic ownership and class stratification, and the material benefits that owning groups acquire give them their own particular basis for wanting and needing a state – protection and enhancement of their privileged position. I would also add that Carneiro seems to ignore, or at least underestimate, the positive feedback that undoubtedly occurs between the evolution of powerful political and economic leaders on the one hand and warfare and political conquest on the other. Once powerful leaders emerge within any society, they develop an interest in warfare and conquest quite apart from population pressure. Given the self-aggrandizing political and economic interests of elites, chiefdoms and states acquire an expansionary logic of their own that is independent of population pressure and environmental circumscription.

Functionalist and conflict theories of the origin of the state

Several social scientists have pointed out that many theories of the rise of the state can be thought of as either functionalist or conflict theories (Service, 1975, 1978; Claessen and Skalnik, 1978a; Gilman, 1981; Haas, 1982; Wenke, 1990). Elman Service (1975, 1978) and Jonathan Haas (1982) have claimed that the distinction between these kinds of theories of sociopolitical evolution is a crucial one with a time-honored history. Indeed, Haas devotes an entire book, *The Evolution of the Prehistoric State*, to analyzing and critically evaluating these theories. Antonio Gilman (1981) and Robert Wenke (1990) argue that the study of sociopolitical evolution has been dominated by functionalist assumptions, and it does appear that many theories, whatever the specific factors that they deem most important, do have a kind of functionalist bias. For instance, of the theories we have been discussing, those of Sanders and Price (1968), Mark Cohen (1981b), and Johnson and Earle (1987) all rest on functionalist premises. All of these theories give population pressure a major role in the evolution of the state, but they do so in a decidedly functionalist way: they assume that higher levels of sociopolitical development are somehow "solutions" to societies' organizational difficulties or stresses. These stresses directly concern societal integration, and they render old integrative mechanisms unsatisfactory. As a result, more advanced sociopolitical systems arise because they are needed to provide a better means of integration. Sanders and Price put it this way (1968:229):

> Given a population of 10,000 [the minimum suggested for the emergence of a civilization], the means of kinship and ceremonial ties used with great efficiency to integrate smaller absolute numbers would become too diffuse to carry out the integrative functions adequately. Other means must be developed, and the result is the social–economic–political hierarchy characteristic of civilization.

Johnson and Earle take a similar view. In discussing the emergence of chiefdoms, they argue that such groups arise because they provide more effective ways of handling risk management (1987:209):

> When population density is sufficiently high to put a population at risk during a shortfall, risk management requires the production of a surplus and, usually, storage. Under some conditions the surplus and its storage can be handled by individual families; when it is centralized under a leader's control, however, risk is averaged across more subsistence producers and the necessary per capita surplus . . . is less. The stored surplus also provides the chief with the means to invest in other political and economic ways, on his own behalf or his polity's. Another environmental source of risk arises from the intensification of shifting cultivation in fragile environments; in such an environment the agricultural cycle must be managed by the chief lest it be mismanaged by his people.

It is clear that these functionalist arguments see the evolution of more complex sociopolitical systems as serving the interests of society in general. Society as a whole is deemed better off with such systems than without them.

The theories of Sanders and Price and Johnson and Earle are functionalist mainly in an implicit rather than an explicit way. A theory that is avowedly functionalist in the most thoroughgoing way has been developed by the well-known social evolutionist Elman Service (1975, 1978). In regard to other theories of the rise of civilization and the state, Service's main complaint is against the Marxian theory. Against Fried, he insists that the state did not arise because of the needs of a ruling class in stratified society, for in fact the earliest state societies were not stratified at all. The main social distinction in these societies was between the governors and the governed, not between wealthy and poor. Service goes on to claim that stratification did not arise until *after* the state had already come into existence.

Service sees the state arising under circumstances in which it could provide a better means of leadership and social integration and provide benefits that could otherwise not be achieved. He claims that the state provided three main types of benefit for the societies they governed. The state is said to play a very important role in economic redistribution. Because of the existence of the state, it is possible for a society to exploit more diverse ecological zones. The products of these diverse zones benefit the court, the bureaucracy, the priesthood, the army, indeed, the people as a whole. The state also introduces new forms of war organization. These can serve as powerful integrative mechanisms because they help to enhance the "national pride." Finally, the state provides a major benefit in the form of public works. Construction projects involving such things as temples, pyramids, tombs, walls, roads, and irrigation systems are carried out by the state, and many segments of society are better off because of them.

Conflict theories of the origin of the state deemphasize the broader societal benefits that the state is often said to generate, concentrating instead on the various ways in which the state is largely intended as a mechanism for the benefit of elite groups. This position historically has seemed to have had fewer adherents than the functionalist view, but it is either implicit or explicit in a number of theories (Fried, 1967; Gilman, 1981; Carneiro, 1970, 1981, 1987a; Haas, 1982).[5] The Marxian theory is, of course, the quintessential conflict theory of the state, explicitly seeing the state as a mechanism designed to preserve ruling class domination of subordinated groups. Carneiro's circumscription theory is also a type of conflict theory. The state emerges as the result of warfare and political conquest, and, Carneiro insists, communities never give up their autonomy voluntarily. They must be *coerced* into doing so, a point to which Carneiro gives great emphasis.

Gilman (1981) takes a conflict view of the rise of stratification and the state, concentrating on Europe. He is highly critical of functionalist arguments, claiming that "the functionalist account of the development of elites may be criticized at once for its failure to explain the hereditary character of the class of 'higher-order regulators' " (1981:3). Gilman contends that "the functionalist account does not match what we actually know about the part played by the ruling classes of stratified societies" (1981:3). In a direct criticism of Service, Gilman also notes that (1981:3), "Warfare, directed by elites, is [seen as] beneficial in functional terms because it supplies scarce resources, such as land, to the victors. If concrete historical cases are any guide, however, very few of the spoils accrue to the mass of the population whose contributions support the military enterprise." To this it might be added that public works projects, seen by Service as a broad society-wide benefit, mainly benefit elite groups. Gilman concludes his argument for a conflict position by saying that, since the actions of elites are so frequently against the interests of the bulk of the population, what really needs explaining is how such groups acquire and preserve their power.

Haas (1982) has made similar arguments against Service's functionalist position and has tried to generate data to demonstrate the superiority of the conflict position. Against Service, Haas tries to show two basic things: that stratification was present at the time of the emergence of the first states, and that these states engaged in considerable coercion of the subordinate population. The data, he claims, show that in the earliest states there was differential access to basic resources. Some people enjoyed significantly higher standards of living than others in regard to food, housing, tools, craft items, and mechanisms of defense. Data also show that force was "actively and regularly applied" to subordinate classes in several of the early states. In Shang China, royalty clearly had the ability to engage in the slaughter of hundreds of people. In the Erh-li-t'ou Culture of ancient China, archaeological evidence shows that some people had been decapitated and others had parts of their limbs missing. In some graves people had been buried, possibly alive, with their hands tied. In South America, Moche ceramics depict persons who had had their noses and lips mutilated, and individuals are also shown with amputated limbs or genitals, bound to a stake or in stockades, and herded in a line by others who were using whips. Haas also draws on ethnographic and ethnohistoric data from aboriginal Hawaii and the Zulu kingdom of Africa to show the extent to which force is used in societies with advanced sociopolitical institutions. In Hawaii, chiefs could dispossess commoners from land and could use physical sanctions against commoners engaged in misdeeds; these sanctions were especially severe if the misdeeds directly affected the chiefs themselves. Haas claims that in the Zulu state the threat and direct use of violence by rulers against commoners played a substantial role. Here people were executed for relatively minor offenses, and at times the Zulu state engaged in the terrorization and slaughtering of thousands of people.

Gilman has also tried to refute Service by showing that stratification emerged before the rise of the state in Europe. He says that, "Even in Greece and the Aegean, where the Minoan and Mycenaean palaces give managerial theories some plausibility, evidence for stratification precedes the development of centers for higher-order regulation by several centuries. In addition, a nonfunctionalist approach explains better the militarism which characterizes the accoutrements of Bronze Age elites throughout Europe" (1981:8). Gilman concludes that an emphasis on exploitation rather than management produces a more realistic view of the primary motives and actions of ancient elites.

My own view is that a conflict view of the rise of the state is far more defensible than a functionalist view. In saying this, I am not denying that the ruling elites of early states may have generated at least some benefits for groups other than themselves. What I would deny is that the early state *can be explained* in terms of the need for such benefits or the desire of elites to provide them. Moreover, while population pressure theories of state formation often have a strong functionalist cast, and while I favor population pressure as a major cause of the emergence of the state, this does not lead to any theoretical contradiction. Population pressure theories can just as well be conflict theories, as indeed Carneiro's is. In conflict versions of population pressure theories, elites and the state arise through a struggle over scarce resources in which the participant groups are actively pursuing their own interests, not because of some need for a higher-level form of management of the affairs of society as a whole.

THE PACE OF STATE EVOLUTION

As a result of the development of the punctuated equilibria theory of biological evolution (Eldredge and Gould, 1972; Gould and Eldredge, 1977; Stanley, 1979), some social scientists (e.g., Collins, 1988) have speculated about its possible application to social evolution. I dealt with this issue earlier in *Social Evolutionism*, and generally my position is that, although there may well be a lot of variation from one epoch of social evolution to another, a gradualist rather than a punctuationalist model is a better fit to most evolutionary events. In chapter 2 I showed that such a model was essential to understanding the Neolithic Revolution: temporally, it was anything but a revolution. But what about the rise of civilization and the state? Might not a punctuationalist model be more appropriate here? Charles Spencer (1990) thinks so, as does Henry Wright (1986). Spencer focuses on the evolution of states in Mesoamerica, particularly on the rise of Monte Albán and Teotihuacán. With respect to the former he says that (1990:19), "In the Oaxaca case, the state emerged over a relatively short period of time and in so doing represented a punctuational change in the Zapotec administrative organization." Regarding Teotihuacán, he claims that "excavations have revealed that an astonishingly large amount of public building construction took place over a fairly short period of time" (1990:22).

However, most social scientists who have closely studied social evolution, including the evolution of the state, have taken a gradualist approach. For example, Morton Fried refers to "the slow, autochthonous growth of the specialized formal instruments of social control" and goes on to say that in the evolution of the state "it is a long time before the wielders of the new power realize its full extent and possibilities" (1967:231). Harris's (1977, 1979) approach is an even more explicitly gradualist one. He describes the formation of the state as "an unconscious process" and claims that "the participants in this enormous transformation seem not to have known what they were creating. *By imperceptible shifts in the redistributive balance from one generation to the next*, the human species bound itself over into a form of social life in which the many debased themselves on behalf of the exaltation of the few" (1977:81; emphasis added).

It is difficult to resolve this issue in any definitive way in the absence of a widely agreed upon operational definition of what constitutes "fast" or "slow." Nonetheless, I am more persuaded by the gradualist view. It is true that, compared to the Neolithic Revolution, the rise of civilization and the state was indeed more rapid. Social evolution is a process that itself evolves, and one way in which this occurs is an acceleration of the pace of evolution as we move from one historical epoch to the next. It is also true that in the case of ancient Egypt the transition from the first agricultural communities to the creation of the state was remarkably fast, taking only about 2,000 years, and that some of the ancient states saw periods of rapid city formation and monument building. But, although the evolution of the state was clearly a more rapid process than the emergence of the first agricultural communities from a foraging economy, it was not rapid in any strictly punctuationalist sense. It was not, that is to say, preceded by a period of stasis that came abruptly to an end with the sudden appearance of something altogether new. As Carneiro (1981) has emphasized, it is not logical to assume, and the archaeological data do not indicate, that human societies could have evolved directly from tribes into states. They had to go through at least one intermediate structure, the chiefdom, and chiefdoms themselves exist at quite different levels of evolutionary development. To me, all of this signals a process that, even though it may be fairly rapid in some instances, is still far more gradualist than punctuationalist. Punctuationalist views of social evolution make sense, if at all, only with the advent of the modern epoch of social evolution, the emergence of the capitalist world-system in sixteenth-century Europe.

CODA: RECONSTRUCTING SOCIAL EVOLUTION
USING THE COMPARATIVE METHOD

In chapter 1 I made the point that archaeological and historical data are always to be preferred in the study of social evolution, but that ethnographic data also frequently need to play a role in evolutionary analyses. By using ethnographic data drawn from many different types of societies to reconstruct and infer evolutionary sequences we are using the comparative method, a method that is justified to the extent that the reconstructed evolutionary sequences correspond to evolutionary sequences derived archaeologically and historically. Here I would like to show that some of our most basic evolutionary typologies derived from the comparative method do, in fact, closely correspond to actual social evolution as it is revealed prehistorically and historically. Since this chapter has been limited to social evolution long before the development of the modern world, capitalist and industrial societies are excluded from consideration.

We have already looked, of course, at Service's (1962, 1971) typology of sociopolitical evolution, which has been used extensively to guide archaeological reconstructions of social evolution. There are several other typologies that are similar in certain basic respects.

For sociologists, probably the best-known evolutionary typology is that of Gerhard Lenski (1966, 1970), who originally developed it to build a theory of social stratification. At the preindustrial level, Lenski distinguishes between hunting and gathering, simple horticultural, advanced horticultural, and agrarian societies. Lenski developed this typology through the extensive use of the ethnographic data in the Human Relations Area Files as well as the use of data compiled by historians.

Hunting and gathering societies are already familiar to us. Here people live entirely or mostly by foraging. Hunter-gatherers ordinarily live in small bands remarkable for their egalitarian structure. Simple horticulturalists rely mainly on agriculture for their subsistence and ordinarily live in small villages. They have more inequalities than are found in hunting and gathering societies, but these inequalities, especially those concerning material wealth, do not tend to be large. Prestige differences between individuals are apt to be more important than wealth differences. Simple horticulturalists use relatively primitive methods of cultivation, such as slash-and-burn, and have no cultivation tools beyond the simple digging stick. Advanced horticulturalists, on the other hand, have a more advanced technology. According to Lenski, they are distinguished from simple horticulturalists by the availability of metal hoes used for cultivation. Advanced horticulturalists are formed into much larger and more complex societies, often at the level of chiefdoms or even rudimentary states and civilizations. They are frequently highly stratified, at least compared to simple horticulturalists. A common pattern is a division into three main social strata: chiefs, subchiefs, and commoners. In these societies, however, there are definite limits placed upon stratification. The severity of the stratification system is usually mitigated by the presence of a chiefly "redistributive ethic." Chiefs are still related to commoners by kinship, and they are expected to be generous and take the interests of their followers into consideration. In agrarian societies, these limitations on stratification are removed and gross inequalities in power, privilege, and prestige develop. Agrarian societies are characterized by intensive agriculture using the plow and draft animals. They normally greatly exceed in complexity most advanced horticultural societies. Virtually all agrarian societies have states, and some of them form multistate empires.

Lenski's typology closely approximates the social evolution that we have examined in this chapter via the data of archaeology.

Elsewhere I have slightly reformulated his typology and tried to show how evolutionary variations in subsistence technology and stratification correspond to modes of property ownership and economic distribution (Sanderson, 1991a: chapters 4–6). I have reformulated Lenski's distinction between simple and advanced horticulturalists into one between simple and *intensive* horticulturalists. Because it relies only on the presence or absence of metal hoes to classify horticulturalists, I argue that Lenski's distinction is too simple and ends up with some extremely questionable classifications. For example, aboriginal Hawaii is placed in the simple category because it lacked metal hoes. My distinction rests on the *level of intensity* of horticulture, which is the extent to which time, energy, and resources are invested in the process of production. Simple horticulturalists use long-fallowing methods of production.[6] Gardens are cultivated only for a year or two and then the site is abandoned for as long as 20 to 30 years before being reused. Intensive horticulturalists intensify production by cutting down on the fallow period. Land may be cultivated for several years in a row and then fallowed for, say, only five or ten years. Intensive horticulturalists may also have developed other ways of intensifying production, such as adopting metal hoes or building irrigation systems, but these are not essential to this form of horticulture. My distinction allows societies like aboriginal Hawaii to be put into the category of intensive rather than simple horticulture. The Hawaiians had no metal tools, but they had a very intensive mode of agricultural production. Irrigation was used, and some plots of land had been given over to permanent cultivation. At the time of European contact, the Hawaiians were making use of practically every available square inch of land (cf. Kirch, 1984).

Using my distinction, simple horticulturalists are generally found to be unstratified, if by stratification we mean Fried's (1967) "differential access to resources." Generally, simple horticulturalists have no true class system. Inequality in these societies ordinarily consists of differences in prestige rather than of power and privilege. Some simple horticulturalists have developed the famous "big man systems" of leadership and competition for status. Fried (1967) considers these to be "rank societies," and I would agree. Intensive horticulturalists ordinarily have evolved differential access to resources and hereditary social strata – true class stratification, in other words. Lenski is quite right, though, to claim that the stratification systems in these societies are relatively mild and strongly mitigated by expectations of chiefly generosity. The Polynesian systems of stratification, as well as those in intensive horticultural societies throughout Africa, have had this important feature.

I have shown that there is a very close connection between subsistence technology and stratification on the one hand and modes of property ownership and economic distribution on the other (Sanderson, 1991a). I believe that, in fact, the mode of property ownership is the crucial determinant of redistribution and stratification, although of course this cannot really be demonstrated conclusively using synchronic ethnographic data. Hunting and gathering societies are notable for having a mode of ownership very close to what Marx called "primitive communism." There is no differential access to productive resources, and elaborate norms of generalized reciprocity often govern the distribution of food (Lee, 1978). Simple horticultural societies have an alternative version of communal ownership that I have termed *lineage ownership*. Here land is owned by large kinship groups – lineages and clans – as corporate property and use of the land is determined by lineage or clan leaders, who act in behalf of the entire group. Reciprocity is an important part of economic life, but so is redistribution, which at this evolutionary stage is what is normally called *pure* or *egalitarian* redistribution (Moseley and Wallerstein, 1978). Village or lineage leaders act as organizers or coordinators of production and redistribute goods so that virtually everyone gets an equal share.

Once we pass to the level of intensive horticulture a critical threshold is crossed. Land comes to be controlled by powerful chiefly groups who can, at least to some extent, dictate the terms under which the bulk of the population is allowed to farm the land for its own subsistence. Chiefly groups can compel surplus production and the transfer of much of the surplus to themselves. A certain amount of redistribution of this surplus may occur, but much or even most of it may be retained by chiefs for their own use and for building up an administrative and military apparatus. This has been called *partial* or *stratified* redistribution (Moseley and Wallerstein, 1978), and it is intimately connected with true class stratification. Agrarian societies are characterized by extreme forms of private property. Land is owned (or at least controlled) either by powerful landlords, by centralized governments, or to some extent by both. The peasants who farm the land must pay heavy penalties – rent, taxes, labor services, or all of these – to overlords for the right to cultivate land for their own use. We have passed the point of redistribution, for nothing is really redistributed in any meaningful sense. *Surplus expropriation* is now the order of the day. The relationship between ruling and subordinate classes becomes extremely imbalanced, and extreme stratification is common.

A slightly different approach to the same set of problems has been developed by the cultural anthropologist/archaeologist team of Johnson and Earle (1987). They develop an evolutionary model that also corresponds well to the data of archaeology. They distinguish between family-level groups, local groups, and regional polities. Family-level groups are societies in which the family is the basic unit of subsistence and social integration. Johnson and Earle distinguish between family-level groups with and without domestication.[7] The !Kung San of southern Africa are undoubtedly the world's leading ethnographic example of a family-level group without domestication. They live in small nomadic bands of 20 to 30 people and are notable for their patterns of communal ownership, intense norms concerning sharing and generosity, and lack of any class distinctions. The !Kung San live at a very low level of population density, well under one person per square mile. The Machiguenga of the Peruvian Amazon illustrate the family-level group with domestication. They live at a higher level of population density than the !Kung San or most other groups without domestication, but they are still sparsely settled on the land. They live in semisedentary hamlets of no more than 25 people, each of which may contain three to five autonomous households. They cultivate crops, but also engage in substantial foraging. The household is a unit of intense generalized reciprocity, and from all accounts the Machiguenga are highly egalitarian.

The local group is integrated by villages or larger kinship units. Most of the groups at this stage live by some sort of relatively simple horticulture, although pastoralism and hunting and gathering may also be subsistence practices. The Yanomama of the Amazon Basin and the Tsembaga Maring of New Guinea illustrate this evolutionary stage. The Yanomama are simple horticulturalists whose main crop is plantains, but who also hunt and gather. They live in highly egalitarian (except for gender) villages ranging from 40 to 250 members, each of which is politically autonomous. The kinship groups are patrilineages, six of which are scattered throughout their territory. They have an informal mode of leadership, no real social ranking, and are egalitarian economically. The Tsembaga Maring are one of some 30 politically autonomous Maring groups occupying the highlands of central Papua New Guinea. They live under fairly crowded conditions – about 35 people per square mile – and as a result there is considerable competition for land. They are simple horticulturalists, but with a somewhat more intensive mode of cultivation than the Yanomama, and a much more intensive mode than the Machiguenga. The Tsembaga Maring number some 200 and are organized into clans. These clans establish ownership rights and restrict access to land, but they are also political and ceremonial units. There is no real evidence of social stratification.

The Yanomama and the Tsembaga Maring are what Johnson and Earle call the "acephalous local group." A more evolutionarily advanced version of the local group is what they call a "big man collectivity." Here leadership has become more elaborate and social ranking has begun. The Central Enga of highland New Guinea illustrate this type. The Enga live in homestead farms spread throughout the territory of a clan. The largest politically autonomous unit contains some 350 people. At 85–250 persons per square mile, the Enga are densely populated. They are fairly intensive horticulturalists whose main crop is sweet potatoes, which are cultivated in permanent gardens, but they also employ a simpler form of horticulture on steep slopes. Enga clans are extremely important social units, being vital to the regulation of access to land, and each clan is led by a highly ambitious "big man." The big man is an economic organizer and a political leader. The status of big man is one of high social rank, and individuals openly compete for this status.

Regional polities represent a considerable evolutionary step beyond local groups. Here villages and other small residential groups lose their autonomy and come to be combined into larger centralized and hierarchical units. The two main types of regional polities are chiefdoms and states. The Trobriand Islanders of Melanesia are organized as a simple chiefdom of about 1,000 members. They have a population density of more than 100 persons per square mile. The subsistence pattern is intensive horticulture, in which yams are the main crop, combined with fishing. Johnson and Earle describe Trobriand society as representing a kind of intermediate evolutionary stage between a big man system and a more advanced chiefdom. Social life is stratified, and one may rise to the position of chief only by being born into a high-ranking kinship group.

The aboriginal Hawaiians represent a more complex chiefdom. The Hawaiians lived in communities of 300 to 400 and were organized into large chiefdoms that sometimes included as many as 100,000 members. Population density was very high, around 310 persons per square mile of arable land, and thus the subsistence technology was a very intensive system of horticulture involving irrigation networks and permanent cultivation. At the top of the sociopolitical hierarchy stood a paramount chief who had enormous control over people and resources, and who was considered divine and thus the subject of ritual taboos. The paramount was the head of the senior lineage of a highly stratified, so-called conical clan. There were subchiefs who were heads of junior lineages within the clan, and these were subordinate to the paramount chief and ranked among themselves. The Hawaiian chiefdoms were highly expansionist in nature, and there was severe competition among paramount chiefs, as well as among the junior chiefs within a chiefdom. The Hawaiian chiefdoms are perhaps the most complex and advanced known to ethnography, and indeed they have sometimes been considered states. At the very least they were chiefdoms quite close to the state level.

Johnson and Earle use the Inca Empire to illustrate the state level of the regional polity. The Inca, of course, were a highly stratified, state-level society organized at their peak into an empire numbering perhaps as many as 14 million persons. Their subsistence technology, a very intensive system of agriculture that combined irrigation with the terracing and draining of fields, was a response to very high levels of population density.

Whether one favors the evolutionary typologies of Lenski, Sanderson, or Johnson and Earle, the crucial point is that these evolutionary reconstructions from ethnographic and historical data correspond remarkably well to the actual evolution of human societies all over the world from the Neolithic Revolution through the rise of civilization and the state. Surely this vindicates one of the primary methodological tools upon which social evolutionists have relied.

NOTES

1 This should not be taken to mean that no society ever assumes a state level of political organization without going through a chiefdom stage. The Aztec, for example, evolved extremely rapidly from a tribe to a state between the late fourteenth to the early sixteenth century, and may well not have passed through a chiefdom stage (or at least not been in such a stage very long). However, political evolution of this rapidity is highly atypical, and in most cases a society that evolves from tribe to state passes through a chiefdom stage.

2 Just to be on the safe side, it might be worth noting that the term civilization as it is used in this book has been entirely stripped of the moral and evaluative baggage that it once carried (and to some extent still carries). Here a civilization is regarded as a type of society with a certain level of organizational complexity, and no assumptions whatever are being made to the effect that it represents a superior form of social life or increased cultural sophistication.

3 Not all archaeologists agree that there were this many centers of independent state formation. Some would limit the list to six (Mesopotamia, Egypt, China, the Indus Valley, Peru, and Mesoamerica), and especially cautious ones might further exclude the Indus Valley, thus stripping the list down to five. So some doubt still remains about the independent rise of the state in Africa outside of Egypt and Europe, and possibly also about the Indus Valley (since little is still known about it). However, I will stick to my guns and I think in due time the independence of these regions will be confirmed.

4 See Sanderson (1987) for a detailed critique of eclecticism as a strategy of theorizing.

5 Timothy Earle has also advocated a conflict–theoretical position at times despite his endorsement of a functionalist logic in his book with Johnson (Johnson and Earle, 1987). For example, in an article on chiefdoms, Earle (1987) refers to chiefs' control over labor and their need to justify their rule ideologically in order to bind the rest of the population to them. He also says that the newer view of chiefdoms, to which he at least in part subscribes, "emphasizes internal conflicts between communities, elite factions, and emergent classes" (1987:298). Earle's inconsistency on the question of whether chiefs serve primarily their own interests or those of the wider society is presumably due to an incompletely resolved endorsement of both positions.

6 Here I am following Ester Boserup (1965, 1981), who argues that the best index of the intensity of agriculture is the length of the fallow period.

7 Obviously, Johnson and Earle are among those recent anthropologists who argue that the distinction between hunting and gathering and horticulture is not necessarily critical. Like some others, they think this distinction is overriden by other factors (Testart, 1982, 1988).

4

Agrarian States and their Evolutionary Dynamics

From the rise of the first states around 5000 BP until the last few hundred years, the dominant form of social organization has been the agrarian state, or what Collins (1990, 1992) has called *agrarian–coercive societies*, Kautsky (1982) *traditional aristocratic empires*, and Marxist-oriented scholars the *tributary mode of production* (Amin, 1976; Wolf, 1982). In this chapter I shall take a close look at this type of society with a special eye to understanding its peculiar evolutionary dynamics. As we shall see, an understanding of these dynamics is essential to comprehending the rise of the modern world.

Regardless of their various differences, agrarian states share at least five fundamental characteristics. First, they are characterized by a class division between a small landowning (or at least land controlling) nobility and a large peasantry. The peasantry is compelled on threat of violence to pay tribute in the form of rent, taxation, labor services, or some combination thereof to the nobility for the latter's economic benefit. This relationship is one of naked exploitation backed by military force. Second, the noble–peasant relationship is the principal economic axis in the society, and it is a relationship of production-for-use rather than production-for-exchange. Production-for-exchange exists to some degree, but it is subordinate in importance, often greatly so, to production-for-use. Indeed, those who dominate production-for-exchange, urban merchants, were typically looked down upon by the aristocracy as money-grubbing individuals who dared to dirty their hands with the soil of commerce. Merchants sometimes enjoyed great wealth, but their social status was almost invariably low. Third, despite the class division between nobles and peasants, there is no overt class struggle carried on between these two classes (Kautsky, 1982; Giddens, 1985). There is, of course, a marked conflict of class *interest*, but this does not manifest itself, other than in the most minimal and sporadic way, in deliberate actions by one class against the other. Fourth, agrarian societies are held together not by any sort of ideological consensus or common world-outlook, but by military force (Giddens, 1985). Agrarian societies are virtually always highly militarized societies, and such militarization is essential to the aims and ambitions of dominant groups. Military might is devoted to the twin aims of internal repression and external conquest. Finally, agrarian states, during the era from about 3000 BC to about AD 1500, have been relatively unchanging societies. But we must be cautious. The key word is *relatively*, and the standard of comparison is the period of social evolution in the several thousand years before 3000 BC and the modern period which began around AD 1500. Agrarian societies lack a strong evolutionary dynamic and tend to persist in relatively unchanging ways generation after generation, century after century, and to some extent even millennium after millennium. Dynasties rise and fall, but the basic structural features of the society change little. Yet agrarian societies have not been as stagnant as has frequently been thought, and in fact have experienced a certain amount of economic, technological, and political change, albeit very slowly and gradually. We will need to pay attention to both why agrarian societies have changed little and slowly and to the cumulative importance – the long-run evolutionary significance – of the small and slow changes that have occurred.

Some of the most important agrarian states in world history have been the ancient empires of Egypt and Babylonia; the Aztec and Inca empires; various Chinese empires; various Persian empires; the Roman and Hellenistic empires; the Byzantine empire; the Arab caliphate; the various empires of the Mongols; the Moghul empire in India; and the Turkic empires of the Ottomans in the fourteenth century (Eisenstadt, 1963; Kautsky, 1982). This list, of course, is only a fraction of the total. Naturally these traditional agrarian states were not all completely alike, and it is important to acknowledge some of their important differences. S.N. Eisenstadt (1963) has distinguished five basic types of agrarian states:

1   patrimonial empires, such as the Carolingian empire;
2   nomad or conquest empires, such as those of the Mongols;
3   city-states, the most important example of which is probably ancient Athens;
4   feudal systems, such as existed in the European Middle Ages and Tokugawa Japan; and
5   historical bureaucratic empires, such as various empires of the Chinese, the Roman empire, and the Moghul empire in India.

Eisenstadt sees the clearest line of demarcation as lying between the historical bureaucratic empires and the rest, with the key difference involving the level of political centralization and bureaucratization. Historical bureaucratic empires, Eisenstadt tells us, are the most prominent form of agrarian state in world history, and there is no reason to question this judgment. Most of what we shall have to say in this chapter concerns this type of agrarian state. The much more decentralized type of agrarian state known as a feudal state is much less common historically than the bureaucratic empire, but its historical importance is highly disproportionate to its frequency of occurrence. It shall be the subject of a detailed analysis in chapter 5.

SOCIAL CHANGE IN AGRARIAN STATES

Agrarian states: growth versus evolution

The economic historian E.L. Jones (1988; Goudsblom, Jones, and Mennell, 1989) has drawn a distinction between *extensive growth* and *intensive growth* in world history. By extensive growth Jones means an increase in economic productivity sufficient merely to provide for an expanding population at roughly the same standard of living. Intensive growth, on the other hand, involves a rise in economic productivity that exceeds the rise in population so that the economic output per capita rises. Using this distinction, Jones notes that extensive growth has been overwhelmingly the norm throughout world history; there have been relatively few instances of intensive growth. Jones nominates early modern Europe, Tokugawa Japan, and Sung China as history's leading candidates for intensive growth. I concur with Jones's nominees and shall explore in great detail in the next chapter the European and Japanese cases. Sung China will be looked at later in this chapter.

Useful though Jones's distinction is, I should like to introduce a similar though importantly different one between *social growth* and *social evolution.* Social growth occurs when there is a *quantitative* change in one or more dimensions within a system of social organization. Increases in, say, the size of a population, military might, technological efficiency, or political power may be regarded as social growth so long as they do not lead a society into a structurally new mode of organization. Jones's extensive growth therefore belongs within my category of social growth. However, intensive growth may also be social growth rather than social evolution if it is not sufficient to produce a qualitative shift to a structurally novel mode of life. The case of Sung China was just that: a powerful economic thrust forward that petered out before it could generate a new mode of social organization. This makes it obvious, then, that by social evolution I mean a *qualitative* transformation, the development of something *new* rather than simply something *greater*.

The crucial question obviously becomes, was there much social evolution during the so-called agrarian era? The answer is no, there was not. As we shall see in more detail later, there was considerable social growth in the spheres of politics and military force, economics, and technology, a lot more in fact than is ordinarily supposed. But throughout some 4,500 years there was no leap forward to a structurally new form of social organization. In fact, only twice did evolution out of the stage of agrarian states occur, once in western Europe beginning around 1500, and once more in Japan during its Tokugawa era (between 1600 and 1868) (these are, of course, Jones's other examples of intensive growth).

This theme of the absence of any real "evolutionary potential" to agrarian states has been enunciated by numerous scholars. Representative of them is Jonathan Friedman, who notes (1982:182; emphasis added):

While there is clearly an ... evolutionary process of the formation of states and civilizations, there is no continuity of social evolution after the emergence of civilization. It would appear that the regional systems of civilizations ... have been stable organizations until the modern period. While centers of accumulation have shifted, *there has been no fundamental change in form*, only differences in dominant economic sectors – state versus private – and the form of exploitation – peasant, serf, slave, or wage labor – that have been prevalent.

Michael Mann (1986) has characterized this view as the *negative view of empires*, and suggests that it is overdrawn. "Although the militarism of imperial states certainly had its negative side," he argues, "it could lead to general economic development" (1986:148). Mann argues that the leading example of militarism having a catalyzing effect on economic development is the Roman empire. In this case, militarism contributed to economic development in a number of ways, but particularly in terms of the consumption needs of the army. These needs greatly stimulated demand and, hence, production (Mann refers to this as a sort of "military Keynesianism"). In the end, though, Mann is forced to admit that militarism led more often to quite different results, and that empires "contained no development, no true dialectic" (1986:161).

Based on earlier evolutionary developments, this is not what one would have expected, at least in the abstract. During and after the Neolithic Revolution the pace of social evolution was accelerating, and in only a few thousand years human societies had evolved from hunting and gathering bands to simple agricultural villages to the state. But after the rise of the state the pace of change slowed greatly and it took four and a half millennia before the agrarian era generated something evolutionarily novel. Why this slowing of the pace of change? What was it about the agrarian world that seemed to inhibit any substantial leap forward?

There is a common way of explaining this "evolutionary inertia" of agrarian societies, and that is to argue that it was the result of the peculiar system of social stratification and state power so characteristic of these societies. This point of view was adopted by Max Weber (1981[1927], 1976[1896/1909]) early in this century, and has been promoted by such recent social scientists as Immanuel Wallerstein (1974b), John A. Hall (1985), Gerhard Lenski (1970), Dietrich Rueschemeyer (1986), John Kautsky (1982), and E.L. Jones (1988). The argument is essentially that the two basic social classes, the aristocracy and the peasantry, had no incentive to alter the underlying mode of economic production. The aristocracy had no incentive for change because they benefitted enormously from the prevailing tributary arrangements. Indeed, commercial activity or technological advancement could be positively threatening to their means of extracting wealth from the subject population. They therefore kept a close watch on the activities of specialists in production-for-exchange, the merchants, and generally acted so as to keep their activities within certain bounds. On the peasants' side, they too had little incentive for change because whatever improvements they may have introduced into the productive process would have gone for the benefit of their lords rather than themselves. Speaking from the peasants' point of view, Gerhard Lenski says (1970:249):

> The development of the state and the growth of social inequality that followed the shift from horticulture to agriculture created a situation in which those who were engaged in the daily tasks of production were gradually reduced to the barest subsistence level, and kept there, by their more powerful superiors. Thus these peasant producers lost the normal incentive for creativity; any benefits that might result from an invention or discovery would simply be appropriated by the governing class.

And speaking from both the peasants' and the nobility's side, John Kautsky claims (1982:7):

> Once the entire small surplus produced by peasants is appropriated for consumption by an aristocracy, nothing remains to be invested in improvements of the process of production. Neither the peasants nor the aristocrats have incentives to seek such improvements, the peasants because they could not retain any resulting gains and the aristocrats because they can augment their gains more easily by increasing the number of peasants and the amount of land subject to their exploitation. Both the acceptance by peasants as well as aristocrats of the productive process as it is and the resort by aristocrats to territorial expansion as virtually the sole means of maximizing their material gains become fortified by ideology – which, in turn, remains unchanging.
>   The process of production, then, rather than being improved, is endlessly repeated.

Lenski and Kautsky are speaking mainly about technological advancement in general, but others have spoken specifically of *capitalist* development. In *The Agrarian Sociology of Ancient Civilizations*, Weber waxed eloquent on how agrarian bureaucratic states stifled capitalism (1976[1896/1909]:62–3):

> The public finance of the ancient states could . . . retard private capitalism in various ways. Above all the general political basis of ancient states typically reinforced the great instability of capital structure and formation inherent in the ancient economies. There were many pressures working in the same direction . . . . Furthermore there was the danger of confiscations, which occurred at every political upset and change of parties in ancient communities . . . .
>   However, much more important than these catastrophes which affected only particular interests or communities, was the general limitation imposed by public administrations on the profits of private capital, and thereby on capital formation. . . . The ancient monarch and members of his court were always great agrarian lords . . .

The line of reasoning employed by Lenski, Kautsky, and Weber can be used to explain another inherent feature of agrarian states: dynastic cycles. Because of the way in which the stratification and political systems of agrarian societies work, military conquest is essential to the economic success of agrarian elites. More than in any other type of society before (and perhaps even since) their emergence, agrarian societies are characterized by the continuous struggle for power. As Kautsky notes, this has given them a remarkably high degree of instability (1982:247–8):

> The process of intraaristocratic politics . . . produces a higher degree of instability of a certain type. Small and large territories change hands, military leaders, bureaucrats, and priests are transferred, promoted, demoted, and killed, and rulers ascend and are removed from thrones. The average length of the reign of Umayyad caliphs (661–750) was only six years and that of Seljuk sultans (1055–1194) was eleven, and the averages for the rulers of a number of other dynasties in various traditional and near-traditional aristocratic empires ranged from thirteen to twenty-one years. . . .

Dynasties themselves are also highly unstable. Rein Taagepera (1990) has calculated the length of duration of 78 agrarian empires over the past 5,000 years and has found it to be 130 years, with no trend toward increase or decrease during this period. Only 16 empires lasted 300 years even at one-half their peak size.

I see no reason to challenge the Weber–Lenski–Kautsky view of agrarian empires, but I would add to it one important point. Assuming that the movement out of the stage of agrarian society was going to be a movement into a specifically capitalist system of social and economic life – and historically, of course, this is the way things have worked out – it needs to be stressed that the emergence of capitalism could not be some sort of sudden leap forward to be achieved in a few dozen or even a few hundred years. It was an economic transformation that required a long period of time because of what might be called the "threshold effect." Because of capitalism's requirement for extensive markets (both foreign and domestic), and because of the general hostility of agrarian elites to it, it could only emerge slowly, and as such would require a lengthy period of incubation before it could reach a kind of "critical mass" essential to a tipping of economic power in its favor. In retrospect we know that the time period actually required was approximately 4,500 years from the beginning of the first agrarian states.

But I am in danger of running ahead of the story, and we must leave the whole issue of the rise of capitalism and the modern world for the next chapter. What remains to be shown in this chapter is the process or processes whereby agrarian societies gradually built up the critical mass needed for eventually crossing the threshold into a genuinely capitalist system.

Forms of social growth in agrarian societies

I would like to suggest that there have been four major forms of social growth during the era dominated by agrarian states:

1 population growth;
2 political growth, which involves both an increase in the size of political units and an increase in the concentration of power within these units;
3 technological growth, with respect to both economics and military force; and
4 economic growth, which has been manifested primarily in an increase in the level of world commercialization and the size and density of trade networks.

Table 4.1 presents estimates of population growth for the period between 3000 BC and AD 1500. As can be seen, population grew steadily during this time, although there were periods of population decline during the time around the collapse of the Roman empire, and again in the fourteenth century AD. Between 3000 and 1000 BC world population remained relatively small, increasing from 14

Table 4.1 *World population growth, 3000 BC–AD 1500*

Date	*Approximate world population (millions)*
3000 BC	14
2500 BC	19
2000 BC	27
1500 BC	38
1000 BC	62
600 BC	110
400 BC	153
200 BC	165
AD 1	252
AD 200	257
AD 600	208
AD 1000	253
AD 1200	400
AD 1400	375
AD 1500	461

Sources: Eckhardt (1992), table 2.1; Livi-Bacci (1992), table 1.3

to 62 million. However, after the latter date world population began to grow to considerable size, and in many areas population densities increased markedly. From 62 million in 1000 BC, world population increased to 110 million by 600 BC and to 257 million by AD 200. After a decline during the second half of the first millenium AD, population began to grow again, reaching 400 million by AD 1200 and 461 million by AD 1500. World population exploded after this time, but that is the subject of another chapter.

With respect to political growth, Rein Taagepera (1978) has studied changes in the size of agrarian empires over approximately the last 5,000 years. He shows that there has been a significant increase in empire size during this time and marks out three phases of empire growth. The first phase begins with the rise of the state itself. Before this time there were no political units with a size greater than 0.1 square megameters (one square megameter = 386,000 square miles). During the first phase of empire building the single largest agrarian empire seemed to maintain a size of at least 0.15 square megameters and to have at least occasionally attained a size of about 1.3 square megameters. A second phase of empire building was inaugurated around 600 BC. After this time the single largest empire was never smaller than 2.3 square megameters, and the maximum imperial size attained was 24 square megameters. Obviously, then, there was a substantial increase in the size of empires after 600 BC.

Table 4.2 *Growth in the size of political empires, 3000 BC–AD 1500*

Date	Size of world's largest empire (square megameters)	Total size of all of world's empires (square megameters)
3000 BC	0.15 (Egypt)	0.15
2500 BC	0.40 (Egypt)	0.43
2000 BC	0.20 (Egypt, India)	0.50
1500 BC	1.00 (Egypt)	2.05
1000 BC	0.45 (China)	1.00
600 BC	5.50 (Persia)	7.85
200 BC	5.70 (Central Asia)	15.15
AD 200	5.50 (China)	14.70
AD 600	9.00 (Mesopotamia)	18.00
AD 1000	5.00 (Central Asia)	17.00
AD 1200	25.20 (Central Asia)	32.70
AD 1300	15.00 (China)	32.80
AD 1400	6.50 (China)	17.10
AD 1500	12.20 (Europe)	24.20

Source: Eckhardt (1992), table 3.4

William Eckhardt (1992) has carried out more detailed calculations on Taagepera's data, and his findings are presented in table 4.2. These data show the size of the world's largest empire for a given date, plus the total size of all the world's empires added together. The steady increase in imperial size is obvious, and it is clear that throughout the agrarian era an increasing portion of the world was filled by large empires.

Taagepera believes that the increase in empire size during the second phase of political growth (600 BC–AD 1600) probably resulted from increasing sophistication in the art of power delegation, especially through impersonal bureaucratic roles rather than personal relationships. But it is also likely that the size increase was made possible by important developments in the areas of transportation and communication, as Taagepera himself notes. Empires could not become effectively larger until the means were available for controlling and integrating much larger areas.

Taagepera sees a third phase of empire growth beginning around AD 1600 with the emergence of the modern capitalist world. However, this phase is the concern of the next chapter rather than this one.

As empires have grown throughout world history there has been a corresponding increase in the amount of power available to agrarian states. Although rejecting an evolutionary view of world history, Michael Mann (1986) nonetheless notes that there has been a long-term, cumulative, and unidirectional increase in power over the past 5,000 years. Mann is talking about what he calls *social power*, which for him comes in four kinds: ideological, economic, military, and political. Our main concern at this point is the latter two types of power, and much of Mann's discussion concerns these two as well. As he says (1986:524):

Seen in the very long run, the infrastructure available to power holders and to societies at large has steadily increased. Many different societies have contributed to this. But, once invented, the major infrastructural techniques seem almost never to have disappeared from human practice. . . .

A process of continuous invention, where little is lost, must result in a broadly one-directional, one-dimensional development of power. This is obvious if we examine *either* the logistics of authoritatively commanding the movement of people, materials, or messages, *or* the infrastructures underlying the universal diffusion of similar social practices and messages. . . . If we quantify the speed of message carrying, of troop movements, . . . of the kill ratios of armies, . . . then on all these dimensions of power (as on many others), we find the same overall process of growth.

Indeed, Mann argues that there has been such a large increase in power capacity that it is difficult to embrace in the same category agrarian societies early in the agrarian epoch and agrarian societies late in that epoch.

Accompanying and closely intertwined with political growth has been technological growth throughout the agrarian epoch. The expansion of technological capacity has had important consequences for economic subsistence and military force. Clearly one of the most important inventions during the agrarian epoch was iron smelting. Iron ore deposits were discovered by the Hittites of Asia Minor sometime around 1800 BC, and soon thereafter the Hittites invented a technique of smelting. After about 1200 BC this technique came to be widely diffused throughout the agrarian world (Lenski, 1970). Iron came to be used for weapons and tools. Lenski (1970) regards its effects on tool production as so important that he distinguishes between simple agrarian societies, which have no iron tools, and advanced agrarian societies, which do. Among the most important tools that were made possible, or at least improved, by iron smelting were hinged tongs, frame saws, anvils for nail making, axes, adzes, chisels, gouges, drills, bits, augers, hammers, saws, picks, and hoes (Coghlan, 1954; Derry and Williams, 1961). The significance of the development of iron tools has been caught by R.J. Forbes (1954:592–3), who has said that

the effect of the introduction of iron was gradually to extend and cheapen production. Iron ores were widely distributed and readily available; iron tools were cheaper and more efficient than those made of bronze. They rendered possible the clearing of forests, the drainage of marshes, and the improvement of cultivation upon a very much wider scale. Thus iron . . . greatly reinforced man's equipment for dealing with the forces of nature.

Iron also made a major contribution to military technology in the form of the sword (Derry and Williams, 1961).

There was a wide range of other important technological developments of course. Among the most important we may list the catapult, the crossbow, gunpowder, the chariot, heavy cavalries, the naval galley, irrigation systems, the spoked wheel on fixed axle, wet-soil plowing, open-sea navigation, printing, the horseshoe, a workable harness for horses, the stirrup, the wood-turning lathe, the auger, the screw, the wheelbarrow, the rotary fan for ventilation, the clock, the spinning wheel, the magnet, water-powered mills, and windmills (Lenski, 1970; Mann, 1986). As can be seen from the list, some of these involved military techniques, but most of them involved economic production and exchange.

Technological change during the agrarian epoch occurred in many parts of the world, and a good many things were probably invented more than once (Ronan and Needham, 1978). However, much of the technological change that occurred in the West was of Eastern, especially Chinese, origin. As Colin Ronan and Joseph Needham (1978:58) have pointed out, "Chinese inventions and discoveries passed in a continuous flood from East to West for twenty centuries before the scientific revolution." Among the many inventions acquired by the West from China may be listed piston bellows, the draw-loom, silk handling machinery, the wheelbarrow, an efficient harness for draft animals, the crossbow, iron casting, the segmental arch bridge, the iron-chain suspension bridge, the canal pound-lock, nautical construction principles, gunpowder, firearms, the magnetic compass, paper, printing, and porcelain (Ronan and Needham, 1978). Many of these inventions had been made by the Chinese a millennium or more before their acquisition by the West.[1]

The final form of social growth during the agrarian era involved important economic changes in the direction of an increase in the level of world commercialization. This involved an expansion in the scale and importance of economic exchange, which can be assessed in terms of growth in the size and density of trade networks. John Kautsky (1982) has drawn a distinction between "traditional" and "commercialized" aristocratic empires, noting that there has been a general trend for the former to give way to the latter. He suggests that, given enough time, virtually all of history's traditional aristocratic empires have tended to become commercialized, describing it as an almost inexorable process. Along similar lines, Andre Gunder Frank (1990, 1991; Gills and Frank, 1991) argues for a long-term process of capital accumulation, based mainly on trade, that has occurred at an increasingly global level since the origin of the first Mesopotamian states 5,000 years ago. Frank sees this process as the central developmental process of world history, and one that is needed in order to explain developments· in the noneconomic spheres of agrarian societies.

It is possible to mark off three major stages in this process of expanding world commercialization (McNeill, 1982; Curtin, 1984). The first stage begins around 2000 BC and ends around 200 BC. During this phase trade was largely local or, at best, regional in scope. By 200 BC there emerged the first truly worldwide trade – not literally incorporating every single part of the globe, but at least being carried on throughout a large portion of the world – with the establishment of a trade axis that ran all the way from China to the Mediterranean. After about AD 1000 there was another big leap forward in which trade networks expanded and deepened, especially in the period 1250–1350.

It is interesting to note that the emergence of a worldwide trade axis after 200 BC corresponds closely to Taagepera's date for a sudden surge in the size of agrarian empires (600 BC). The two are undoubtedly causally related, for as E.L. Jones (1988) has argued, truly long-distance trade networks only became possible with the rise of very large empires. Only empires of that size had developed the technology of communication and transportation needed to facilitate worldwide trade.

Philip Curtin (1984) has described some of the basic characteristics of the worldwide trade network that was in effect between 200 BC and AD 1000 (cf. Chaudhuri, 1985). As he notes, during this period trade became regularized between the Red Sea/Persian Gulf region and India, between India and southeast Asia, and between southeast Asia and both China and Japan. In the middle Han period, Chinese merchants traveled to the West through central Asia and established an overland trade route between east Asia and Europe. Chinese trade with India had become extensive by the first century AD, and Chinese goods were being sold widely in the Roman empire. During Roman times trade between India and the Mediterranean was carried on through three different routes: an overland route through Parthia, the Persian Gulf combined with an overland route, and the Red Sea combined with an overland route to Egypt or some part of the Fertile Crescent region. Maritime trade flourished in the South China Sea and the Bay of Bengal, with Canton being an important port for trade to the south.

William McNeill (1982) has described almost breathlessly what he regards as a new and major burst of world commercialization beginning around AD 1000, and centering heavily on China. It was during this time that China had by far its greatest burst of economic activity prior to modern times, one that lags behind only late medieval Europe and Tokugawa Japan in scale and scope. Mark Elvin (1973) has referred to this as an "economic revolution," most of which occurred during the period of the Sung dynasty (AD 960–1275). Elvin sees the Sung economic revolution as involving agriculture, water transport, money and credit, industry, and trade (both domestic and foreign). Elvin argues that improvements in agriculture gave China by the thirteenth century the most sophisticated agricultural system in the world, and one that provided a foundation for major thrusts forward in commercial activity. Commercial activity was also greatly aided by improvements in water transport. These improvements involved both the construction of better sailing vessels on the one hand and the building of canals and removal of natural obstacles to navigation in streams and rivers on the other. Industry flourished, especially the production of steel and iron. The economy became much more monetized. There was a much greater volume of money in circulation, and the money economy even penetrated into peasant villages. Foreign trade, especially with southeast Asia and Japan, flourished. Markets proliferated and became hierarchically organized. At this time China was the world's most economically advanced society, and many observers have suggested that it was on the brink of the world's first industrial revolution. However, beginning sometime in the fourteenth century China began to decline and stagnate economically and gradually to withdraw from foreign trade. It became increasingly isolated and inward looking, a process that had become fairly complete by the middle of the fifteenth century. The reasons for this economic downturn are still very imperfectly understood today. Discussion of the downturn is beyond the aims of this chapter, but we shall meet up with it again in the next chapter in the context of the rise of modern capitalism.

McNeill sees the enormous economic growth in Sung China as part of a larger picture of world commercialization. As he says, "China's rapid evolution towards market-regulated behavior in the centuries on either side of the year 1000 tipped a critical balance in world history" (1982:25). And he elaborates (1982:50–4):

Though the capitalist spirit was ... kept firmly under control, the rise of a massive market economy in China during the eleventh century may have sufficed to change the world balance between command and market behavior in a critically significant way. ... Moreover, the growth of the Chinese economy and society was felt beyond

China's borders; and as Chinese technical secrets spread abroad, new possibilities opened in other parts of the Old World, most conspicuously in western Europe. . . .

What seems certain is that the scale of trade through the southern seas grew persistently and systematically from 1000 onwards, despite innumerable temporary setbacks and local disasters. Behavior attuned to the maintenance of such trade became more and more firmly embedded in everyday routines of human life. . . .

What was new in the eleventh century, therefore, was not the principle of market articulation of human effort across long distances, but the scale on which this kind of behavior began to affect human lives. New wealth arising among a hundred million Chinese began to flow out across the seas (and significantly along caravan routes as well) and added new vigor and scope to market-related activity. Scores, hundreds, and perhaps thousands of vessels began to sail from port to port within the Sea of Japan and the South China Sea, the Indonesian Archipelago and the Indian Ocean. . . .

As is well known, a similar upsurge of commercial activity took place in the eleventh century in the Mediterranean, where the principal carriers were Italian merchants sailing from Venice, Genoa, and other ports. They in turn brought most of peninsular Europe into a more and more closely articulated trade net in the course of the next three hundred years. It was a notable achievement, but only a small part of the larger phenomenon, which, I believe, raised market-regulated behavior to a scale and significance for civilized peoples that had never been attained before. . . .

It was precisely in the eleventh century, when China's conversion to cash exchanges went into high gear, that European seamen and traders made the Mediterranean a miniature replica of what was probably happening simultaneously in the southern oceans. . . . These separate sea networks were then combined into one single interacting whole after 1291.

Janet Abu-Lughod (1989) has picked up the story where McNeill left it. She describes in great detail for the period 1250–1350 the structure and operation of a vast worldwide trade network from western Europe to east Asia. This huge network contained eight overlapping subsystems that can be categorized into three larger circuits centering on western Europe, the Middle East, and the Far East. Abu-Lughod refuses to be drawn into a discussion of whether this system was "capitalistic" or not, but she does claim that it provided the basis for the development of modern capitalism after about 1500 (we will take up this part of her argument in chapter 5). Furthermore, she claims that this world trade network (1989:353)

was substantially more complex in organization, greater in volume, and more sophisticated in execution, than anything the world had previously known. . . .

Sophistication was evident in the technology of shipping and navigation, the social organization of production and marketing, and the institutional arrangements for conducting business, such as partnerships, mechanisms for pooling capital, and techniques for monetization and exchange.

Additional corroboration for the notion of expanding world commercialization throughout the agrarian era comes from research on trends in world urbanization. Using data compiled by Tertius Chandler (1987), David Wilkinson (1992, 1993) has shown that urbanization is a striking trend in world history. Of course, commercialization and urbanization cannot be strictly equated, but it is likely that urbanization is more a function of increasing commercialization than of anything else. Cities may grow and expand to fulfill important political functions, of course, and certainly for various other reasons, but commercialization seems to be the main driving force behind urbanization (Bairoch, 1988).

Table 4.3 presents data on world urbanization trends from 2250 BC to AD 1500. It is clear that urbanization has been a striking feature of agrarian social growth over a period of nearly 4,000 years. A particularly large leap in urbanization occurs in the period between 650 BC and 430 BC. During this period the number of cities of 30,000 or more inhabitants increased from 20 to 51, and the total population represented by these cities increased from 894,000 to 2,877,000, a more than threefold increase. It seems very noteworthy that this period marks the early beginnings of Greco-Roman civilization and is the same period that Taagepera has identified as associated with a major increase in the size and scope of political empires. There is another major urbanization spurt between 430 BC and AD 100, during which the number of cities of 30,000 or more inhabitants increased from 51 to at least 75, and also during which the total population of these cities expanded from 2,877,000 to 5,181,000, an 80 percent increase. This period is essentially the same period that McNeill and Curtin refer to as involving the emergence of the first truly long-distance trade network between east Asia and the Mediterranean.

It cannot escape attention that world urbanization suffered a setback between AD 100 and AD 500. There were fewer large cities (those with 30,000–40,000 or more inhabitants), and the total population of these cities fell from 5,181,000 to 3,892,000. This was, of course, the period of the decline and eventual collapse of the Roman empire. However, world urbanization and commercialization suffered only a minimal and quite temporary setback. By AD 800, the total population of the largest cities (5,237,000) had regained the level achieved in AD 100. It took longer for the number of large cities to return to the level reached in AD 100 – there were 70

Table 4.3 *World urbanization, 2250 BC–AD 1500*

Year	No. largest cities	Pop. range of largest cities	Estimated total pop. of largest cities	Civilizations represented
2250 BC	8	c. 30,000	240,000	Mesopotamian, Egyptian
1600 BC	13	24,000–100,000	459,000	Mesopotamian, Egyptian, Aegean
1200 BC	16	24,000–50,000	499,000	Central,ᵃ Aegean, Indic, Far Eastern
650 BC	20	30,000–120,000	894,000	Central, Aegean, Indic, Far Eastern
430 BC	51	30,000–200,000	2,877,000	Central, Indic, Far Eastern
AD 100	75*	30,000–450,000	5,181,000	Central, Indic, Far Eastern
AD 500	47	40,000–400,000	3,892,000	Central, Indic, Far Eastern
AD 800	56	40,000–700,000	5,237,000	Central, Indic, West African, Far Eastern, Indonesian, Japanese
AD 1000	70	40,000–450,000	5,629,000	Central, Indic, Far Eastern, Indonesian, Japanese
AD 1300	75*	40,000–432,000	6,224,000	Central, Indic, West African, Far Eastern, Japanese, Indonesian
AD 1500	75*	45,000–672,000	7,454,000	Central, Indic, West African, Far Eastern, Japanese

ᵃ Central civilization is Wilkinson's name for the expanded civilization originally centered on Mesopotamia and Egypt. By 200 BC it had engulfed Europe.
* Denotes the upper limit on the number of cities set by Chandler (1987).
Sources: Wilkinson (1992, 1993); Chandler (1987)

such cities in AD 1000 and 75 or more cities in AD 1300 – but not that much longer. Moreover, after AD 1000 the scale of world urbanization was clearly very large and continuing to grow, and, as already noted, the period after AD 1000 has been seen by McNeill and Curtin as involving another major leap in world trade networks.

Wilkinson has also constructed maps that show in a very graphic

tent of world commercialization between 2250 BC and AD
veral of these maps are reproduced here as figures 4.1
4.6. It can clearly be seen that not only was there a major
e in the size and number of large cities, but also that the
es between these cities grew and deepened dramatically over
period. For the most part, these linkages would have been
mercial in nature. There can be no serious doubt that the scope
density of world trade increased enormously throughout this
riod.

It is my view that expanding world commercialization was the
nost important form of social growth that occurred during the
approximately four and a half millennia of the agrarian epoch, at
least in terms of its ultimate world-transforming significance. It was
to a large degree an autonomous process in its own right, driven by
the desires of merchants for greater wealth and economic power.
But to an extent it was also driven by population growth. As populations grew and the size and density of urban areas expanded, the
size of markets increased proportionally, as did the availability of
workers and of various resources necessary to industrial production.
In the next chapter we shall have an opportunity to examine the
implications of this change for bursting the agrarian epoch asunder
and issuing in the modern capitalist and industrial world.

AGRARIAN STATES AS PRECAPITALIST WORLD-SYSTEMS

We now turn to an issue that is closely related to – actually, inextricably intertwined with – the whole question of trade and trade
networks in the agrarian epoch. Because of the enormous fruitful-
ness of Immanuel Wallerstein's (1974a,b, 1979, 1980a, 1989) world-
system model of modern capitalism (see chapter 5), a number of
scholars have begun to ask whether or not this model, or something
like it, could be usefully applied to historically earlier societies. Are
there, in other words, "precapitalist world-systems," and, if so, what
are they like? How are they similar to or different from the modern
capitalist world-system? And, if there are world-systems in the
precapitalist world, are they the basic unit of social change?

The first scholar to raise questions like these was Jane Schneider
(1977). Schneider claimed that one of the main difficulties
with Wallerstein's work was that it "suffers from too narrow an

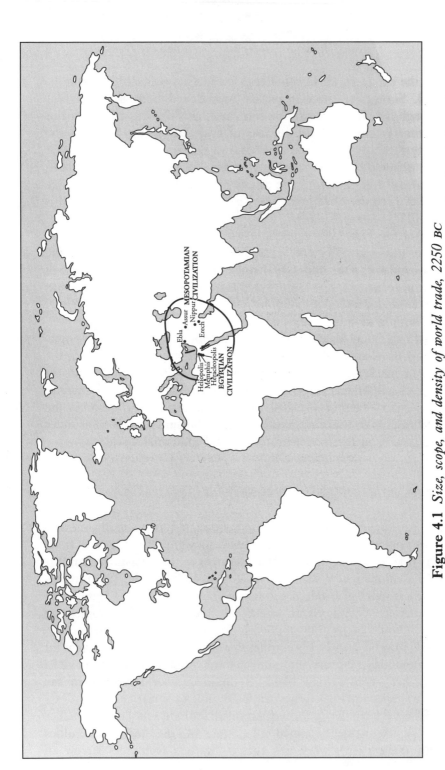

Figure 4.1 *Size, scope, and density of world trade, 2250 BC*

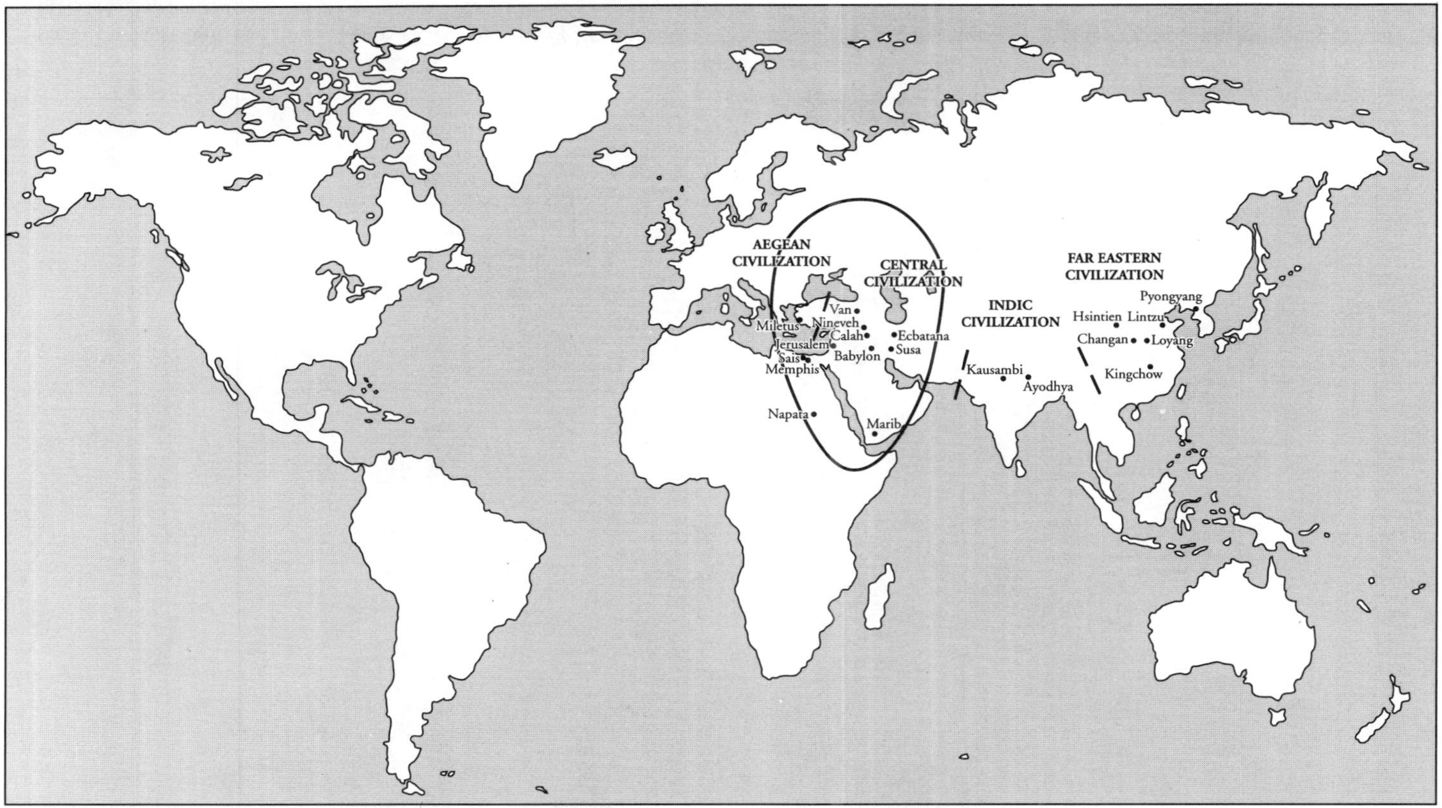
AEGEAN
CIVILIZATION
CENTRAL
CIVILIZATION
FAR EASTERN
CIVILIZATION
INDIC
CIVILIZATION
Van
Miletus
Nineveh
Calah
Jerusalem
Ecbatana
Susa
Babylon
Sais
Memphis
Napata
Marib
Kausambi
Ayodhya
Pyongyang
Hsintien
Lintzu
Changan
Loyang
Kingchow

Figure 4.2 *Size, scope, and density of world trade, 650* BC

Source: David Wilkinson (1992), figure 11. (Copyright © 1992 by David Wilkinson. License to reproduce granted gratis, only for use in works themselves distributed at no charge, and in which this map is reproduced in full, including this note. All other rights reserved.)

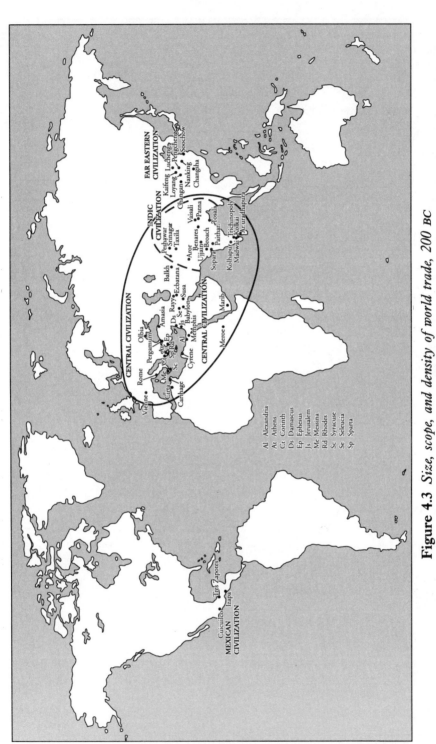

Figure 4.3 *Size, scope, and density of world trade, 200 BC*

Al Alexandria
At Athens
Cr Corinth
Ds Damascus
Ep Ephesus
Js Jerusalem
Mc Messina
Rd Rhodes
Sc Syracuse
Se Seleucia
Sp Sparta

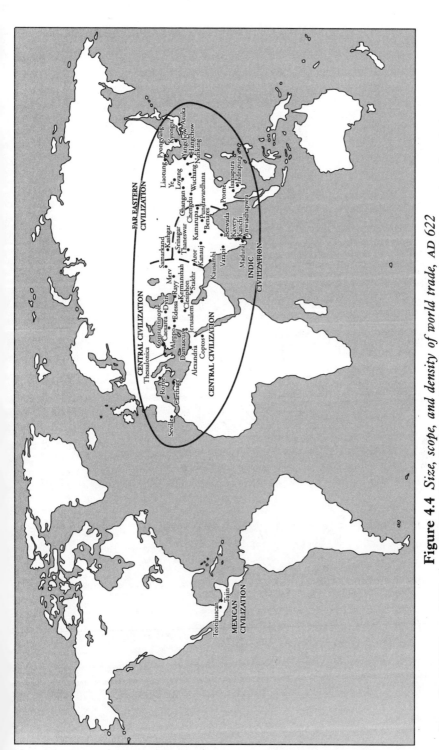

Figure 4.4 *Size, scope, and density of world trade, AD 622* (Copyright © 1992 by David Wilkinson. License to reproduce granted gratis, only for use in works themselves distributed at no charge, and in which this map is reproduced in full, including this note. All other rights reserved.)

Source: David Wilkinson (1992), figure 17.

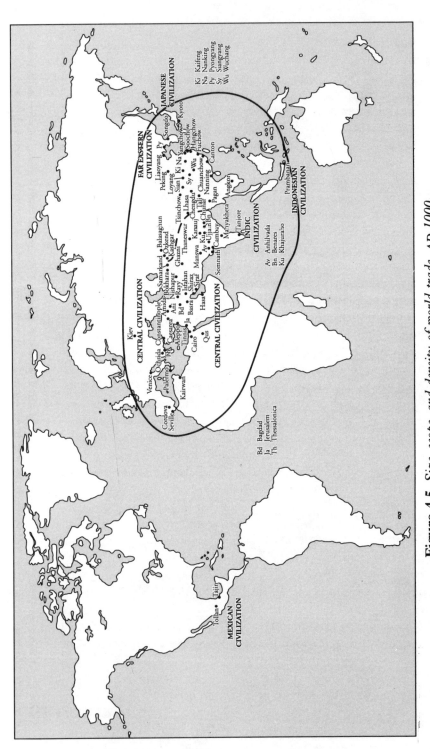

Figure 4.5 *Size, scope, and density of world trade, AD 1000*

Source: David Wilkinson (1992), figure 20. (Copyright © 1992 by David Wilkinson. License to reproduce granted gratis, only for use in works themselves distributed at no charge, and in which this map is reproduced in full, including this note. All other rights reserved.)

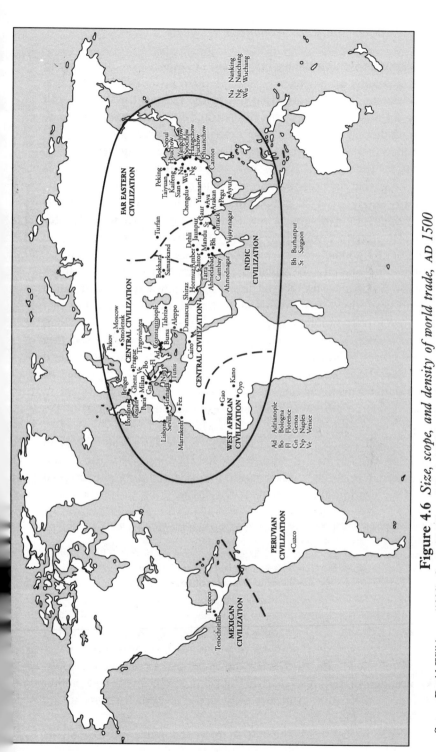

Figure 4.6 *Size, scope, and density of world trade, AD 1500*

application of its own theory" (1977:20). That is, it sees the capitalist world-economy as having no parallels during the precapitalist era. Schneider went on to argue that one of the reasons for Wallerstein's stance on this matter concerns his distinction between the exchange of fundamental goods and the exchange of preciosities and his insistence that a world-economy is based on the former rather than the latter. Indeed, for Wallerstein the exchange of preciosities is something that is nonsystemic, or that occurs between a world-economy and its external arena. This leads him to exclude precapitalist Europe from involvement in a world-economy, since its exchanges with other regions were largely exchanges of luxuries rather than fundamental goods.

Schneider objected to Wallerstein's diminution of the importance of trade in preciosities. She claimed that such a trade is of much greater significance than Wallerstein was willing to grant, and that therefore it is "possible to hypothesize a *pre-capitalist* world-system, in which core-areas accumulated precious metals while exporting manufactures, whereas peripheral areas gave up these metals (and often slaves) against an inflow of finished goods" (1977:25). She saw precapitalist Europe as deeply involved in a large world-system in which it was peripheral to the better-established civilizations of the Levant and Asia.

Other scholars were soon to follow Schneider's lead. Jonathan Friedman and Michael Rowlands (1978:271) argued that the notion of "external relations" was central to understanding the original rise of civilization and the state:

The development of the early central civilizations clearly depended on the productive activity of very large areas, and in order to fully understand the evolutionary process it is necessary to take account of these larger systems of reproduction. The transformation of societies does not occur in a vacuum and the relation between units in a larger system may determine the conditions of evolution of any one of them.

This idea has been substantially elaborated by Friedman and Kajsa Ekholm (Ekholm and Friedman, 1982; Ekholm, 1981). Ekholm and Friedman see world-systems as very general historical phenomena, and as the basic unit to which evolutionary analyses should apply. Ekholm denies the relevance of focusing on individual societies, claiming that "evolution occurs only at the level of the system as a whole" (1981:245).

In more recent years the notion of precapitalist world-systems has continued to find strong proponents. In 1987 an important conference was held on this topic, and the conference proceedings were published (Rowlands, Larsen, and Kristiansen, 1987). The authors of the individual essays try to demonstrate the existence of world-systemic networks in ancient times in such places as the ancient Near East, Scandinavia, and ancient Rome.

The most extensive single work applying a world-system perspective to a precapitalist situation is Janet Abu-Lughod's celebrated *Before European Hegemony* (1989). We have already encountered this work in the context of our discussion of increasing world commercialization during the agrarian era. Abu-Lughod is in essence applying Jane Schneider's argument in great detail. She identifies a vast thirteenth-and fourteenth-century world-system with eight overlapping subsystems and three major trade circuits. Within this system, Asia (especially China) acted as a core, and Europe was peripheral. In later years the relative positions of Asia and Europe were reversed, and the only way to understand how this happened is to look at the system as a whole, not at its individual (societal) units.

Andre Gunder Frank (1990, 1991; Gills and Frank, 1991) has made the boldest argument concerning the application of a world-system perspective backwards in time. He argues that there has been, continuously, for some 5,000 years a *single* world-system that now encompasses the whole world. This world-system began with the rise of civilization in Mesopotamia and has expanded slowly and gradually so as now to be literally worldwide in scope. According to Frank, the basic mechanism driving this world-system forward is the accumulation of capital, and what we need to be studying are the variety of ways in which this process has worked.

Guillermo Algaze (1989) and Mitchell Allen (1992) have used world-system theory to analyze the structure of Mesopotamian civilization after about 1900 BC. They both claim that there existed a world-system remarkably similar to the modern capitalist world-system, and that the difference between the two was only a matter of degree. They identify core and peripheral areas and claim that the "development of underdevelopment" was a significant feature of the system. Like other world-system theorists, they believe that the evolution of Mesopotamian civilization could only be understood from the perspective of the system as a whole, not in terms of its individual parts.

The most systematic work on precapitalist world-systems has been carried out by Christopher Chase-Dunn and Thomas Hall (1991, 1993; Hall and Chase-Dunn, 1992). They are in the process of developing a comparative sociology of world-systems, which they recognize requires at the precapitalist level modifications of Wallersteinian world-system theory. Wallersteinian theory cannot, they claim, be imported wholesale into the study of the precapitalist world. Chase-Dunn and Hall distinguish *kin-based, tributary,* and *modern capitalist* world-systems, and differentiate four types of tributary systems: primary (pristine) state-based world-systems; primary world-empires in which a number of autonomous states have been unified by conquest; multicentered world-systems composed of empires, states, and peripheral regions; and commercializing world-systems, or those within which a high level of commodification has been achieved. Chase-Dunn and Hall are much concerned with core–periphery relations and raise the important question as to whether or not all world-systems have core–periphery hierarchies. They also make an interesting innovation in pointing out that some core–periphery hierarchies may lead to "spread effects" – development in the core carrying over into development in the periphery – whereas others may lead to "backwash effects" – the development of underdevelopment. Chase-Dunn and Hall see precapitalist world-system analysis as having important implications for theories of social evolution and unsurprisingly claim that the basic unit of social evolution is the world-system, not its individual societal units.

What can be made of these various efforts? There are a number of things that need to be said on the more critical side. First, there is a serious danger in applying terms like core and periphery to systems for which they were never originally designed or intended. Although Chase-Dunn and Hall's approach gets around this problem to some extent – they recognize important differences in core–periphery relations in different types of world-systems – it is not entirely free of it. Samir Amin (1991), for instance, has remarked that it is stretching things beyond the breaking point to argue that the competition between societies in the precapitalist world is like the competition between societies in the modern capitalist world. He also argues that the kind of polarization we see in the modern world is far different from what we see in earlier eras. Philip Kohl makes a similar point with respect to an analysis of a Bronze Age world-system (1987:16):

There is little reason to doubt that patterns of dependency . . . were established as a result of intercultural exchange in the Bronze Age world system. . . . Dependency could lead to exploitation, and . . . the more powerful urban societies could dictate the terms of the exchange. But the relations between ancient cores and peripheries were not structurally analogous to those which underdevelopment theorists postulate are characteristic of First–Third World relations today. Unless conquered (i.e., incorporated into a larger polity), ancient peripheries could have followed one of several options ranging from withdrawal from the exchange network to substitutions of one core partner for another. Archaeological and historical evidence converge to suggest that most intercultural exchange systems in antiquity were fragile, lasting at most a few generations before collapsing. This inherent instability is related to the relative weakness of the bonds of dependency that existed between core and peripheral partners.

Christopher Edens (1992:134) agrees, claiming that "center–periphery relations in antiquity simply were not adequately encompassing, even leaving aside logistical problems, to create 'world-systems.'"

An examination of Janet Abu-Lughod's work shows that terms like core and periphery are often thrown about loosely, and thus either have a meaning different in important respects from that originally given to them by Wallerstein or no clear meaning at all. Abu-Lughod refers to China as "core" and Europe as "periphery" in her thirteenth-and fourteenth-century world-system. But in this context what do these terms actually mean? They cannot possibly have the same meaning that they do for Wallerstein. China was not using Europe as a raw-material-producing dependent partner to enhance its own developmental status. Europe was not being subjected to "coerced cash-crop labor" for the benefit of Chinese land-lords and entrepreneurs.

Consider also another kind of difficulty in using the terms core and periphery in the precapitalist context. Thomas Barfield's *The Perilous Frontier* (1989) describes in great detail the political, military, and economic interactions that took place between Chinese civilization and the nomadic peoples occupying its northern steppe fringe over a period of two millennia. From Barfield's analysis it seems clear that the tribes of the steppe benefitted more from these interactions than Chinese civilization itself. Was, then, one group core and the other periphery? If so, which was which? I submit that these are very difficult if not impossible questions to answer, at least within the framework of Wallerstein's meanings.

A second difficulty with precapitalist world-system analyses concerns their claim to be contributing to a theory of social evolution.[2]

Most of the scholars whose work we have discussed have made this claim, and none more strongly than Chase-Dunn and Hall (who open their 1992 article with a discussion of social evolution). However, in these analyses there is no development of any important theoretical conception of social evolution, other than the very general (though certainly not unimportant) notion that world-systems are the units that are doing the evolving. To be contributing to a theory of social evolution one must do more than merely identify the evolutionary unit; one must also identify a mechanism or set of mechanisms responsible for whatever evolutionary changes are taking place. Two examples may help to clarify my point. Think back for a moment to Carneiro's theory of the origin of the state, a theory that Chase-Dunn and Hall refer to favorably and one that certainly emphasizes the importance of intersocietal relations (although in this case the relations are political and military rather than economic). What makes Carneiro's theory evolutionary is that he identifies the specific kinds of factors that he believes are crucial for pristine state development: population pressure, warfare, and environmental circumscription. So far as I can tell, precapitalist world-system theorists fail to do anything comparable. Or take Wallerstein's theory of the modern world-system. Wallerstein has convinced me that social evolution in the modern era must be understood in the context of the world-system as a whole, but he does more than this. He goes on to identify the specific mechanisms and processes inherent within capitalism that account for its evolution and expansion and that predict its ultimate demise. Again, I fail to see anything comparable being produced by advocates of precapitalist world-system analysis.

I should hasten to say that I agree that one must take intersocietal relations, especially world trade, seriously when studying the precapitalist, and especially the agrarian, world. My earlier analysis of rising world commercialization should put this beyond doubt. However, we must be careful not to exaggerate the importance of intersocietal networks or "external relations" for social change in the agrarian world. Internal or endogenous factors are important as well and cannot be ignored. The unit of social change in the agrarian world is in many respects just as much the society as it is the intersocietal network. The question of the relative significance of endogenous versus exogenous factors is, I should think, always an empirical one that must be taken case by case. Depending on what we are studying, endogenous factors may be more important, exogenous factors may be more important, or it may be crucial to grasp some concatenation of the two. The theory of evolutionary materialism recognizes the importance of both kinds of factors throughout social evolution and does not privilege either kind on *a priori* grounds.

Yet despite all these criticisms, I want to acknowledge one extremely important contribution made by those who urge precapitalist world-system analysis, although it is secondary to their major point: they have rightly asked us to pay more attention to the importance of mercantile activity in agrarian societies. Precapitalist world-system thinkers are not claiming that "capitalism" existed long before the sixteenth century AD, but they are showing that mercantile activity of a "protocapitalist" sort was much more important in the last few thousand years than many of us are accustomed to think (see especially Ekholm and Friedman [1982] on this point). We are in the habit of thinking of agrarian societies as resting on production-for-use economies, and indeed this is so. However, agrarian societies all had mercantile sectors within their economies as well, and in many agrarian states this sector was of substantial significance. I myself must confess that I have been one of those guilty of not taking mercantile activity in agrarian states seriously enough. More was going on in the period of world history from 3000 BC to AD 1500 than many, myself included, thought. There was no genuine evolutionary shift to a qualitatively new stage of social organization, but there was a lot of political and economic growth, the significance of which will soon become apparent.

SOCIAL DEVOLUTION AND THE COLLAPSE OF AGRARIAN STATES

Antievolutionists often like to point to numerous instances of the regression or collapse of societies as contradicting the basic logic of evolutionary theories (Runciman, 1989). It would be an extremely rigid and simplistic type of evolutionism, though, that would deny regression. In fact, most evolutionary theories, and certainly the theory of evolutionary materialism, not only make allowance for regression, but try to explain it in terms of the same general principles that are called forth to account for forward evolutionary movement.

It is true, nonetheless, that the phenomena of regression and collapse have not received the attention they deserve (Yoffee, 1988). However, there have been some important recent studies that we can draw upon. First, though, we need to be clear about the meanings of terms. I use the words *devolution* and *regression* synonymously. These terms refer to a situation in which a sociocultural system loses organizational complexity and reverts to a stage of historical development normally characteristic of earlier societies. Some people, such as Joseph Tainter (1988), prefer to use the word *collapse*. Tainter defines collapse as occurring when a sociocultural system displays a rapid and substantial loss of its established degree of sociocultural complexity. It is difficult to argue for any real difference between the word collapse on the one hand and the words regression and devolution on the other. We might say that two key ideas contained in Tainter's notion of collapse – "rapid" and "substantial" – are not necessarily connoted by the words regression and devolution. However, it is difficult to think of any examples of regression/ devolution that would also not ultimately be examples of collapse. I shall therefore use all these terms interchangeably, though taking note, of course, that some instances of collapse/devolution/ regression are more rapid and substantial than others.

Devolution or collapse should not be confused with the fall of dynasties. The fall of dynasties amounts simply to a changing of personnel without any, or at least any major, structural reorganization of the sociopolitical system. As we have seen, dynasties rise and fall all the time, and there are many more examples of this process than of collapse. When a complex society collapses most or all of the following consequences eventuate (Tainter, 1988):

1 there is a breakdown of authority and centralized control;
2 small states emerge within the territory that was formerly unified, and these often contend with each other for domination;
3 the construction of monumental architecture and other publicly-supported works slows greatly or ceases altogether;
4 palaces and central storage facilities are abandoned, along with market exchange and the centralized distribution of foodstuffs;
5 subsistence and other material needs come to be provided for in terms of local self-sufficiency;
6 technology reverts to simpler forms that can be maintained at the local level;
7 there is a marked and usually rapid reduction in population size and density;
8 many settlements are abandoned.

Collapse is obviously not a phenomenon limited to agrarian states; it can occur, and generally has occurred, throughout the entire evolutionary range of human societies. (Industrial societies have yet to collapse, of course, but they are potentially at least as subject to this possibility as is any other type of society. We shall be looking at this possibility in chapter 9.) It is just that our concern in this chapter is only with agrarian states, and so our discussion of collapse will be limited to that type of society.

The best examples of societal collapse are the final disintegration of the Roman empire in the late fifth century AD and the collapse of Mayan society in the ninth and tenth centuries AD. We shall focus on these instances of collapse in the discussion that follows. Among other good examples of the collapse of complex societies are the Harappan civilization around 1750 BC; the Egyptian Old Kingdom after the end of the Sixth Dynasty in 2181 BC; the Hittite empire in the thirteenth century BC; Mycenaean civilization after about 1200 BC; the Olmec civilization sometime in the last few centuries BC; and Teotihuacán about AD 700 (Tainter, 1988).

Tainter has carried out the most comprehensive analysis of the collapse of complex societies to date. Before presenting his own theory, Tainter reviews 11 other explanations of societal collapse commonly found in the literature. These are:

1   resource depletion;
2   excessively bountiful resources;
3   natural catastrophes, such as hurricanes, earthquakes, or epidemics of disease;
4   insufficient response to circumstances as a result of the basic limitations of social, economic, and political systems;
5   competition with other complex societies;
6   foreign intrusion, especially of barbarians;
7   class conflict, internal contradictions, or elite mismanagement;
8   social dysfunction as the result of mysterious internal processes;
9   mystical factors (e.g., "decadence," "loss of vigor");
10 chance concatenation of events;
11 economic explanations, such as declining advantages of complexity, increasing disadvantages of complexity, or increasing costliness of complexity.

Tainter finds all of these explanations wanting, some of them severely so. Unfortunately space does not allow discussion of all of Tainter's counterarguments (but see Tainter, 1988:44–90). Suffice it to say that he believes that the economic explanations come closest to the mark because they recognize the need to identify factors contributing to a society's internal weaknesses, because they identify a specific mechanism or mechanisms held to be responsible for collapse, and because they establish a definite causal chain connecting the causal mechanism and the observed outcome.

In fact, Tainter's own theory is rather similar to some of these economic explanations. This theory holds that as a society becomes increasingly complex the costs of maintaining the administrative apparatus of complexity increase to the point where declining marginal productivity is eventually reached and even frequently exceeded with the occurrence of decreased overall benefits to the population as a whole. The costs of maintaining such a complex administrative apparatus eventually become impossible to bear, and a society caught in this situation will be unable to prevent itself from collapsing. As the point of diminishing marginal returns is reached a society is in a weakened condition that makes it especially vulnerable to any particular stresses or shocks, and it is probably only a matter of time before it collapses. In essence what Tainter is describing is a kind of dialectic in which societies are hoist on their own petard; the more they invest in complexity, the more difficult it is for them to pay the costs of that complexity, and the very nature of the evolutionary trajectory they follow is self-undermining in the long run. Social evolution thus proceeds from lower to higher cost, a fact that Tainter regards as an "immutable fact of societal evolution."

Tainter's theory is a very general and parsimonious one that is deemed to be applicable, at least in principle, to all complex societies and even to simple ones. A little inspection will show that it is remarkably similar to Ester Boserup's (1965, 1981) theory of agricultural intensification and Mark Cohen's (1977) theory of the worldwide origins of agriculture. In fact, Tainter regards these latter theories as special instances of his own theory. This makes Tainter's theory highly compatible with the strategy of evolutionary materialism.

Tainter applies his theory to understand the collapse of the Roman empire and Mayan civilization. It was during the reign of Marcus Aurelius (AD 161–80) that the structure of the empire first began to show signs of cracking. In the early third century the empire was plagued by bands of military deserters, and order was beginning to break down. The period between 235 and 284 was one of severe crisis during which the empire came very close to collapsing. This period was witness to foreign and civil wars, barbarian invasions, financial exigency and increased taxes, debasement of the currency, and massive inflation. It was a time of extreme political instability; there were 20 emperors during this half-century, 18 of whom died violent deaths (P. Anderson, 1974a). At the end of the third century there was something of a recovery, but this was only partial and temporary. By the fifth century the civil service had grown so large that it was a tremendous burden on an extremely weakened empire, as were huge military costs. Since population had declined, the increased military and administrative costs had to be borne by fewer individuals. Tainter shows that for some time the burdens of maintaining the empire were felt throughout Roman society, and a large segment of the population was hopeful that the invading barbarians would destroy the empire and free them from its over-whelming burdens. By the end of the fifth century, in AD 476 to be exact, the last emperor was deposed, and the empire can be said to have officially ended. Tainter sees this outcome as virtually inevitable (1988:150):

The cost of saving the empire was extremely high for a non-industrial population. And as in the third century, payment of this cost yielded no increase in benefits. Yet what happened during the fourth and fifth centuries was more than simply a further decline in the marginal return. The Empire was by this time sustaining itself by the consump-tion of its capital resources: producing lands and peasant population. Continued invest-ment in empire was creating not only a drop in marginal output, but also a drop in *actual* output. Where under the Principate the strategy had been to tax the future to pay for the present, the Dominate paid for the present by undermining the future's ability to pay taxes. The Empire emerged from the third century crisis, but at a cost that weakened its ability to meet future crises. At least in the West, a downward spiral ensued: reduced finances weakened military defense, while military disasters in turn meant further loss of producing lands and population. Collapse was in the end inevit-able, as indeed it had always been.

As is well known, the eastern part of the empire, Byzantium, did not collapse. Tainter claims that this is because it was more economically developed and populous, as well as because it had a much smaller frontier to defend against barbarian incursions. Therefore its invest-ment in complexity could be financed more easily.

Tainter's explanation for the Roman collapse is similar in import-ant respects to the theory developed early in this century by Max Weber (1976[1896/1909]) and elaborated more recently by Perry Anderson (1974a). Weber and Anderson may, in fact, supply a critical factor missing in Tainter's theory. The Weber–Anderson argument rests upon the overwhelming importance of slavery in the Roman economy. The Roman slave labor force was not one that was self-reproducing, and therefore Rome had to acquire new slaves continually. These came mainly from foreign conquest. However, a point was eventually reached beyond which foreign conquest could no longer go, and thus the supply of slaves began to dry up. The increasing shortage of slaves dealt a severe blow to the functioning of the economy, and the worsening economic situation had major spillover effects on the political system and the society more generally. The collapse of Rome, then, was the result of a severe internal contradiction within the mode of production.

Many explanations of the Roman collapse have concentrated on the barbarian invasions as the chief culprit (e.g., Mann, 1986). However, the theories of Tainter, Weber, and Anderson see the barbarian invasions as important only in the context of a severely weakened empire. By themselves the invasions could not have brought the empire down.

As I said above, the Tainter and Weber–Anderson explanations are similar in that they refer to the dialectical contradictions of a system – how the Roman system was self-undermining. Actually, the Weber–Anderson explanation is but a special instance of Tainter's more general theory. Is the addition of the factor of the exhaustion of the slave labor force essential to understand the Roman collapse? Tainter makes no mention of this factor and would probably claim that even without the drying up of the slave labor force Rome was destined to collapse. This may well be true, for this was surely one of the more complex and militarily and administratively top-heavy societies of all time. It may have been simply that the decline of slavery hastened the process of collapse but did not directly determine it.

As I mentioned earlier, one of the great attractions of Tainter's theory is its remarkable generality and parsimony. We can see the theory at work also in the case of the collapse of Mayan civilization. Here Tainter's specific argument converges almost precisely with a particular kind of evolutionary materialist argument: population pressure and its effects. The beginning of the Mayan collapse may be dated to the end of the eighth or beginning of the ninth century AD. After this time the construction of monumental architecture slowed and eventually stopped altogether, tomb burials grew fewer in number and less elaborate, and population declined massively and rapidly (one estimate [Tainter, 1988] is that population was reduced over a 75-year period from 3 million to 450,000). Moreover, stela construction stopped, luxury items were no longer manufactured, and the calendrical and writing systems were lost (Tainter, 1988).

At its peak Mayan civilization was an extremely densely populated preindustrial society. Tainter and a leading expert on the Mayan collapse, T. Patrick Culbert (1988), attribute the collapse to enormous population pressure and its reverberating effects on economic and sociopolitical life. The Maya had been investing for hundreds of years in sociopolitical complexity, and the costs of this investment had to be borne entirely by the peasant agricultural population. With the buildup of severe population pressure over time, the bulk of the population had great difficulty meeting their own daily needs, let alone providing for the support of a large administrative superstructure. Declining marginal productivity set in, soon to be followed by absolute declines in productivity. As Culbert (1988:77) explains, "The Maya never attained equilibrium. They were a growth system, changing continually and subject to the possibility that the very processes that generated growth might lead to distintegration if the trajectory continued." Like the Romans and many other complex societies, the Maya's commitment to greater and greater complexity turned out to be inherently self-defeating. And thus we see that social devolution can only be understood as a process that is inextricably intertwined with the very nature of social evolution itself.

The frequency of societal collapse in world history surely provides a reason for having extreme doubt about the allegedly *adaptive* benefits of social complexity. Many evolutionists – functionalist evolutionists in particular – argue that the key dimension of social evolution is growing differentiation or complexity, and that such a process produces increasingly well-adapted societies (Parsons, 1966, 1971; Carneiro, 1972). In *Social Evolutionism* I argued vigorously against such a notion, and here is yet another good reason to question it. Growing complexity may be a good thing for elites, in whose interests it is generally carried out in the first place. But it is of dubious worth, or actually maladaptive, for the bulk of the population who must pay the costs of complexity. And, as Tainter shows, it is maladaptive over the long run even for elite groups. Tainter suggests that in this light there is no particular reason to view negatively the collapse of a society to a simpler level of organization (1988:197–8):

Most of the writers whose work has been considered seem to approve of civilizations and complex societies. They see complexity as a desirable, even commendable, condition of human affairs. Civilization to them is the ultimate accomplishment of human society, far preferable to simpler, less differentiated forms of organization. . . .

With such emphasis on civil society as desirable, it is almost necessary that collapse be viewed as a catastrophe. An end to the artistic and literary features of civilization, and to the umbrella of service and protection that an administration provides, are seen as fearful events, truly paradise lost. The notion that collapse is a catastrophe is rampant . . . .

Complex societies . . . are recent in human history. Collapse then is not a fall to some primordial chaos, but a return to the normal human condition of lower complexity. The notion that collapse is uniformly a catastrophe is contradicted, moreover, by the present theory. To the extent that collapse is due to declining marginal returns on investment in complexity, it is an *economizing* process. It occurs when it becomes necessary to restore the marginal return on organizational investment to a more favorable level. To a population that is receiving little return on the cost of supporting complexity, the loss of that complexity brings economic, and perhaps administrative, gains.

Tainter's theory is rife with implications for the future of industrial capitalist societies, indeed for the entire modern world. It will become relevant again in that context (chapter 9).

CONCLUSION: THE EVOLUTIONARY DYNAMICS OF AGRARIAN STATES

This chapter has been concerned with tracing out the evolutionary dynamics, or what might be called the "evolutionary logic," of agrarian states. To the question, What is the evolutionary logic of agrarian states?, the answer is, They have no evolutionary logic, at least not in the sense of some mechanism or mechanisms creating powerful pressures for the shift to a fundamentally different mode of social organization. Long-term stasis and devolution are just as common as, if not much more common than, any tendency to forward directional change. It is important to stress once again, though, that despite the absence of any powerful evolutionary impetus, many agrarian societies have expanded demographically and geographically and grown in size and scope. They have also, over the long haul of nearly five millennia, expanded the scale of their mercantile activities. Thus the level of world commercialization, as assessed mainly by the size and density of trade networks, has increased, not necessarily regularly or along some smooth curve, but at least in an overall sense. Agrarian societies cannot therefore be characterized as truly stagnant. The rate of social evolution slowed down during the period of their world-historical reign, but things were happening that would prepare the way for a qualitative evolutionary leap greater than the world had ever seen. This leap is the subject of the next chapter.

NOTES

1 For extensive amplification of this all too brief discussion of technological change, see especially Singer, Holmyard, and Hall (1954), Singer, Holmyard, Hall, and Williams (1956), Derry and Williams (1961), Lynn White (1962), Kranzberg and Pursell (1967), Daumas (1969), Hodges (1970), Needham (1954–86), Ronan and Needham (1978–81), Pacey (1990), and Dudley (1991).

2 It might be wondered how this could be possible at all, given the tendency of many thinkers to consider Wallersteinian world-system theory as historical and nonevolutionary (perhaps even antievolutionary). I regard Wallersteinian theory, however, as genuinely evolutionary, as do Hall and Chase-Dunn (1992) and various other precapitalist world-system theorists. My argument for the evolutionary character of world-system theory is developed in Sanderson (1990, 1991b).

5

The Capitalist Revolution and the Beginnings of the Modern World

Throughout most of the history of sociology it has been the standard wisdom that the modern world was the creation of the Industrial Revolution of the late eighteenth and early nineteenth centuries. Indeed, sociology was born as a discipline largely as a means of understanding the impact of industrialization on the structure of social life. In recent years, however, some scholars have shifted the origins of modernity backward in time to the sixteenth century, and have seen the modern world's beginnings in the transformation that Marxists call the transition from feudalism to capitalism (Wallerstein, 1974a,b, 1989). This is the viewpoint adopted here. Industrialization in Europe, North America, and elsewhere did not occur in a vacuum, but emerged only within the context of a prior shift toward a capitalist form of economic organization.

Most scholars who have studied the capitalist transition have seen it as a unique occurrence, possibly even as an extraordinary historical accident or a "miracle" (Mann, 1986; E.L. Jones, 1987). But if it was an accident or miracle, it was a most unusual one, for this miracle occurred not once but twice – or at least so it will be argued here. A number of scholars have noted that medieval Japan underwent a transition from a feudal to a largely capitalist society that was remarkably similar to the European transition, and so I am hardly the first to draw attention to Japan as a case comparable to Europe. Nonetheless, the extent to which Japan was similar to Europe has never been fully appreciated, nor has the significance of the Japanese case ever been properly understood in terms of its implications for a general theory of the emergence of modernity.

In this chapter I hope to rectify these problems by using the following strategy. First I will discuss the controversial issue of the nature of feudalism and the extent of its prevalence as a political and economic structure in world history. I will try to show that feudalism proper was found only in medieval Europe and Japan. This will then lead into a descriptive analysis of the European and Japanese transitions to capitalism. The stage will then be set for a discussion of the many theories that have been offered to explain the rise of capitalism. Nearly all these theories focus on the European case, although there have been some attempts to explain the Japanese transition. In analyzing these theories, I will argue that priority must be given, as it virtually never has been previously, to a theoretical interpretation that best explains both cases, this being consistent, of course, with the principle of parsimony. In this context I will set forth my own interpretation of the beginnings of the modern capitalist world.

FEUDALISM IN WORLD HISTORY

Debate has raged for decades, indeed, since the eighteenth century, as to whether feudalism is a phenomenon unique to European history or a more general characteristic of societies throughout world history. The debate depends at least partly on what is meant by feudalism. Marxist scholars have generally conceived feudalism to be any mode of economic production in which landlords subordinate a class of dependent peasants. Given this very general conception of feudalism, it is not surprising that Marxists have tended to see it as being widespread throughout human history. However, this notion of feudalism is much too broad to be useful as a classificatory device, and in fact is inconsistent with Marx's own writings. Marx emphasized that European feudalism was quite distinct from what he called the "Asiatic mode of production."

The classic study of feudalism is, of course, Marc Bloch's (1961). Bloch saw feudalism as having five basic characteristics:

1   a peasantry subjected to the control of a landlord class;
2   the fief rather than a salary as a mode of payment of landlords' officials;
3   the political supremacy of a class of specialized warriors, with landlordship and military leadership fused;
4   vassalage, or the close personal tie between a vassal and his overlord, signified by the vassal's swearing of an oath of fealty;

5   the fragmentation of political authority.

Bloch's analysis of feudalism was based on its medieval French version, which has often been said to be the classical form of feudalism. However, Bloch made special mention of medieval Japan as having a form of feudalism, and he speculated that feudalism may well have been a common feature of world history.

One of the most systematic analyses of feudalism is that carried out by Rushton Coulborn and his collaborators (Coulborn, 1956). In this work, feudalism was defined as basically a method of government rather than a type of economic or social system. Feudalism's essential characteristic was the lord–vassal relationship, which led to political authority being treated as a private possession, something personal rather than institutional. Yet despite this definition, in the course of applying it other notions seemed to be smuggled in, with a feudal system also being seen as the disintegrated phase of an empire, as being highly characterized by barbarian attacks, as evincing political disunity, or as strikingly lacking in commerce. Armed with such a broad notion of feudalism, Coulborn and his associates found evidence for its historical generality, with Chou China, ancient Mesopotamia, and Muscovite Russia being added to the western European and Japanese cases. Coulborn et al. admitted that not all of these societies were feudal to the same degree (some being "feudalistic" rather than truly feudal), but they insisted nonetheless on seeing feudalism as a "repetitive phenomenon in history."

John Critchley (1978) and Perry Anderson (1974a) have helped to clarify both the nature of feudalism and the extent of its world-historical frequency. Critchley argues that the military tenure dimension of feudalism – the granting of land in return for military service and protection – has been relatively common historically. However, he argues, the close personal bond between lord and vassal signified by the vassal's taking an oath of fealty was a unique feature of European feudalism. He also claims that European feudalism was a unique amalgam of characteristics found nowhere else in just that form. Critchley sees Japan as having a form of feudalism that was the nearest to a replica of European feudalism.

Anderson's analysis of feudalism stresses that it is neither strictly an economic system nor strictly political. Instead, it involves the inextricable fusion of the economic and the political. For Anderson, the critical features of feudalism are vassalage, the fief, and, most significantly, the "parcellization of sovereignty." Feudalism combines landlordship with military service, and as such leads to a political arrangement in which authority is fragmented among a variety of lords, and thus highly decentralized. According to Anderson, this parcellization of sovereignty created towns that were characterized by a striking autonomy. As he puts it with respect to medieval Europe (1974a:150–1):

> The feudal mode of production . . . was the *first* to permit it [the town] an *autonomous development* within a natural-agrarian economy. The fact that the largest mediaeval towns never rivalled in scale those of either Antiquity or Asian Empires has often obscured the truth that their function within the social formation was a much more advanced one. In the Roman Empire, with its highly sophisticated urban civilization, the towns were subordinated to the rule of noble landowners who lived in them, but not from them; in China, vast provincial agglomerations were controlled by mandarin bureaucrats resident in a special district segregated from all commercial activity. By contrast, the paradigmatic mediaeval towns of Europe which practised trade and manufactures were self-governing communes, enjoying corporate political and military autonomy from the nobility and the Church. . . . Thus a *dynamic opposition* of town and country was alone possible in the feudal mode of production: opposition between an urban economy of increasing commodity exchange, and a rural economy of natural exchange, controlled by nobles and organized in manors and strips, with communal and individual peasant enclaves.

Anderson argues, as have a number of scholars, that the heartland of feudalism was northern France, which was of course the homeland of the Carolingian empire. Feudalism also was highly characteristic of other areas of western Europe, especially southern France, Italy, Spain, England, Germany, and Scandinavia. It emerged in the late eighth century AD and lasted until approximately 1450. According to Anderson (1974b), only one other area outside Europe was characterized by a truly feudal mode of social organization, and that was medieval Japan.[1] Beginning perhaps as early as AD 1185, a classical feudal system had become well established in Japan by the early fourteenth century and lasted until the nineteenth century. Anderson sees Japanese feudalism as strikingly similar to its European counterpart, even in terms of the autonomy of the town, a point also made by Critchley (1978). As Anderson says (1974b:44), "In the gaps left by the political fragmentation of Japan, autonomous merchant towns reminiscent of those of mediaeval Europe – Sakai, Hakata, Otsu, Ujiyamada and others – were able to flourish: the port of Sakai was to be termed an oriental 'Venice' by Jesuit travellers." It can even be argued that Japanese feudalism was, like European feudalism, based on a close personal bond between lord and vassal.

Anderson has convinced me that feudalism, at least in the sense intended by him, has been found only twice in world history. Other societies at other times have had some of the elements of feudalism (and thus might be called "feudalistic"), but only medieval Europe and Japan had a form of feudalism based on a close personal bond between lord and vassal and an economic arrangement in which towns had remarkable autonomy. As we shall see, this latter feature is one that seems to have had great significance for the future evolution of the respective societies.

THE NATURE OF CAPITALISM

Before beginning our discussion of the rise of capitalism, we must first try to establish just what capitalism is, a task that is complicated by substantial controversy and debate. Is capitalism unique to the modern world, or has it been found throughout much of world history? If it is unique to the modern world, what makes it so? What distinguishes modern capitalism from earlier forms of mercantile activity, and just when did modern capitalism begin?

Many scholars have used the word capitalism quite loosely and have generally assumed that it has been characteristic of much of world history. Thinkers working in the Marxist tradition, however, have been at pains to emphasize the uniquely modern nature of capitalism. Marx himself (1967[1867]) made two essential distinctions in this regard. On the one hand Marx distinguished between "simple commodity production" and "capitalist production." He argued that the former has been found widely throughout world history, while the latter is uniquely characteristic of modern times. Simple commodity production is represented, of course, by the formula C–M–C. In this form of economic activity, commodities are produced because of their use-value. A producer sells a commodity wanted or needed by someone else, and then turns around and uses this money to purchase another commodity that he himself wants or needs. One starts with commodities and ends with commodities. Capitalist production, by contrast, is represented by the formula M–C–M or, more accurately, M–C–M'. Here one produces commodities for their exchange-value rather than their use-value. One uses a supply of money to produce commodities and then sells these commodities on the market for an ever greater quantity of money. One starts with money and ends with even more money. The purpose of creating commodities is to enhance the quantity of money under one's control.

Marx's other critical distinction was that between "merchant capital" and "industrial capital," a distinction that rested on his use of the labor theory of value to formulate his theory of surplus value. In developing this theory Marx argued, of course, that commodified labor is the only source of the capitalist's surplus value. Surplus value cannot exist until labor has become commodified and turned into wage labor. The worker's labor power is the only commodity that the capitalist can purchase at less than its full value, and thus it is the only source of surplus value. According to Marx, when producers create goods for sale in the market by exploiting the labor power of workers through the wage–labor nexus, then and only then has "true" capitalism – industrial capitalism – begun. Marx saw this occurring only after the English Industrial Revolution of the second half of the eighteenth century, and thus "true" capitalism begins only then. However, there was a period of merchant capitalism that began in the sixteenth century and paved the way for the development of industrial capitalism. Here, however, Marx tells us, wage labor did not yet exist on any scale and profits were obtained through mercantile activity – buying and selling on the world market – rather than through exploitation of labor power through wage labor. Marx often referred to this period of merchant capital as the period of the "primitive accumulation" of capital. Merchant capitalism involved only the circulation or exchange of commodities, and those who sold them were not their producers. Industrial capitalism, by contrast, was capitalism-in-production: those who sold commodities were also their producers.

For Marx, then, capitalism begins no earlier than the sixteenth century in western Europe, and its "true" or industrial form does not emerge until the late eighteenth century. Industrial capitalism for Marx depended on three things: private ownership of the means of production by a social class known as a bourgeoisie; the existence of wage labor as the basis of production; and the profit motive and long-term accumulation of capital as the driving aim of production.

A rather similar conception of capitalism was offered by Max

Weber in his posthumously published *General Economic History* (1981[1927]). Weber argued that various forms of capitalism had existed throughout history, but modern capitalism was importantly different from all these (1981[1927]:276):

> While capitalism of various sorts is met with in all periods of history, the provision of the everyday wants by capitalistic methods is characteristic of the occident alone and even here has been the inevitable method only since the middle of the 19th century. Such capitalistic beginnings as are found in earlier centuries were merely anticipatory, and even the somewhat capitalistic establishments of the 16th century may be removed in thought from the economic life of the time without introducing any overwhelming change.

Weber went on to argue that modern capitalism had six basic characteristics generally absent in earlier forms of capitalism:

1 appropriation of the means of production as the property of autonomous private industrial enterprises;
2 the absence of irrational constraints on market exchange;
3 rational development of technology in the form of mechanization;
4 calculable law;
5 free labor; and
6 the general commercialization of economic life.

Weber was, like Marx, adamant about the importance of free labor, arguing that there had to be a class of persons forced to sell its labor in order to live. Unfree labor made capitalism impossible.

A more recent conceptualization of capitalism has been advanced by Immanuel Wallerstein (1974a,b). Although himself working in the Marxian tradition, Wallerstein's notion of capitalism is in some respects very "un-Marxist." For Wallerstein, capitalism is simply an economic system in which commodities are produced for sale in a market and in which the economic objective is to realize a profit and to accumulate capital over time. Wallerstein makes no mention of the need for free labor, nor does he make private ownership of capital essential. Indeed, he specifically argues that capitalism can take place, and in fact has taken place, with the use of forced labor (slavery, serfdom, and their variations), and he points to modern "socialist" economies as having a form of "state capitalism" in which there are no private entrepreneurs, but simply one big capitalist in the form of the state. Wallerstein says little about the existence of capitalism in earlier periods of history, but presumably he would see a certain amount of it there. He makes it quite clear, though, that the modern form of capitalism began in the "long" sixteenth century (i.e., after about 1450). He rejects Marx's distinction between merchant and industrial capital as useful, holding that the so-called Industrial Revolution was simply a phase in the development of world capitalism, not something particularly new and certainly not any sort of "great divide" in world history.

Wallerstein has aroused the ire of a number of more orthodox Marxists (e.g., Brenner, 1977), who have hurled the label "neo-Smithian Marxism" at him as a term of abuse. Nonetheless, it is my view that Wallerstein's conception of capitalism is more useful than the orthodox Marxist or Weberian conceptions. The proof of the pudding is in the eating, and I argue here, and will try to show later in the chapter, that Wallerstein's flexible conception of capitalism illuminates more of the last 500 years of world history than its competitors.

We still need to say as clearly as we can, though, what the critical distinctions between modern capitalism and earlier forms of capitalism are. I propose to call these earlier forms "protocapitalism" and to suggest that protocapitalism differed from modern capitalism in three crucial respects. First, modern capitalism's scale of operation is far greater than the protocapitalism of earlier periods of world history. Second, modern capitalism pervades both economic and noneconomic life, whereas protocapitalism touched directly upon the lives of only a small fraction of the population. Finally, modern capitalism has an evolutionary dynamic overwhelmingly greater than anything protocapitalism may have possessed. Modern capitalism is truly world-transforming in a way that protocapitalism never was.

THE ORIGINS OF EUROPEAN CAPITALISM

A classic analysis of the rise of capitalism in Europe has been presented by Maurice Dobb (1963). As a Marxist, the distinction between merchant and industrial capital is relevant for Dobb. He sees merchant capitalism as beginning in the fourteenth and fifteenth centuries with the rise of the towns within the context of the breakdown of the feudal mode of production. The rise of the towns is also the rise of a new social class, the bourgeoisie, or at least an elevation of its economic importance. A critical question concerns the source of wealth acquired by the bourgeoisie. Dobb's answer to this question points to plunder and monopoly (1963:88):

In the first place, so much commerce in those times, especially foreign commerce, consisted either of exploiting some political advantage or of scarcely-veiled plunder. Secondly, the class of merchants, as soon as it assumed any corporate forms, was quick to acquire powers of monopoly, which fenced its ranks from competition and served to turn the terms of exchange to its own advantage in its dealings with producer and consumer. It is evident that this twofold character of commerce at this period constituted the essential basis of early burgher wealth and of the accumulation of merchant capital.

The early bourgeoisie drew its wealth primarily from trade rather than production, and as such Dobb argues that its role in the late medieval social order was not truly revolutionary. Nonetheless, it clearly helped pave the way for a more revolutionary development, the early beginnings of industrial capital, which can be seen by the sixteenth century. In agriculture, estates began to be treated as capitalist investments and run with hired workers along the lines of a capitalist farm. City merchants invested in manors, many landowners transformed themselves from aristocrats to bourgeois, and a class of yeoman farmers rose from the ranks of the peasantry. In manufacturing, many merchant capitalists turned toward control over production in such trades as the textile, leather, and smaller metal industries. Dobb notes that it is here, in the beginning of the bourgeoisie's control over production, that "the real qualitative change appears" (1963:128). This qualitative change involved not only the bourgeoisie's increasing control over production, but also the subordination of a labor force to the bourgeoisie's demands and requirements. Dobb continues (1963:143):

The domestic industry of this period . . . was in a crucial respect different from the guild handicraft from which it had descended: in the majority of cases it had become subordinated to the control of capital, and the producing craftsman had lost most of his economic independence of earlier times. References become increasingly common at this time to craftsmen being "employed" or "maintained" by the merchant-manufacturing element. . . . The craftsman's status was already beginning to approximate to that of a simple wage-earner; . . . The subordination of production to capital, and the appearance of this class relationship between capitalist and the producer is, therefore, to be regarded as the crucial watershed between the old mode of production and the new, even if the technical changes that we associate with the industrial revolution were needed both to complete the transition and to afford scope for the full maturing of

the capitalist mode of production and of the great increase in the productive power
of human labour associated with it.

Dobb does go on to note, however, that what was occurring in
England in the sixteenth century could already be found to some
extent in the Netherlands and several Italian cities at a much earlier
date, perhaps as early as 1200. Capitalist-controlled cloth manufacture was going on at Antwerp, and enterprises involving iron smelting and coal mining were found in the districts of Liège, Namur,
and Hainault. Although cottage industry was the predominant way
of organizing a work force, some factories did exist: "In Florence
in 1338 there were said to be as many as 200 workshops engaged in
cloth manufacture, employing a total of 30,000 workmen or about a
quarter of the whole occupied population of the city" (Dobb,
1963:157). Jere Cohen (1980) has picked up on this theme, noting
that in Renaissance Italy there was a form of capitalism that satisfied
most of Weber's criteria for modern rational capitalism. Cohen
claims that capitalism was born in Renaissance Italy and then copied
by northern Europe. Fernand Braudel (1984) also prefers an early
starting point for the beginnings of capitalism, although he does
suggest that this was still a form of protocapitalism rather than
capitalism proper (Braudel, 1984:92): "The birth of Europe, that
monstrous shaper of world history, took place not in 1400 . . .
but at least two hundred years earlier." Just as for Cohen, for
Braudel capitalism was born in Italy, and it was Venice that was the
greatest of all the early Italian capitalist city-states (1984:127–
8):

Venice was no isolated phenomenon, but had grown up surrounded by a network of
thriving towns, all inspired to similar responses by the age they lived in. . . .
. . . Venice succeeded in establishing a system which from the very first raised all
the problems of the relations between Capital, Labour and the State, relations which
would increasingly come to be identified with the word *capitalism* in the course of its
long subsequent development.
    By the late twelfth or early thirteenth century, and *a fortiori* by the fourteenth, the
Venetian economy was already well-equipped with institutions: it had markets, shops,
warehouses, the Ascensionide Fair (*la Sensa*), the Mint (the *Zecca*), the Doges' Palace,
the Arsenal, the Doganna.

It also had very well developed financial and banking institutions,
and, as we have seen, it had factories and wage labor.
    Easily the most important recent analysis of the rise of European

capitalism is that of Immanuel Wallerstein (1974a,b, 1979, 1980a, 1989). For Wallerstein, the capitalistic developments of late medieval Europe differed in a critical way from what began to develop after the sixteenth century: they were focused heavily on trade in luxury goods or preciosities rather than staples, and thus they could not form the basis for a world-economy based on a world market. This point is a linchpin of Wallerstein's analysis of capitalism.

Wallerstein's most fundamental contribution to the analysis of modern capitalism is, of course, his notion that capitalism emerged as, and has continued to expand and evolve as, a *world-system*. To understand capitalism, one must focus on the systemic relations among its parts rather than on the parts – individual societies – themselves. This principle applies to the birth of capitalism in the sixteenth century as well as to its character in the late twentieth century.

Capitalism emerged as and has always remained a world-economy rather than a world-empire. A world-empire has a centralized political and military structure that coordinates the whole system, whereas a world-economy is politically decentralized and is held together by relations of economic production and exchange. As a world-economy, capitalism contains three major components that are probably best termed *zones*. The *core* consists of those societies that have the greatest economic power within the entire world-economy. Capitalist entrepreneurs in the core extract great amounts of the surplus value that is produced within the system, both within the core and in the other two zones. This means that the core is the most prosperous zone. It is also the zone that concentrates on the most advanced productive activities that go on within the system, and it uses the most advanced forms of productive technology. The core zone produces finished goods, and it tends to rely on wage labor as the mode of labor control (or at least makes more use of wage labor than do the other zones). The societies of the core also generally contain the most politically and militarily powerful states within the world-system.

The *periphery* of the capitalist world-economy consists of those societies or regions that are the economically least powerful and most severely exploited. A peripheral region is one that has been invaded by the core (and to some extent the one remaining zone) for purposes of producing commodities containing extremely high levels of surplus value. Inasmuch as the periphery is the most exploited zone, it follows that it is the least economically developed or prosperous. The periphery has historically been, and to a large degree still is, economically specialized in terms of the production of raw agricultural or mineral products, generally with the use of forced labor or what Wallerstein calls "coerced cash-crop labor." Coerced cash-crop labor is either slavery, serfdom, or some variant of these that is devoted to the production of commodities for sale on the world market. The nature of economic activity within the periphery is such that technological advancement is generally inhibited, and so we find that the periphery is the least technologically developed zone. Politically and militarily, peripheral regions are weak, and in some cases may lack political sovereignty altogether.

Wallerstein proposes a third zone which he calls the *semiperiphery*. This zone is intermediate between core and periphery and generally contains mixtures of both core-like and periphery-like elements. The semiperiphery thus has an intermediate level of technological and economic development, an intermediate level of political and military power, and an intermediate level of prosperity. It will contain activities devoted to the production of finished goods along with activities devoted to producing raw materials. As such, it will contain both wage labor and coerced cash-crop labor in substantial amounts.

Wallerstein sees capitalism emerging in the "long" sixteenth century, by which he means the period between 1450 and 1640. The first capitalist states were Spain and Portugal, which were also the first European powers to establish colonies (peripheral regions) in the New World. The Spanish colonies in Peru, Mexico and other parts of what is now Latin America were heavily given over to gold and silver mining relying on the forms of forced labor known as *encomienda, repartimiento*, and *hacienda*. Gold and silver ore was used in the production of bullion, which greatly increased the supply of money in the European economy. The Portuguese colony in Brazil rested on sugar cane production using slave labor drawn from Africa through the Atlantic slave trade.

Spain and Portugal, however, were not destined to attain true core status in the world-economy. They faltered and slipped into the semiperiphery. The first society to achieve true core status was the Netherlands, which, as we have seen, had a very advanced form of protocapitalism as early as the thirteenth century. The Netherlands was followed by England, and then by the northern region of France. These were the three members of the core in the early seventeenth century. In these societies capitalist agriculture and early forms of capitalist industry predominated.

We have already seen that Spain and Portugal belonged to the semiperiphery by the end of the long sixteenth century. They were joined by southern France and Italy, the latter, of course, long the center of a vigorous protocapitalism. Here sharecropping was the major mode of labor control, and capitalist production centered on high-cost industrial products such as silks. In addition to Spanish and Portuguese America, the periphery at the end of the long sixteenth century included eastern Europe. Here there occurred what historians have called the "second serfdom," which involved a reenserfment of the peasantry only a historical moment or so after they were being liberated. Wallerstein views the second serfdom as dictated by the logic of the world-economy that was just coming into existence. Eastern European peasants were being reenserfed, but in the context of the capitalist production of grain and other primary products for export to western Europe. Eastern European peasants were thus not acting any longer, at least economically speaking, as feudal peasants, but as coerced cash-crop workers within a capitalist system.

In 1640 it is likely that the entire capitalist world-economy did not constitute more than 15 or 20 percent of the inhabitable surface of the globe, and this would not change much until approximately a century later. Yet a major transformation was occurring that would soon greatly accelerate the rate of evolutionary change. Capitalism had not come to dominate economic activity wherever it was found, at least in the sense that it had penetrated into every nook and cranny of economic life. A good deal of economic life remained outside the realm of capitalist production and exchange. However, things had changed enough so that we may speak of a capitalist mode of production as having come into existence.[2] A qualitative evolutionary shift had begun, and it is a great challenge to a theory of social evolution to be able to explain this shift. I will take up this challenge, but first let us look at the remarkably similar shift that occurred in Japan at a very similar point in history.

THE JAPANESE TRANSITION FROM FEUDALISM
TO CAPITALISM

Although the Japanese transition from feudalism to capitalism has been much less studied and is less well understood than the European transition, enough is now known about the development of capitalism in Japan so that a fairly detailed story can be told. Japanese culture and civilization owe much to China, but politically Japan has developed in a very different way. As I have already shown, Japan was the one society outside Europe to develop a genuine feudal system. Many Japanese scholars see Japanese feudalism beginning with the Kamakura Shogunate in 1185, although it is commonly argued that the full development of feudal institutions occurred only with the establishment of the Ashikaga Shogunate in 1338 (J.W. Hall, 1970; Reischauer, 1956). Edwin Reischauer (1956) calls the feudalism of the Kamakura period "protofeudalism" and argues that the period from 1338 to 1600 was the age of classical feudalism in Japan. With the establishment of the Tokugawa Shogunate in 1603 Japan entered into its late feudal period, which was to last until the middle of the nineteenth century.

During its feudal period the Japanese nobility was divided into an upper nobility, the *daimyo* or great lords, and a lower nobility known as the *samurai*, who were vassals of the *daimyo*. Japanese merchants, or *chonin*, were an important part of the economic situation in feudal Japan, but, as in all agrarian states, they were generally looked down upon, if not despised, by the nobility. As we shall see, though, they played a critical role in the economic evolution of medieval Japan.

European contact was established with Japan by the middle of the sixteenth century. Some trade was carried on between the two regions, and Christian missionaries established themselves in Japan. However, not long after the establishment of the Tokugawa Shogunate Japan began to embark on its famous policy of isolation from the West. This seclusion policy took effect in several stages (Pearson, 1991). In 1606 Christianity was forbidden, in 1623 the English left, and in 1624 this was quickly followed by the expulsion of the Spaniards. In 1630 Japanese were no longer allowed to engage in foreign trade or travel. The Dutch were allowed to stay, but in 1639 they were restricted to a small area and were very closely supervised. It is usually assumed that after 1639 the Japanese were virtually totally isolated from the rest of the world, but Ronald Toby (1984) has shown that this is erroneous. Japan continued to carry on important trade relations with China and other nearby parts of Asia, and was thus still involved in foreign trade. Daniel Spencer (1958:212) suggests that the remaining trade was "still quite comparable to a good sized colonial trade of the period." Indeed, the Sino-Japanese trade may actually have increased by the end of the seventeenth century (Atwell, 1986). And Marius Jansen (1992:41) comments that

the China trade . . . was an important factor in the political and economic history of both China and Japan in the seventeenth century. It financed much of the resistance of Taiwan and south China to the Manchu takeover. It provided luxury goods for a growing Japanese market whose elite wanted more of everything the ships could bring. It helped to consume the impressive stocks of precious metal that Japanese had mined during the consolidation of political power.

The Tokugawa regime seemed to be motivated by several factors in establishing its seclusion policy toward the West. One of these was fear of Christianity and its influence. However, economic and political factors probably played a bigger role. As Charles David Sheldon (1958) has suggested, the Tokugawa regime suspected the Europeans of having designs on Japanese territory, and the regime also feared the potential for growing power on the part of those *daimyo* involved in significant trade relations with Europeans. Whatever the exact reasons, the isolationist policy had become a firm reality by 1639, and this policy would come to have a major influence on the course of Japanese economic development.

Until about the 1960s it was generally assumed by scholars of Japan that the Tokugawa period was one of economic stagnation that was only overcome with the arrival of the Europeans and the reopening of Japan in the mid-nineteenth century. Recent scholarship, however, shows that this older view was wrong, and badly so. Many scholars now stress the economic vitality of the Tokugawa period and see it as contributing significantly to Japanese economic developments in the second half of the nineteenth century. One of the first to adopt this newer view was Daniel Spencer (1958). Spencer described a series of interrelated processes involving large-scale urbanization, commercialization of agriculture, increasing flight of peasants into the towns and cities, the worsening economic condition of the nobility, growth in the wealth and economic importance of the merchant class, increased monetization of the economy, and the beginnings of the factory system. He concluded that Japan experienced a level of economic growth during this period that paved the way for the even greater economic development of the Meiji era (Spencer, 1958:213):

> By the end of the seventeenth century, Japan was a money economy whose high development led Kaempfer, that astute observer from the then leading country of Europe, to marvel at its cities, its highways, commerce and general conditions. Here is the broad foundation for later growth.
>
> The essence of this preparation was the institutional change which mobilized the social surplus in the hands of a monopolistic class of entrenched big merchants.

In a more recent study Kozo Yamamura (1980) has shown that the period from 1550 to 1650 witnessed an agricultural and commercial revolution. The large rise in agricultural productivity during this century was made possible by several proximate conditions: increasing effectiveness of water use, development and dissemination of higher-yielding varieties of rice, availability of inexpensive hoes, and increased use of fertilizers. Yamamura stresses in particular the importance of better methods of water management involving irrigation dikes, banks, and dams. Lurking behind these proximate causes of increased agricultural productivity, Yamamura claims, was a change in property rights involving giving peasants more individual control over their land. What Yamamura is essentially describing is the beginning of a shift toward more capitalistic land tenure. With these changing property rights there arose a class of independent farmers closely akin to the yeoman farmers of early modern Europe. Yamamura holds that greater control over their own land gave peasants increased incentives to make the land productive.

The commercial revolution of the mid-sixteenth century involved deliberate measures undertaken by the state to promote commerce. These measures included such things as decrees to protect merchants and to eliminate various restrictions on the operation of markets, active development of transportation networks and facilities (which eventually involved the creation of a nationwide network of sea and river transportation), and standardization of measurements.

Yamamura is quick to point to the parallels between Japanese and English economic development in this period. Indeed, for Yamamura these parallels are close enough to allow him to assert that "what becomes increasingly evident is the fact that, as our knowledge of the earlier period of Japanese economic history increases, the crucial

question which we should have asked is not why Japan was the first
to industrialize in Asia, but why did the Japanese industrialization
begin so late in the nineteenth century?" (1980:104). So from Yamamura's research we learn not only that there are important parallels
between Japan and Europe, but that these parallels can be found
even before the beginning of the Tokugawa period.

Sheldon (1958) has traced the rising economic importance of the
merchant class throughout the Tokugawa period, but, like Yamamura, notes that important economic developments were taking
place in the century before Tokugawa. Sheldon sees the Genroku
period (1688–1703) as the critical one in the merchants' economic
evolution. By this time there was a vigorous money economy and
the merchant class had finally become strong enough to force the
nobility to regard it as a serious economic competitor (Sheldon,
1958:99):

The general prosperity and increased standard of living experienced in the Genroku
period meant a great increase in the manufacturing and sale of commercial goods. Not
only did the merchants benefit from this, but the Genroku period saw the draining of
feudal treasuries into merchant coffers. The *daimyo* and ordinary samurai alike became
more deeply indebted to the merchant money lenders. This gave the merchants a high
degree of economic security and permitted the development of a type of merchant
nobility.

John Whitney Hall (1970) sees the growth of mercantile activities
during the Tokugawa epoch in similar terms, pointing out that it
was during this time that a bourgeoisie first rose to national prominence. Like Sheldon, he is concerned to trace the general outlines of
the evolution of the merchant class (1970:208–9):

The merchant community of Tokugawa times went through certain stages of development in its rise to economic prominence. In the early years, the important merchants
were those specially patronized by the Shogun and daimyo, the so-called "house
merchants." By the eighteenth century a number of great commercial houses had
grown up in Osaka and Edo [modern Tokyo] whose diversified activities focused upon
moneylending and exchange. By the nineteenth century, houses based on manufacturing
and cottage industry had begun to make their appearance. The growth of commercial
capital is revealed in the estimate that by 1761 there were in Japan over two hundred
commercial houses each valued at over 200,000 gold *ryo*. . . . Thus in total capital
worth the great merchants had become the equivalent of many daimyo.

By the middle Tokugawa period most of the outstanding *chonin* houses which were
to retain their status into modern times had been established.

It is interesting to note that an especially important commodity in Japan in the sixteenth and seventeenth centuries was silver ore (Flynn, 1991; Barrett, 1990), which was exported to Korea and China. Only Spanish America was a bigger producer of silver during this time (Flynn, 1991; Barrett, 1990). Flynn (1991) notes that this made Spain and Japan major competitors in the world market. Once silver waned, Japan became a major exporter of copper, with the biggest buyer being China.

An inextricable part of Japanese economic development during the Tokugawa era was extensive urbanization. This was particularly the case during the seventeenth century. Hall (1970) calls the urbanization of this time "astounding," and suggests that it is quite possibly without historical precedent (cf. Goldsmith, 1987). Gilbert Rozman (1974:98) puts the matter this way:

> While rural Japan shared in the dynamism with respect to population growth, to commercial specialization, and to social differentiation in the seventeenth century, it was overshadowed by the unparalleled transformation within the urban sector. With Edo, Osaka, and Kyoto leading the way, new patterns of consumption and new modes of social organization developed in Japanese cities. If any period of premodern history anywhere can properly be labeled urban-centered, it is this period from about 1600 to the 1720's in Japan.

The growth of Edo was truly spectacular. At the end of the sixteenth century it was not much more than a small village, but by the early eighteenth century it had reached half a million persons and by the end of that century it was well over a million in population (Spencer, 1958). Edo had become the world's largest city. Spencer (1958) estimates that in the eighteenth century between 10 and 13.3 percent of the Japanese population lived in large towns or cities, a remarkable figure, he suggests, when we recognize that in the United States in 1790 the urban population constituted only 3 percent of the total, and only 16 percent of the total as late as 1860. Japan was even more urbanized than Europe, which in 1800 had only 22 cities above 100,000 in population, and these cities together constituted only 3 percent of the total population (Spencer, 1958).

The full extent to which capitalism was emerging in Tokugawa Japan can also be seen by examining one of the most important aspects of capitalist development: proletarianization of the labor force. Gary Leupp (1992) argues that during the Tokugawa period Japan was becoming an increasingly impersonal, money-dominated society with a larger and larger part of its labor force being compensated in the form of wages. In fact, by the end of the Tokugawa period Leupp suggests that wage labor had become the major form of compensation, at least with respect to urban workers.

Thomas Smith (1959) has shown that wage labor became increasingly important during the Tokugawa period even in agricultural work, and that by the end of the period feudal peasants were no longer the predominant form of farm worker. Agricultural workers gradually became *hokonin*, workers who were part way between traditional feudal peasants and fully free workers. Smith distinguishes between three grades of *hokonin*. The least free of the *hokonin* were workers who were given to a family for an indeterminate period of time in return for a loan. The worker received no compensation other than his keep and had to work until the loan was repaid. A second type of *hokonin* was like the first except for the fact that he received at least some compensation. However, he was not paid an hourly or daily wage; instead, a sum was agreed on in advance and this sum was then deducted from the debt remaining at the end of the loan period. Obviously neither of these types of labor is much like wage labor, but nonetheless the second type does show an economic value of its own that could be rationally calculated. Moreover, both types of *hokonin* possessed at least some degree of freedom denied the traditional peasant. Smith tells us that the second type of laborer became increasingly common as the Tokugawa period advanced.

The third type of *hokonin* marked a further advance toward free labor. This type of worker was still "bound by debt for the duration of the loan, but his labor during that time constituted repayment of it in full: at the end of the stipulated period neither any part of the principal of the debt nor unpaid interest remained to hold him" (T.C. Smith, 1959:114). Smith goes on to note that throughout the Tokugawa era there was a gradual shortening of the length of time for which workers were bound. It may once have been of indefinite duration, then shortened to 10 or 15 years, then to no more than three years, and then finally to only one year or possibly even a single season. Smith argues, correctly in my opinion, that this shortening of the employment period shows that work was increasingly regarded as having its own economic value (i.e., a value independent of particular social relations), and that the worker was increasingly being regarded as a hired hand to be employed just for the time that his labor was needed. Eventually, true wage labor in agriculture evolved after having first been applied to industry and trade. Smith suggests that by the end of the Tokugawa era it was quite common, although certainly by no means the universal form of labor.

It is only in recent decades that scholars have recognized the deep historical roots of Japan's development of industrial capitalism in the twentieth century. At one time virtually no one thought of looking backward in time beyond the Meiji Restoration (1868) in order to trace Japan's modern transformation. Of course it is now recognized that the entire Tokugawa era contained major economic changes, and that many of these changes began even in the century before Tokugawa (Yamamura, 1980). But even the sixteenth century may be starting too late, for there is evidence that important economic developments were occurring in Japan as early as the thirteenth century. Several scholars have shown that Japan was deeply enmeshed in a network of foreign trade with other parts of Asia at this early period (Sansom, 1961; Reischauer, 1956; J.W. Hall, 1970). Edwin Reischauer (1956) notes that trade with China and Korea became an important part of the Japanese economy in the thirteenth century. The lead in financing the larger commercial ventures was taken by Buddhist monasteries, but these ventures had been taken over by the shogun and feudal lords by the end of the fourteenth century. During the fifteenth and sixteenth centuries foreign trade grew rapidly in intensity and trade ventures were extended to other parts of the Far East, even as far as the Straits of Malacca. Some feudal lords, especially those in coastal areas, depended on foreign trade for much of their income. Japanese traders became a virtual part of the warrior nobility and came to be renowned throughout the Far East for both their martial abilities and their commercial endeavors.

John Whitney Hall has also not overlooked the importance of the economic developments of the three centuries before Tokugawa. He notes that (1970:113; emphasis added):

One of the fascinating and seemingly paradoxical aspects of the history of the fourteenth and fifteenth centuries in Japan is that, despite the instability of the political order, the country at large gave evidence of remarkable cultural and economic growth. . . . *The same centuries saw Japan emerge as a major maritime power in East Asia activated by a vigorous internal economic expansion.*

And he continues (1970:121, 123, 126):

We should not suppose that Japan remained economically stagnant during the Kamakura period, and it is in the early years of the Ashikaga period that our attention is again attracted by evidence of dramatic economic growth in Japan. . . .

The increase in trade, of which the spread of money was a symptom, brought with it a number of major consequences. Wealth, for instance, was no longer tied solely to the land but could be accumulated in other ways and stored in the form of precious metals or goods. A merchant class, congregating in a few important administrative and trade centers, was able to establish itself as a class of wealth outside of the confines of aristocratic society. . . .

In Japan as in Europe the growth of the commercial and service classes was marked by the rise of new towns and cities which contrasted sharply in their prime functions with the older administrative centers. . . .

. . . The trade also reveals a great deal about the state of the Japanese economy. Exports to China were now mass commodities and artifacts such as refined copper, sulfur, folding fans, screens, painted scrolls, and above all swords. Single missions carried tens of thousands of Japanese steel swords to China. In return the Japanese ships returned with strings of cash (50,000 strings in 1454), raw silk, porcelains, paintings, medicines, and books. All of this gave evidence that Japan was no longer an underdeveloped member of the Chinese world order. In fact the limited trade permitted by a reluctant China was eventually to prove too restrictive for the Japanese. After 1551 the tally trade broke down, and Japanese traders in unrestrained numbers began to ply the China seas . . .

It is important to situate this early Japanese economic thrust in its world-systemic context. It seems that Japan was involving itself in a vigorous Far Eastern trade at basically the same time that late Sung and early Ming China were withdrawing from world trade and declining economically. These events are undoubtedly connected. A large economic vacuum was created, and Japan was quick to fill it (Collins, 1990). Japan picked up the Asian economic impetus where China left off.

No one should think I am suggesting that Japan was becoming a capitalist society in the thirteenth and fourteenth centuries. Far from it. But it was involving itself in economic networks and undergoing economic changes that would be of momentous importance in the centuries to come.

By the end of the Tokugawa Shogunate in 1868 Japan had become an essentially capitalist society in economic terms despite retaining basically feudal social and political arrangements. But this is not surprising: superstructures commonly lag behind and change more slowly than infrastructures. I say that Japan had become essentially capitalist for several reasons. The merchant class had grown tremendously in economic importance. Japan had undergone tremendous commercialization, both in agriculture and in industry, and had become one of the most urbanized societies in the world. Spencer (1958) claims that by the end of the eighteenth century fully fifteen sixteenths of Japan's wealth was in the hands of the merchants, a remarkable indication of the extent of the economic changes. It was the merchant class that was in economic, if not political, control of late Tokugawa Japan.

The rising economic significance of the merchants meant the simultaneous decline of the nobility, both the great *daimyo* and the lesser *samurai*. The *samurai* eventually became little more than paid administrative officials of the *daimyo*, thus losing their former close association with the land. Both the *samurai* and the *daimyo* had to rely increasingly on loans from the merchants, and their indebtedness grew throughout the Tokugawa period. The worsening plight of the nobility caused many of them to go over to the merchant class, with many former nobles becoming bankers, manufacturers, and other types of entrepreneur. This situation in which many nobles turned bourgeois to adapt to the changing economic conditions is highly reminiscent of the situation in Europe, and yet one more important parallel between the European and Japanese transitions to capitalism.[3]

THEORIES OF THE TRANSITION TO CAPITALISM

We are now faced with the formidable task of explaining the capitalist revolution that took place in western Europe and Japan in the fifteenth, sixteenth, and seventeenth centuries. It is important to say at the outset that, although this is a problem to which a great deal of attention has been given, it has seemingly been intractable to our best theoretical efforts. Numerous theories have been set forth, but there is little consensus concerning them. A further problem is that most of these theories have been constructed with only the European case in mind. I should like to run through all of the major theories in some detail, pointing out their strengths and weaknesses, and in the end I will advance my own interpretation. This interpretation is based on the assumption that any good theory of the capitalist revolution must apply to *both* the European *and* the Japanese cases. I reject the notion, set forth by historical particularists (or historicists as they are usually called by sociologists), that different historical events must be explained by different concepts and theories. Any social science worthy of the name must push nomothetic explanation as far as it can go. It is my view that, although there were important differences, the European and Japanese trajectories toward modern capitalism were sufficiently similar to constitute essentially the same kind of event occurring more or less independently in two different world regions at approximately the same time in world history. This cannot be an accident of history, and thus the European advance cannot be a "miracle," as some scholars have argued (E.L. Jones, 1987, 1988). I have no patience at all with the incredible dismissal by Eric Jones (1987) of the relevance of the Japanese case to an understanding of the rise of the modern capitalist world, especially inasmuch as he himself has recognized the existence of important parallels between Europe and Japan. Jones may rest content with his version of Eurocentrism, but for me it is a serious barrier to understanding the rise of modernity.

Marxian theories

A variety of contrasting Marxian theories have been put forth to explain the European transition from feudalism to capitalism. Let us start with the famous debate between the Marxists Maurice Dobb and Paul Sweezy that was conducted shortly after the end of the Second World War. In his classic *Studies in the Development of Capitalism* (1963; first edition 1947), Dobb set forth a theory of the transition that emphasized the internal contradictions of feudalism as a mode of production. What led the feudal system into crisis and ultimately tore it apart, Dobb argued, was the growing class struggle between landlords and peasants. By late feudal times landlords had significantly increased their exploitation of the peasantry, and this intensified exploitation provoked a peasant flight from the land that created a "crisis of feudalism" and set in motion a transition to a capitalist mode of production.

Sweezy (1976[1950]) questioned the basic logic of this theory by asserting that it improperly concentrated on endogenous forces. He argued that there were no forces within feudalism strong enough to transform it and went on to propose as an alternative a basically exogenist theory. It was the revival, from about the eleventh century, of long-distance trade between Europe and other world regions that he saw as the impetus for the feudal crisis and the move toward capitalism. The revival of trade caused feudalism to be increasingly involved in a market economy. As towns grew in size and importance, serfs were increasingly attracted to them and they fled the land in large numbers. Moreover, feudal lords themselves were increasingly attracted by the possibilities inherent in the market economy for the generation of large fortunes. For Sweezy, a market economy was inherently superior in efficiency to a feudal one, and it is his view that this greater efficiency was clearly recognized by landlords. In a sense, then, Sweezy was saying that it was the inefficiency of feudalism that led it to be destroyed in the end by a capitalist form of economic organization.

One serious difficulty with Dobb's theory is that it provides no convincing explanation of landlords' increased exploitation of the peasantry over time. His basic argument is that nobles were caught up in a game of spiraling status emulation that required greater and greater levels of surplus extraction from the peasantry, but I do not find this argument persuasive. The game of status emulation was played by landlord classes throughout the agrarian world without necessarily resulting in increased levels of exploitation and peasant flight. Peasant flight from the land was an important aspect of the breakdown of feudalism and the shift toward capitalism, but it will need to be explained in different terms.

Sweezy's purely exogenist theory suffers from a serious underappreciation of the dynamics of feudalism. Sweezy argued that feudalism was an inherently stagnant mode of production. On its own it lacked any mechanism that could transform it, and thus it could only be transformed from the outside. But as Wallerstein (1974b) has argued, feudalism should not be thought of as necessarily antithetical to a system of trade. We have learned in recent years that feudalism was a lot more dynamic than was once thought. Considerable growth and change occurred within European feudalism, and by no means can all of this be attributed to external influences. Nonetheless, as we will see later, Sweezy's theory is particularly useful in pointing us in the direction, if only implicitly, of the importance of rising world commercialization for the transformation of feudalism.[4]

Wallerstein has offered an interpretation of the transition to capitalism that, unsurprisingly, fits neatly into his general world-system perspective. Wallerstein gives special emphasis to the "crisis of feudalism" to which many scholars of late medieval Europe have referred. For Wallerstein, this crisis was primarily one of revenue collection on the part of the feudal nobility. The severely declining ability of feudalism to create wealth necessitated the shift to a new mode of production, and this involved the creation of a capitalist world-economy based on the world market. A critical aspect of the creation of this world-economy was geographical expansion into areas outside Europe. What caused the feudal crisis in the first place? Wallerstein says it was the result of the simultaneous occurrence of three basic events. First, there was the downside of an economic cycle. The feudal system had been expanding between 1150 and 1300 but had reached a point beyond which it could no longer go. A contraction then set in. Second, there was a long-term secular trend. After nearly a millennium of surplus expropriation within the feudal mode of production a point of diminishing returns had been reached. Finally, there were unfavorable climatological conditions that lowered the productivity of the soil and increased epidemics.

Like Sweezy's theory, Wallerstein's is not a Marxist one in any orthodox sense. It contains some obvious Marxian elements but also imports notions foreign to the Marxian tradition. It has been severely criticized by more orthodox Marxists for concentrating on "exchange relations" rather than relations of production (Brenner, 1976, 1977; cf. Holton, 1981, 1985; Mooers, 1991). In two famous articles, Robert Brenner (1976, 1977) has referred to Wallerstein as a "neo-Smithian Marxist" for his alleged neglect of production (class) relations in favor of exchange relations. Brenner's own preferred interpretation stresses the role of class relations and levels of class power. The breakthrough to the self-sustaining development of capitalism was made possible by the creation of a set of capitalist class relations, and this in turn depended upon the outcome of class struggles within feudalism.

My sympathies lie much more with Wallerstein rather than Brenner. Brenner seems to view class relations as somehow self-levitating because he ignores the larger social, economic, and political context in which they emerge, exist, and get transformed. He has made a shibboleth of the Marxian notion of class struggle. I do, however, see two problems with Wallerstein's argument. First, there is what I regard as his undue emphasis on the role of a feudal crisis. As we shall see more clearly at a later point, it is sensible to talk of the existence of a feudal crisis in Europe between approximately 1300 and 1450, but the extent to which this crisis was critical for the transition to capitalism is by no means clear. Doubt is cast on this possibility when we recognize that there was no feudal crisis in Japan, at least of the sort that occurred in Europe. Second, the capitalist world-economy seems to be virtually a creation *ex nihilo*. Wallerstein discounts the prior role, emphasized by Sweezy, of long-distance world trade as an explanation of the expansion of European commerce in the sixteenth century. This trade, Wallerstein says, was based on preciosities, and only a trade in bulk goods could have sustained the expansion of the Atlantic economy and the formation of something as large as a capitalist world-economy. Perhaps so, but the earlier world trade, which had become globally both extensive and intensive by the thirteenth century, could still have provided *a context for* the kind of expansion that Wallerstein is talking about. I will show the significance of this point in the presentation of my own interpretation of the rise of modern capitalism.[5]

Weberian theories

Numerous Weberian interpretations of the rise of modern capitalism have been presented. Of course, the most famous Weberian explanation is the one offered in 1904 by Weber himself in *The Protestant Ethic and the Spirit of Capitalism* (1958[1904]). This argument is so well known that it needs no elaborate elucidation. Weber's basic point was that the rise of capitalism was a unique Western occurrence that benefitted greatly from the Protestant Reformation of the sixteenth century. The Protestant work ethic, particularly in its Calvinist form, stimulated an entrepreneurial attitude toward the world on the part of believers because it glorified hard work, devotion to one's "calling," frugality, avoidance of the ostentatious display of wealth, and the continuous reinvestment of profits in one's business. Success in the world of business through strict adherence to the work ethic did not gain one salvation, but nonetheless it served as a sign from God that one had been placed among the elect. Weber, of course, never argued that Protestantism was the sole cause of the rise of capitalism, only that it was one crucial stimulus among others.

Robert Bellah (1957) has applied Weber's thesis to Japan in order to explain its unique economic development in the Asian world. He claims that the Japanese versions of Buddhism and Confucianism displayed a strong inner-worldly asceticism of the type Weber closely associated with Protestantism, and that this religious outlook had a powerful effect in conditioning an entrepreneurial attitude. Bellah's argument is a somewhat ironic twist on Weber inasmuch as the latter considered Eastern religions to hold to an other-worldly outlook that inhibited economic development.

There are good reasons for being highly suspicious of Weber's argument and its extension to Japan. One of the early core powers of European capitalism was France, a largely Catholic country. Moreover, Jere Cohen (1980) has shown that Renaissance Italy, the heartland of Catholicism, gave rise to a vigorous merchant capitalism that contained most of the elements of modern rational capitalism as indicated by Weber. So Protestantism could not have been a necessary cause of capitalism. Moreover, Janet Abu-Lughod (1989) has suggested that it is difficult to draw much of a connection between religion and economics. She has pointed out that "Christianity, Buddhism, Confucianism, Islam, Zoroastrianism, and numerous other smaller sects often dismissed as 'pagan' all seem to have permitted and indeed facilitated commerce, production, exchange, risk taking, and the like. And among these, Christianity played a relatively insignificant role" (1989:354–5). Wallerstein is also skeptical of drawing too close a connection between religion and economics, but suggests that if there is one the causal arrows are more likely to be pointing in the opposite direction (1974b:151–3):

The central pan-European ideological controversy of the sixteenth and seventeenth centuries – Reformation versus Counter-Reformation – was inextricably intertwined with the creation both of the strong states and of the capitalist system. It is no accident that those parts of Europe which were re-agrarianized in the sixteenth century were also those parts of Europe in which the Counter-Reformation triumphed, while, for the most part, the industrializing countries remained Protestant. . . .

This is no accident, not because, following Weber, we think Protestant theology is somehow more consonant with capitalism than Catholic theology. No doubt one can make a case for this argument. On the other hand, it seems to be true in general that any complex system of ideas can be manipulated to serve any particular social or political objective. Surely Catholic theology, too, has proved its capacity to be adaptable to its social milieu. There is little reason at the abstract level of ideas why one couldn't have written a plausible book entitled "The Catholic Ethic and the Rise of Capitalism." And Calvinist theology could be taken to have anticapitalist implications. The point I am making is a different one. By a series of intellectually accidental historical developments, Protestantism became identified to a large extent in the period of the Reformation with the forces favoring the expansion of commercial capitalism within the framework of strong national states, and with the countries in which these forces were dominant. Thus when such forces lost out in Poland, or Spain, or "Italy," or Hungary, Protestantism declined too and often rapidly. The factors which favored the expansion of export agriculture favored the reassertion of Catholicism.

Weber's Protestant ethic argument was put forth relatively early in his career, and in later work he seems to have given the Protestant ethic a smaller role and moved in the direction of emphasizing the role of the nation–state (Collins, 1980). In his *General Economic History* (1981[1927]) he gives the nation–state a prominent role in the development of capitalism because it rationalized law, freed land for the capitalist market, eliminated barriers to markets, and standardized taxation and currencies. The nation–state also helped lay the foundations for a reliable system of banking, investment, property, and contracts. In general, it was the key to the development of the basic institutional structures of modern rational capitalism (Collins, 1980).

This later theory, though, has its own difficulties, the most significant of which is that it begs the question as to what gave rise to the modern state. Weber argues that the early modern nation–state arose because it was the most effective means available of pacifying a large territory (Collins, 1980). Such an argument, though, leaves us wondering why this kind of highly efficient state did not arise in other places and at other times. It would seem just as logical, if not more so, to argue that the early modern nation–state was the product of a system that was already becoming capitalist (in chapter 7 I shall develop just such an argument).

The spirit of Weber has been kept alive in recent years by various scholars who have proposed neo–Weberian interpretations of the rise of modern capitalism. Daniel Chirot (1985, 1986) offers a multidimensional explanation that emphasizes three main factors: Europe's unique geographical conditions, the highly decentralized character of feudalism, and the increasing rationalization of law and religion in late feudalism. Similar interpretations have been offered by John A. Hall (1985) and Michael Mann (1986), who give particular emphasis to the role of religion. Both go beyond the Protestant ethic thesis to claim that it was Christianity in general, and not just Protestantism, that played a major role in the emergence of capitalism. Mann claims that Christianity was important because it led to the "normative pacification" of Europe, which allowed economic activity a freer rein, and because it contained an ideology or spirit of "rational restlessness." This restlessness, Mann claims, stimulated a strong orientation toward rational human action in the world, one part of which was religious action.

These theories contain some insights, but in general their highly eclectic nature seems to complicate unnecessarily the search for a coherent and parsimonious understanding of the transition to capitalism. This is carrying multidimensionality too far. And serious doubts can be raised about some of the proposed factors, especially Christianity. As we have already noted in our discussion of the views of Abu-Lughod and Wallerstein, there is no necessary connection between religion and economics, and other religions besides Christianity have been seen to stimulate forms of rational economic growth. It is also difficult to accept Chirot's claim that capitalism was spurred along by some sort of spirit of rationality that was unique to Europe. This argument simply begs the question as to the origins of such a spirit. What is to prevent us from arguing that it was capitalism itself that spurred a new spirit of rationality?

World-system theories

Some of the most recent and provocative theories of the rise of capitalism employ a world-system approach similar to Wallerstein's (Schneider, 1977; Ekholm, 1981; Abu-Lughod, 1988, 1989; Frank, 1990, 1991). These theories are similar to Sweezy's in emphasizing the importance of world trade external to Europe, but they go considerably further.

A somewhat extreme version of this kind of theory has been developed by Andre Gunder Frank (1990, 1991; Gills and Frank, 1991). Frank rejects the very notion that there was a qualitative shift from feudalism to capitalism in the sixteenth century, claiming that there has been a continuous process of capital accumulation within a single world system for some 5,000 years. He even argues against continued employment of terms like feudalism or capitalism to indicate distinct modes of production in world history. What happened in Europe in the sixteenth century was simply the quantitative continuation of a very long-term historical process. Frank puts his case most forcefully (1991:24):

Is it still possible or sensible to argue that there was a qualitatively different "transition" to and creation of a "modern-world-capitalist-system" around 1500? Or that this "transition" arose essentially out of the "transition from feudalism to capitalism" in Europe? No! and No again! It is time to relegate the latter debate to the parochial European history to which it rightly belongs. . . .

Then is it still sensible to hold on for dear life to the supposedly scientific historical categories of . . . feudalism, capitalism, socialism – or indeed any such "scientifically" defined "modes of production" or ideologically defined "systems" and "isms?" I believe NOT!

So for Frank there really is nothing special about the sixteenth century, and thus nothing particularly worth explaining concerning that time. What is worth describing and explaining in great detail is the general process of world capital accumulation since 3000 BC.

A more typical world-system approach to the rise of the modern world is that of Janet Abu-Lughod (1988, 1989). In her splendid *Before European Hegemony*, Abu-Lughod argues that Wallerstein's world-system argument starts too late and that there was a major world-system in effect as early as 1250. As we saw in chapter 4, for Abu-Lughod this system was truly global and consisted of eight interlocking subsystems combined into three regional trade networks. The core of the system was Asia, especially China, and Europe was in a peripheral position. By 1350 the system had substantially distintegrated, with China withdrawing from participation and declining economically. Abu-Lughod claims that to understand the rise of Wallerstein's capitalist world-economy in the sixteenth century we cannot focus our attention only on Europe, as has typically been the case. There was nothing special about Europe, and indeed concentration on it has been a kind of obsessive Eurocentrism. To understand the emergence of the modern world-system we must look at the global system that preceded it. Europe rose not because of any internal characteristics that made it special, but because of major geopolitical shifts within the world as a whole. The "rise of the West" was simultaneously the "fall of the East." Trade links between the eastern Mediterranean and the Orient were ruptured at the same time that trade relations between the Mediterranean and northwest Europe were deepening. These phenomena were not independent events but simply two different sides of the same world geopolitical coin.

These theories are especially valuable in calling our attention to the importance of world trade networks prior to the sixteenth century. Frank's argument is particularly significant in that it points to an important process of world commercialization going on for several millennia. Nonetheless, Frank's argument goes too far in identifying this process as one of capital accumulation essentially like the process of capital accumulation after 1500. It also goes too far in rejecting the notion of a qualitative shift in the sixteenth century, as well as the notion of distinct feudal and capitalist modes of production. While in some sense what happened after the six-teenth century was a quantitative extension of what had been going on for a very long time, in another sense there was a massive break with the past. There was a huge acceleration of the intensity of commercial activity and the shift to a mode of economic production in which capitalism became the *dominant* activity for the very first time. A truly "world-transforming" capitalism was coming into existence and it would set in motion processes never seen before in the world. There is indeed something vital about the sixteenth century that has to be explained.

Abu-Lughod's analysis is more measured, and her notion that there was a thirteenth-century world-system is of great importance. However, the real problem with her attempted explanation of the sixteenth-century transition is that it is really no explanation at all. It is simply a new way of *describing* certain processes. If the relations between the eastern Mediterranean and the Orient frayed while those between the Mediterranean and northwest Europe deepened, then we need to know *why* such geopolitical shifts occurred, and Abu-Lughod never tells us. To identify the existence of a system within which different things go on at different times is only the beginning of the analysis. To stop things at that point is to make no contribution to a *theory* of economic development. Moreover, Abu-Lughod is quite wrong when she suggests that there was nothing distinctive about Europe. It was indeed different from the rest of the world, or at least most of it, since Japan was different too. It is not a matter of distinguishing the West from the East, but of distinguishing the particular combination of characteristics found in Europe and Japan on the one hand from the rest of the world on the other. No Eurocentrism in that!

Demographic theories

A particularly prominent line of thought concerned with the break-down of feudalism and the rise of capitalism in Europe has focused on demographic factors. A demographic explanation has been put forward by such scholars as Postan (1972), Wilkinson (1973), Le Roy Ladurie (1974), Harris (1977), and Perry Anderson (1974a). The argument is not always completely clear, but it seems to go something like this. From about the eleventh until the end of the thirteenth century, European feudalism was undergoing significant economic, ecological, and demographic expansion. As population grew new and more marginal lands were increasingly brought under cultivation until eventually Europe became "filled up." By about 1300 a serious state of population pressure had been reached, and this led to declining yields from the land and increasingly severe economic difficulties for both landlords and peasants. An economic, ecological, and demographic "crisis of feudalism" had developed. Nonetheless, in a sense the demographic aspect of this crisis turned out to be its own "cure." Increasing famine, malnourishment, and other disease – especially the Black Death that first swept Europe in 1348–50 – led to a sharp population decline that continued until around 1450. The demographic collapse generated a severe labor shortage, which caused a dramatic fall in the incomes of the landlord class and shifted the balance of class power in the direction of the peasantry. Economically, this made matters even worse for the feudal nobility. The nobles reacted to their worsened economic fortunes in a number of ways, but especially by expropriating the peasantry from the land and turning their estates over to the raising of sheep in order to sell their wool on the market. Landlords were moving more in the direction of becoming capitalist farmers. The increasing power of the peasantry allowed many peasants to flee into the towns where their labor was much in demand by the merchants, whose economic power was growing. However, many of the peasants who stayed on the land did not do so as traditional serfs (feudal social relations were essentially dead by 1450, at least in England). They were transformed into wage-earning farmhands who assisted their former landlords in running a capitalist agricultural enterprise. Some peasants even became transformed into capitalists – yeoman farmers – themselves.

A critical question concerns why the demographic and economic crisis of feudalism got resolved in the particular way that it did. Why did the nobles react to their worsening economic situation by gradually transforming themselves, and many of their serfs, into capitalists? Why did they not respond to the growing power of the peasants by intensifying their repression and exploitation of this class? Michael Mann (1986:411) has offered a very plausible answer to these questions:

If the feudal mode of production gave to the lords a monopoly of the means of physical violence, could they not respond with military force at times when relative product and factor values did not favor them?

. . . This is not an idle question, for in many other times and places the response of lords to labor shortages has been to increase the dependency of their laborers. . . . The immediate answer to these questions is that the European lords did try repression and they nominally succeeded, but to no avail. Returning to the example of late-fourteenth-century labor shortages, there was a wave of landlord reaction. The lords attempted with violence and legislation to tie the peasantry to the manor and to keep down wages (just as late Roman landlords had). All across Europe the peasantry rose up in rebellion, and everywhere (except Switzerland) they were repressed. But their lords' victory proved hollow. The lords were compelled not by the peasants but by the transformed capitalist market and by opportunities for profit, and threat of loss, within it. The weak state could not implement legislation without the local cooperation of the lords; it *was* the lords. And individual lords gave in, leased out their demesnes, and converted labor services into money rents. . . . The feudal mode of production was finally broken by the market.

Marvin Harris (1977) has asked a similar question. Why, Harris wants to know, did the demographic decline of the fourteenth and fifteenth centuries not become part of a cyclical process of demographic and economic ups and downs? Why was there not a return to feudalism instead of a forward movement into capitalism? Here is Harris's answer (1977:173):

In the crisis of European feudalism . . . the problem lay in the landlessness of the victims of enclosures and the raising of animals on lands that were needed to raise food crops. The first order of business of the manorial lords turned merchants and manufacturers could not be to drive out the sheep, restore the peasants to the land, and stop manufacturing woolens. The maximization of their own immediate political and economic welfare lay not in going backward but in going forward into larger and more uninhibited attempts to make money and accumulate capital by raising more sheep and manufacturing more woolens.

In other words, a new economic path had already been set, and under the circumstances it was more rational to follow the logic of that path than to return to the earlier path. And Mann shows us one of the major reasons why: the changes within late feudalism were occurring within the context of an expanding world economic market – the major new phase of world commercialization that developed after AD 1000 – and this market drew feudal lords into it like a magnet.

One difficulty with the demographic argument is that it is never completely clear whether the demographic crisis of feudalism was due to overpopulation, underpopulation, or both. Harris (1977) seems to be giving more emphasis to overpopulation, while Postan's (1972) analysis seems to focus more on the underpopulation that occurred after 1300 (cf. Brenner, 1976). Perry Anderson (1974a), on the other hand, seems to be talking about both. This question is especially critical in view of the somewhat different demographic patterns displayed by Japan throughout its feudal and early capitalist periods.

Less work has been done on the demographic history of Japan than on Europe, but we now seem to have a fairly good picture of the former. Between the end of the twelfth and the end of the sixteenth century the population of Japan essentially doubled, rising from approximately 9.75 million in the period 1185–1333 to about 18 million in the period 1572–1591 (Taeuber, 1958). Major population growth continued throughout the first half of the Tokugawa era, with the population increasing to perhaps 30 million by 1725 (Jannetta, 1987). It used to be thought that population stagnated after this time throughout the remainder of the Tokugawa period (Hanley, 1972), but a new consensus has emerged that population continued to grow, albeit more slowly, from 1721 to 1868 (Hanley and Yamamura, 1972). Hanley and Yamamura (1972) estimate that during the period 1721–1872 the Japanese population grew at an average annual rate of 0.16 percent.

Ann Bowman Jannetta (1987) claims that in 1600 Japan already had one of the world's most densely settled populations, and it would appear that this pressure intensified during the Tokugawa era. There is much evidence of infanticide during this time, and, as in Europe, considerable land reclamation was carried out. Hanley and Yamamura (1972) have summarized the evidence for a generally increasing rate of land reclamation from before the beginning of the Tokugawa period. Between 1551 and 1600 there were 28 *shinden* ("new fields") created. This number rose to 243 during the period

1601–1650 and to 434 during the period 1651–1700. During the eighteenth century the number of *shinden* dropped sharply, but then rose again to 788 during the period 1801–68. Land reclamation during the Tokugawa period approximately doubled the amount of total arable land. As in Europe, it is likely that a large portion of this land reclamation was due to population pressure, although we must acknowledge that a certain amount would have resulted from economic changes such as the growing commercialization of agriculture, or from the government's efforts at increasing its tax base (Hanley and Yamamura, 1972).

The picture so far of Japanese demographic change is remarkably similar to the European picture before 1300. But at this point the picture changes drastically. There never was a period of significant decline in the Japanese population even remotely comparable to the European demographic collapse of 1300–1450 (Jannetta, 1987). The reason for this appears to be that Japan was never subjected to the two great killer diseases that beset medieval Europe, bubonic plague and typhus. The absence of these diseases no doubt stems from Japan's relative isolation from Europe. The black rat that carried the flea responsible for bubonic plague followed the overland caravan trade, and there was no caravan trade to Japan (Jannetta, 1987).

The demographic regimes of Europe and Japan are different, then, in one crucial respect, and this means that a "crisis of underpopulation" that would have shifted the balance of class power away from the nobility in favor of the peasantry could not have been a causal factor in Japan's capitalist transition. That should make us doubt that the population crash of late medieval Europe played an important role in the European transition. However, it is still possible that *over*population could have been a factor in Japan, and in the European capitalist transition as well.

A NEW INTERPRETATION

All of the theories we have discussed have significant weaknesses that preclude any of them offering a satisfactory explanation of the transition to capitalism. However, some of the insights of these theories can be drawn on in constructing a new interpretation. I proceed in a twofold manner. I begin by identifying several basic characteristics of Europe and Japan that I think operated as important preconditions facilitating their transition from a feudal to a capitalist economy. These preconditions, however, did not operate in a vacuum, but occurred only within the context of a particular historical juncture that marked the conclusion of a great historical trend. It was the interaction of these factors – the five preconditions on the one hand and a major historical trend on the other – that combined to produce the transition to modern capitalism when and where it occurred.

The basic similarities between Europe and Japan that operated as preconditions for capitalist development were:

1 *Size*: Japan and two of the three leading capitalist countries of early modern Europe – England and the Netherlands – were small, and as such contrast markedly with such Asian societies as China and India, which were large empires. This may be very significant. Fernand Braudel (1984) has argued that the reason France lagged behind England and the Netherlands in her capitalist development was because she was "a victim of her size." France was thirteen times as large as the Netherlands and three to four times the size of England. Braudel points out that France's size created problems of transportation that England and the Netherlands did not have. Moreover, it is costly to maintain a large state because resources are drained away that could be used more directly for economic development. I think there is a parallel situation with large Asian societies like China and India. They were simply so big that obstacles were put in the way of economic development. In Asia Japan's much smaller size gave her a decided advantage.

2 *Geography*: Japan and the leading capitalist countries of north-west Europe were located on large bodies of water that allowed them to give predominance to maritime rather than overland trade. Samir Amin (1991) has noted that the societies containing the greatest amount of protocapitalism in the long agrarian era tended to be those in which maritime trade was characteristic. And Braudel has pointed to the greater capitalist possibilities of maritime trade specifically with respect to Japan (1982:582):

If Japan seems rather different from the rest of eastern Asia, it is in the first place because it is surrounded by the sea, which made communications easier; the Seto no Uchi was a tiny Japanese Mediterranean and a very lively one. (Imagine an inland sea between Lyons and Paris.) I am not seeking to explain the entire development of Japan by the virtues of salt water – but without them, the processes and sequences of events in this singular history would be almost impossible to imagine.

It is noteworthy that the protocapitalism of China tended to be located along its southern coast, and that the great Indian Ocean trade linking the Mediterranean and east Asia between the rise of Islam in the seventh century and the beginnings of early modern Europe was indeed centered precisely there – in the Indian Ocean (Chaudhuri, 1985). And where was the greatest economic development in late medieval Europe concentrated but in the city-states of Italy on the Mediterranean. The presence of maritime trade by itself determines nothing, but it is a very important precondition for capitalist development. Edward Whiting Fox (1991) and Peter Hugill (1993) have also noted the advantages of maritime over land-based trade. Hugill (1993:105) has said that the "development of ships has been crucial to the development of trade in any goods other than preciosities and at any distance beyond the few miles a person can walk." Moreover, Hugill quotes Adam Smith to the following effect (Smith, 1776; quoted in Hugill, 1993:48):

As by means of water-carriage a more extensive market is opened to every sort of industry than what land-carriage alone can afford it, so it is upon the seacoast, and along the banks of navigable rivers, that industry of every kind naturally begins to subdivide and improve itself. . . . A broad-wheeled waggon, attended by two men, and drawn by eight horses, in about six weeks time carries and brings back between London and Edinburgh near four ton weight of goods. In about the same time a ship navigated by six or eight men, and sailing between the ports of London and Leith, frequently carries and brings back two hundred ton weight of goods.

3 *Climate*: Europe and Japan both had temperate climates. This is important when we recognize that the bulk of the world colonized by Europe had tropical or subtropical climates. These regions were most suitable for the development of the kinds of peripheral economic activities – production of raw materials for export using forced labor – European states wanted to pursue in those zones. Alfred Crosby (1986) has argued that an important reason for the economic success of British settler colonies like the United States, Canada, and Australia was the fact that the settlers were inhabiting regions remarkably similar to western Europe. Most of North America and Australia had climates poorly suited to peripheral economic activities (the southern United States is the exception that proves the rule: its warm climate was suitable for plantation agriculture, and it was peripheralized). Japan may have escaped peripheralization by Europe at least partly because of its climate or

its distant northerly location. In any event, it wasn't climatologically suited for peripheral development.

4 *Demography*: Both Europe and Japan underwent dramatic population growth during their feudal and early capitalist regimes. We have already noted the extent of population growth in Japan between the twelfth and the nineteenth centuries. The total population of Europe in AD 1000 was approximately 30 million. By 1340 that had increased by some two and a half times to 74 million. Total population dropped to 52 million by 1400, but began to grow again in the fifteenth century, reaching 67 million by 1500. By the eve of the Industrial Revolution the total European population stood at approximately 111 million (Livi-Bacci, 1992).

The buildup of population pressure may have contributed to the declining efficiency of feudalism and the shift toward capitalism in both the European and Japanese cases. However, the growth of population is probably more significant in another way. At least in Europe and Japan, population growth led to increasing urbanization, which in its turn provided a larger pool of workers and promoted expansion in the size of real and potential markets. Increased urbanization also permitted and encouraged increased economic specialization and, in many respects, a more efficient utilization of various resources. Ester Boserup (1981:102, 104) explains further:

The increasing population density in Europe facilitated development of specialized crafts and manufactured goods. In areas of dense population, a large number of customers lived within a relatively small territory. Direct contact with customers was possible and transport costs for products could be kept at a minimum. A densely populated area, moreover, offered the advantages that levels of infrastructure investment were high according to the standards of the time, and that the market was large enough for specialization among the craftsmen, who were therefore more skilled than those in sparsely populated areas.

Manufacturing industries were even more dependent upon good infrastructure and a large market than were crafts. They required skilled workers and traders as well as the financial services and management and administrative skills which were concentrated in urbanized areas. Therefore, the areas in Europe which first developed manufacturing industries were those with the highest population densities – Tuscany, and the Low Countries – where there was already a tendency to concentrate production processes under one roof in the form of a manufactory in the Middle Ages. Such concentration occurred only later in France and England. . . .

However, with increasing population size and urbanization in England, the home market became large enough to support processing industries. England changed from a deliverer of wool to a large center of woolen industries, which produced both for the growing home market, including the army, and for exports to the Continent and to the colonies.

5 *Political structure*: Europe and Japan had the only true feudal regimes in world history in the sense that feudalism was defined earlier in this chapter. In fact, there is more similarity than that. The feudal systems of Europe and Japan arose at about the same time in world history and persisted for a remarkably similar length of time. If we use the earliest and latest dates ordinarily given for feudalism in Europe and Japan, we arrive at essentially the following results. The earliest date ordinarily given for the beginnings of feudalism in Europe is 768, the beginning of the Carolingian state (Anderson, 1974a), and it is generally agreed that feudalism proper did not last beyond 1450. This gives a feudal period lasting 682 years. For Japan, the earliest date given is normally 1185, the beginning of the Kamakura Shogunate (Sansom, 1961; Reischauer, 1956; J.W. Hall, 1970). It is a bit difficult to date the end of Japanese feudalism, but everyone would agree that it was finished no later than 1868, the year of the Meiji Restoration. This gives a feudal period lasting 683 years, remarkably only one year more than the length of feudalism in Europe! Now I am not suggesting that we can really date the length of Japanese and European feudalism that precisely, but a striking similarity is clearly there.

The significance of the feudal experiences of Europe and Japan lies in the substantial freedom they gave to their merchant classes to operate economically. There is widespread agreement that large bureaucratic empires stifle mercantile activity because it is a threat to the tributary mode through which the state extracts surplus. Europe and Japan were strikingly different from the rest of the agrarian world. Their high levels of political decentralization meant that mercantile activities could not be controlled as they normally were in large bureaucratic states. Anderson (1974a,b) has called attention to the freedom of the towns in medieval Europe and Japan, their remarkably independent role within the total economies of these societies. Likewise, Norman Jacobs (1958) has stressed the remarkable freedom and independence of Japanese merchants in contrast to the tight control of merchants in China. Indeed, it was not just that the Japanese merchants enjoyed considerable economic freedom, but that the whole conception of the importance of mercantile activity was distinctive in Europe and Japan. As Jacobs

(1958:118–19) has remarked by way of a comparison of China with Japan and Europe:

> In China, commerce – and its successor, industry – were viewed as necessary but morally inferior, and not primary to the operation of the division of labour. The occupational interests of commerce were subordinate to those of the literati and agriculture. . . .
>
> [I]n Japan (as in western Europe) in contrast, the significance of commerce and of the merchant, even under feudalism, derived from an appreciation of the role of the merchant and his money in the struggle for control of independent political or economic power. Consequently the merchant, and his successor, the capitalist-industrialist, received in return a respected and sought-after position in the division of labour.

The freedom given to merchants may well be the most important of the five preconditions that helped push Europe and Japan forward as the first states to undergo a capitalist revolution.[6]

There were of course differences between Europe and Japan, the two most important of which seem to be the following:

1 There was no demographic collapse in late medieval Japan as there was in late medieval Europe. The Japanese population remained large and dense and continued to grow throughout the Tokugawa period.
2 One does not really get a sense of a crisis of feudalism in Japan that corresponded to the European crisis. Perry Anderson (1974b) suggests that there was a feudal crisis in early-nineteenth-century Japan, but what he is describing looks more like a crisis of *capitalism*, probably induced by the relative isolation of the country from foreign markets. In any event, even if there was a Japanese crisis, it was not of the same type as the European crisis.

These differences between Europe and Japan provide some suggestions about what won't work in explaining the capitalist transition. The absence of an underpopulation problem in Japan raises doubts about the importance of such a factor in Europe. There was a labor shortage in Japan in Tokugawa times, but it was not the result of insufficient population. Rather, it was an urban rather than a rural problem and stemmed from the rapid commercialization and urbanization of the country.

My basic explanation of the transition to capitalism, which is deemed to apply equally to western Europe and Japan, is this: modern capitalism resulted from the interaction between the five preconditions discussed earlier – small size, location on a large body of water, temperate climate, growing population density, and feudal political relations permitting mercantile freedom and independence – and the process of long-term historical expansion of world commercialization that occurred between 3000 BC and AD 1500. *The level of world commercialization had finally built up in the centuries after AD 1000 to a critical density sufficient to trigger a massive capitalist takeoff.* A threshold of commercialization as the result of expanding urban networks and extensive and intensive trade density had been achieved, and this led to an explosive capitalist takeoff in those two regions of the world, western Europe and Japan, that were most hospitable to capitalist activity.

The increasing level of world commercialization over the very long run is the truly critical factor in all this, for as Fernand Braudel (1984:96) has said, "There could be no world economy until there was a dense enough urban network with trade of sufficient volume and regularity to breathe life into a central or core zone." Braudel is speaking of Europe, but the same argument applies to Japan. Although Japan did not trade with Europe in the centuries before Tokugawa, and although it was isolated from the West during most of the Tokugawa epoch, it did carry on a very significant trade with east Asia during this entire period, and it has been described by several economic historians as one of the great maritime powers of east Asia in the thirteenth, fourteenth, and fifteenth centuries (J.W. Hall, 1970; Braudel, 1982). The seeds of capitalism had clearly been sown by Ashikaga times (i.e., after 1338) (Jacobs, 1958; Braudel, 1982). Of the preconditions that interacted with this expanding level of world commercialization the most important was the freedom given to mercantile activity by feudal political relations. Although the other conditions were certainly important in stimulating commercial activity, European and Japanese merchants could not have gotten as far as they did at the time that they did without a favorable political climate.[7]

It is of the greatest importance to note that my theory says that *capitalism would eventually have developed anyway* given enough time for the further buildup of world commercialization. Europe and Japan were the first to have genuine capitalist takeoffs because they had the most suitable preconditions, but even if there never had been any feudal societies in the world an explosive capitalist spurt would eventually have occurred. My argument is made quite consciously in terms of an analogy with Carneiro's theory of the origin of the state. Carneiro has said that the pristine states arose when

and where they did because they were the world's most circumscribed regions at those times. But he claims that the state would
eventually have emerged anyway even in regions that were not
circumscribed at all in 5000 BP. Eventually *some* region would have
become circumscribed, and it would have witnessed the development
of the world's first state. Given the nature of the conditions determining political evolution, the rise of the state was inevitable.

My point about capitalism is a very similar one. It may have taken
a good deal more time – say another millennium or two – for
capitalism to emerge because of the lack of suitable preconditions,
but the expanding level of world commercialization would eventually
have gotten its way. It was a force that could be slowed down,
but it could not have been stopped. Eventually the level of world
commercialization would have become such that the tipover into
world-transforming capitalism would have occurred even under generally unfavorable preconditions. Capitalism was a force that could
not be denied. Its rise was inevitable at some point or other.

The rise of capitalism was a matter of the *growing economic power*
of the mercantile classes, a matter of these classes insinuating themselves into the sinews of agrarian-coercive societies with their tributary modes of production and finding the best home they could.
Since merchants were looked down upon by agrarian ruling classes,
their advancement could only be difficult and slow. Nonetheless,
agrarian elites could not dispense with merchants because they
provided goods and services that agrarian elites greatly desired.
They had to be tolerated, if not encouraged. And merchants took
whatever they could get. Some anthropologists have said, correctly
in my opinion, that in egalitarian band and tribal societies "inequality
is always struggling to get out." By analogy, I would say that in
agrarian-coercive societies "capitalism is always struggling to get
out." Merchants could be hemmed in here and there, could have
their wealth expropriated by this and that bureaucratic elite, but
they could not be denied forever. Gradually their economic power
grew, until, some 4,500 years after the origins of the first states and
quite probably the first genuine merchants, they were able to conquer
and subdue the very kind of society that gave them birth. It wasn't
easy, and it took a long time, but eventually it happened. It happened
first in western Europe and Japan, but if it had not happened there
it would have happened somewhere else at a later time. In my view,
capitalism was born of class struggle. However, it was not, as the

Marxists would have it, a struggle between landlords and peasants. Rather, it was the struggle between the landlord class and the merchants that was fundamental to the rise of capitalism.

I regard my interpretation as a highly parsimonious one that accomplishes the following things:

1   It explains why capitalism first emerged when and where it did.
2   It explains why it took a full 4,500 years for capitalism to emerge. This is an important accomplishment because the question as to why it took so long for capitalism to emerge after the rise of the first agrarian states has been a central one.
3   It explains why there was such remarkably similar timing in the emergence of capitalism in Europe and Japan. The buildup in world commercialization, especially in the centuries after AD 1000, was the critical context for capitalism. Some might think it a "coincidence" or a mere "historical accident" that the transition to capitalism was made in two distant parts of the world at, in world-historical terms, almost the same moment. But for any nomothetically oriented scholar the timing is too close to be explained in that way.
4   It dispenses with the hoary debate concerning whether the rise of capitalism in Japan was the result of endogenous or exogenous factors. Clearly both kinds of factors were important. The one big external factor was the intensified level of world commercialization, whereas the internal factors were the five basic preconditions. Perry Anderson (1974b) claims that Japan made its capitalist transition only as a result of the forced reopening of the country in the middle of the nineteenth century, an all-too-common view even today. Frances Moulder (1977) also claims that Japan never could have made the transition under its own impetus. But both scholars seriously underappreciate Japan's internal strengths and the degree to which it had already become essentially capitalist by the time of Commodore Perry's arrival in 1853. Norman Jacobs (1958) and Fernand Braudel (1982) show that there was a substantial endogenous evolution toward capitalism in Japan. As Braudel puts it (1982:591), "An early form of Japanese capitalism, clearly self-generated and native to the country, did nevertheless appear of its own accord." "Everything conspired," he claims, "to produce a kind of early capitalism which was the product neither of imitation of foreigners, nor of initiatives by any religious community" (1982:592). Moreover, "this capitalism emerged in the first instance from the development of a market economy which was long-standing, lively, and expanding: markets, fairs, sea-voyages, and exchange (if only the redistribution of fish to inland towns) and finally long-distance trade which was also an early development, particularly with China, and which yielded fantastic rewards (1100 per cent on the first voyages of the fifteenth century)" (1982:592–3).

What would have happened in Japan if it had not been forcibly reopened by the West? Moulder's (1977) answer is that it would have continued to stagnate under archaic feudal relations. My answer, though, is that by the mid-nineteenth century Japan was extremely close to opening itself up under its own volition. In the nineteenth century the Japanese had enormous interest in Western technology, and Japan was ripe for the shift to industrial capitalism. If this shift had not begun in the late nineteenth century, as we know it actually did, then it would not have taken much longer. Japan would have opened itself up voluntarily, inserted itself into the world capitalist market, and begun its own independent process of industrialization.

Consider what happened in China in the fourteenth and fifteenth centuries. It withdrew from world trade and declined economically, short circuiting the advance toward capitalism that some scholars think was soon in store for it. Contrast this with what happened in Japan when it embarked on its isolationist path in the seventeenth century. During the more than two centuries of its isolation it underwent enormous economic expansion, surely an indication of the strength of the endogenous forces pushing it toward capitalism.

I know that some readers may be wary of my theory because the notion of capitalism's slow but inevitable emergence will conjure up for them an underlying image of "economic man" who has a "tendency to truck, barter, and exchange." The theory will be branded as yet another version of a "neo-Smithian" argument. But this would be a misreading of my intent. I do not hold to a view of human nature that says that humans have some sort of inborn tendency to exchange things for profit. Humans are not inherently "capitalistic" in their outlook on the world. Indeed, if I thought such a thing shouldn't I expect capitalism to have appeared much earlier than it did, and shouldn't there have been much less resistance to it? My argument is that, when after a certain historical point mercantile activity became feasible (about 3000 BC), at least *some* people wanted to pursue it and at least *some* other people wanted it maintained because they could benefit from it. Once in existence, mercantile activity tended to expand of its own accord, and thus the class power of the merchant classes slowly, but surely, increased. And at some point it reached a level beyond which it could not be stopped.

I take no particular pleasure in holding this view, and such a view should by no means be interpreted as tantamount to a "procapitalist" ideological position. I am just as aware as my Marxist friends of the unpleasant and objectionable features of the capitalist mode of production. To explain the rise of capitalism is one thing, to evaluate its moral and political significance quite another.

NOTES

1 Many scholars have characterized medieval Japan as feudal, and as having the form of feudalism that most closely resembled the European version. See in particular Duus (1969), Reischauer (1956), J.W. Hall (1970), and T.C. Smith (1959).

2 The phrase "mode of production" is deliberate and should be taken literally. Most Marxists, of course, argue that the capitalist mode of *production* did not emerge until after the Industrial Revolution of the late eighteenth century, and that the mercantile capitalism of the sixteenth to eighteenth centuries was based only on relations of exchange. This notion is what is lurking behind Brenner's (1976, 1977) famous assertion in his extended critique of Wallerstein that Wallerstein's analysis is "un-Marxist" and unacceptable because it views capitalism as a system of exchange rather than production. I flatly reject Brenner's claim that Wallerstein is a "circulationist" and therefore a "neo-Smithian Marxist," as does Wallerstein himself (see especially Wallerstein 1979:147). While it must be admitted that much of what goes on among Wallerstein's zones of the capitalist world-economy involves exchange, much also involves production. When, for example, core capitalists peripheralize a region in order to extract surplus value from it, they are doing so through the direct establishment of productive activities that they ultimately control. How can such an economic relationship between core and periphery be regarded as based only on exchange?

  Brenner's circulationist charge against Wallerstein is one of several important criticisms of his world-system model that must be addressed. However, I postpone discussion of the other criticisms until chapter 6, where they can be taken up in the context of a much longer discussion of the nature and implications of world-system theory.

3 This discussion of the development of capitalism in Japan has relied exclusively on English-language sources, and almost exclusively on the work of Western historians. Undoubtedly there is a large Japanese-language literature on the subject, but very little of it has been translated. According to Gary Leupp (Tufts University, personal communication), for many decades there has existed a large Japanese-language litera-ture written by Marxist historians, but the vast majority of this remains untranslated. Germaine Hoston (1986) has summarized a good deal of this literature in her *Marxism and the Crisis of Development in Prewar Japan*.

  As Hoston notes, in the early 1930s a vigorous debate was carried on among Japanese Marxists concerning internal versus external causes of Japanese capitalistic development, as well as concerning the degree to which Japan had achieved a capitalistic status by the time of the opening of its ports in 1853. This debate preceded by nearly twenty years the famous Dobb–Sweezy debate on internal versus external causes of the development of Western capitalism; moreover, those Japanese historians who saw a strong indigenous capitalism developing during the Tokugawa era were well ahead of their Western counterparts, who even into the 1950s and

1960s continued to cling to the view that the Tokugawa period contained a stagnant feudalism that was overturned only with the opening to the West.

The debate in the early 1930s was carried on among many thinkers, but the leading representatives were Shiso Hattori and Takao Tsuchiya. Hattori argued that Japan had a strong indigenous capitalism by the time the ports were opened, and that the effect of Western intrusion was only to accelerate the capitalistic development that had already been taking place for some time. Hattori thought that by mid-Tokugawa times Japan had achieved the stage of capitalist manufacture. He believed that by the 1840s "capitalist production in Japan had already advanced beyond the stage of small handicraft industry and was preparing for the transition to large-scale mechanized industrial capitalism" (Hoston, 1986:101). According to Hoston (1986:114), Hattori thought that capitalism in Japan "evolved spontaneously out of mechanisms of the transition from feudalism to capitalism that Japan shared with Western Europe. To Hattori, there was no question that the course of capitalist development in Japan fit neatly the paradigm outlined in Marx's *Capital*: like England and France, Japan required no external impetus to assure its participation in the world-historical development of capitalism."

Hattori's argument was attacked most prominently by Takao Tsuchiya, who argued that Japan at the time of Western contact had not gotten to the stage of capitalist manufacture, but was still stuck in the stage of the putting-out system and domestic labor, at least with respect to the Japanese silk and cotton industries. Oddly, though, Tsuchiya went on to present examples of spinning and weaving manufactories; noted the existence of manufacture in magnetic sand refining, wax making, and the cast iron industry; and mentioned that large-scale manufacture was applied to the whale-processing industry. Apparently Tsuchiya's thinking was governed more by how the textile industry was organized, but it should not escape our notice that he does indeed provide evidence of a good deal of capitalist development during the Tokugawa era.

Hattori apparently had numerous supporters, but some of his critics also thought that he drew too close a connection between Japanese and Western capitalist development. Hoston has observed that Hattori's argument had a very positive influence on Japanese historiography in forcing "the participants of the larger debate on Japanese capitalism to speak to the issues in more concrete terms and to lengthen their historical perspective by tracing the roots of Japanese capitalism back further into the Edo period than they had done hitherto" (1986:124–5). At the same time, she notes that the work of Hattori's critics (1986:125) "also demonstrated that the existence of manufacture in general must not obscure the peculiarities of its manifestation in Japan: its extraordinarily heavy reliance on domestic labor through the putting-out system, the significant role of feudal lords in promoting capitalistic production, and the absence of thorough change in feudal landownership relations in the early stages of capitalist development."

Since I do not read Japanese, it is impossible to know with certainty the views held today by historians in Japan concerning the process of Japanese capitalist development. However, I strongly suspect that they support what Western historians have been saying for the past three decades about Japan's precocious capitalist development. In two articles that have been translated, Yataro Sakudo (1990) and Satoru Nakamura (1990) argue for vigorous capitalist development during the Tokugawa epoch. Sakudo speaks of the period as witnessing the "dramatic development of commercial capital," and goes on to claim that it was during the Tokugawa period that a type of family business management system developed that was the prototype for contemporary *zaibatsu*. Nakamura argues that "in the late seventeenth century, a new breed of large merchant, exemplified by the Mitsui house, appeared in the three largest cities of Edo, Osaka, and Kyoto," and that by "the eighteenth century [these merchants] controlled a nationwide system of commodity distribution" (1990:84).

Unfortunately, I am unaware of any translations of Japanese-language works that attempt directly to theorize the development of capitalism in Japan; thus, the theoretical discussion to come must rely entirely on the works of Western scholars. Even most of these theorize only about the West.

4 It is worth noting that there is nothing really very Marxist about Sweezy's theory, except in the most general (but essentially meaningless) sense that it pays attention to economic determinants. The essence of a Marxist theory of social transformation lies in the emphasis on dialectical contradictions, especially as they are expressed in "class struggle." These elements are completely missing in Sweezy's theory, indeed are declared to be either lacking in the feudal mode of production or incapable of explaining its transformation into capitalism. Probably the only reason that Sweezy's theory is classed with other Marxist theories is because Sweezy himself is a well-known Marxist.

5 In a recent essay, Wallerstein (1992) has altered his argument somewhat. He now offers what he calls a "conjunctural" explanation in which feudalism disintegrated via the simultaneous collapse of the economy, the state, and the Church. Although this argument is different from his original one, it still relies crucially on the notion of capitalism as a solution to a "crisis of feudalism." Indeed, the notion of feudal crisis has been broadened and thus looms even larger. Moreover, the rise of capitalism is still seen as a unique European phenomenon.

6 My historian colleague Larry Miller, while agreeing that a feudal politico-economic arrangement promotes capitalist development, has suggested that the point should be reframed in terms of political decentralization more generally, of which feudalism is simply one type. He points out that the Netherlands in late medieval/early capitalist Europe was not really feudal, but it did have a highly decentralized mode of government. Miller's point seems quite sensible and can easily be extended to include the Italian city-states of late medieval Europe.

7 We can now see the reason why a capitalist takeoff did not occur in the Phoenician city-states or Hellenic Greece. Although they were highly decentralized politically, and thus very favorable to mercantile and commercial activity, they existed too early in world history to generate a major capitalist advance. The level of world commercialization had not yet built up sufficiently for this to be possible.

6

The Evolution of the Modern World, I: The Expanding and Evolving Modern World-System

The modern world is first and foremost a capitalist world, and it has evolved as a result of both processes at the level of the world-system as a whole and processes endogenous to particular societies or nation-states. The evolution of the modern world cannot be understood, as has usually been assumed, simply by analyzing the historical development of individual societies or nation-states considered more or less independently of one another. It is critical that the evolution of nation-states be viewed from the perspective of their embeddedness within the modern world-system. But neither can the modern world be understood, as world-system theorists often seem to imply, by looking only at the world-system considered as a single indivisible entity. The world-system and its individual societal units are inextricably intertwined, and both must be studied in full. This chapter focuses on the evolution of the modern world-system as a whole; the next chapter looks at the development of the main institutional sectors of modernity as characteristics of the individual nation-states that comprise the world-system.

THE STRUCTURE AND DYNAMICS OF THE MODERN WORLD-SYSTEM

What we call the modern world-system is a structure composed of two complementary pillars, the capitalist world-economy and the interstate system (the following formulations are drawn largely from Wallerstein, 1974a,b, 1979, 1980a, 1983, 1984, 1989 and Chase-Dunn, 1989). The *capitalist world-economy* is the economic side of the system and the side that is given more attention by world-system theorists. As noted in chapter 5, it is a structure containing three principal zones. The core consists of those nation-states that dominate the world-economy and concentrate on the production of the most advanced (or leading-sector) goods using the most advanced technologies and employing wage labor. It is the most economically developed zone. The periphery is the least developed zone. Nation-states and regions within this zone use the most backward and outdated technologies and concentrate on backward or declining sectors of economic production. Historically, the periphery has concentrated on the production of raw mineral and agricultural products for export using one or another form of forced labor. The semiperiphery is an intermediate zone consisting of those nation-states and regions that combine elements of core and peripheral economic activity. It is at an intermediate level of economic development. The three zones are also characterized by different levels of political and military development. In the core we find the strongest states and military forces, whereas in the periphery the weakest political and military units are to be found. The semiperiphery is, once again, at an intermediate level with respect to these entities. The three zones also display strikingly different levels of intellectual and cultural development, especially as these are measured by the advancement of modern science. Science developed earliest and farthest in the core, last and least in the periphery, and in between these two extremes in the semiperiphery.

Around the edges of the capitalist world-economy there exists an *external arena*, which is a region (there may be more than one) that interacts with the world-economy but that has not been truly incorporated into it. Wallerstein argues that an external arena is a region that engages in trade of nonessential goods with the world-economy but that otherwise maintains a high level of economic and political autonomy. Then there is the rest of the world, consisting of regions not interacting at all with the capitalist world-economy. Oftentimes the movement of a region into the external arena is a prelude to its full incorporation as a peripheral segment of the world-system.

The three zones of the world-system carry on characteristic

relationships with each other, four of which are most noteworthy. First, the core uses its control over the means of economic production and its superior political and military power to dominate and exploit both the semiperiphery and the periphery (but especially the periphery). The semiperiphery, in its turn, is capable to some extent of using its relative economic and political superiority to dominate and exploit the periphery. There is thus created a complex hierarchy that we may call a core–semiperiphery–periphery hierarchy, or more simply, a core–periphery hierarchy. Such a hierarchy has existed throughout the 500–year history of capitalism and appears to be a permanent characteristic of capitalism as a world-system. Second, there is intense economic rivalry within the core that is expressed not only economically, but also in terms of antagonistic political and military relations. Nation-states within the core compete among themselves for economic dominance. Third, according to Wallerstein at least, the semiperiphery is said to mediate the sharp polarization and antagonism between the core and periphery. The argument is that any highly polarized system is unstable and needs some sort of intermediate unit to prevent it from exploding. Finally, and of crucial importance, is the fact that both ascent and decline go on within the system. Nation-states have various opportunities for mobility within the system, both upward and downward, and some movement does occur. However, this statement must be sharply qualified. In fact, most nations do not move over time, and when they do they do not move very far. The vast majority of mobile nation-states move only to an adjacent position, and there are few examples of countries that move all the way from the periphery into the core (the reverse has never occurred). Giovanni Arrighi and Jessica Drangel (1986) studied the issue of ascent and decline within the world-system by comparing the world-system position of nation-states in 1938–50 with their position in 1975–83. They found that 71 percent of nation-states were in exactly the same position in the second period that they occupied in the first, meaning that only 29 percent of states moved at all. Moreover, of the states that did move, many moved only within a zone (say from the edge of the semiperiphery to the middle of the semiperiphery) rather than from one zone to another. They concluded that fully 95 percent of states during this period either remained in the same portion of the same zone or moved only to the boundaries of that zone.

There are three kinds of dynamics that the world-system has displayed from its very beginnings to the present. First of all, it has been a continually (if not continuously) expanding system, undergoing the process known as the *broadening* of capitalist relations. This means that the system has been expanding geographically to incorporate more and more of the entire habitable earth. In 1500 the system was only just beginning to come into existence, and by 1640 it had expanded to include only about 20 percent of the habitable globe. It continued to expand slowly throughout most of the seventeenth and the first half of the eighteenth century. After about 1760, however, it underwent a quantum leap in expansion and by the beginning of the twentieth century had incorporated most of the globe. Virtually the entire earth today is part of the system. This process of expansion has been relentless, but it is now coming very close to reaching its geographical limits.

In addition to expansion or broadening, the world-system has also undergone the *deepening* of capitalist relations, or the increasing extension of the logic of capitalist production, the capitalist marketplace, and capitalist norms and values to economic relationships. This is what I prefer to call the *evolutionary dynamics* of the world-system. The process of deepening is the chief evolutionary process within the capitalist system and is ultimately responsible for many of the structural changes that have occurred both to the system itself, and to its constituent parts, over its 500–year history. It is possible to distinguish at least five fundamental evolutionary subprocesses that comprise the overall evolutionary process of deepening:

1   *commodification*, or the increasing extent to which factors of production and human relationships come to be characterized by the goal of buying and selling in order to realize a profit; this process is the most fundamental evolutionary process within the world-system; it involves both the commodification of things previously not commodified and the increasing commodification of what is already commodified; several important subtypes of commodification can be identified: (a) increasing size and scale of economic enterprises, (b) increasing transnationalization of capital, or its increasing movement across state boundaries, and (c) increasing proletarianization, which is sufficiently important to be listed by itself below;

2   *mechanization*, or the increasing application of advanced technological means to the process of production; this process occurs most rapidly and extensively in the core and least rapidly and extensively in the periphery, with the semiperiphery being in an intermediate position;

3   *contractualization*, or the increasing application of formalized rules and legalistic

norms to the human relationships that are a fundamental part of the capitalist production process;

4 *proletarianization*, or the increasing replacement of various forms of forced labor (slavery, serfdom and their variations) by wage labor; as noted above, this is a subtype of the process of commodification, i.e., it represents the commodification of labor;

5 *polarization*, or the increased widening of the gap between core and peripheral states.

The capitalist world-economy is also characterized by cyclical as well as linear dynamics, the most important of which are Kondratieff waves (or long waves), and hegemony cycles. *Kondratieff waves*, so called because they were first identified and described by the Russian economist Nikolai Kondratieff (1984[1928]) in the 1920s, are economic cycles of approximately 50 years' duration. The first part of a long wave consists of a cycle of economic boom and prosperity that crests after about 25 years, a downswing then beginning and bottoming out after another 25 years, only to give way to another upswing. Such waves have been shown to be remarkably regular for Western capitalism since at least the beginning of the nineteenth century, and in at least one case have been traced back to 1495 (Goldstein, 1988). These waves are controversial and still not particularly well understood. Their existence seems well established, but exactly why they occur and what they represent is still hotly debated. *Hegemony cycles* are better understood. They are instances of the economic rise of particular nation-states to extreme dominance within the world-economy and their subsequent fall from that position of dominance. There have so far been only three instances of hegemonic rise and fall: Holland (the United Provinces) in the seventeenth century, Great Britain in the nineteenth century, and the United States in the twentieth century. These will be discussed in some detail later in this chapter.

The modern world-system also has a political side, which is usually known as the *interstate system*. This is the system of competing and colluding nation-states that began to evolve more or less simultaneously with the emergence of the capitalist world-economy. Wallerstein has stressed that the world-system has always been politically decentralized and that this has been critical to its survival and continued expansion. It has never been turned into an empire politically and militarily dominated by a single state, although attempts at imperium have been made from time to time. The capitalist world-economy and the interstate system have been inextricably intertwined, virtually unable to exist without each other. We will shortly explore the nature of this connection and why it persists. States systems have not been unknown in history, but they have usually been short-lived and fragile, empire being far more common. This makes the modern interstate system unique, a fact that cries out for explanation.[1]

THE EVOLUTION OF THE CAPITALIST
WORLD-ECONOMY, 1500–1995

Wallerstein (1974a) has distinguished four major stages in the development of the capitalist world-economy. In the first phase, dated from approximately 1450 to 1640, the world-economy was only just emerging from the remnants of feudalism. By the end of this period a capitalist world-economy can be said to have formed. The second phase, running from 1640 to 1760, marked the consolidation and solidification of the system. Little expansion occurred, the system at the end of the period being only slightly larger than it was at the beginning. This was a period of growth, but slow growth. The third stage marked what Wallerstein (1989) has called "the second era of great expansion of the capitalist world-economy," and can be dated between 1760 and approximately the beginning of World War I. During this period there was dramatic expansion to include the bulk of the globe. In terms of the evolution of the system, large-scale mechanization, known usually as the Industrial Revolution, began. This marked the beginnings of a radical transformation of social life. The fourth phase, which we are still in, can be dated from the First World War. Tremendous capitalist deepening occurred in this phase but with relatively limited expansion of the system. Industrialization continued apace in western Europe, in the newly formed Soviet Union, and in North America, Australia, and Japan. Let us look at each of these major stages in more detail.

Stage 1: 1450–1640

At the beginning of this period the most powerful European actors were Spain and Portugal. They led the way in the geographical expansion of the European world to include the New World and, of course, established important colonies mainly in what we now call Mexico, Peru, and Brazil. The Spaniards encountered the Aztec in Mexico in 1519 and conquered them in 1521; the Inca in Peru were subdued a decade or so later. The Spaniards conquered the native ruling classes of these societies and took control of their economies, establishing forced labor systems that concentrated on the production of raw agricultural and mineral products. The Portuguese in what became Brazil established plantations devoted initially to the production of sugar and using slave labor imported from west Africa.

Why Spain faltered as a central European actor and was destined to remain in a semiperipheral position has been the subject of much discussion among historians. Many have suggested that Spain's difficulties lay in her cumbersome state apparatus. Wallerstein (1974b:191), for example, argues that "the cause, in our terms, seems to be that Spain did not erect (probably because she could not erect) the kind of state machinery which would enable the dominant classes in Spain to profit from the creation of a European world-economy, despite the central geographical–economic position of Spain in this world-economy in the sixteenth century." More to the point, Spain had a highly parasitical state bureaucracy that engaged in an enormously high level of luxury expenditure.

When Spain faltered, Holland (the United Provinces)[2] picked up the slack (Wallerstein, 1980a; Israel, 1989). Holland steadily increased its economic power and importance throughout the second half of the sixteenth century, and by the turn of the seventeenth century it was clearly a force to be reckoned with. World trade was the key. By 1590 the Dutch Republic had come to dominate the Baltic trade, and had also become a significant force in the Mediterranean rich trades (Israel, 1989). In 1602 the *Verenigde Oost-Indische Compagnie* (VOC, or Dutch East India Company) was established, which gave the Dutch Republic important trade relations with the East Indies. The Dutch Republic had become a world entrepot. But it was also important as a financial and manufacturing center. It controlled or came close to controlling certain key sectors of textile production, and also had a variety of highly specialized industries in which it outperformed its rivals: glaze and dye processing, tobacco spinning and blending, diamond cutting, whale oil refining, sugar refining, and lens grinding (Israel, 1989). After about 1625 the Dutch

Republic had achieved a truly hegemonic position in the world-economy. The nature of that hegemony, and the reasons for the Dutch Republic's success, will be discussed shortly.

The Dutch Republic's chief economic rivals were Spain, England, and France. As the period wore on, England and France became increasingly important as economic competitors. As Dutch economic strength increased, and especially as it became truly hegemonic, the intensity of political and military conflict among these three countries increased and in the second half of the seventeenth century became especially acute. It was especially the Dutch Republic's stranglehold on world trade that drove England and France to strong measures to improve their own economic situation.

After about 1250 the Italian city-states were the dominant economic forces in Europe, and their position rested on their Mediterranean location and their enormous specialization for trade. With the shift of economic dynamism to northwest Europe after the sixteenth century, the Italian city-states lost their former economic sparkle and declined to a semiperipheral position. Wallerstein asks whether Italy could have played the role assumed by the Netherlands, and answers his own question in the following terms (1980a:220–1):

Possibly, but there was probably not room for them both, and Holland was better suited for the task for a host of reasons than Venice or Milan or Genoa. Nor could Italy follow the path of England and France, for one thing for a lack of political unity. When the plague hit Italy in 1630, it reduced the pressure on food supply, but it also drove wages up still higher. It served as the last straw. Northern Italy thus completed the transition from core to semiperiphery.

In addition to Iberian America, the other major segment of the periphery in this first phase was eastern Europe. It underwent in the sixteenth century the famous "second serfdom," which involved the reenserfment of the peasantry at about the same time that western European peasants were losing their serf status permanently. According to Wallerstein, eastern Europe came to be economically focused on grain farming for export to the core. The import market for grain grew in western Europe as economic advancement there allowed it to concentrate on other forms of production. Eastern Europe as a result remained much less urbanized and industrialized than its western counterpart, and forced labor (what Wallerstein calls "coerced cash-crop production") remained dominant. The economic gap between the two halves of Europe grew. However, we should not be led into thinking that the division between these two halves was simply a creation of the capitalist world-economy. On the contrary, the economic, political, and cultural differences between western and eastern Europe existed long before the sixteenth century (Gunst, 1989; Kochanowicz, 1989). Nor did the specialization for the export of raw materials emerge only with the creation of a capitalist world-economy in the sixteenth century. Péter Gunst (1989) notes that as early as the fourteenth century eastern Europe was involved in large-scale cattle export to western Europe. The relationship between eastern and western Europe that is described by Wallerstein seems to be real enough, except that he is too late in his timing. Gunst (1989:62) explains further (he is speaking of the fourteenth century):

The Western economic impact on East Central Europe made itself felt from the very start in raw agricultural products and ores. The latter could be purchased in these centuries only from East Central Europe. The surge of copper and precious metal mining in Hungary, Bohemia, and Silesia is explained by this demand. Precious metals were exported to the West either in raw form or as coins; in return, consumption goods and articles such as dresses, textiles, and arms were imported. . . .

Similar to the demand for precious metals and copper, yet greater and longer lasting in importance, was the demand for agricultural products that began in the fourteenth century. The growth of towns and the increase in population produced a demand for food products that could not be satisfied by West European supplies alone. The demand for meat, especially, could no longer be met from nearby areas. At the same time meat was the product that could be delivered relatively easily on its own legs to the markets. In the fourteenth century cattle exports began to take place from a wide area. This marked the beginning of the development of market towns in Eastern and Central Europe.

From the next century onward a new feature was included with the former two: an increasing demand for grain and timber. The demand for grain from Dutch towns, to which it could be delivered by water, exerted an influence everywhere. From the end of the fourteenth century this influence spread over England, Denmark, and Southern Sweden on one side, and East German, Polish, and Baltic areas on the other.

The capitalist world-economy made up only a small portion of the world in the sixteenth and early seventeenth centuries and would not get much bigger until after the middle of the eighteenth century (I would estimate that about 20 percent of the habitable globe was part of the system by the first half of the seventeenth century). Most of the world was outside the system, and a good deal was even outside the external arena. Slave trading had begun in Africa during this period, but Africa still related to Europe as an external arena rather than as a genuine periphery. There was luxury trade with China and India, but they, along with the rest of Asia, were still outside the system. The capitalist world-system was only in its early stages.

Stage 2: 1640–1760

The second stage in the evolution of the modern world-system involved little geographic expansion and only moderate evolution. One of the striking features of this stage, especially its first half, was the intense rivalry between England and France on the one hand and the Dutch Republic on the other. The former were intensely determined to destroy Holland's hegemonic position, and war was a frequent outcome of the economic means by which they tried to do so. For example, in 1652 war broke out between the English and the Dutch as a result of English attempts to put restrictions on Dutch imports into England. Economic conflict between the Dutch Republic and France led to war between these nations in 1672 (Wallerstein, 1980a). These and other wars over time weakened the Dutch Republic, causing it first to lose its hegemonic position (after 1672) and then eventually to cede economic dominance to the English and French (by the middle of the eighteenth century). As their separate conflicts with the Dutch Republic continued to weaken it, the English and French began to see Holland as less of a rival and to focus increasingly on each other. Indeed, this rivalry was already in full swing even as the conflict with the Dutch remained intense. As Wallerstein (1980a:245) remarks, "The period of 1689 to 1763 . . . bounds a time of unbroken Anglo-French rivalry." And he continues (1980a:246): "The rivalry seemed a round of almost unending wars over the issues of land, allies, and markets in Europe and over supplies (of slaves, of tropical and semitropical products such as sugar, and of furs and naval stores) in the periphery and the external arena (the Americas, West Africa, India)." As the first half of the eighteenth century wore on, England continued to get the upper hand, and by 1760 had clearly emerged as the world-system's dominant (if not yet hegemonic) power.

Three new nation-states entered the world-economy as semiperipheral powers during this second phase: Sweden, Brandenburg-

Prussia, and the northern colonies in America (Wallerstein, 1980a). According to Wallerstein, it was during the reign of Gustavus Adolphus (1611–32) that Sweden made its move, and copper was the key. Copper mining became Sweden's leading economic activity and Sweden emerged as Europe's leading copper producer. Later in the seventeenth century copper gave way to iron, which was used in the manufacture of artillery, and also in the production of household ware. "The state encouraged iron production and was the chief customer, using the products for its military equipment," and Sweden acquired virtual monopolies over the production of copper and high quality iron (Wallerstein, 1980a:209).

The state of Brandenburg-Prussia also moved from a peripheral position in the world-economy during this time. It had achieved semiperipheral status by the eighteenth century, and Wallerstein attributes its rise to its development of strong state machinery and the fact that there was "room" for a semiperipheral power in central Europe. The English colonies of America, which were not even part of the world-economy until after the middle of the seventeenth century, had moved themselves into a semiperipheral position by the end of the second phase. Wallerstein attributes their rise to such factors as their role as competitive shipbuilders and their involvement in several important triangular trades involving Africa, the West Indies, England, and southern Europe. These trades were facilitated, of course, by their location on or near a major body of water.

This period in the evolution of world capitalism also saw the extension of the periphery to include what Wallerstein (1980a) calls the "extended Caribbean," which stretched all the way from northeast Brazil to Maryland. In the latter part of the first phase of capitalist advance the English, French, and Dutch had all begun to occupy various Caribbean islands, and in the second phase the use of these islands as peripheral regions for the production of one major agricultural product, sugar, expanded greatly. Sugar plantations were established throughout the Caribbean islands and in the southern colonies of North America, and Africans were imported through the slave trade to be the primary laborers. The European demand for sugar as a sweetener for coffee and tea and as an additive to cacao to make sweet chocolate was strong and continued to get stronger, and so its production was extremely profitable. Slavery had already been established in Portuguese America (Brazil), and its large-scale extension meant that this form of production and labor organization had become a fundamental part of the capitalist world-economy. Indeed, New World slavery was a fundamentally capitalist institution that would last well into the nineteenth century.

Stage 3: 1760–1917

After about 1760 the capitalist world-economy began to undergo a dramatic transformation. Most importantly, this transformation involved a major burst of mechanization, the Industrial Revolution; intense rivalry between the English and the French that led to Britain's achievement of hegemony by 1815; the incorporation of most of the rest of the habitable globe into the world-economy as peripheral regions; and the settler decolonization of the Americas. The Industrial Revolution will be discussed in the next chapter, but let us take a brief look at the other features of this stage.

By the beginning of this period – indeed, well before it – the Dutch Republic's position in the world-economy had declined significantly and the English and the French concentrated primarily on each other and worried much less about the Dutch. Wallerstein (1989) argues that the period between 1792 and 1815 was the last crucial phase of Anglo-French competition for hegemony in the world-economy, and that the triumph of Britain by 1815 was achieved to a large degree because of the superior strength of its state machinery and military power. As he notes (1989:112–13), "It was these politico-military victories [of Britain over France] that critically increased the economic gaps – in agriculture, in industry, in trade, and in finance." He adds that it was the wars between the two countries that gave a tremendous advantage to Britain's exports of its cotton textiles and thus to a major trading advantage in world markets.

In a sense the most significant development of the third stage was the incorporation of most of the rest of the world into the world-system. Latin America, of course, or at least much of it, had already been incorporated in the first stage. But Asia and Africa remained outside the world-economy proper (they were at best in the external arena) until after 1750. In Asia, the Ottoman Empire, China, the East Indies, and India came to be incorporated in these years, the last eventually becoming a formal colony of Britain. The British incorporation of India, as is well known, resulted in severe deindustrialization of the native Indian cotton industry, an outcome deliberately designed by the British to allow them to be able to sell their cotton goods there. Wallerstein remarks, however, that such deindustrialization was not limited to India but was in fact widespread throughout the newly incorporated areas. In the East Indies, incorporated and eventually formally colonized by the Dutch, native production was massively reorganized to allow for the production of coffee as the major cash crop. West Africa was gradually incorporated throughout the nineteenth century in conjunction with the abolition of the slave trade and slavery. Wallerstein makes the point that Africans were beginning to become more valuable as workers in their own land rather than as slaves in some foreign land, and thus the abolition of the slave trade was an important prerequisite for the shift of Africa from the external arena to a peripheral region producing raw materials for export. The full-scale incorporation of Africa did not occur until the late nineteenth century, through the famous "scramble for Africa" engaged in by several European powers. With the incorporation of Africa, most of the world was now functioning in one way or another within the framework of the capitalist world-economy. There was indeed a massive increase in the size, scope, and scale of the world-system.

Russia was also incorporated during this period, but as a semiperipheral rather than peripheral region. Russia's trade with western Europe underwent a notable upsurge in the period between 1750 and 1850; its main European trading partners were England, France, and Scotland, and it also carried on a significant trade with the United States. Wallerstein (1989:187) comments that Russia "was incorporated into the capitalist world-economy in ways that guaranteed and promoted the famous 'backwardness' of which later authors would write. But Russia still enjoyed a less weak interstate position than other incorporated zones, and this fact would result eventually in her ability to pursue the Russian Revolution."

The settler decolonization of the New World was one of the other historical occurrences of this third stage, just as the decolonization of Asia and Africa was to be a major occurrence within the fourth stage. The British colonies declared their independence in 1776, although they still had to fight militarily to make it a final reality. The colonies of Latin America attempted to gain their independence in the first decades of the nineteenth century, with the last colony gaining independence in 1830. Wallerstein (1989:226–7) explains the significance of these events:

Thus it was that, following the Treaty of Paris in 1763, in less than 20 years the Americas – all the Americas – seemed inescapably headed down the path of the establishment of a series of independent settler states. The next 50 years was merely the unfolding of a pattern whose general lines, if not detailed etching, had been drawn. Why this was so probably lies less in the heroics of some devotion to "liberty" on the part of the settlers or in some "errors" of judgment of the metropolitan powers – two favorite lines of argument – as in the cumulation of successive evaluations of costs and benefits (on all sides) in the context of the newly emerging British world order. . . .

The final outcome was beneficial in different ways simultaneously to the British and to the settlers in the Americas, both north and south.

. . . The principal losers were the Iberian states and the non-white populations of the Americas.

Spain and Portugal's loss of their colonies in Latin America proved to be not only highly detrimental to them, but also highly advantageous to Britain, for now it was free to pursue its economic interests in that region during a period of major expansion of the world-economy.

Stage 4: 1917–present

A detailed history of the present stage of the expansion and evolution of capitalism has yet to be written, but its outlines are clear enough. First, core rivalry became such that two major wars (or, as some would have it, two phases of the same war) were fought over their colliding interests. Several semiperipheral countries seeking upward mobility within the system were caught up in these wars as well. In addition, before the end of the First World War (in 1917) the Bolshevik Revolution transformed Russia into the Soviet Union, creating the world's first "socialist" state. This was to have a major impact after World War II when Soviet military power drew eastern Europe into the state socialist world.

There was little expansion during this stage, inasmuch as most of the world had already been incorporated by the beginning of the period. However, Britain, which had lost its hegemonic position in the 1870s, continued to decline so that today it is in the lower reaches of the core, dangerously near the semiperiphery. Its main rivals in the late nineteenth and early twentieth centuries were the United States and Germany, and it was, of course, the United States that succeeded Britain, becoming hegemonic by the end of the Second World War. This was a short-lived hegemony, however, for it was not to last beyond 1970.

The core today is made up of the leading industrial capitalist countries of western Europe, North America, Australia, and Japan, with the United States, Germany, France, and Japan being the four leading economic powers. Much of Latin America has been upwardly mobile into the semiperiphery, as have some Asian countries, such as Taiwan, South Korea, Hong Kong, and Singapore. Most of Africa, though, remains deeply embedded in the periphery with little hope in the foreseeable future of much improvement.

Two other major events need to be mentioned. First, there has been a massive mechanization of capitalist production and an intensification of its size and scale; the latter has involved the increasing globalization of production and the rise, in the middle of the period, of the transnational corporation as the major world economic actor. The globalization of production has become so extensive in the last few decades that several scholars have suggested that we have entered a new structural phase, variously called *the new international division of labor* (Fröbel, Heinrichs, and Kreye, 1980), *flexible accumulation* (Harvey, 1989), *post-Fordism* (Liepitz, 1992), *disorganized capitalism* (Lash and Urry, 1987), and *global capitalism* (Ross and Trachte, 1990). Although what these authors are speaking of is probably only an intensification of existing structures rather than a shift to something qualitatively new (Gordon, 1988; Chase-Dunn, 1989), it represents an important phenomenon nonetheless, for it is associated with the simultaneous industrialization of parts of the periphery and semiperiphery and the deindustrialization of parts of the core.

Finally, one of the more momentous events within the current period is the collapse of Communism in the Soviet Union and eastern Europe and the apparent movement of these state socialist countries back into the capitalist fold (see chapter 7 for a discussion of these events). This part of the world appears, at present, to be reopening itself to major capitalist investment from the West, and thus completing the process of the extension of capitalist commodity relations to the entire habitable earth.

HEGEMONY IN THE WORLD-ECONOMY

So far I have alluded to the rise and fall of hegemonic powers in the world-system, but the phenomenon of hegemony deserves to be discussed more thoroughly. Wallerstein calls a nation-state hegemonic when it has achieved a superiority over all other nations simultaneously in three major economic activities: production, commerce, and finance. He conceives of hegemony as more than merely economic dominance within the world-economy. It is a dominance so great that a hegemonic power is capable of competing effectively even in the domestic markets of its major competitors. "Hegemony in the interstate system," Wallerstein (1984:38) says, "refers to that situation in which the ongoing rivalry between the so-called 'great powers' is so unbalanced that one power is truly *primus inter pares*; that is, one power can largely impose its rules and wishes (at the very least by effective veto power) in the economic, political, military, diplomatic, and even cultural arenas." Instances of hegemony in the world-economy have been relatively few and far between, and for most of its existence the world-system has lacked a true hegemon. It is generally agreed among world-system theorists that there have been three major instances of hegemony: the Dutch Republic from 1625 to 1672, Great Britain from 1815 to 1873, and the United States from 1945 to about 1970. Let us look at the rise and fall of each of these hegemonic powers with a special eye toward explaining why hegemons are unable to sustain their hegemony.

That the Dutch were truly hegemonic in approximately the middle third of the seventeenth century is widely recognized (Wallerstein, 1980a; Israel, 1989). They were Europe's leading agricultural producer as well as its leading industrial producer. The Dutch dominated one of the critically important industries of the day, shipbuilding, and controlled several other industries as well. They controlled commerce to such an extent that their major rivals, England and France, had, as already noted, to drive them from their superior position by force. The Dutch fleet ruled the seas. The Dutch Republic was easily the most densely populated and urbanized society in Europe. In 1622 60 percent of the population lived in towns rather than in the countryside, and mostly in towns of 10,000 or more inhabitants (Wallerstein, 1980a). The Amsterdam stock exchange was the "Wall Street of the seventeenth century" (Wallerstein, 1980a), and this made Holland the financial center of

Europe. It was, in short, Europe's leader in the three critical economic categories of production, commerce, and finance.

Several factors have been identified as critical to Dutch success (Wallerstein 1980a; Israel, 1989). First there was the Dutch Republic's extremely favorable geographical location. As Israel (1989:14) notes, "The Republic was situated at a conjunction of northern waterways connecting the Atlantic, Baltic, and Rhine, a particularly crucial intersection once the Mediterranean ceased to be the pivot of intercontinental commerce." In addition, the Dutch Republic enjoyed low freight charges and low shipbuilding costs, the one reinforcing the other. Numerous authors have also called particular attention to the special design of Dutch trading ships, the famous *fluyts* or "flyboats." These were well constructed, large-capacity ships that could be handled by a crew approximately 20 percent smaller than those needed for other ships, and they thus allowed the Dutch to save costs on labor and provisions for shiphands (Wallerstein, 1980a; Braudel, 1984; Hugill, 1993). The highly specialized and productive character of Dutch agriculture must also be regarded as an important contributor to its commercial and financial position, for it provided the basis for a densely populated and highly urbanized society (Israel, 1989). As Israel points out, this made possible the freeing of a substantial portion of the rural workforce for work in nonagricultural activities. And we should not overlook the interest rates available to Dutch merchants, which were much lower than those available to merchants in other countries. Israel says that this feature of the Dutch economy was "universally admired" and gave Dutch merchants a tremendous economic advantage.

But, as important as these factors were, perhaps none was more important than the character of the Dutch state. Both Wallerstein and Israel regard this as absolutely crucial to Dutch success. They both note that the Dutch state was an especially strong and highly efficient state. Israel (1989:411) refers to the "unique suitability and aptitude of the Dutch federal state for the advancement and protection of trade." He also notes that it supervised a surprisingly broad range of economic activities, much more than other states did, and that its regulation of business practices was much more extensive than what was found in other states. Of great importance, it intervened again and again with other states to protect Dutch merchants from their rivals.

After 1672 Dutch hegemony came to an end and Holland began a slow decline, although for awhile it remained the dominant economy in the world-system. But even this was soon to end, and by 1740 its primacy in world trade had been destroyed at the hands of its rivals (Israel, 1989). Great Britain replaced the United Provinces as the next hegemonic power in the world-economy, enjoying a hegemonic position between 1815 and 1873. This was a hegemony on an even grander scale than that of the Dutch. During this time Great Britain became the world's leading industrial producer (the "workshop of the world") and commercial and financial power. Its navies ruled the seas and enforced its position. It was not only dominant within Europe, but indeed carried out extensive economic interactions with much of the less-developed world, and formally colonized a good deal of it. Wallerstein (1989:122) gives us a feel for the greatness of British hegemony:

With the end of the [Napoleonic] wars, Britain was finally truly hegemonic in the world-system. It consolidated its world power by acquiring a set of maritime bases, which added to what it already had, and meant that it now circled the globe strategically. Between 1783 and 1816 Britain acquired, in the Atlantic Ocean area, St. Lucia, Trinidad, Tobago, Bathurst, Sierra Leone, Ascension, St. Helena, Tristan da Cunha, and Gough Island; in the Indian Ocean, the Cape Colony, Mauritius, the Seychelles, the Laccadive Islands, the Maldive Islands, Ceylon, the Andaman Islands, and Penang; in Australasia, New South Wales, New Zealand, Macquarie Islands, Campbell Islands, Auckland Island, Lord Howe Island, and Chatham Island; and in the Mediterranean, Malta and the Ionian Islands.

Furthermore, Britain had in the process of the war been able to end the last vestiges of Holland's one-time hegemony, her role as a financial center of Europe. Through her dominance in commerce and finance, Britain now began to earn massive invisible credits – earnings of the merchant marine, commercial commissions, remittances from technicians and colonial officials abroad, earnings from investments – which were enough to compensate a continuing, even expanding, trade deficit, one that existed despite the size of her export trade. Britain, therefore, could maintain a favorable balance of payments. She commenced too her new role as the "schoolmaster of industrial Europe," while nonetheless still maintaining her high protectionist barriers.

And this was only at the beginning of British hegemony, for Britain was able to solidify and extend this hegemony in later decades. However, by the last quarter of the nineteenth century Britain's hegemony came to an end; it began to decline, and in fact markedly so. In 1870 its share of world industrial production was 32 percent, but by 1914 this had fallen to 14 percent, and by 1930 to 9 percent (Chirot, 1986). Since 1930 Britain has continued to decline, but only very slowly. It is now one of the poorest countries in all of western Europe, with a per capita Gross National Product about the size of Italy's. Further decline might slip it into the semiperiphery. Indeed, Michael Mann (1988:235) wryly observes that "by the year 2000 it will be as difficult to remember the Greatness of Britain as it is now to remember the Empire of Spain."

Britain's successor hegemon has, of course, been the United States, which has enjoyed the shortest-lived hegemony to date (1945–70). The United States achieved its hegemony on the heels of World War II, although it was clearly on the road well before that date. In 1870 the United States held a 23 percent share of world industrial production, a figure that rose to 38 percent by 1914 and a full 42 percent by 1930 (Chirot, 1986). The United States was able to back up its control over world industry, commerce, and finance with the world's largest military force, which helped the United States achieve a "Pax Americana" analogous to the famous "Pax Britannica" of Britain's hegemonic period (Chirot, 1986). In order to provide itself with huge markets for its goods, it played the leading role (via the Marshall Plan and Bretton Woods) in the economic reconstruction of Europe and Japan (Wallerstein, 1987). Approximately two-thirds of its foreign aid in the period 1945–66 went to Europe (Chirot, 1986). But it also helped guarantee markets and access to cheap labor in the less-developed world, as well as secure a world geopolitical situation favorable to its interests, by giving out huge amounts of aid and loans to less-developed countries. In the period 1956–75, 42 percent of its aid went to south, east, and southeast Asia, 24 percent to the Near East, and 17 percent to Latin America; in the period 1976–82, 49 percent of its aid was going to the Near East (mostly to Israel and Egypt), 15 percent to south, east, and southeast Asia, and only 8 percent to Latin America (Chirot, 1986). And we should not overlook the enormous prestige the United States attained in the postwar period, as well as the extraordinary Americanization of much of the rest of the world (Wallerstein, 1987).

The United States still has much of this prestige, but it is obvious to everyone that it has slipped. By 1970 (Wallerstein prefers the year 1967) US hegemony had come, or was coming, to an end. One sign of this has been the deindustrialization that has gone on throughout the country, especially in the highly urbanized and industrialized northeast, and the export of many jobs to the Third

World (Bluestone and Harrison, 1982). Another sign is the fact that the United States is no longer feared politically and militarily as it once was. A much more systematic analysis of the decline of American hegemony has been carried out by Bergesen, Fernandez, and Sahoo (1987). They examined the world's 50 largest industrial firms in 1956 and again in 1980. They found that the United States contained 42 of these firms in 1956, but by 1980 only 23 such firms were US firms. Looking at different industries represented by these 50 firms, they discovered that in 1956 the United States was producing in 13 industries, but by 1980 it was producing in only 7. Who picked up the slack? It was western Europe and Japan. In 1956 Europe had only 8 of the top 50 firms, but by 1980 20 such firms were located in Europe. The number of European industries represented by these firms remained about the same from 1956 to 1980 at 6 to 7. Japan contained none of the top 50 firms in 1956, but had 6 such firms in 1980. Similarly, Japan was represented in none of the industries in the top 50 firms in 1956, but was producing in 3 top 50 industries in 1980. It is clear from these findings that the United States is still the dominant economic actor in the world-economy, but it is no longer hegemonic and its primary rivals have made major strides. Albert Szymanski (1981) carried out a similar study with respect to banking. He showed that in 1970 6 of the world's 10 largest commercial banks (as measured by assets) were based in the United States, whereas in 1978 the United States contained only 2 commercial banks that were among the world's 10 largest.

We have already seen some of the factors basic to Dutch hegemony, but what kinds of characteristics are in general associated with hegemonic states? Christopher Chase-Dunn (1989) suggests four. Geographical location is one. We have seen how the Dutch location on the North Sea was highly favorable, and of course Great Britain had the same kind of maritime location, as did the United States. A second characteristic is that hegemons have been able to develop technologies that have enabled them to produce mass consumption goods more efficiently and cheaply than their competitors. In addition, rising hegemonic powers have developed at an early stage diversified and highly capital-intensive agriculture for domestic consumption as well as for export, and they have acquired access to inexpensive imports of staple foods and raw materials produced in peripheral regions. Finally, Chase-Dunn emphasizes the importance of the state. Hegemons have tended to have states that are neither too small nor too large and, more importantly, that are relatively pluralistic. In the case of the United States and the United Provinces, we find in fact states that were federations.

Hopkins and Wallerstein (1982) note that a hegemonic position is always fragile, and indeed that a nation starts to decline almost from the moment it achieves hegemony. What accounts for the loss of hegemony and, indeed, the fact that hegemony is always relatively short-lived? Several reasons may be suggested (Hopkins and Wallerstein, 1982; Wallerstein, 1984; Mann, 1988; Goldfrank, 1983; Szymanski, 1981). First, a hegemon always has rivals and these rivals do their utmost to undercut a hegemon's dominant position. We have seen how England and France used various economic measures to undercut the Dutch Republic's trade dominance and shifted to military measures to the extent that the economic measures failed. Likewise, Germany and the United States were Great Britain's chief rivals in the late nineteenth century and they were ultimately able to undercut it. In this regard it should be noted that hegemons generally favor an open world-economy, the better to maximize their world trade. But this is a two-edged sword, for it helps rivals along by giving them a better chance of learning to imitate the hegemon and defeat it at its own game.

Second, hegemons must bear the high costs of hegemony. These involve such things as the costs of developing new forms of technology and, perhaps more importantly, military costs. Military costs were an important factor in Britain's loss of hegemony, and they have undoubtedly been important in the American loss of hegemony. A strong military is usually critical to the maintenance of hegemony, and the more that funds are spent on the military the more they must be diverted from direct investment in economic growth. The United States, for example, spends an amount on defense that is equivalent to approximately 25 percent of its Gross National Product (US Bureau of the Census, 1992).

Third, a hegemon's productive efficiency inevitably declines over time. Industrial plants, for example, get old and have to be replaced, and competitors with newer plants gain a productive advantage. This applies especially to the United States. It was a world leader in steel production until recent decades, just as it was a leader in the production of automobiles. The United States currently produces much less steel with its decrepit steel mills, and much steel production has been shifted to Japan and less-developed countries like Brazil. The Japanese have shown the capability of producing steel much more efficiently, which of course gives them a tremendous advantage in world markets.

Fourth, just as productive efficiency wanes, so may organizational superiority. Walter Goldfrank (1983:147–8) notes that

> the optimal scale and organizational form of leading-sector enterprises are pioneered by the up-and-coming industrial states. In the nineteenth century, it was the trust and cartel movement giving way to the giant corporation, a movement that went further and faster in the United States and Germany than it did in Britain. At the present time, it is the integration of large firms with state planning and banking agencies, which the Europeans and Japanese are accomplishing while the United States resists and even, under Reagan, renounces.

As hegemons cling to the organizational forms that made them hegemonic, they can be eclipsed by rivals adopting forms that have become more suitable to new circumstances.

Fifth, hegemons create a high mass standard of living that in the long run forms part of the costs of maintaining hegemony. This point applies particularly well to the United States. A major part of the "Pax Americana" was the relative labor peace that could be achieved by high wages. However, over time, wage costs rose to such a level that they reduced the United States's competitiveness, leading to deindustrialization and the export of jobs to Third World countries with much lower wage levels.

Finally, the very basis for a hegemon's original success may easily turn into a fetter on its continued success. In Great Britain, for example, industrial production could be carried out by small-scale businessmen using relatively simple techniques. Industry did not require large external financing, and so most capital went into commercial ventures (Mann, 1988). As a result, British commercial and financial institutions became highly developed relative to industry and were hugely successful in Britain's world dominance. Britain's economy became heavily skewed toward the so-called City of London – Britain's trade and banking interests (Tylecote, 1982; Mann, 1988). This type of economic structure came to haunt Britain after about 1875, as Michael Mann explains (1988:229; emphasis added):

> When German and American competition hit hard, from the 1880s, the response came from an essentially commercial political economy. Industry hit back through its own

resources, largely unaided by government. Mergers, at first cooperative, then often contested, attempted to find investment funds through concentration. Though British firms became proportionately the biggest in the world, this was not a very efficient route to greater productivity. . . . But industry's efforts were further harmed by government economic policy, dominated by commercial reasoning and actually implemented by the City/Treasury/Bank of England nexus. Industry has been left unprotected from either foreign competition or the vagaries of international currency movements. The positive side of the balance is that British capitalism's essential commercialism enabled the City to retain considerable power as the main money middlemen of the whole world. With the rise of Europe relative to the United States from the 1960s the offshore island in the Thames has been well placed and organized to bring great prosperity to its members. *Commerce prospers while industry decays.*

DEVELOPMENT AND UNDERDEVELOPMENT IN THE WORLD-SYSTEM

In the early days of the capitalist world-economy, Wallerstein has argued, the economic gap between core and periphery was not very large, but it has increased over time so that it is now dramatic. Small differences have become widening scissors, and global polarization has occurred. Paul Bairoch (1981) has shown Wallerstein's argument to be right on target. Bairoch has demonstrated that in 1750 the differences in national income between the most developed and the least developed countries were very small, with the ratio of the richest country to the poorest country being only about 1.8:1. By 1860 the ratio had increased to 5:1, by 1913 to 10:1, by 1950 to 18:1, and by 1977 to 29:1. We now live in a world in which the income gap between core, peripheral, and semiperipheral nations is dramatic and continuing to increase. This is indeed one of the most significant trends in the evolution of world capitalism. How do we explain this trend and, indeed, what is the origin of underdevelopment within the world-system? There are several well-known theories.

Modernization theory

Modernization theory originated in the years after World War II and dominated thinking about underdevelopment during the 1950s and 1960s. Linked mostly to the field of economics, modernization theory has found many adherents among political scientists, sociologists, and anthropologists as well. This approach starts from the assumption that underdevelopment has been humankind's historical fate until at least the past few centuries, when some European countries began to overcome it. Societies can be divided into "traditional" and "modern." Traditional societies are those of the preindustrial world. These societies consisted mostly of peasant farmers who lived relatively conservative lives and remained committed to traditional modes of technology, economic practice, and social and cultural life. In such societies there was little impetus for change, and whatever economic development may have occurred was only sufficient to provide for expanding populations, not for real economic growth. These societies remained in an underdeveloped state because they lacked the key ingredients of true economic development. They remained trapped in traditional ways of doing things. They clung to old-fashioned modes of technology and business organization, lacked modern entrepreneurial attitudes and skills, and embraced values and religious traditions that were conservative rather than forward-looking.

After the sixteenth century in western Europe, however, and especially after the middle of the eighteenth century, certain key groups began to shed traditional norms and values and adopt a forward-looking worldview that emphasized economic growth based on modern science and technology. Their societies began to embark on a process of economic development that became self-sustaining, and these societies became the ones that now comprise the industrial capitalist world. Modernization theorists held that economic development was an evolutionary process that only some societies had gone through, but in principle it could be undergone by any society. They were optimistic that in time the less-developed societies of the world would acquire, mainly through the actions of various groups in the developed countries, the ingredients necessary for development, and eventually the whole world would become developed.

Modernization theory is really a broad theoretical strategy that contains a number of specific theories. These theories agree on general principles but part company on the specific mechanisms basic to development. Probably the most famous modernization theory is that of W.W. Rostow (1960). He sees development as a process that proceeds through five basic stages: traditional society, preconditions for takeoff, takeoff, drive to maturity, and high mass consumption. Societies can be jolted out of the complacency of the stage of traditionalism by some affront to their national dignity caused by the intrusion of a foreign power. This sets them on the path to development, which involves acquiring the preconditions for an economic takeoff. These include such things as the spread of ideologies declaring that development is both possible and desirable, the expansion of education, the emergence of individuals with strongly entrepreneurial personalities, the appearance of banks and other capital-mobilizing institutions, the development of modern science, and the building of effective centralized governments. The combination of these things may propel a society into the takeoff stage, which is reached when the rate of investment and savings has reached 10 percent or more of the national income. The takeoff is followed by the drive to maturity, a stage which may take 60 years to traverse. During this stage a society expands and diversifies its economy beyond the original industries that launched its takeoff. The pinnacle is reached when the consumption of numerous consumer goods becomes possible for the mass of the population.

A more sociological type of modernization theory has been offered by Bert Hoselitz (1960), who has applied the famous pattern variables of Talcott Parsons (1951) to the development process. Underdevelopment is a result of the holding of certain value-orientations, and development becomes possible through a shift in these orientations. Underdeveloped societies are oriented toward values that emphasize particularism, the functional diffuseness of roles, and self-orientation. This means that social roles are built around ascription rather than achievement, that roles are highly general rather than functionally specialized, and that individuals are concerned with maximizing self-interest rather than the larger social good. Economic development occurs when universalism (achievement) replaces particularism, highly differentiated roles replace undifferentiated ones, and the interest of the collectivity gains prominence over self-interest. Promoting development, then, means changing the value-orientations of the people, especially elite groups, in particular ways.

David McClelland (1961) produced a psychological version of modernization theory. He identified a psychological motive he called the "need for achievement" as fundamental to development. The degree to which individuals have such a motive varies within a society and between and among societies. High levels of the need for achievement are produced within individuals by particular kinds of child-rearing practices, particularly those that emphasize individual independence and self-reliance in the context of a warm and loving relationship, and these child-rearing patterns stem from certain family patterns. When many individuals in a society, or at least an elite group of individuals, acquire this motive, they constitute a strong force that can lead their society into sustained economic development. McClelland actually went so far as to design training programs for individuals in Third World countries (India in particular) that would increase their need for achievement and thus their entrepreneurial talents (McClelland and Winter, 1969).

Dependency theory

Dependency theory originated in Latin America and was introduced into the developed world through its chief spokesman, Andre Gunder Frank (1966, 1969, 1978, 1979). It rejects the simple distinction between traditional and modern societies, the notion that a society's underdeveloped state is the result of its own internal deficiencies, and the belief that the developed world can assist the underdeveloped world in the attainment of a high level of development. It has argued instead that development is not a matter of internal deficiencies, but rather of economic dependency, or the penetration of a country's economy by some foreign society that comes to dominate it and manipulate it for its own economic purposes. Dependency exists when the economy of a less-developed country has been inserted into a more-developed society's economy and functions only as an appendage of it. There arises a relationship between dominant and dependent countries in which the economic surplus created in the dependent country is siphoned off, leaving it in a perpetual state of underdevelopment (or perhaps even worsening its underdevelopment). It is, in Frank's memorable phrase, the *development of underdevelopment*. Economic underdevelopment thus results from domination and naked exploitation, and for development to occur the fetters of dependency must be removed.

Dependency theorists have viewed dependency as a phenomenon that has taken different forms in the historical development of capitalism. The first form of dependency was colonialism, the formal political domination of a less-developed region by a European power. The ending of colonialism – in Latin America by 1830 and in Asia and Africa after World War II – did not eliminate dependency but only changed its form. Neocolonialism replaced colonialism, the former involving extensive economic penetration without formal political rule. Theotonio Dos Santos (1970) has distinguished two forms of neocolonial dependency, financial–industrial dependency and the "new" dependency. Financial–industrial dependency began in the nineteenth century and involved heavy investment by big capitalists in the developed world. The new dependency originated after World War II and involved the penetration of Third World economies by transnational corporations. In the colonial phase of dependency, less-developed regions functioned primarily as raw material producing and exporting regions. This function has continued to a considerable extent during the neocolonial period, but less-developed countries have also become sites for industrial production organized by capitalists from the developed world.

Like modernization theory, dependency theory is a broad paradigm that includes theories that differ on specifics. Just how dependency leads to underdevelopment is conceived differently by different dependency theorists, and at least four basic mechanisms have been proposed (Chase-Dunn, 1975; Delacroix and Ragin, 1981; Barrett and Whyte, 1982). Andre Gunder Frank has stressed an exploitative relationship in which earnings of developed countries in the less-developed world are repatriated. Elite complicity has also been prominently suggested as a mechanism. This involves close agreements between capitalists of the developed countries and capitalists in the less-developed world. These agreements benefit both groups while at the same time perpetuating or even worsening underdevelopment. The notion of structural distortion has also been suggested, most prominently by Samir Amin (1974). Developed countries, Amin argues, have highly articulated economics in which there is a close and dynamic relationship among the various economic sectors. Growth in one spills over into growth in others, and a dynamic process of positive feedback is set up that leads to high levels of economic growth. Less-developed countries, on the other hand, have disarticulated economies. The various economic sectors are weakly related, one sector tending to develop while others are neglected. It is the sector devoted to the production and export of raw materials that is most developed, and this sector is closely tied to the economies of developed countries rather than to the other economic sectors of the less-developed country. The economy thus comes to be distorted in such a way that growth in the most prominent sector benefits the developed economies to which it is linked but leads to the failure of other sectors to develop significantly. Finally, some dependency theorists have emphasized market vulnerability as a mechanism of underdevelopment. Because less-developed countries commonly rely on one major export product, they are often harmed by the tendency for the world demand for this product to decline over time.

Some dependency theorists, dissatisfied with what they perceive to be unnecessary rigidities in early dependency theory, have worked out an alternative version of dependency theory. I propose to call these two versions of dependency theory *strong* dependency theory and *weak* dependency theory (these might also be called *hard* and *soft* dependency theory). The strong version, associated most closely with Frank and Amin, tends to see economic development as impossible so long as a condition of dependency exists and views core capitalism as always detrimental to the less-developed world. The weaker or softer version, developed primarily by Fernando Henrique Cardoso (Cardoso, 1982; Cardoso and Faletto, 1979) and Peter Evans (1979), rests on Cardoso's concept of "associated dependent development," or simply "dependent development." This is a type of economic growth that occurs in less-developed countries as a result of the operation of foreign transnational corporations. The argument is that a certain degree and type of economic development is not incompatible with the continuation of dependency. Soft dependency theorists are able to point to such countries as Brazil and South Korea as examples of dependent development in recent decades. They are also able to emphasize that, since following a socialist path has produced such meager results for most of the less-developed countries that have tried it, staying within the capitalist system rather than cutting ties to it may be on the whole a better choice for less-developed countries. The weaker or softer version of dependency theory is different from the stronger or harder version, but we should be careful not to overemphasize their differences. Countries like Brazil and South Korea are exceptional cases. Even then development has only gone so far, and in the case of Brazil has been associated with sharp rises in economic inequality. In some cases of dependent development, the economic growth that occurs may benefit only a minority of the population, leaving the majority no better off or, in some instances, even worse off. Dependent development is not the same thing as the genuine article, that which has occurred in western Europe, North America, Australia, and Japan.

World-system theory

World-system theory is similar to dependency theory and actually arose in part from it. It holds that it is the world-system as a whole, rather than individual societies, that develops. Basic to this system is a core–periphery–semiperiphery hierarchy that will last as long as capitalism lasts. Over time the gap between the core and the periphery increases because of the very logic of the world-system itself. Once a society's position within the system has been determined, it tends to remain in that position permanently. However, at various points in the historical evolution of the system various opportunities are created for some countries to become upwardly mobile. Wallerstein (1979) suggests three strategies that a country may use to take advantage of these opportunities. First is *seizing the chance*. During periods of contraction in the world-economy (Kondratieff B phases), some core countries will be in a weakened position, and a few peripheral or semiperipheral countries may be able to move aggressively (economically speaking) against these core countries. Russia adopted such a strategy in the late nineteenth century, and Brazil and Mexico tried it in the 1930s. In addition, there is *development by invitation*. During an upswing (Kondratieff A) phase of the world-economy, the higher level of world economic demand creates more "room" or "space" for some countries to develop. Less-developed countries with a particularly favorable combination of characteristics (one of which is the presence of mind to recognize an opportunity when it comes) may be able to undergo substantial development. Scotland pursued such a strategy in the late eighteenth century, and it has been followed by South Korea and Taiwan in the post-World War II period, as we shall see in more detail later. Finally, there is the strategy of *self-reliance*. This involves cutting ties to the capitalist system and going it alone, usually along some type of socialist path. Russia followed this strategy in the early twentieth century, as did China and Cuba in the middle of the twentieth century, and as have about three dozen other less-developed countries. It worked reasonably well for Russia for a time, but not very well for most of the others that have tried it, and so it has been a very limited strategy.

World-system theory is different from dependency theory, especially the hard or strong version, but it is not all that different. (Hard and soft dependency theory and world-system theory are really a family of closely related theories.) When Wallerstein speaks of the possibilities for upward mobility within the world-system he stresses that these possibilities are sharply limited. They exist only at certain times, are only possible for a few countries, and often produce very limited development. Wallerstein believes that the best opportunities for the less-developed world occur over the long haul, that is, in the long-term disintegration of the capitalist system and its conversion into some other (most likely socialist) world-system.

Marxist modernization theory

Most radical thinkers today, including those who see themselves as Marxist in one way or another, subscribe to one of the versions of dependency theory or to world-system theory. However, two contemporary radical Marxists have eschewed these theories and striven to return to the original ideas of Marx on underdevelopment and develop theories from that baseline. The thinkers are Albert Szymanski (1981) and Bill Warren (1973, 1980), whose views are quite similar, but yet diverge in some important respects. Their ideas provide a challenge to dependency and world-system theories from *within* the radical camp rather than from outside it.

Szymanski and Warren assert that Marx held that the impact of capitalist imperialism on the less-developed countries would ultimately be to lead them along the same evolutionary path the developed countries had followed. Szymanski argues that, although Marx saw colonialism as detrimental to the less-developed world, he saw the achievement of political independence as creating conditions within which the effect of continuing imperialism would be favorable rather than unfavorable, and he believes that Marx has turned out to be right.[3] Szymanski himself argues that capitalist imperialism has in fact led to the greater industrialization and economic development of the less-developed world. Countering Frank's argument that the flow of economic surplus has been from the less-developed to the developed world, Szymanski claims just the opposite has occurred. Szymanski also charges that the economic gap between the developed and less-developed countries, as measured by national income (Gross National Product or Gross Domestic Product), has been shrinking rather than widening. However, there are respects in which Szymanski's overall position bears a resemblance to dependency and world-system theory. He notes that there are some important differences between the development of the Third World today and the development of Europe and North America a century ago, the most important of which is the structural distortion of Third World economies: the encouragement of the growth of the raw materials producing sector at the expense of manufacturing. Even more significantly, Szymanski argues that despite the economic development of the Third World there has been little if any change in living standards, and abject poverty still abounds. In addition, economic inequality has increased. Szymanski (1981:365) reaches conclusions that look much like those reached by dependency and world-system theory:

Hypothetically, if the rates of economic growth of the less-developed countries were to continue at their 1970–77 rate, the less-developed countries would finally catch up to the developed countries around the year 2175, although they would attain the late 1970s levels of GDP per capita of the developed countries around 2050. . . .

However, it is most unlikely that the current tendency for the less-developed countries to catch up with the developed will proceed very far; likewise, the possibility of current trends in the living standards of workers in the less-developed countries being reversed and eventually converging with those of developed countries is unlikely to be realized (at least in most countries). The massive social disruption, aggravated social inequality, and political repression that imperialist development entails are very likely to result in social revolutions that will break with imperialism and establish socialist or at least noncapitalist paths of development.

Szymanski's style of thinking might be termed "Marxist modernization theory," but it is obvious that some of its conclusions are radically at odds with those of conventional modernization theory.

Warren's view is very similar but leans more toward conventional modernization theory. Warren maintains that the notion of underdevelopment is a fiction and that Western imperialism has stimulated a genuine process of development in the less-developed world by such means as destroying premodern cultures and modes of production, stimulating new aspirations, and implanting the economic and cultural elements of modern civilization. He sees numerous indicators of economic development in the less-developed world:

increasingly adequate modern health care, expansion of the supply of consumer goods available to large segments of the population, and the expansion of access to education. The less-developed world is being industrialized and GNP per capita is definitely on the rise. Furthermore, he claims, this has been occurring, contrary to the dependency and world-system theorists, without increases in economic inequality. He adds that worldwide economic power is becoming more dispersed and that the gap in living standards has clearly been shrinking. The alleged marginalization of significant segments of Third World populations – a key part of the argument of dependency and world-system theory – is not occurring. Warren concludes that "the period since the Second World War has seen titanic strides forward in the establishment, consolidation, and growth of capitalism in the Third World, with corresponding advances in material welfare and the expansion of the productive forces" (1980:252).

Evaluating the theories

Modernization theory was severely criticized in the 1960s and 1970s, and it has seemed to some that it was dealt a fatal blow. But it never died and, indeed, I think it has always remained the dominant approach among social scientists, even if the label tends to be avoided. Some now talk of "neomodernization theory" (Apter, 1987; So, 1990), but it does not differ in principle from plain old-fashioned modernization theory. It is just old wine in new bottles.

Modernization theory has numerous defects that have long been known. First, theories like Rostow's end up being more descriptive than explanatory, and even his descriptive stages seem of little use. Isn't it obvious that a society must develop the preconditions for economic growth before it will begin to experience growth itself, and isn't it fairly obvious that a drive to maturity cannot occur until growth begins? What we really want to know is not that for a society to grow it must have the preconditions for growth – that is a mere truism – but what those preconditions are and, more importantly, how a society can acquire them. Rostow of course does suggest that a "reactive nationalism" is the key, but this is a very vaguely formulated notion; moreover, such a phenomenon has likely occurred throughout history without producing any significant economic development. Why should it have become so important in just the last few centuries?

Hoselitz's theory fares little better than Rostow's. The accuracy of his characterization of traditional and modern societies can be seriously questioned (Frank, 1967). Is it really the case that modern societies emphasize collectivity-orientation over self-orientation? Elsewhere I have suggested that there are some very good reasons for believing that the very opposite may be true (Sanderson, 1990). In McClelland's theory we have an extreme form of psychological reductionism. Is it really plausible to believe that massive macrohistorical changes can be brought about simply by changing our child-rearing practices so that we can alter people's psychological needs and drives? Often modernization theorists produce arguments that are little more than intellectual sleight of hand. A favorite theme among sociological modernization theorists is the importance of certain value-complexes, especially religious ones. For example, the tremendous economic development of Japan in this century is often ascribed to Confucianism (cf. Kahn, 1993); this leaves us scratching our heads, though, in wondering why it took so long for Confucianism to have its impact (it is a very old religion), or why it did not have a similarly salutary effect in China, where it originated (Yoshihara, 1986; Ellison and Gereffi, 1990).

The biggest problem with modernization theory, though, is its almost complete neglect of the political and economic relations that have been carried on between developed and less-developed countries for several centuries. Modernization theorists seldom mention colonialism, let alone give it systematic and sustained attention. They lump all societies into one of two categories, "traditional" or "modern," and thus treat ancient Rome, medieval Europe, Heian Japan, or Sung China as if they were only modestly distinguishable from British India in 1850 or the Dutch East Indies at the same time. Surely it is not possible to understand the contemporary underdeveloped world without considering in a detailed and systematic way its colonial and neocolonial relationships with the developed world. Why do serious social scientists look for hidden cultural orientations or psychological motives and ignore massive political and economic realities that are obvious to even a casual observer? It boggles the mind.

Marxist modernization theory, or at least Szymanski's version of it, holds up considerably better. Despite Szymanski's strong stand against dependency theory, as already noted his conclusions about Third World development do not differ that much from those of dependency theory in terms of the quality of life in less-developed countries and the likelihood of these countries catching up with the developed world. The main difference concerns whether or not foreign investment inhibits or promotes development in the Third World. Warren's position is really not significantly different from ordinary modernization theory in its prediction that the gap between the developed and less-developed countries is closing now and will eventually close. Virtually the only thing that makes Warren's view distinct from conventional modernization theory is his disapproval of capitalism, which is the sole remaining reason why he can continue to call himself a Marxist. The problem with Warren's argument is that the facts are simply against it, or at least that part of his argument that declares the First World–Third World gap to be closing. Warren is correct when he says that education is expanding, per capita GNP is growing, health care is improving, and infant mortality is declining in less-developed countries (phenomena we shall look at in some detail in chapter 8 in the context of a discussion of immiseration in the world-system). However, he is most certainly *not* correct when he asserts that there is no polarization in the world-system (as measured by per capita national income) but in fact just its opposite. A publication of the United Nations shows that the ratio of the per capita national income of the richest 20 percent of the world's countries to the poorest 20 percent was 30:1 in 1960 and that it had climbed to 59:1 by 1989 (United Nations, 1992a). It must be acknowledged that on a variety of indicators a certain amount of development has been occurring in the underdeveloped world. Nevertheless, it is still an open question the extent to which such development is benefiting the mass of the population. And it is still an open question whether the development that is occurring is going on because of or in spite of foreign penetration by the developed economies.

In the last two decades various researchers have conducted elaborate and methodologically sophisticated studies designed to determine whether or not economic dependency, conceptualized as the extent of foreign investment in underdeveloped economies, retards or stimulates development. These studies have produced contradictory results that have been difficult to interpret. Fortunately, research by Volker Bornschier, Christopher Chase-Dunn, and Richard Rubinson

(1978) has been devoted to determining the reason for the inconsistent findings. Looking at 16 studies in 1978, and then at a larger group of 36 studies in 1985 (Bornschier and Chase-Dunn, 1985), the authors came to the conclusion that the results obtained depended on how economic dependency was conceptualized and measured. Studies that measured dependency in terms of the *short-term flow of capital investment* generally found that foreign investment stimulated economic growth. On the other hand, those studies that measured dependency in terms of the *long-term buildup of stocks of foreign capital* tended to find that foreign investment had a negative effect on economic growth. The authors concluded that the findings were not, in fact, contradictory. Rather, short-term capital investment does stimulate development initially as capitalists move in and purchase land, labor, and materials, but this initial growth spurt soon peters out and over the long haul the effect of the buildup of stocks of capital investment is negative rather than positive. The authors then carried out their own independent study and found that the short-term effect of foreign investment was to stimulate economic growth whereas the long-term effect of the accumulation of stocks of foreign capital was to decrease growth.

These conclusions have been challenged in a recent study by Glenn Firebaugh (1992), who claims that previous studies have been statistically and methodologically flawed. He has carried out his own study using the same data base used by Bornschier, Chase-Dunn, and Rubinson and correcting what he believes to be the earlier flaws. His findings show that foreign investment stimulates rather than retards economic growth. Domestic investment, he reports, stimulates a higher lever of development than foreign investment, but the effects of foreign investment are nonetheless positive. Foreign investment, in other words, is not as good as domestic investment, but it is better than no foreign investment at all.

It appears that at the present moment we are unable to say definitively exactly what the impact of current foreign investment is on the underdeveloped world. If it is eventually shown to most everyone's satisfaction that the effect is favorable, this is certainly a strike against one element of dependency theory, but a modified dependency argument would still be plausible and empirically supportable. We have to bear in mind that dependency theory is not only a theory about the present, but even more significantly a theory about how world capitalism has developed in an extremely uneven way over the past few centuries. Even here there are problems, however, and, although they are certainly not insurmountable, we need to take note of them before moving on. Six weaknesses of dependency theory can, in particular, be noted (Roxborough, 1979; Hoogvelt, 1982; Leys, 1982; Blomstrom and Hettne, 1984; So, 1990):

1 Although they have criticized modernization theory for its ahistorical approach, dependency theorists have something of an ahistorical outlook of their own. They tend to ignore the history of societies before they were incorporated into the world-system. However, it is likely that the precapitalist histories of these societies are very important in conditioning the way in which they will be incorporated and their various developmental possibilities and prospects after incorporation (Chase-Dunn, 1989). Gerhard Lenski and Patrick Nolan (1984), for example, have argued that the technological level a society has reached at the time of its incorporation has a significant effect on its developmental future.

2 Dependency theory tends to stress external factors to the relative neglect of internal factors. It tends to overgeneralize about the underdeveloped world and treat under-developed societies as if they are all essentially alike, ignoring differences among societies involving such things as population size, geography, political structure, and class structure. These differences may play a large role in shaping a country's developmental prospects.

3 Dependency theory has been too pessimistic and rigid in its claim that economic dependency renders economic development impossible. This claim is belied by the startling amount of economic development occurring in recent decades in such Asian societies as Singapore, Hong Kong, Taiwan, and South Korea, as well as in such Latin American societies as Brazil, Mexico, and Argentina.

4 The dependency theorists have made as their major policy recommendation cutting the economic umbilical cord that ties the less-developed countries to the developed world and "going it alone," usually along a socialist path. An appreciable number of less-developed countries have tried this strategy, but for the most part it has not been very successful.

5 Dependency theorists often imply, and sometimes state directly, that the poverty of the less-developed world is the product of their dependent relations with developed societies. But the precapitalist societies that were incorporated into the world-system often had forms of class inequality in which the mass of the population existed in a very degraded state. It is possible that dependency could have worsened poverty in some cases, but it cannot be regarded as some sort of original cause of poverty.

6 Early versions of dependency theory implied that the developed countries only became developed by virtue of their exploitation of a periphery – that capitalist imperialism was necessary for economic development. However, even some dependency and world-system theorists now regard this proposition as indefensible (Szymanski, 1981; Chase-Dunn, 1989; Chirot, 1977). Capitalist imperialism may have been useful, and may still be, but it should not be regarded as a prerequisite for development.

Most of these criticisms, which I will happily accept as essentially valid, apply largely to the earlier, hard version of dependency theory and leave soft dependency theory and world-system theory relatively untouched (even such architects of dependency theory as Frank now admit that the earlier version has serious limitations and have cast their lot with the more flexible dependency and world-system theorists; see Frank, 1987). My own view is that these latter theories are the best we have to date to make sense of the patterns of economic development and underdevelopment that have been formed in the last few centuries. New and better ones will come along in the future, but until then I would urge the following general conclusions:

1   The modern world is quintessentially a capitalist world, and the principle of capital accumulation has been for several hundred years the main (although certainly not the only), engine of social evolution. An understanding of the logic of capital accumulation is an essential starting point for an understanding of the economic development and underdevelopment of the modern world. (It is also essential for understanding the evolution of the noneconomic dimensions of the modern world, which is the subject of chapter 7.)

2   This capitalist world has developed in an extremely uneven fashion; those societies that, for one reason or another, had advantages that gave them a favorable starting position have been able to improve that position, and those that had unfavorable starting positions have often ended up much more unfavorably, often as clients or dependents of the better-off societies.

3   Once a society's position within the world-system has been set, it has a certain permanence. However, some societies, because of a favorable combination of characteristics valuable in certain historical circumstances, can move up within the system, although in most cases they can move up only so far.

4   Despite the fact that the gap in national income between the developed and the less-developed countries continues to widen, most less-developed countries have experienced a process of development relative to their own past. They have developed in absolute terms even while they have fallen farther and farther behind in relative terms. The less-developed societies have experienced, among other things, growth in their manufacturing sectors, decline in the proportion of the labor force in agriculture, real increases in per capita GNP or GDP, declines in infant and child mortality and increases in longevity, expanding education, and increasing literacy. However, the degree to which these developmental changes extend to and benefit the broad mass of the population, rather than particular segments of the population, is still very much an open question.

5   Although the less-developed countries are developing relative to their own past, the vast majority will never catch up with the developed countries, and in fact can only fall farther and farther behind those countries. The whole world cannot develop equally; this is impossible not only on economic grounds, but on ecological grounds as well. Barring a major technological revolution, the earth cannot sustain some 175 societies at high levels of economic development. (The issue of the

ecological sustainability of human societies in the present and the near future is explored much more fully in chapter 9.)

6   There can be no question but that the relations between the developed and the less-developed countries have been, and still are, characterized by high levels of exploitation. However, even if such exploitative relations did not exist, the less-developed countries would still be at a significant disadvantage vis-à-vis the developed countries. The developed countries retain their advantage because they developed first and because their sheer presence in world markets impedes the operation of less-developed countries. This is so simply because there is only so much world economic demand, and thus room for only so many societies at a high level of commodity production.

SOME TEST CASES

Perhaps the best way to evaluate these propositions is to look at a fair sampling of test cases. Let us first take a general look at the integration of Latin America into the world-system.

Latin America

As we have already seen, that region of the world now known as Latin America was the first non-European region to be incorporated into the emerging capitalist world-economy. It was colonized by Spain and Portugal in the sixteenth century and made into a classical periphery, or one devoted to the production of raw agricultural and mineral products for export. The coercive labor systems known as *encomienda, repartimiento,* and *hacienda* were established (Frank, 1979). By 1830 the colonial system had come to an end and Latin America became formally independent. However, it continued to play a role in the world-economy as a raw materials exporter and consumer goods importer. After about 1880 a process of significant economic expansion began that produced remarkable prosperity for the elite segments of the society. Throughout the nineteenth century Latin America's major trade partner was Britain, the world-system's hegemonic power (Skidmore and Smith, 1989).

In the 1930s Latin America began its first major attempt at industrialization, using the strategy known as ISI, or *import substitution industrialization* (Skidmore and Smith, 1989; Villareal, 1990). This marked an attempt to achieve greater economic autonomy by establishing high tariffs on foreign goods coming into the country and building up and protecting domestic industry. The ISI strategy was effective in producing a significant degree of industrialization, but by the 1960s it had petered out, as ISI has seemed to do wherever it has been tried. Its limitations are reasonably well known (Landsberg, 1979; Blomstrom and Hettne, 1984; So, 1990; Haggard, 1990). Because of their limited capital, domestic firms must rely on developed countries for loans. They must also import technology and capital goods (such as machine tools), and thus they end up investing many of their profits in the developed countries. This leads to growing balance of payments problems. In addition, because of the highly underdeveloped nature of the economy, underdeveloped countries have very limited markets for consumer goods. Only a relatively small segment of the population can afford to purchase these things. Finally, because ISI is capital-intensive rather than labor-intensive it has a very limited capacity to create jobs.

In the 1960s many Latin American countries turned toward the development strategy known as ELI, or *export-led industrialization* (Skidmore and Smith, 1989). This strategy involves producing goods for the world market rather than the domestic market. For this strategy to be workable, it is essential that labor costs be held down to keep the price of manufactured goods low so as to allow them to be competitive in the world market. It is also essential that any country using this strategy have access to foreign markets. In Latin America the period of ELI was closely associated with the rise of governments that have been called "bureaucratic–authoritarian" states (O'Donnell, 1973). These military-led states crushed the working classes and drove wages down and, in general, engaged in a severe repression of the population. Since Latin American ELI was outward-looking rather than inward-looking, close associations were formed with foreign multinationals, and extensive foreign investment in Latin America occurred. This strategy did produce results and led to a certain amount of development ("dependent development"), but the results were very short-lived, not lasting beyond the late 1970s. Latin America is today in a period of relative stagnation, although the military dictatorships have given way to civilian governments that are ostensibly more democratic.

The Latin American situation can be nicely illustrated with the case of Brazil (Skidmore and Smith, 1989; Evans, 1979). In colonial times, Brazil produced sugar cane for export using slave labor on

large-scale plantations ("factories in the fields," as they have sometimes been called). In the immediate postindependence era
(1821–30) sugar comprised 30 percent of exports but declined
throughout the nineteenth century and only constituted 5 percent
of exports in 1900. Sugar was replaced by coffee, which by the
beginning of the twentieth century accounted for nearly 75 percent
of the total world supply. Coffee has since declined markedly, and
in 1978 accounted for only 18 percent of total world production.

During the era of ISI Brazil's industrial sector underwent extensive expansion. It moved into such heavy industries as steel and
automobiles, and by 1975 industrial production totalled almost 30
percent of GDP. Between 1964 and 1985 Brazil was ruled by a
series of bureaucratic–authoritarian states that were military-led and
embarked on a large-scale ELI development strategy. Economic
growth was impressive, and so much so that the period from the
mid-1960s to the mid-1970s has frequently been referred to as
the "Brazilian miracle." During the period between 1968 and 1974
the rate of economic growth averaged 10 percent per year.

By the late 1970s, however, economic growth had faded, and
stagnation and new economic problems arose. One of these was
inflation, and another was the growth of a massive foreign debt
incurred by borrowing huge sums of money from the leading financial institutions of the developed world (the World Bank and the
International Monetary Fund). In 1986 Brazil's foreign debt was
82.6 billion dollars, the largest in the world.

Brazil has experienced a certain amount of economic development
in the period since the 1930s, and especially since the 1960s, but
this development has clearly been dependent development (Evans,
1979). Brazil is today and has been for some time a semiperipheral
country whose per capita GNP in 1990 was only $2,680, well below
some other semiperipheral countries, and far below the developed
economies of the core, whose per capita GNPs in 1990 averaged
$20,683 (World Bank, 1992). Moreover, the question of who has
benefited from this economic growth is fundamental. Has it been
the large mass of the population, or has only a minority, already
better off before the "Brazilian miracle," benefited? The fact that
income inequality increased sharply in Brazil between 1960 and
1980 suggests that the benefits have been highly disproportionate.
In 1960 the richest tenth of the population received 40 percent of
the national income, whereas the bottom half received only 17

percent, already a severely unequal distribution. But by 1980 this distribution had become much more unequal: the top tenth had increased its share to 51 percent of the national income, while the bottom half's share had fallen to 13 percent (Skidmore and Smith, 1989). Brazil today is in a sense two different societies. There is a modern sector of middle-class and upper-class individuals who live in cities and enjoy comfortable standards of living. But alongside this sector there is also a traditional sector of peasants and poor urban workers who have reaped few of the benefits of Brazilian industrialization.

Asia

Asia presents an apparent paradox for development theory since it contains many very poor countries along with one economic giant and several less-developed countries that have made major developmental strides in recent decades. In Asia we find the world's two biggest countries (demographically speaking), China and India, which are also two of the world's poorest countries (China's per capita GNP in 1990 was $370, India's $350). But we also find the world's fastest-growing country, Japan (with a 1990 per capita GNP of $25,430, third-highest in the world), as well as the so-called east Asian Newly Industrialized Countries, or NICs: South Korea, Taiwan, Hong Kong, and Singapore (with, respectively, 1990 per capita GNPs of $5,400, $7,390, $11,490, and $11,160) (World Bank, 1992; US Bureau of the Census, 1992). Let us look at China and India first.

China was never a formal colony, but it was incorporated into the world-economy as a peripheral region from approximately the late eighteenth or early nineteenth centuries on (Moulder, 1977; So, 1984; Wolf, 1982). During this time the luxury trade between China and Europe, which had gone on for many centuries, was replaced by a trade in staple goods between China and Great Britain. China lost its former economic autonomy as it was sucked into the world capitalist system. Tea was initially the most important staple item traded between China and Britain. By the middle of the nineteenth century, duties on tea imports had become an important source of revenue for the British government. Britain also established a three-way trade relationship between itself and both China and India.

After the middle of the eighteenth century Britain gained control over opium production in India and sold this opium in China after it succeeded in addicting a segment of the Chinese population to the drug. The British also produced raw cotton in India and exported much of this to China.

The incorporation of China also involved using it as a market for the sale of British textiles, and to facilitate this the British needed to deprive the Chinese of a home market for their own textile production. British, rather than Chinese, textiles were the ones that came to be more prominently sold in China. Britain was followed in the late nineteenth century by several other core countries – the United States, Germany, and France in particular – that successfully sought to sell their manufactured goods in China. But the incorporation of China did not involve only trade, for foreign investment was also undertaken. Shipbuilding, especially under the direction of the British, was an especially important form of foreign investment, and by the 1930s over half of the tonnage that was being built in China was the result of the efforts of foreign firms. Railroads and mining were even more important forms of foreign investment. As Frances Moulder (1977:114) notes, "by 1911, 41 percent of the railway mileage in China was owned by foreigners," and "numerous mining concessions were granted from 1896 to 1913 to the British, Germans, Russians, French, Americans, Belgians, and Japanese."

India's incorporation begins around 1750, and it was made a formal colony of Britain about a century later (Frank, 1978; Wolf, 1982; Palat, Barr, Matson, Bahl, and Ahmad, 1986). In general, Britain's control over the Indian economy meant that the latter lost its economic autonomy and its economy began to function according to the rhythms of the capitalist world-economy in general and the British economy in particular. The Indian economy became a peripheral region exporting raw materials and importing foreign goods. Much of Indian agriculture was restructured so as to produce commercial crops: sugar, tobacco, spices, cotton, jute, indigo (Wolf, 1982). We have already spoken of British opium and cotton growing in India and the export of these items to China. One of the most devastating consequences of British control in India involved the destruction of the flourishing Indian textile industry, which was undertaken so Britain could sell its own finished textiles there. The Indian textile industry was ruined, which increased the number of landless laborers (Wolf, 1982). In general, there was significant deindustrialization and deurbanization throughout the subcontinent (Palat et al., 1986). After the middle of the nineteenth century "shipbuilding and railroad construction . . . speeded up the growth of commercial crop production in the countryside, prompting exports of wheat from the Punjab, cotton from Bombay, and jute from Bengal, as well as a shift from the production of food crops to industrial crops such as cotton, peanuts, sugarcane, and tobacco" (Wolf, 1982:251). From the seventh century until around 1750 there was a flourishing south Asian economy that was integrated into an even larger Indian Ocean world-economy stretching all the way from the Red Sea/Persian Gulf region to southeast Asia and eastern China (Chaudhuri, 1985). After India's incorporation into the European world-economy, "the 'reversal' of the political economy of South Asia had become historical reality" (Palat et al., 1986:184).

The current levels of economic development in China and India have no doubt been significantly affected by their historical incorporation into the world-economy since the eighteenth century. However, we should be careful not to overstress this. These were large agrarian empires in which the peasantry was severely oppressed and exploited before European capitalism arrived, and thus poverty and misery were already widespread. Moreover, as suggested in chapter 5, the immense size and scope of these agrarian empires probably inhibited indigenous capitalist development within them, and so, leaving the Europeans quite out of the picture, their developmental prospects were not good. However, it might be argued that China's current developmental prospects are rather favorable. Being such a huge country, China represents a potentially gigantic market for Western capitalist investment. Even if only 20 percent of the society were consuming mass consumer goods on something like a Western scale, that would still mean a market of more than 200 million customers. Indeed, since China reembarked on the capitalist road after the mid-1970s there has been great interest in Western capitalist investment there, and a great deal has already occurred. In today's world-economy, large countries have an advantage over small ones as locations for capitalist investment, and this may well work to China's advantage.

From China and India to Japan is a long developmental road. Japan is the only highly industrialized, highly developed country not only in Asia, but in all of the world outside western Europe, North America, and Australia. I believe it is no mystery why this is the case: Japan escaped incorporation into the European world-economy and subsequent peripheralization. As we have already discussed, Japan began to close itself to the European world (and much of the non-European world as well) in the early seventeenth century with the coming to power of the Tokugawa regime. By 1639 this closure had become almost complete. Japan carried on an extremely limited economic exchange and cultural contact with Europe primarily through the Dutch, a few of whom were permitted to live in Japan isolated from the Japanese. As we saw in chapter 4, it was during the period of isolation, which extended to 1853, that Japan underwent very substantial development away from feudalism toward a capitalist society. When Japan entered the world-economy after 1853 under Western threat, it was able to do so as a semiperipheral rather than peripheral country. And after it entered it rapidly took major steps to ensure that it would operate within the world-economy on its own terms as much as it could. The Meiji Restoration, launched in 1868, was a deliberate attempt by Japan to begin industrialization on its own terms (Yoshihara, 1986). There was foreign investment in Japan after its opening to the West, but this was much more limited than in China and India, and Japan was able to maintain an autonomy that was never possible for the former (Moulder, 1977).

   This brings us, then, to the east Asian NICs, easily the most successful examples ever of the economic development of Third World countries: poor, peripheral countries that in the 1950s began to achieve extraordinary economic growth. These countries have not merely achieved high levels of national income, but have also acquired many of the other features of development: low infant mortality rates and good health care, high longevity, a small percentage of the labor force in agriculture, widespread access to education, and high levels of literacy. Moreover, they now have some of the lowest levels of income inequality found anywhere in the world (Haggard, 1990). The NICs are especially important to us because their success has been widely touted as a refutation of dependency and world-system theories of underdevelopment (Barrett and Whyte, 1982; P. Berger, 1986). But as I shall show, this is not so, and the developmental success of the NICs can in fact be explained only by using the principles of world-system theory. The NICs are a splendid example of Wallerstein's development by invitation (Bienefeld, 1981; Cumings, 1984). I shall concentrate on South Korea and

Taiwan, because Hong Kong and Singapore are really city-states with no significant agricultural sector.[4] South Korea and Taiwan have benefited from the coming together of several circumstances at a particular historical juncture. These circumstances have been both exogenous (characteristic of the world-system at a particular time) and endogenous (characteristic of the societies themselves) in nature (Bienefeld, 1981; Cumings, 1984; Crane, 1982; Koo, 1987; Evans, 1987).

1 Although Taiwan and Korea became colonies of Japan around the turn of the twentieth century, the nature of Japanese colonialism was different from European colonialism. The Japanese built up a tremendous infrastructure of transportation and communication in these colonies, and even developed industry, concentrating on such heavy industries as steel, chemicals, and hydroelectric power. Japan brought the industry to the raw materials, the reverse of the pattern of European colonialism. This provided an important technological and economic base on which to build. As Bruce Cumings (1984) has pointed out, at the end of the Second World War Korea had one of the best industrial infrastructures in all of the Third World.

2 Both South Korea and Taiwan carried out extensive land reforms that have almost never been carried out elsewhere in the Third World. After the Chinese Revolution in the late 1940s the defeated Kuomintang fled to Taiwan (then known as Formosa) and undertook a redistribution of land in a much more egalitarian direction. South Korea undertook a similar land reform in the early 1950s. Actually, there was an even earlier series of land reforms carried out by the Japanese, between 1898 and 1906 in Taiwan, and between 1910 and 1918 in Korea (Cumings, 1984). These reforms were of dramatic significance, for they helped create entrepreneurial farmers with strong economic incentives to increase agricultural output, a basic prerequisite for industrialization.

3 Taiwan and South Korea benefited enormously from the geopolitical world situation of the late 1940s and early 1950s. China had just elected to take the socialist path of development and the United States was extremely fearful that socialism would spread to adjacent Asian regions. To keep South Korea and Taiwan in the capitalist fold, it provided massive aid and loans designed to build up the domestic economies in these countries and prevent a Communist takeover. Cumings (1984:24) describes just how much money was pumped into the two Asian countries: "Since 1945 South Korea has received some $13 billion in American military and economic aid, and Taiwan some $5.6 billion ($600 per capita in the ROK, $425 per capita in Taiwan). To gauge the true dimensions of this munificence comparative figures are helpful. The ROK's total of nearly $6 billion in U.S. economic grants and loans, 1946–78, compares with a total for all of Africa of $6.89 billion and for all of Latin America of $14.8 billion; only India, with a population seventeen times that of South Korea, received more ($9.6 billion). U.S. military deliveries to Taiwan and the ROK in 1955–78 (that is, excluding the Korean War) totaled $9.05 billion. All of Latin America and all of Africa received $3.2 billion; only Iran got more, and

most of that was pumped in after 1972 (the figure is \$10.01 billion)."

4 We also need to understand Taiwan's and South Korea's spectacular development in its historical context. These societies began their development during what was the greatest upswing in the history of the capitalist world-economy. This meant that there was more room available – not exactly at the top, but nearer the top – for those countries with favorable characteristics that could recognize their opportunities. South Korea and Taiwan began their developmental push using an ISI strategy, but by the 1960s they had switched to ELI (Cheng, 1990). Since this was the period of American hegemony, and because of the United States's geopolitical concerns, the US opened its domestic markets to South Korean and Taiwanese products, which was crucial for the sale of their manufactured goods. Had this been a downswing in the world-economy, the United States could have ill afforded to encourage competition from two rising powers.

5 Finally, Taiwan, and South Korea even more, had very strong states that had been built on the Japanese model of a strong state, and these states took an active role in capital investment. The state not only played a major role as an investor, but it also provided the labor discipline and repression of the working class necessary to making the ELI strategy work.

It is widely believed that Taiwan and South Korea provide a model for the development of other Third World countries, but this is very dubious. The development of these countries is a historically unique phenomenon that is unrepeatable in that form. What works at one time in the history of the world-economy often does not work at another time. Because the South Korean and Taiwanese cases result from a unique combination of circumstances, a repetition of their experience is extremely unlikely. Moreover, we have to recognize that Taiwan and South Korea are still a far cry from being members of the capitalist core. They are prosperous semiperipheral countries, but their growth has slowed in recent years and may be running into firm limits (Bello and Rosenfeld, 1993). How much farther they can go is very much an open question. South Korea has also acquired a huge foreign debt as a result of borrowing to finance its development, and this is likely to prove a serious obstacle to further development.

As a final point, it might be worth noting that North Korea has been one of the more successful Third World countries following a socialist path. Although its level of national income is considerably lower than either South Korea's or Taiwan's, it is higher than that of most other Third World socialist countries, and North Korea compares quite favorably with South Korea and Taiwan on the other standard development indicators. This success is likely linked to the heritage of Japanese colonialism. Of course, North Korea has never had the benefit of US aid and loans. Where might it be if that factor had been supplied as well?

Africa

The continent of Africa, especially sub-Saharan Africa, remains the most underdeveloped of the entire underdeveloped world, and there are few bright spots. Following Amin (1972) and Wallerstein (1985), we can distinguish several stages of Africa's involvement with the European world-economy. Africa's first real contact with the world-economy came via the European slave trade, lasting approximately from 1500 to 1860, with the major period of slave trading being the eighteenth century. Was Africa part of the periphery or the external arena during this period? Early on Wallerstein (1974b) suggested that it was only part of the external arena, but in later work (e.g., Wallerstein, 1985) he seems to have changed his mind and come to regard it as part of the periphery, at least by 1750. This is a difficult question. External arenas interact with the world-economy via luxury trade, and slaves are certainly not luxuries. Yet a periphery is a region *within* which the production of raw materials for export is going on. During the era of the slave trade this was not yet happening in Africa. Slaves were being exported for work elsewhere. My conclusion is that Africa at this time was really neither external arena nor periphery, but had some characteristics of each (whoever said Wallerstein's categories were fully adequate to the task of classification).[5]

In any event, by the early nineteenth century the slave trade was winding down (Britain abolished its role in it in 1807) and the real peripheralization of Africa began. Throughout the nineteenth century Africa came to be used, albeit slowly and gradually, as a region producing raw agricultural products for export. The full-scale peripheralization of Africa did not begin until around 1880. At this time we see the "scramble for Africa," as the European powers vied for colonies there. Britain and France were the big colonizers, but Belgium and Portugal played some role. Different styles of colonialism, labor control, and productive organization developed in different regions of Africa (Amin, 1972; Wallerstein,

1985), but all were devoted to the production of cash crops for the world market using cheap labor.

Decolonization began in the 1950s and lasted until 1974, but most of the decolonization took place between 1957 and 1965 (Fieldhouse, 1986). With decolonization, development efforts began in earnest using ISI. Hopes were great at the beginning of the period, but they were soon dashed as ISI produced little in most African countries. In the current world economic downswing that began around 1970 Africa has stagnated perhaps more than any other part of the world, and development prospects look grim. Wallerstein (1985:54) sees continuing underdevelopment and worsening standards of living for most of Africa, saying that there will be "acute suffering for truly peripheral areas, whose nonessential exports will find a very weak world market and whose internal food production may collapse further. They will bear the brunt of death from famine and major transfers of remaining populations from rural areas to bidonvilles. The corresponding political regimes will almost certainly be that of corrupt and repressive pretorians."

Africa is a region that core capital penetrated in the last few centuries, distorting and restructuring it as a result, but that now seems to be in the process of being largely ignored. Most African countries are very small and have few resources to attract significant investment from the core (Wallerstein, 1985; Leys, 1982), and thus little chance at even the kind of dependent development that several Latin American countries have experienced (not to mention the east Asian NICs). These countries have been dominated and exploited and are now being cast aside. A few of the bigger African countries – such as Egypt, Nigeria, Algeria, and Zaire – might have better prospects. Because of their much bigger markets and possession of important raw materials, they could emerge as significant producers of manufactured goods for their domestic markets and possibly for those of neighboring countries (Wallerstein, 1985).

Latin America versus Asia and Africa

As table 6.1 shows, as a region Latin America is significantly more developed than both Asia and Africa. Compared to these other two regions, Latin American countries have higher per capita GNPs, a smaller percentage of the labor force in agriculture, lower infant mortality rates, longer life expectancies at birth, higher levels of adult literacy, and higher levels of educational attainment for their citizens. In terms of a three-way comparison, Latin America is at the highest developmental level, Africa is at the lowest level, and Asia (or at least most of Asia) is in between. What lies behind these developmental differences?

Table 6.1 *Levels of economic development in Latin America, Asia, and Africa, 1990*

Region	GNP	LFA	IMR	LEX	LIT	SCH
Latin America	1,582	29.6	44.9	67.7	85.7	5.4
Africa	695	68.4	103.9	52.5	49.0	1.7
Asia	2,472	41.4	59.8	61.4	67.3	4.1
(excl. NICs)	885	45.3	66.4	59.5	64.6	3.8
(Developed countries)	20,683	5.4	7.5	76.6	98.9	10.9

GNP = Gross National Product per capita in $US; LFA = percentage of the labor force in agriculture (these data are for 1986–9); IMR = infant mortality rate, defined as the number of infants who die in their first year of life per 1,000 babies born; LEX = life expectancy at birth in years; LIT = percentage of the adult population that is literate; SCH = mean years of schooling. *Sources*: World Bank (1992), tables 1, 28; United Nations (1992a: 127–9, 134–5, 158–9, 189, 195)

In a pair of articles, Gerhard Lenski and Patrick Nolan (1984; Nolan and Lenski, 1985) have argued that a society or region's technoeconomic heritage at the time of incorporation (or shortly after incorporation) into the world-system has an important effect on its developmental success. They are able to show that those societies they call "industrializing agrarian societies" are superior on a variety of developmental indices to "industrializing horticultural societies." It turns out that the differences between these two types of societies closely corresponds to the distinction between Latin America and Asia on the one hand and Africa on the other. Most Asian societies had already achieved an agrarian level of technoeconomic development – defined largely in terms of the presence of the plow and traction animals for plowing – at the time of incorporation into the world-system, and the plow was introduced into Latin America shortly after it was colonized by the Iberian powers. Africa at the time of incorporation, on the other hand, consisted mostly of societies at no higher than a horticultural stage of technoeconomic development – the cultivation of gardens using hand tools – and all of sub-Saharan Africa contained economies that were devoted to either horticulture, pastoralism, or hunting and gathering. Lenski and Nolan then go on to compare "new agrarian societies," or those that did not adopt the plow until after incorporation, with "old agrarian societies," or those that had adopted the plow much earlier, and found that the new agrarian societies were developmentally superior. They interpret this difference largely in demographic terms, arguing that the older agrarian societies have lagged behind the newer ones because the former had greater population densities that negatively affected their developmental progress in the modern era. As they say (Nolan and Lenski, 1985:343), "Societies that were slow to make the shift from horticulture to agriculture have brought less of a demographic burden into the industrial era and therefore have been in a better position to take advantage of the new opportunities that industrialization has provided."

Lenski and Nolan are probably right to stress technoeconomic heritage as a factor significantly affecting economic development, and this is undoubtedly a good part of the reason why Africa has lagged so far behind the rest of the Third World. However, the developmental difference between Latin America and Asia is less easily explained in terms of technoeconomic heritage. Lenski and Nolan's distinction between old and new agrarian societies is virtually a distinction between Asia and Latin America. In their sample of 23 old agrarian societies, all but three are in Asia (the others are in north Africa: Morocco, Tunisia, and Egypt), and all but one of their 14 new agrarian societies are in Latin America (the one exception is the Philippines). Lenski and Nolan do not consider the fact that Latin America was incorporated into the world-system far earlier than Asia and Africa; in fact, at the time the Latin American countries were gaining their independence from Spain and Portugal, Asia and Africa (especially Africa) were only just being incorporated and had not yet even become formal colonies. This difference in the timing of incorporation and independence may well be highly significant. Although the gap between the developed and the less-developed countries has continued to widen over the years, as we have seen most Third World societies have experienced some development relative to their own past. It therefore stands to reason that the longer a society has been participating in the world-system the farther along on the developmental path it should be expected to be. The early date of Latin American political independence may be an especially important aspect of this. Neocolonialism notwithstanding, *ceteris paribus* politically independent nations should have better developmental potential than nations still under colonialism.

Scotland

Just as numerous social scientists have argued that the cases of the east Asian NIC's refute dependency and world-system theory, T.C. Smout (1980) has challenged world-system theory with the case of Scotland. Smout claims that in the eighteenth century Scotland was a poor peripheral or semiperipheral country that was highly dependent on England. Following Alan Gilbert (1974), Smout proposes four criteria that define a dependent status: reliance on exporting a limited range of goods, usually agricultural and mineral products, to a richer country from which a country imports finished goods; technological dependence on richer countries; capital dependence on richer countries; and, finally, identification on the part of a country's elite with the cultural elite of a richer country. Smout argues that Scotland was dependent on England in all these ways.

Yet beginning in the late eighteenth century Scotland was nonetheless able to undergo significant economic development. Smout notes that by 1825 Scotland was already an extraordinary economic success story and had significantly closed the gap between England and itself. He further notes that in the late eighteenth century Scotland was a leader in the intellectual movement known as the Enlightenment, the Scottish universities having surpassed Cambridge and Oxford in reputation. Scottish banks came to be used as a model for Swedish economic reformers, and Scottish plows became a model for Finnish farmers. He concludes that "development of the most brilliant kind had taken place, economic, intellectual, cultural, all separate yet each connected" (1980:614). And, of course, it is well recognized today that Scotland hardly belongs to the Third World. Lowland Scotland is about at the same level of economic development as England, and the Scottish highlands, though less developed than the lowlands, hardly merit classification with Third World countries. All this development has occurred under conditions that are, Smout alleges, supposed to constitute severe obstacles to development.

Wallerstein (1980b) has argued in reply that Scotland does not refute dependency and world-system theory but that, on the contrary, Scottish development must actually be explained in terms of those theories. Scotland was an early example of development by invitation. It was not truly dependent as Smout claims it was, but was, rather, a region whose natural resources were not coveted by

England. As a result, its economic elites were not put under the thumb of English elites, and this gave it a certain autonomy of action. This put it in a position to make use of the economic boom of the late eighteenth century to become upwardly mobile within the world-economy. As Wallerstein has put it (1980b:635):

> If you live in an area whose natural resources are not sought after, you may not attract as much the imperialist thrust of other states. You may instead be left relatively alone, keep your social and political structures relatively intact, and thus be able to operate better in the world-economy at a later moment in time. Far from refuting Andre Gunder Frank, this turns out to be a confirmation by Smout of the essence of Frank's hypothesis of the "development of underdevelopment."

The major error made by Smout, as I see it, is that he conflates the notion of peripheral or semiperipheral status with dependency. Wallerstein himself is sometimes guilty of the same logical error. I suggest we use the term periphery (or semiperiphery) to refer to a low level of economic development, reserving the term dependency for a situation in which the economy of a country or region has fallen under the domination and direction of some foreign economy (production of raw materials for export and importation of consumer goods are usually taken as the crucial identifying characteristics of dependency). Thus, although being a periphery and being dependent often correspond, it is possible for a country to be peripheral (or semiperipheral) without necessarily being dependent, and I think that was exactly the situation of Scotland in the mid-eighteenth century. It was poor and economically backward compared to England, but nonetheless its economy had not fallen under the direction of England in any meaningful sense. Indeed, Smout himself seems to recognize the distinction I am drawing, as the following statement reveals (Smout, 1980:625):

> England was not interested in developing Scotland in the way that she could be said to have been interested in developing the West Indies as sugar plantations or Virginia for the production of tobacco.... Consequently, there was no attempt by southern merchants or the London government to mold the Scottish economy in a way that had only the short-term interests of England at heart, which would not necessarily have been in the long-term interests of Scotland. No one in Scotland could have alleged, as Jefferson did of Virginia plantations, that their lands were "a species of property annexed to certain merchant houses in London," or, as modern employees of a multinational in Chile might, that they are the pawns of a boardroom meeting in New York. Scotland was simply not endowed with the kind of natural resources that would have lent themselves to "robber exploitation" from the outside.

The economic relationship between Scotland and England was, in one fundamental respect, very similar to the way in which England's settler colonies related to it, and this type of relationship turns out to be highly significant for economic development.

The "neo-Europes"

Alfred Crosby (1986), speaking of what he calls the "neo-Europes," or the European settler colonies in other parts of the world, has argued that the regions that were selected for settler colonization had to meet several criteria. The most important of these was similarity of land and climate so that the Europeans and their plants and animals could adjust as swiftly and efficiently as possible to life in the colonies. The British settler colonies, of course – the North American colonies, Australia, and New Zealand – clearly met this criterion. And it can hardly escape attention that each and every one of these regions is today among the most highly developed countries of the world. A primary reason for that, as Adam Smith noted over two hundred years ago, and as Andre Gunder Frank (1979) has argued more recently, is that these colonies escaped the fate of becoming true economic dependencies in the world-economy. Because they lacked the climate or the resources critical to being made a dependent region, Britain had little economic interest in them and they were subjected to the fortuitous process of "benign neglect." Adam Smith put it this way in his *Wealth of Nations* (quoted in Crosby, 1986:195): "The colony of a civilized nation which takes possession, either of waste country, or of one so thinly inhabited, that the natives easily give place to the new settlers, advances more rapidly to wealth and greatness than any other human society."

In the American colonies in the New World, those in the south had a climate suitable to growing cash crops for the world market, and they did become truly dependent, being devoted to plantation capitalism using slave labor. However, in the northern colonies, and in those further north that became Canada, the climate was too cold and the resources too few to be worth bothering with, and they were left relatively alone. As Frank (1979:60) has argued, it was the relative *poverty* of the land and climate, as well as of course the non-existence of mines, in the North-east which explains why access to land was less foreclosed than it was in the South and elsewhere. Determinant in differentiating these regions was the possibility of extracting a profit from the land in the South – essentially through production for export – much more than in New England even in the grain regions of the Middle Atlantic States.

Note also that Argentina, one of the most developed countries in Latin America, was different from most other parts of Latin America. It was and still is today the most "Europeanized" country in Latin America. In its early stages it was largely a settler colony of Spain and only little devoted to the types of dependent production that characterized the rest of Latin America (Frank, 1979). And then there is the strange case of South Africa. Classified by most world-system theorists as a semiperipheral country, South Africa is perhaps more aptly described as a core sitting atop a periphery. It slowly emerged as a type of white settler colony after the middle of the seventeenth century when it began to be used as a naval refreshment station by the Dutch on their way to the East Indies (Ehrensaft, 1985). South Africa's industrialization began in the late nineteenth century on the basis of the gold mining industry, and Africans, already conquered and colonized, provided much of the labor in the gold mines. The rigid system of apartheid that emerged from this context (Ndabezitha and Sanderson, 1988) provided the basis for the development of two relatively distinct societies, one white and relatively well off, the other black (or at least nonwhite) and suffering a wretched existence.

In a recent article on Canada's position in the world-economy, Heather-Jo Hammer and John Gartrell (1986) try to explain that nation's economic success despite the large amount of foreign investment from the United States and elsewhere in its economy during the twentieth century. They conclude that Canada, although dependent, has had a different type of dependency that they call "mature dependency." They conceptualize mature dependency as differing from conventional dependency in several ways. A society characterized by mature dependency retains an economy that is functionally complete, and mature dependency does not involve the economic exclusion of the masses. In addition, in mature dependency foreign investment occurs within an economy that has demonstrated a clear capacity for self-sustained capital accumulation. I would suggest that what Hammer and Gartrell are describing is not economic dependency at all, but the absence of dependency. There is nothing about foreign investment *per se* that makes a country dependent. (After all, there is today a great deal of Japanese investment in the United States, but the latter has scarcely become a dependency of the former.) Canada has been able to develop into an advanced industrial nation because it has escaped dependency.

In sum, it is possible for countries and regions to be peripheral in the world-economy – at a low stage of development of the productive forces and the capacity for creating wealth – and yet nondependent. Such countries, as long as various other conditions favorable to development are also present, have been able to become some of the most economically advanced countries in the world.[6]

THE INTERSTATE SYSTEM: THE POLITICAL SIDE OF THE MODERN WORLD-SYSTEM

So far our discussion of the modern world-system has focused entirely on its economic side: the capitalist world-economy. But it also has an important political side that we call the interstate system. This is the now elaborate system of interdependent states that began to evolve at approximately the same time as the capitalist world-economy. Today there are something on the order of 175 states bound together in a worldwide web of interdependence. The critical point to be made about the interstate system is that it has never succumbed to attempts to convert it into an empire under the control of one immensely powerful state. Wallerstein has stressed that the interstate system has been vital to the maintenance of the capitalist world-economy, and that had a world-empire been created capitalism would have collapsed. The reason is that only an interstate system is capable of maintaining the vigorous economic rivalry and competition that is necessary for capitalism. The formation of a world empire would have restored an economic system along the lines of old agrarian empires in which tributary relations of production dominated capitalist relations. Actually, Wallerstein's point was anticipated long ago by Max Weber. Weber argued that it was the "national state which afforded to capitalism its chance for development – and as long as the national state does not give place to a world empire capitalism will also endure" (1981[1927]:337; quoted in Collins, 1980:940).

What exactly is the relationship between the capitalist world-economy and the interstate system? We know that they are seemingly bound inseparably, but do they maintain some degree of autonomy? Weberian-oriented scholars have charged that world-system theorists view the interstate system simply as an epiphenomenal reflection of the world-economy: that states are simply the servants of their capitalist classes and the world-system in which they act (Skocpol, 1977; Modelski, 1978; Zolberg, 1981). This is, of course, the familiar criticism that world-system theory is "class reductionist" and "economistic," and Weberian scholars want to give geopolitics an autonomous role in the modern world. World-system theorists, in reply, have rejected this characterization, claiming that they see the modern world as more or less equally made up of its economic and political dimensions, and that the modern world is, after all, built around the "political economy" of capitalism. Chase-Dunn (1989:134), for example, has said that

Wallerstein's work suggests a reconceptualization of the capitalist mode of production itself such that references to capitalism do not point simply to market-oriented strategies for accumulating surplus value. According to Wallerstein the capitalist mode of production is a system in which groups pursue both political–military goals and profit-making strategies, and the winners are those who effectively combine the two. Thus the interstate system, state-building, and geopolitics are the political side of the capitalist mode of production.

But is the recognition of the crucial importance of politics (including geopolitics) tantamount to acceptance of its autonomy? It would appear not, for Chase-Dunn also declares that geopolitics and capitalism do not constitute two separate logics, but are inextricably bound into a single logic. And what kind of logic is it? The logic of capital accumulation, of course. Chase-Dunn (1989:155) says that "a particular kind of political structure is most suitable for the continued operation of this competitive economic system" and that "the multicentric interstate system is important to the maintenance of a capitalist systemic logic and to the specific institutions which most directly embody this logic: markets for labor, capital, and commodities." This makes it look very much as if world-system theory is, as its critics charge, actually economically reductionist for the most part even if it does take geopolitics into account. However, I do not see this as a flaw but as a virtue. It is my own view that there is indeed a single logic of the modern world-system, and that this logic is precisely that of capital accumulation. This is what drives the system and accounts for its expansionary and evolutionary trends. Geopolitics enters into the matter, of course, and is not simply reducible to the economics of core–periphery–semiperiphery relations[7]. But geopolitics most of the time plays the secondary role and hardly has the kind of autonomy that the Weberians see it having.

Two questions remain to be answered. First, why does the inter-state system persist in spite of the occasional efforts to turn it into a world empire? Second, how do states relate to the core–periph-ery–semiperiphery hierarchy of the world-economy? How and why are core, semiperipheral, and peripheral states different?

Why do efforts at imperium fail? Before answering this question it should be pointed out that there is really a logically prior question: Why have there been so few efforts made by any given state to establish imperial control over the entire system? The answer seems to be that most states recognize that the maintenance of an open world-economy and an interstate system will best promote their economic interests, or at least the economic interests of their leading capitalists (which amounts to more or less the same thing). Because capitalists may have investments in many states, they are reluctant to support efforts on the part of their own national state to bring other states within an imperial orbit (Chase-Dunn, 1989). There have, though, been three major attempts at imperium within the modern world-system: by the Hapsburgs in the sixteenth and seventeenth centuries, by Napoleonic France in the early nineteenth century, and by Germany in the twentieth century. The reason all of these attempts failed is basically the same as the reason why so few attempts at imperium have been made: it is in the economic interests of most core capitalists and their states to maintain an open world-economy. Therefore, when any country attempts imperium many of the others will form a coalition against it in order to defeat it. To this point, these coalitions have always been successful.

Finally, how does the logic of the core–periphery–semiperiphery hierarchy get translated into the structure of the state? One way is in terms of the relative strength of the state. As Wallerstein has stressed, in the core states tend to be strong whereas in the periph-ery and semiperiphery they are usually weaker. This has been a controversial argument that has been strongly challenged (e.g., by Skocpol, 1977), but when the criteria for state strength are properly recognized then I think it holds up fairly well (cf. Chase-Dunn, 1989). Critics have often taken the major historical form of the strong state to be the absolutist state, but Wallerstein has suggested that this can be very misleading. Absolutist states are not necessarily particularly strong, and more decentralized states, such as the Dutch Republic of the seventeenth century, can be very strong. Wallerstein (1980a:113) has suggested five criteria for the identification of a strong state:

1   the extent to which state policy facilitates the competitiveness of capitalists in the world market;
2   the extent to which a state can weaken, by military power, the capacity of other states to compete in the world market;
3   the extent to which a state can use sound public finance to perform the above two tasks at an efficient level of cost;
4   the extent to which a state can create an administrative bureaucracy that will allow tactical decisions to be carried out rapidly;
5   the extent to which a state's political rules reflect a balance of interests among different capitalist class fractions so that the capitalist class–state relationship allows for the formation of an effective "hegemonic bloc."

I would argue that if states are evaluated in these terms then it will be shown that core states are generally strong and peripheral and semiperipheral states much weaker. Indeed, strong states have generally been essential to the achievement and maintenance of core status in the past, and peripheral and semiperipheral societies that are able to enhance the strength of their state apparatuses may be successful in their attempts at upward mobility.

In addition to the relative strength of the state there is its level of democratization. The pattern is one in which democracy has become universal in the core but much less frequently found in the periphery and semiperiphery. The primary reason why democracy has become universal in the core has to do both with capitalists' desire for a parliamentary system of government and the fact that industrial capitalism transforms the class structure in the direction of greatly enlarging the size and organizational potential of the working class. (This is a subject that will be discussed in considerably more detail in chapter 7.) Peripheral and semiperipheral states are commonly highly repressive in one way or another, and even the formal democracy that prevails in many – such as in contemporary Latin America – contains little real, substantive democracy. The relative absence of genuine substantive democracy outside the core to a large extent involves the small size and limited political power of the working classes of peripheral and semiperipheral societies. Peasants may greatly outnumber industrial workers, and the political ineffectiveness of peasants throughout history is well known. Moreover, the highly repressive nature of the peripheral or semiperipheral state also derives from the extreme economic inequalities and resultant tension and unrest that plague such societies. High levels of state repression are often necessary, from the standpoint of economic and political elites, to maintain simple law and order and keep subordinate groups in line. World-system theorists also suggest a third reason why some peripheral or semiperipheral states may be so repressive. Strong states that repress the masses may be very useful strategically in societies whose elites are striving to become upwardly mobile within the world-system. For example, as seen earlier many have argued that a key to South Korea's recent economic development has been its very strong state apparatus that repressed the working class so as to keep wages down and make the country highly competitive in the world-economy, and a similar strategy seemed to be followed in Brazil in the 1960s and 1970s.

NOTES

1 What I have been describing to this point are essentially the basic principles of world-system theory as formulated by its principal architects, Immanuel Wallerstein and Christopher Chase-Dunn. As everyone knows, this perspective has remained deeply controversial. It has attracted strong adherents from far and wide, but its detractors are numerous and often strident. Many criticisms have been made. Some of these are relatively easy to answer, but others are more troubling. Below is a list of some of the major criticisms and my response to each. My grand conclusion is that world-system theory is a flawed but nonetheless critically necessary perspective if we are to have any hope of understanding the modern world. We must recognize that it is an abstract theoretical model that is only an approximate fit to reality, as all abstract models in any science (natural or social) necessarily are. The question is not whether the model fits reality imperfectly, for obviously it does. The question is whether we are better off with this model than with other models or with no model at all. My answer is that we are decidedly better off with this particular model.

(a) *Economic reductionism*: This has been perhaps the most persistent and most stressed criticism, made by numerous critics but especially by Skocpol (1977) and Zolberg (1981). The argument, of course, is that world-system theory does not give politics an autonomous role in the development of the modern world, a role that it clearly deserves. States are reduced to their economic functions. Such an argument is frequently made by political scientists, or by sociologists of Weberian orientation who emphasize the importance of state power and military might in their own terms. Some world-system thinkers have tried to respond to this criticism by playing down the alleged economic reductionism of world-system theory, but I myself would not choose this route. As I see it, world-system theory *is* economically reductionist; however, I regard that not as something to bemoan, but rather as something to defend. The modern world is first and foremost a capitalist world and, although states cannot be fully reduced to their economic functions, these functions overshadow any others. The nature of the capitalist world-economy cannot explain everything, but it can explain far more than its next closest competitor.

A particularly important version of the economic reductionism criticism, made in particular by Skocpol (1977), is that there is no especially close association between core position in the world-economy and the possession of a strong state. It is argued, for example, that early modern Sweden was peripheral in the world-economy but had a strong state, or that the United Provinces were in the capitalist core (indeed, were hegemonic) in the seventeenth century but had a relatively weak state. Chase-Dunn (1989), however, shows that core societies generally *do* have strong states. The problem here seems to be largely a matter of how the notion of strong state is operationalized. Strong states can be decentralized and on the surface look weak, whereas absolutist states may be much weaker than surface appearance suggests. Later I will suggest several criteria whereby strong states can be identified.

(b) *Historical accuracy*: Historians have often been put off by world-system theory, claiming that it commits many errors with respect to historical accuracy. It has been claimed that Wallerstein has been willing to perpetrate many historical errors in order to keep his model afloat. In response, it must be said that historians in general do not like any type of abstract model, and so it is hardly surprising that many of them object to the world-system approach (quite a few do favor it, however). Nomothetic sociologists are not obliged to accept this idiographic logic, however, and it can be argued that so long as any model does not violate reality too severely it can fruitfully be used. I believe the world-system model passes this test. In a sense the point is the same one that was made with respect to the previous criticism: the model is certainly imperfect, but are we better off with it than we are without it?

(c) *Excessive holism*: It is sometimes charged that the world-system perspective exaggerates the extent to which characteristics of the world-system itself, and thus factors that are external to individual societies, shape the development of these societies. Although world-system theorists have usually argued that they recognize the importance of endogenous factors in social evolution, this criticism is perhaps justified. In principle world-system theorists generally do recognize endogenous factors, but in practice they often lose sight of them. The solution is to give explicit attention to both exogenous and endogenous factors and make it an empirical question as to which is dominant in any particular situation (or whether both are equally significant).

(d) *Difficulty corroborating the notion of unequal exchange*: Several critics have charged that the concept of unequal exchange between core and periphery, which is usually thought to be a vital element of world-system theory, has never been empirically demonstrated. To some extent this is a damaging criticism, but it should not be taken too far. It is often the case in the history of the sciences that empirical demonstration of just how a postulated mechanism works is only slowly forthcoming. Moreover, the concept of unequal exchange may not be all that vital. Perhaps all that need be shown is that core–periphery hierarchies do exist and have a remarkable persistence over time (this has definitely been demonstrated), and that those nation-states that have particular advantages allowing them to achieve a core position early on will be able to perpetuate and even extend their prominent position. This point will be pursued later in the chapter in a discussion of unequal levels of economic development within the world-system.

(e) *Necessity of the periphery for core development*: Early versions of dependency theory (from which world-system theory evolved), and perhaps even world-system theory itself, have suggested, either explicitly or implicitly, that the periphery has been necessary for the economic development of the core. This argument is probably wrong. However, an easy solution is to drop back to a milder version of it: that peripheral development has been *useful* to the core in a variety of ways. Chase-Dunn (1989), for example, suggests that the existence of a highly exploitable periphery has allowed core capitalists to maintain labor peace by offering workers higher wages.

(f) *Ambiguity of the concept of semiperiphery*: Numerous scholars have suggested that the concept of semiperiphery is poorly formulated and altogether lacking in precision, a criticism with which I have no difficulty agreeing (see in particular Arrighi and Drangel, 1986). First, there is Wallerstein's notion that the semiperiphery mediates the relationship between core and periphery. I have difficulty visualizing this and understanding how it is supposed to happen. There is the additional problem of the rather "grabbag" or "dumping bin" nature of the semiperiphery concept. It appears that societies are placed in the semiperiphery when they do not fit well within either core or periphery. This leads to a situation in which many highly diverse societies are treated as semiperipheral. Thus we have sixteenth-century Italy, the nineteenth-century United States, and Russia, South Africa, and Brazil in the twentieth century all being classified as semiperipheral societies. What seems to be needed is a more precise formulation in which the semiperiphery is subdivided into two or more categories. However, refined conceptual development has been lacking, and at this point this seems to be a difficulty with which we will simply have to live for a while longer.

(g) *Immiseration of the periphery*: Wallerstein has emphatically stated that the periphery has experienced an absolute decline in its standard of living over time. This argument has appeared questionable to many critics, who claim that economic development has in fact occurred within the periphery and semiperiphery. This argument appears valid. However, it is still possible to claim that immiseration is occurring in the periphery *in relative terms*, that is, that although the periphery is better off relative to its own past it is in fact worse off with respect to the level of development of the core. This argument, the relative immiseration argument, is plausible and can be defended, as we will see in chapter 8.

(h) *Teleological reasoning*: It is often claimed that Wallerstein perpetuates a kind of functionalist reasoning in that he frequently talks about those things that are necessary for the world-system to survive. This criticism has a certain amount of validity, and it is to be regretted that Wallerstein (and Chase-Dunn as well to some extent) often lapses into this kind of thinking. However, I see no reason why world-system theory cannot be purged of this flaw and hold up well. We could even argue that the teleological reasoning is mainly a form of talk that is not essential to the perspective. At least that is my argument.

(i) *Circulationism*: Finally, there is the famous charge, made first by Robert Brenner (1977) and repeated many times since, that world-system theory rests upon a "circulationist" rather than "productionist" conception of capitalism. The argument is that Wallerstein's world-system takes into account only relations of economic exchange (via trade) and ignores production (and thus class) relations. This is, quite frankly, a silly and quite false charge (Blomstrom and Hettne, 1984; Chase-Dunn, 1989). As Chase-Dunn (1989:5) has said, "Contrary to the popular misconception that world-system theory emphasizes exchange relations over production relations, capitalism is defined as a system in which commodity production for profit occurs in the context of differentiated forms of labor control." Indeed, in the world-system perspective capitalism is a vast system of hierarchically organized production. Core states do not merely exchange products with the periphery, but play a crucial role in establishing various forms of production there.

2 The state in question should really be called the United Provinces or the Dutch Republic. It was a loose confederation of seven provinces – Holland, Zeeland, Friesland, Groningen, Overijssel, Utrecht, and Gelderland – of which Holland was the most economically central and politically powerful. Henceforth I shall use the terms Holland, United Provinces, and Dutch Republic synonymously.

3 In several articles he wrote in the 1850s for the *New York Daily Tribune* (Marx and Engels, 1959[1850–94]), Marx argued that the ultimate effects of British rule in India would be to lead India along the developmental path already traveled by Britain. He commented specifically that the railways would be the basis for the industrialization of India. However, when he looked at the effects of British imperialism in Ireland, he came to a conclusion much more like that of contemporary dependency or world-system theory (Marx and Engels, 1959[1850–94]). Jorge Larrain (1989) suggests that Marx was not being inconsistent or contradictory, but that he actually changed his view over time. This exegetical issue cannot be settled here, but suffice it to say that there is sufficient warrant for Szymanski's and Warren's use of Marx.

4 It seems fairly clear that Hong Kong's and Singapore's recent development is closely linked to their unique roles as financial centers and entrepots in the world-economy in general and the east Asian economy in particular. To a considerable degree, these roles stem from their geographical location. The fact that they have never had to worry about the agricultural sector and problems of agrarian reform is also important (Haggard, 1990).

5 The question as to why Africa was chosen as the source of labor for the slave plantations of the New World is an interesting one. Wallerstein (1974b) argues, and I agree, that slave labor needed to be drawn from a region of the world that was not being used by Europe for indigenous production, but that was still close enough to keep the costs of acquiring and transporting slaves down. Africa, he says, fit the bill best. Race had nothing to do with it. Why not Chinese or Indians? Because the cost of exporting them was too great.

6 There are other examples of peripheral but nondependent countries besides the

European settler colonies. Sweden, for example, is described by Wallerstein (1980a) as peripheral in the sixteenth century, but it is of course a highly developed country today. It was peripheral but not dependent.

7 For example, who in their right mind would try to interpret the political conflicts of the contemporary Middle East in terms of the simple logic of capital accumulation and core–periphery–semiperiphery relations? There are a lot of other instances, too, in which geopolitics looms large. But if we add all these instances together we still have a total effect on world social evolution that is considerably less than that produced by the logic of capital accumulation. Most world social evolution today is, and for the past 500 years has been, driven by the logic of capitalist economic relations, and most geopolitics has been adapted to that logic. The later in history we look, the more accurate this statement turns out to be.

7

The Evolution of the Modern World, II: The Emergence of the Institutions of Modernity

The story of the evolution of the modern world is just as much the story of the development of the primary institutions of modernity as it is the story of the expanding and evolving modern world-system. To tell the story of the rise of the institutions of modernity shall be my task in this chapter. I shall divide the chapter into seven sections dealing with five institutional sectors, and will discuss the creation of industrial economies, the rise and ultimate collapse of state socialist economies, the evolution of the modern industrial class structure and patterns of mobility, the development of the modern state, the creation of systems of mass education, the rise of modern science, and the argument that Western society is currently in the process of moving into a postindustrial phase of social evolution.

INDUSTRIALIZATION IN THE WEST AND JAPAN

The Industrial Revolution

The Industrial Revolution has been treated by most sociologists as the "great divide" between the premodern world and the world of modernity. I believe this to be a mistaken claim and would give the role of "great divider" to the capitalist revolution of the sixteenth century. It was capitalism, not industrialism, that really introduced the modern world and, indeed, it was capitalism that made industrialism possible. Nevertheless, the Industrial Revolution was a dramatic event and did bring about radical changes in economic life and social organization, and is therefore deserving of considerable attention in any discussion of the rise of modernity.

What was the Industrial Revolution? Peter Stearns (1993:11) says that an industrial revolution is "a massive set of changes that begin when radical innovations in technologies and organizational forms are extensively introduced in key manufacturing sectors and that end, in the truly revolutionary phase, when these innovations are widely, though not necessarily universally, established in the economy at large." Stearns's definition is obviously meant to apply not only to the original Industrial Revolution in Britain, but to any subsequent industrial revolution elsewhere. David Landes (1969), speaking specifically of Great Britain, says that the Industrial Revolution involved a series of innovations that transformed manufacturing and gave rise to the factory system. These innovations, he tells us (1969:41), were threefold, involving

the substitution of machines – rapid, regular, precise, tireless – for human skill and effort; the substitution of inanimate for animate sources of power, in particular the introduction of engines for converting heat into work, thereby opening to man a new and almost unlimited supply of energy; [and] the use of new and far more abundant raw materials, in particular, the substitution of mineral for vegetable or animal substances.

The Industrial Revolution was, in short, both a revolution in technology and one involving the organization of the economy. It introduced the factory system and brought about enormous increases in the productivity of labor. Sidney Pollard (1981) notes, for example, that in Britain the productivity of spinning rose approximately 150-fold by 1800 and approximately 300-fold by 1825. It was a revolution within capitalism.

As everyone knows, the Industrial Revolution was originally centered in Britain, being dated usually from about 1760. The most important technical innovations introduced were the spinning jenny, the waterframe, and Crompton's mule – all these relating to the textile industry, of course – and, most importantly, James Watts's steam engine, which had wide application. The most important industries were textile manufacturing (especially cotton), metallurgy and chemicals, machine building, and coal mining (Landes, 1969). All of these technical inventions, combined with the emergence of the factory system, gave Britain a huge advantage as the world's leading producer of manufactured goods, which it exported throughout the world.

Industrial revolutions also occurred in the early to mid-nineteenth century in parts of continental Europe – most particularly in France, Belgium, and Germany – as well as in the United States. Although the French cotton industry lagged well behind the British – the French industry had smaller plants, older and less efficient machines, and lower labor productivity – it was still the continental leader in the production of cotton goods (Landes, 1969). The Industrial Revolution in France was heavily concentrated in the northeast, and industrialization spilled over from this region into adjacent parts of Belgium. As Pollard (1981) has pointed out, the Belgian industrializing zone contained all of the major industries that we associate with the Industrial Revolution – cotton and wool manufacturing, coal mining, and iron production – as well as such others as glass making and chemicals. In Germany, early industrialization was centered in Saxony, although the great center of industrialization in Germany was the Ruhr region. Although it developed late, when it started to industrialize "its development came with a rush. Within half a century it had become the most important industrial region on the Continent" (Pollard, 1981:99). In the United States industrialization began around 1820, or perhaps slightly later. It was centered in the northeast and driven largely by textile manufacture (Stearns, 1993).

There were several important differences between Great Britain and the earliest continental industrializers in their patterns of industrialization. These largely involved the industries that were given prominence. In Britain, textile manufacturing drove the industrialization process, whereas on the continent this industry was less important and heavy industry – mining and metallurgy, and then later railroads – was the focus of industrialization (Landes, 1969). And, of course, continental industrialization lagged behind British in several important respects, as David Landes (1969:187–8) explains:

At mid-century . . . continental Europe was still about a generation behind Britain in industrial development. The relative disparity showed clearly in the population figures. Where in 1851 about half of the people of England and Wales lived in towns, in France and Germany the proportion was about a quarter; not until the last years of the century did urban population pass rural in Germany, and in France the even point did not come until after the First World War. The occupational distribution tells the same story. At mid-century, only a quarter of the British male working force (twenty years and older) was engaged in agriculture. For Belgium, the most industrialized nation on the Continent, the figure was about 50 per cent. Germany took another twenty-five years to reach this point; indeed as late as 1895, there were more people engaged in agriculture than in industry. And in France industry was outnumbered until the Second World War and the economic recovery that followed.

By the same token, the continental proletariat was very different from the British. The concentration of large numbers of workers in huge factories was only just beginning, and then more in heavy industry than in textiles. There was nothing yet like the new slums of Manchester and Leeds, filled with pallid mill hands crowding into a smokestack jungle. Continental slums were different. They were usually the run-down older quarters, comparable to the wynds of Edinburgh, and were inhabited primarily by artisans and domestic workers – handloom weavers in the damp cellars of Lille or the tenements of Liege; woodworkers in the Faubourg Saint-Antoine. Here and there were new mill towns on the British pattern; but Roubaix, Mulhouse, and the cities of the Wuppertal were so much smaller than their counterparts in Lancashire and the West Riding that they were really a different species.

Industrialization came even later to other parts of Europe. It began toward the end of the nineteenth century (or even later) in the Netherlands, Czechoslovakia, Austria, the Scandinavian countries, and Italy, and Russia. In Iberia and eastern Europe, especially the Balkans, industrialization came latest of all. On the eve of the First World War there was still very little industrial development in these regions.

In Japan industrialization began around 1880 and was heavily orchestrated by the Meiji government that had taken power in 1868. The government promoted industrialization in several ways (Moulder, 1977): it established and administered pilot projects; it subsidized industries, especially heavy industry, railway construction, shipping, and mining; and it helped create a system of national banks that would provide low-interest, long-term loans to investors. It also established a number of model factories devoted to the production of textiles, glass, cement, and machine tools (Stearns, 1993). Peter Stearns (1993) reports that considerable industrialization was occurring by the 1890s, and that another major industrial spurt occurred between 1905 and 1918.

Some years ago Alexander Gerschenkron (1962) put forth the thesis that the patterns of industrialization for early and later industrializers differed in several significant respects, the most important of which were the type of industry (light versus heavy) and the source of capital investment (private entrepreneurs versus the state).

Early industrializers, he argued, relied extensively on private capital and concentrated on the production of light to medium manufactured goods. Later industrializers, by contrast, focused more on heavy industry and the state played a major role as a source of investment capital and as an orchestrator of development. Gerschenkron's thesis seems to fit the facts reasonably well. The classic early industrializer, of course, was Britain, which industrialized primarily via private capital and concentrated on textile manufacturing. The United States, Belgium, and France fit this pattern reasonably well too, although the last two concentrated more than Britain did on heavy industry. Germany comes closer to the pattern of the later industrializers, and Russia and Japan, which were truly late industrializers, were indeed countries that concentrated on heavy industry and in which the state played a major role. The modes of industrialization adopted by later industrializers seem to be rooted in the fact that they are in the process of "catching up" with earlier industrializers. Private capital is often in short supply, and thus the state must play a role as a major investor. Heavy industry is preferred to light or medium industry because of its greater scale and thus its impact on technological and economic growth.

So far we have been discussing the Industrial Revolution as if it were a historical "event" in the sense that political revolutions or wars are events. But this is misleading. It is better to speak not so much of an Industrial Revolution, but of a *process of industrialization* that began at a certain point and that has continued right up to the present (Lenski, 1970). Industrialization is a process of mechanization within capitalism that has been a constant feature of the evolution of capitalism. Indeed, it has not only been a constant process, but actually an accelerating one. The pace of industrialization has advanced over time. Five major stages of industrialization can be distinguished (Chirot, 1991):

1   textile manufacturing, which was dominated by Britain and ran from 1760 to about 1830;
2   railroads and iron, which was also dominated by Britain, but the United States and several European countries were also prominent; it can be dated from 1830 to about 1870;
3   steel and organic chemistry, a stage which also saw the emergence of new industries based on producing and using electrical machinery; it is dated from 1870 to World War I and was dominated by the United States and Germany;

4 automobiles and petrochemicals, which ran from World War I to about 1970 and was dominated by the United States; and
5 electronics, information, and biotechnology, which began in the early 1970s and will continue into the early part of the next century; it is still dominated by the United States, but with increasing encroachment on that dominance by Japan and western Europe.

Protoindustrialization and the Industrial Revolution

The analysis presented above conforms closely to what might be called the "conventional interpretation" of the Industrial Revolution: the Industrial Revolution was a dramatic technological upheaval that began in Britain in the 1760s, spread from there to continental Europe, the United States, and Japan in the nineteenth century, and radically transformed the nature of social and economic life. This interpretation is not especially wrong, but it can be misleading in some very important respects. Immanuel Wallerstein (1989) has challenged the very concept of the Industrial Revolution in three major ways. First, he suggests that British dominance has been exaggerated, and that France was not all that far behind. Second, he notes that much recent evidence has accumulated to show that there was a great deal of industry in Europe well before the Industrial Revolution proper. Significant industrialization in parts of Europe was occurring as early as the sixteenth century. The process of industrialization was not so much one that began in a revolutionary way in 1760, but rather one that was much slower and more gradual and was drawn out over a longer period of time. Finally, Wallerstein suggests that the emphasis on Britain "being first" puts all the emphasis on industrialization as a process of development that occurs within nation-states, when in fact it is a process that occurs within the world-economy as a whole. Wallerstein ends up concluding that there really was no industrial revolution, at least not in the sense in which it has been conventionally understood.

Wallerstein's argument has considerable force, I believe, but I am not quite prepared to accept all of it. I agree that it is the world-economy as a whole that develops or evolves, and thus that industrializes, and that we should therefore be careful not to put too much emphasis on "who was first." Industrialization occurs unevenly within the world-economy: the core industrializes earliest and fastest, the periphery latest and slowest, and the semiperiphery, as usual, is in between. However, as Wallerstein well knows, industrialization, like core status itself, is still made possible because of the existence of certain kinds of states, and therefore it does make sense to talk in terms of states. Where this kind of talk becomes dangerously misleading is when we say that industrialization occurred in one place and then "spread" from there to another. This makes it appear as if the Industrial Revolution occurred just once and then was diffused to other states, which were mere imitators that otherwise would not have been able to industrialize. (This is analogous to the specious old argument, reviewed in chapter 2, that agriculture was "invented" once and then diffused to other regions that had known nothing of it.)

I also think that Wallerstein underrates the degree to which the technological and economic changes that occurred after 1760 were dramatic in both scale and social and economic impact. It is quite true that a good deal of industrialization had already occurred throughout Europe by 1760, about which I shall say more in a moment. However, it is also true that after 1760 technology evolved, the factory system expanded, and the productivity of labor increased on a scale and with a rapidity never before seen in the history of capitalism. The Industrial Revolution was not a revolution in the sense that it was something that emerged out of the blue in societies that had previously known only agriculture. But it was a revolution in the sense that some rather dramatic technological and economic changes occurred within a short period of time. And, as every sociologist knows, these changes produced dramatic changes in the organization of social life. The word "revolution" in Industrial Revolution can be misleading, but it is not wholly inappropriate.

The part of Wallerstein's argument that I think is most significant is his emphasis on the early industrialization that had already occurred in Europe well before 1760. Indeed, a number of recent historians have over the past two decades studied this earlier industrialization process with care. The process even has its own name, over twenty years ago being dubbed "protoindustrialization" by the economic historian Franklin Mendels (1972). Protoindustry was largely rural and was organized mainly in terms of the putting-out system, or what German historians have called the *Verlagssystem* (Braudel, 1982). Rural producers, many of whom were peasant farmers, remained in their homes and were advanced raw materials and part-wages by the merchants who organized the process. Factories were not unknown during this time, but they were few and far between and contributed far less to industrial production than the putting-out system.

Charles Tilly (1983) provides considerable evidence that protoindustrialization was a very significant process before the Industrial Revolution. He notes, for example, that as early as 1502 in the Dutch region of Twente some 25 percent of the population was working outside of agriculture, a figure that had climbed to 48 percent by 1795, well before the Dutch Industrial Revolution. In the Kingdom of Saxony in 1750 nearly half of the population consisted of gardeners and cottars, who constituted the majority of the textile workers in the region. In Basel in 1774 the rural labor force was constituted as follows: 18 percent peasants, 27 percent petty tradesmen, 29 percent handicraft workers, and 26 percent shop workers. In Bavaria, in a cluster of villages around Dachau, as early as 1675 22 percent of the labor force consisted of peasants, 36 percent of dependent workers, 10 percent of independent day-laborers, and 32 percent of nonagricultural tradesmen and craftsmen. Tilly (1983:128) concludes that "a generation's research has made it clear that important parts of the eighteenth-century European countryside teemed with non-peasants and hummed with manufacturing."

Fernand Braudel (1982) also provides much evidence of protoindustrialization and shows that protoindustry could include some very large enterprises. He says, "By the eighteenth century, industrial activity was widespread, virtually ubiquitous, and trading links had proliferated. There was not a town or city, no market town in particular, no village even, without its own looms, forges, brick or tile works, or sawmill" (1982:309). He notes that the coal industry in Newcastle employed 30,000 workers, that in 1680 the Languedoc region of France contained 450,000 weavers, and that in 1795 fully 1,500,000 textile workers were employed in the provinces of Flanders, Artois, Hainaut, Picardy, and Cambrésis. "Industry and trade," he says, "were reaching truly colossal proportions" (1982:309). Looking at specific firms rather than entire industries, Sidney Pollard is also able to show how far rural industry had developed (1981:77–8):

At its peak, rural industry included some enormous enterprises. The Abbeville firm of van Robais employed 1,800 in central workshops, 10,000 in their homes, and in 1780 Puech of Carcassone and Montel of Bédarieux, some 1,000–5,000 each. In Silesia,

Heymann of Breslau employed 71 in, 1,400 out in cottons, Sadebeck, a Reichenau employer, 6,000 spinners, 1,200 winders and shearers, 2,400 weavers. Wegely, in Berlin, in 1782 had 3,466 workers, Lange 3,534, and the royal Lagerhaus some 5,000. Von Leyen's Krefeld silk enterprise had 3,000 workers in 1768. Scheibler in Monschau (Montjoie) 4,000 in 1760, and Schüler, the leading calico-printer in Augsburg 3,500 at about the same time. The famous Calw woollen-mills employed in 1787, 168 in, 933 weavers and 3–4,000 spinners out. In Bohemia . . . J.J. Leitenberger employed 5,000 in 1791 and J.M. Schmidt about 1,700 in 1775 and over 7,500 in 1838, of whom 7,000 were outworkers. The largest Austrian cotton firm, at Schwechat near Vienna, employed 23,549 spinners, and a total of 25,181 in 1785, and there were others nearby employing 13,711, 12,613, and 7,913 spinners, respectively. Probably the largest single firm of all was the Linz woollen manufactory, acquired by the Austrian state in 1754. In 1786, at its peak, it employed 34,935 workers, of whom 29,338 were domestic spinners. Of the latter, 16,820 lived in Bohemia, requiring an elaborate transport system to supply them. Even in Russia, a firm like Garélin employed 120 calico-printing tables, 900 looms, and 1,400 workers.

Evidence has also begun to accumulate to suggest that protoindustrialization was an important process in Japan in the centuries before it began to industrialize. Thomas Smith (1988) has studied what he calls "farm family by-employments" in Kaminoseki County, Japan, in the first half of the nineteenth century. These were forms of nonagricultural work – most commonly some type of craft work or manufacturing – engaged in by farm families as a means of supplementing their farm incomes. Although 82 percent of the families in the county were agricultural, 55 percent of total family income came from nonagricultural pursuits. Smith (1988:92) also notes that by-employments were common in many other parts of Japan as well: "Scattered around the country were hundreds of rural merchants – employers of part-time labor – whose operations rivaled all but the largest merchants in Edo and Osaka." David Howell (1992) provides additional confirmation of the significance of Japanese protoindustry. He points to the importance of protoindustry in such areas as textile manufacturing, papermaking, sake brewing, iron working, and the processing of agricultural and marine products. "Rural industry," Howell says, "was an important and widespread phenomenon in nineteenth-century Japan" (1992:276).

A number of authors have made the claim that protoindustrialization prepared the way for the industrialization of the late eighteenth and nineteenth centuries (Mendels, 1972; Pollard, 1981; Kriedte, Medick, and Schlumbohm, 1981). Peter Kriedte, Hans Medick, and Jürgen Schlumbohm (1981) have suggested five ways in which protoindustrialization contributed to later industrialization:

1 Protoindustrialization created a broad group of skilled handicraft workers that came to comprise a labor force that could be drawn on to supply the labor for the early factories.
2 Protoindustrialization led to the emergence of merchant-manufacturers, middlemen, and artisans who became some of the agents of industrialization.
3 The putting-out system brought merchant capital into contact with the sphere of production; it was, of course, the entry of merchants into the production process (rather than their remaining in the sphere of exchange) that provided the basis for the industrial capitalist mode of production.
4 Protoindustrialization led to the development of a symbiotic relationship between agrarian regions and densely populated industrial regions, a development that made it possible to supply the industrial sector with food once the process of industrialization was under way.
5 Protoindustrialization led to the creation of a hierarchical network of local, regional, national, and international markets that were crucial to the success of industrial capitalism.

Protoindustrialization in Japan also seemed to help prepare the way for full-scale industrialization (T.C. Smith, 1988; Howell, 1992). Thomas Smith (1988) has remarked that the by-employments of farm workers helped to provide them with usable craft skills, and possibly even with managerial skills. By-employments "also helped prepare the rural population, in response to market incentives, to leave their villages and to adapt to new work authorities and social groups" (T.C. Smith, 1988:98).

One risk in employing the concept of protoindustrialization, and especially of seeing it as a preparatory phase in the emergence of full-scale industrialization, is that we may come to see industrialization and protoindustrialization as being connected in too linear a way. Protoindustrialization did not always lead to industrialization, and some regions that were centers of rural industry often declined and deindustrialized after full-scale industrialization commenced (Tilly, 1983; Ogilvie, 1993). Nevertheless, even though industrialization may not have followed protoindustrialization in some regions, the two processes were clearly linked in an *evolutionary* sense. As a technoeconomic *stage* of development, protoindustrialization preceded and prepared the way for full-scale industrialization. Like many other evolutionary processes, the process of industrialization was one that was much more gradual and drawn out than we have been accustomed to think, despite its major burst in the second half of the eighteenth century.

Industrialization: mechanization within capitalism

We come now to the problem of explaining industrialization and protoindustrialization. One line of thought that is always popular when it comes to technological change is to see industrialization as a kind of self-levitating and self-perpetuating process. A favorite ploy of historians interested in the industrialization process is to produce elaborate "multifactor" explanations. Gerhard Lenski (1970) combines the two. He lists the conquest of the New World, the Protestant Reformation, and the eighteenth-century agricultural revolution as the primary causes of the Industrial Revolution. The conquest of the New World was important, he says, because it hastened the spread of a cash economy and improved the social and economic position of merchants relative to landlords. Moreover, the colonies served as new and expanding markets for European goods. The Protestant Reformation was important because, following Weber, Protestantism had a salutary effect on economic development. And the agricultural revolution in eighteenth-century Britain increased the food supply and allowed for the release of a large segment of the agricultural population so they could provide manpower for the factories.

Undoubtedly the first and third of these factors are important (I would demur on the second, for reasons indicated in chapter 5), but Lenski has still another fish to fry. Of crucial significance, he tells us, is the fact that technological change is cumulative, and by the eighteenth century enough technological knowledge had finally accumulated to allow for a great breakthrough. As he tells us (1970:335):

Because sociocultural innovation is cumulative and because the number and type of inventions are a function of the already existing store of technical knowledge, the chances for some kind of major technological breakthrough were bound to be greater in the eighteenth century than in the fifteenth, and greater in the fifteenth than in the first century AD or the tenth century BC.

Another common explanation of the Industrial Revolution is

demographic. Richard Wilkinson (1973) and Ester Boserup (1981) have argued that it was the buildup of population pressure and subsequent environmental depletion and a declining standard of living that led people to adopt industrial innovations. Wilkinson argues that it was the shortage of land and other resources that was crucial. Particularly important was the exhaustion of the supply of timber as a fuel source, and thus the need to turn to coal for fuel. The need to mine more coal led to mines being sunk deeper and deeper, and the steam engine was a response to the problems that deep mines posed. He also suggests that the growth of the cotton industry was a response to the growing need to substitute one material for another, in this case cheaper cotton for more expensive wool.

Wilkinson's argument is an almost strictly demographic/ecological one that fails to take economics into consideration. The fact that it was a capitalist class that was carrying out the shift to industrial capitalism because it was highly profitable is almost completely ignored. Boserup also proposes a demographic explanation but in a way that at least leaves room for the fact that we are dealing with a capitalist mode of production. She notes that the first European countries to develop manufacturing industries in the later Middle Ages were Tuscany and the Low Countries, the regions with the highest population densities. As does Wilkinson, she also notes that the shift from wood to coal was made under increasing demographic pressures, and argues that "many of the technological innovations in the eighteenth century were the result of attempts to develop substitutes for wood as fuel and as raw material for industry and construction" (1981:106). However, she also goes on to say the following (1981:110–11):

As a result of the new iron technology and the changes which went with it, a period began in which Western and Central Europe were technological leaders, owing to their large deposits of coal and ore in favorable locations. These deposits had the double advantage of attracting both raw-material-oriented and market-oriented industries. The result was a snowballing effect in England and the valleys of the Rhine and its confluents, where the rapid growth of industry attracted population from less favored areas. England prospered from depopulation of Scotland and Ireland, and the Rhine valley absorbed the population surplus from eastern Germany. This migratory movement made the industrial regions even more attractive for labor-oriented and market-oriented industries, and it became difficult for other areas to compete with them for new industries.

The shift of industry in Europe from south to north started long before the industrial revolution and proceeded gradually during the whole period of early industrialization. With increasing population densities in northwestern Europe, the southern areas lost much of their advantage with respect to material and human infrastructure and also their attractiveness for market-oriented industries. Italian industries suffered from competition with industries north of the Alps, and Italian shipbuilding suffered earlier than others from forest shortage.

I am prepared to accept much of what Boserup is saying about the importance of population pressure so long as we understand just how the process very likely worked. The industrialization process was much more than just the substitution of coal for wood or cotton for wool, and it involved much more than just a reaction to environmental depletion and lowered standards of living. Even more, it was a process whereby the owners of capital within a capitalist mode of production innovated because technological expansion brought increases in productivity and the size of markets, and thus increases in profitability. Population pressure contributed to this process in the sense that greater concentrations of people meant larger labor forces that could be drawn on and greater numbers of people to consume manufactured products. But population pressure outside a capitalist mode of production would have produced very different results. The substitution of coal for wood, or even of cotton for wool, yes; but the growth of large-scale industry selling in a world market, no. The Industrial Revolution and the whole process of protoindustrialization were distinctly different from the Neolithic Revolution, where population pressure *was* the driving force. There were no capitalists in the late Mesolithic, and very few (and of an altogether different type) at the point of origin of civilization and the state. If population pressure directly caused the Industrial Revolution because of environmental depletion and lower living standards, then Holland should have been in the forefront, because it was the most densely populated country in Europe. But, as we have seen, it lagged not only behind Britain, but behind several other less densely populated countries on the European continent, not beginning its full-scale industrialization until after 1870. Or how could we explain the industrialization of the United States with a purely demographic model? True enough, industrialization began in the most densely populated and highly urbanized areas, but it spread quickly beyond those regions to parts of the country with very thin populations.

What I am saying is that demographic pressure helped spur the industrialization process in Europe, but only in the context of the rapidly expanding capitalist mode of production. Industrialization was a process of "mechanization within capitalism" that occurred to a very great extent because mechanization increased profitability, and it could not have occurred outside a highly advanced form of capitalism. However, to understand the specifics of industrialization – where it occurred earliest, etc. – we need to take into account one more factor: the role of natural resources. The two most critical were coal and water. Coal provided the energy source needed to drive the industrialization process, and the earliest regions of industrialization had large coal deposits. As Pollard (1981:4) has said, "The map of the British industrial revolution, it is well known, is simply the map of the coalfields." Regions deficient in coal were delayed in their industrialization process. But water was also critical, especially for transport (Pollard, 1981).

Before closing this discussion of causation, I should perhaps say a word about the extent to which countries imitated each other in the industrialization process. Putting it another way, what role did the process of diffusion play in industrialization? It must have played some role. The fact that Britain was first caused other European countries to respond in order to quicken the pace of their industrialization so as to maintain their role in the capitalist world market. These countries borrowed a good deal of their technology from Britain. Yet diffusion or imitation should not be overemphasized. The continental European countries would all eventually have industrialized, although it would have taken longer and occurred somewhat differently had Britain not been there to act as a model. Thus to say that the Industrial Revolution "spread" elsewhere from Britain, while perhaps not totally incorrect, is highly misleading. The countries of northwest Europe and Japan were on parallel evolutionary courses and did not need each other as "examples" in order to industrialize. Industrialization was built into the evolutionary logic of their mode of economic production.

THE RISE AND DEMISE OF STATE SOCIALISM
The nature of state socialism

The world's first society to take the name "socialist" came into existence when the Bolshevik Revolution of 1917 transformed Russia into the Soviet Union. Several new socialist societies were created in eastern Europe after World War II, either by internal revolution or, more commonly, through occupation by the Soviet army, as well as in parts of the less-developed world (e.g., in China in 1949 and Cuba in 1962). Perhaps some 40 societies have at one time or another officially declared themselves to be socialist in one sense or another. Here I shall concentrate on the Soviet Union and the relatively industrialized socialist states of eastern Europe.

The precise nature of these societies has been the subject of a great deal of dispute. To me, the most central question is the extent to which these societies have embodied a genuine Marxist ideology and set of social practices. One of the reasons this question is so important is, of course, that the Soviet Union and eastern Europe have referred to themselves as "Marxist" or "Marxist–Leninist" societies. Marx, of course, was deliberately vague in his pronouncements about the future socialist society he thought was to come, arguing that there was no single road to socialism and that no one should prescribe in advance precisely what any of the roads to be taken ought to be like. Nevertheless, he did have certain fundamentals in mind. For Marx, socialism would be characterized by the following general features:

1 abolition of private property in the means of production;
2 abolition of social classes and the class struggle;
3 centralized ownership of the means of economic production in the hands of the state and state administration of the economy;
4 abolition of the capitalist labor process, and thus of alienated labor; and
5 a temporary "dictatorship of the proletariat" in the initial transition to socialism, which would give way to the "withering away of the state" as socialism matured and the threat of a capitalist counterrevolution disappeared.

Numerous views of the extent to which modern state socialist societies have embodied Marxian philosophical and political principles have been stated (cf. Lane, 1984), but rather than try to deal with all of these in a short space I shall discuss only two: Albert Szymanski's view that the state socialist societies, the Soviet Union in particular, actually are genuinely Marxist versions of socialism, and the world-system argument that the state socialist societies are really semiperipheral capitalist societies.

Szymanski's (1979, 1982) view is that the Soviet Union is and has been for a long time genuinely socialist in the Marxian sense.[1]

Its economy is organized around production-for-use rather than production-for-exchange and it maintains a very high level of autonomy from Western capitalism. To defend his view Szymanski offers four main lines of evidence. First, he points out that, although the Soviet Union and Western capitalist states have entered into various agreements regarding the exchange of goods and technology, these agreements have been made on terms favorable to the Soviet Union. Such agreements do not significantly affect the Soviet Union's economic functioning because they do not allow Western capitalists to have any direct investment or management rights in Soviet enterprises. Second, the degree of Soviet investment in peripheral capitalist enterprises is miniscule compared to such investment by Western capitalists. Third, the state socialist societies have their own trading bloc and trade far more among themselves than do any of them with Western capitalist societies. Finally, Szymanski argues that the cyclical economic fluctuations so characteristic of capitalist societies have generally not been characteristic of state socialist societies, suggesting that the latter are truly distinct from Western capitalism. Szymanski notes in particular that during the great capitalist depression of the 1930s the Soviet Union was enjoying very rapid industrial growth.

The world-system position, which has been most forcefully articulated by Christopher Chase-Dunn (1982), is quite different. It holds that the state socialist societies, although having forms of internal economic organization different from Western capitalism, nonetheless have essentially created an alternative version of capitalism. Although Chase-Dunn does not use the term, this might be called "state capitalism" inasmuch as the state is said to act as a rational capitalist. The Soviet Union and eastern Europe engage in the production of commodities using forms of the labor process very similar to Western capitalism. These commodities are exchanged in a world market in which the objective is to realize an enhancement of their value and, indeed, state socialist enterprises, especially those in eastern Europe, have very important dealings with Western capitalism. The Soviet Union and eastern Europe are integrated into the capitalist world-economy as semiperipheral states. Although led by socialist political parties espousing a Marxist-Leninist ideology, on economic grounds they do not behave in the manner that Marx had in mind when he predicted and hoped for a future socialist society.

I agree with the position taken by Walter Goldfrank (1982) when he suggests that both of these positions are flawed, but that the world-system position is the better of the two. But first let us see what may be of value in Szymanski's argument. It must be recognized that the state socialist societies organize their economies in ways quite different from Western capitalism. Private property in the means of production has been almost completely abolished, and the state has taken over the administration of the economy. It sets wages and prices and decides what and how much is produced. Centralized economic planning has replaced the market as the means of making economic decisions. As János Kornai (1992:115) has written, "The 'life or death' of a firm as a collective organization or organism is determined not by the 'natural selection' of market competition but by the bureaucracy. There is a complete absence of . . . entrepreneurs who introduce new products or new technologies, establish new organizations, and conquer new markets, while obsolete production and ossified organizations are squeezed out." What Kornai is saying, of course, is that state socialist economies, being nonmarket economies, do not respond to the basic laws of supply and demand, and thus cannot use such laws as indicators of what they should be producing and how much of it they should produce. This would indeed make state socialism quite distinct from Western capitalism. Of course, this description applies more to the Soviet Union than to eastern Europe. Although the eastern European societies have been based for the most part on the Soviet model, in the 1970s their economies started becoming more open to market-oriented activities (Abonyi, 1982). They have used market principles alongside command principles, even if the latter have been dominant.

Another bit of evidence in support of Szymanski is the behavior of the Soviet Union toward less-developed socialist states. There is no evidence that the Soviet Union has ever acted as a socialist "core" that has treated less-developed socialist countries as economic "peripheries" (it has militarily dominated and politically controlled some of these countries, but that is another matter). In its relationship with Cuba, for example, the Soviet Union has actually bought sugar from the Cubans at prices well above the market price (Eckstein, 1986), strongly suggesting that Soviet policy has been directed toward the economic development of Cuba. As we saw in chapter 6, this is not the way that developed capitalist countries behave toward the Third World.

While the above is supportive of Szymanski's position, his argument falters badly on other grounds, the most obvious of which concerns state socialism's form of political organization. With its extremely high levels of political repression, which Szymanski more or less glosses over, state socialism has experienced neither the "dictatorship of the proletariat" nor the "withering away of the state." Instead, what we see is a "dictatorship *over* the proletariat." Moreover, it has not abolished social classes and the class struggle but simply generated another form of class stratification based on the political power of the *apparatchiki* rather than the economic power of a bourgeoisie. Nor has it abolished the capitalist division of labor and its highly alienating effects, but in fact reproduced it with zeal. In all these ways state socialist societies are not Marxist at all. Rather, they are "Leninist regimes" (Jowitt, 1978) whose most important use of Marxism–Leninism is as a legitimizing ideology.

What then of the world-system argument? I would suggest that the main flaw in this argument is its inclination to gloss over the enormous differences between capitalism's and state socialism's modes of internal economic organization. Whereas state socialist societies have behaved very much like capitalist states in retaining the Taylorist division of labor (so as to be able to produce goods with the capacity to augment their value), their striking lack of market principles (at least the Soviet Union's) has made them crucially different from Western capitalism and has led, as we shall see, to dramatic consequences. However, the world-system position does capture a very important truth. As Chase-Dunn (1982) points out, the state socialist societies have had great difficulty existing within an "ocean of capitalism." Because there have been few socialist states, such states have regularly encountered many more states committed to a capitalist economic strategy, and the capitalist states have shown marked hostility toward socialism. As a result, the socialist states have tended to be either crushed by capitalism or gradually shifted back toward a capitalist mode of production. The socialist states have been compelled to interact with Western capitalism, and over the years have gradually lost most of the socialist content that they originally may have had (Frank, 1980; Abonyi, 1982). Andre Gunder Frank (1980) has shown in detail the remarkable extent to which the state socialist societies have, over the past quarter century, become reintegrated into the capitalist world-economy and increasingly adopted capitalist economic principles. The pace of this reintegration picked up enormously in the 1980s and has led to major economic reforms and political transformations, a matter to be discussed shortly.

On the whole, then, I favor the world-system position despite its tendency to ignore or at least downplay state socialism's unique form of internal economic organization. Moreover, as the state socialist societies have changed over time I think that the world-system position has turned out to be increasingly accurate. The state socialist societies have increasingly behaved in precisely the way that world-system theory has predicted, and world-system theory is capable, I think, of answering another important question about state socialism: why it has been so politically repressive. The nature and extent of this repression are so well known that they need no discussion here. Its most important aspects are that the Communist party has claimed a monopoly of political power (allowing no other parties to exist), that the party has acted as the ultimate interpreter of truth, and that strong restrictions have been placed on the individual's freedom to think, speak, move, and associate as he or she pleases.

The highly repressive character of eastern European states has, of course, been to a large extent the result of Soviet political and military domination, but this does not explain why the Soviet Union itself has engaged in such domination and been so repressive. The world-system position on this issue (cf. Chase-Dunn, 1982; Wallerstein, 1984) is that political repression has resulted from the extreme economic and military threat that has been posed to the Soviet Union and other state socialist societies from Western capitalism. Although I once dismissed this argument as a case of special pleading, it is my view now that the argument has some impressive evidence in its favor. The period of greatest repression in the Soviet Union was, of course, the Stalinist period, which ran from the late 1920s to the mid-1950s. This period suffered through the horrors of Stalin's "reign of terror." It was a period during which the Soviet economy detached itself as much as possible from Western capitalism and followed its own economic path in hopes of catching up with the West. After Stalin died in 1953, the new regime under the leadership of Nikita Kruschchev began to open itself to the West economically, and it was Kruschchev who put an end to the Stalinist reign of terror and tried to create a less repressive regime (Nove, 1989). In the period that began in the mid-1980s, we see a continuation of this process of economic and political change. At the same time that the Soviet Union has moved toward greater *rapprochement* with the capitalist world-economy it has been undertaking dramatic political changes. All of this suggests to me that political repression has been a mechanism used by state socialist societies to deal with the external economic, military, and political threat posed by capitalism. This relates to Chase-Dunn's point that state socialist societies have extreme difficulty surviving in a hostile sea of capitalism. The external threat of capitalism must be dealt with if socialist states are to survive, and political repression has been the means to accomplish that. Marx made much the same point with his "dictatorship of the proletariat" thesis. New socialist societies would be highly unstable, he thought, and there would always be a risk of a capitalist counterrevolution, and the "dictatorship of the proletariat" was the means to prevent that from happening.

One of the most reasonable alternatives to this viewpoint is the Weberian argument that socialism requires large-scale bureaucracy, and that large-scale bureaucracy implies a concentration of power so great that it would be almost impossible to break. Until recently I favored this argument, but what turned me against it was the rapid collapse of Communist regimes in eastern Europe after 1989. Such an event seemed virtually impossible, especially with such rapidity, from a Weberian point of view. Moreover, the changes seemed to be coming largely from within the regimes themselves. From a Weberian standpoint it is extremely difficult to understand why powerful bureaucrats would voluntarily remove themselves from power.

The shift to postsocialism

What we have been describing above is state socialism as it looked up through the late 1980s. As is well known, after Mikhail Gorbachev came to power in the Soviet Union in 1985 state socialism began a series of economic reforms known as *perestroika*, or "restructuring." Similar reforms also were occurring in eastern Europe and, in fact, had begun even earlier. These reforms have all been in the direction of reducing the role of centralized economic planning and giving much more emphasis to market principles. Individual firms were to be given more freedom to make economic decisions; firms would be required to compete with one another according to the criterion of profitability, and insufficiently profitable firms would be eliminated; managers of firms were to be elected instead of simply gaining their positions through the traditional system of political patronage; the wage structure would be overhauled so as to increase wage differentials, the idea being to provide incentives for workers to work harder and better; and new joint ventures were to be undertaken with Western firms in order to attract Western capital and increase the production of consumer goods (Lapidus, 1988; Kushnirsky, 1988; Leggett, 1988; Zemtsov and Farrar, 1989).

A major reason why these economic reforms were undertaken involved the deteriorating economic conditions – indeed, the economic crisis – that the Soviet Union began to face in the 1980s (Zemtsov and Farrar, 1989; Kaneda, 1988; Mandel, 1989). The Soviet Union was increasingly plagued by declining productivity, harvest failures, bottlenecks in industry, energy and labor shortages, chronic shortages of basic necessities, black markets, and widespread bribery and corruption (Leggett, 1988; Kaneda, 1988). The declining standard of living brought about by these problems contributed to low worker morale, rising rates of crime, alcoholism and drug use, and overall popular discontent (Leggett, 1988).

According to János Kornai (1992), these were inevitable problems of the state socialist economy. They were predetermined from the very beginning, and it is simply that they took awhile to manifest themselves. Kornai argues that the critical economic defect in state socialism is its absence of a market principle for making basic economic decisions, especially decisions about pricing. With prices being set by administrative fiat rather than by the level of consumer demand, economic planners have no way to adjust supply so as to bring it into harmony with demand. The command principle of state socialism guarantees that whatever is produced will be sold, and as a result producers have no incentive to increase supply, and a situation of chronic shortage is automatically produced. Because state socialism has always given priority to the production of means of production rather than consumer goods, shortages of the latter have tended to be especially acute. Two other deficiences of state socialism noted by Kornai are its failure to produce a large-scale indigenous technology and thus its need to borrow most of it from the West, and its generally low levels of product quality, a difficulty stemming from its emphasis on the quantity rather than the quality of goods.

The recent economic and political turmoil in the Soviet Union and eastern Europe has led many observers to claim that state socialism has never worked as an economic system. But this is claiming too much. As Chase-Dunn (1992) and Szelenyi and Szelenyi (1992) have shown, the Soviet economy worked well in its first decades, and indeed was capable of producing a remarkably high level of industrialization in a very short period of time. However, although state socialism seemed to be capable of producing a successful industrial economy built around such heavy industries as steel, electrical machinery, and organic chemistry, it seemed capable of producing little else (Chirot, 1991). It seemed to lack the capacity to move into the stage of the production of such mass consumer goods as televisions, washing machines, and automobiles. For Kornai, this failure has been the result of the strategy of forced industrialization, a strategy that, he claims, eventually begins to undermine its own performance. As he says (1992:202), "Even where a high growth rate is attained initially, it cannot be kept up; sooner or later, the growth rate starts to fall more and more conspicuously. Each generation leaves a baleful legacy for the next – of grave, postponed, and increasingly urgent tasks, and of an economy with a disharmonious structure."

It seems clear, then, that the great emphasis on centralized economic planning to the neglect of market principles has had woeful results for state socialism. But the problems of state socialism cannot be laid solely at the feet of its internal economic organization. We cannot overlook the constraints imposed by the capitalist world-economy, within which state socialism, like it or not, has had to function. These constraints – such as the costs of the military buildup needed to protect against the military threats of hostile capitalist powers, or embargoes against trade – have put serious obstacles in the path of state socialism's economic functioning. A fair test of the adequacy of state socialism as an economic system would be one in which external obstacles were removed. Only then could we see the extent of the damage done by the neglect of the market.

In any event, regardless of the exact mix of internal and external factors in state socialism's economic problems, there appears little doubt that the Soviet Union has attempted to deal with these problems by vigorously reinserting itself into the capitalist world-economy. A key aspect of *perestroika* has been the shift toward exporting goods in the world market. As a former economic advisor to Gorbachev announced a few years ago (Aganbegyan, 1989:186), "The Soviet Union will specialize increasingly in the export of industrial goods, particularly machinery, equipment and chemicals, and also of a large selection of services. . . . We have elaborated a special long-term programme for developing our export base for the future." This has represented a tremendous departure from past economic practices, and it is obvious that there has been in recent years a dramatic transformation in the economic outlook and interests of the Soviet elite, or at least of a significant segment of it. As we shall see in a moment, this shift in economic outlook has had a major impact on the politics of state socialism.

János Kornai (1992) has referred to the Soviet Union (Russia, etc.) and eastern Europe of the 1990s as "postsocialist" societies. This is an apt term, for it tells us more about what these societies are not than about what they are. They are "after socialism," and they have taken major steps toward embracing Western capitalism, but it is still too early to say exactly what they are. We know, of course, that they are in a state of transition, and thus are mixtures of the old state socialism and the "new" capitalism. But how this drama will play itself out is still unclear. My expectation is that the postsocialist societies will gradually become fully reintegrated into the capitalist world-economy, but how long this will take, and how much more turmoil it will involve, are matters that cannot be safely predicted.

The collapse of Communism

So far I have been talking of the Soviet Union largely in the present tense, but of course it is no more. Communism collapsed there in 1991 after a failed coup d'état against Gorbachev, and Boris Yeltsin took power. The Communist party was delegitimized to a large extent and lost its monopoly on power. Nationalist movements broke the old Soviet Union apart into Russia and numerous other sovereign states. Of course, similar events occurred in eastern Europe in 1989. Communism has now, as a social and political ideology and movement, largely collapsed, although it is always possible that it might be restored in some places. The collapse of the Soviet Union and the Communist movement came on the heels of the political reforms in the Soviet Union known as *glasnost*. Like *perestroika*, these too were introduced by Gorbachev. *Glasnost* involved greater openness in social and political life, which largely meant less government repression and more toleration of individual expression of opinion.

The collapse of Communism beginning in 1989 took almost everyone by surprise. I was totally unprepared for it, and even while it was happening I tried to deny that it would go very far. But, of course, I was wrong, for it has gone very far indeed. One reason everyone was taken by surprise is that we lacked good theories of what state socialism really was, especially how it related to capitalism. As mentioned earlier, before the events of 1989 I held to a Weberian interpretation of Soviet politics, and I greatly underestimated state socialism's growing participation in the capitalist world-economy. Another reason for our surprise is that the events seemed to happen suddenly and to come out of nowhere. But this was an illusion. Pressures had been building up for a long time toward this conclusion, but most of these were far enough below the surface to make them difficult to detect.

There are numerous interpretations of the collapse of Communism, but I shall concentrate here on just the two that I think are the most sensible. One argument is that of Randall Collins and David Waller (1992), who focus on the Soviet Union and view its collapse as a contemporary example of what have recently been termed *state breakdowns* (Goldstone, 1991), or crises within a state that lead to widespread political conflict and the crippling of the state's capacity to govern. Collins and Waller claim that the Soviet Union broke down because it created an empire that was overextended and whose costs, especially military costs, could no longer be borne. At the level of proximate causes this theory is a type of economic theory: it was the economic problems induced by the overextension of empire that brought the Soviet state down. However, at the level of ultimate causes the theory is a Weberian geopolitical theory, because the economic problems are theorized to be rooted in Soviet geopolitics rather than in any defect of the Soviet economy *per se*.

This theory may capture part of the picture, especially the nationalist movements within the Soviet Union, but only just part. I am extremely dubious that the difficulties of state socialism can be ascribed simply to geopolitics. The most obvious difficulty is the fact that Collins and Waller concentrate only on the Soviet Union, whereas the collapse of Communism has been a much wider phenomenon than this. How can such a theory explain the extraordinary events of 1989 in eastern Europe? I am more persuaded by an economic argument, in the sense of both proximate and ultimate explanation. As we have noted, state socialism has had severe internal economic problems that have been exacerbated by the constraints of the capitalist world-economy. Gorbachev's economic reforms after 1985 were motivated by these problems, and *glasnost* was the political side of *perestroika*. Greater political openness was seen as a necessary means to opening up the economy. What was intended was the gradual shift to a more capitalistic economy and a more democratic polity. However, with his economic and political reforms Gorbachev unleashed a monster he couldn't control, especially in eastern Europe. The political reforms were also associated with a relaxation of the Soviet Union's military domination of eastern Europe, and at some point it began to be clear to dissident factions that the Soviet Union would not intervene to support the eastern European regimes against popular rebellion. This allowed people to take to the streets to demand the overthrow of Communist regimes, and forces were unleashed that couldn't be stopped.

It is absolutely crucial, I feel, to establish the extent to which the events of 1989 in eastern Europe and 1991 in the Soviet Union were determined by popular rebellion, as they have often been made out to be. Were these "people's revolutions" or "rebellions from below"? I am completely sympathetic to the case made by Krishan Kumar (1992) that these were "revolutions from above" that were affected very little by popular protest. They derived primarily from shifts in the economic and political outlook of key segments of the Communist party elite. If we are to make a case for "people's revolutions" as the agents of the collapse of Communism then we have to ask why the popular rebellion against the Communist regime in Hungary in 1956 was repressed by the Soviet military, or why the attempted liberalization of the Dubček regime in Czechoslovakia in 1968 met a similar fate. The reason for these failures is, I believe, that popular desires were incompatible with the economic and political outlook of the Communist party elite, and as a result that elite, having control of military power, prevailed. In 1989 and 1991 the outlook of key segments of the party elite had fallen into line with popular desires, although it appeared to many observers as if these popular desires had in fact determined the outlook. But no, not at all. It was the elite's desires that won the day, for without them the system would not and could not have changed. To the extent that popular dissent figured in the matter, it was only at the end when everything had basically been determined. Kumar (1992:321) puts it beautifully:

> It is only when the ruling structures of society are in a clear state of decay or dissolution that popular discontent can express itself in a confident way. Then we usually find spokesmen from the upper classes urging on popular feeling against the regime. Revolutionaries, often released from prison or returned from exile abroad, busy themselves with organizing the mass discontent. After the success of the revolution, the idea of a popular uprising against a hated tyranny becomes the official myth of the new regime. This conceals the fact that the old regime has died, often by its own hand, rather than been overthrown in a popular outburst of indignation.

Kumar goes on to provide extensive evidence that the Soviet elite was actually closely involved in deposing leaders throughout eastern Europe, even to the extent of virtually orchestrating some events. This was true in East Germany, Czechoslovakia, Hungary, Poland, Bulgaria, and Romania (see Kumar, 1992:345–9).

The collapse of the Communist movement in the Soviet Union and eastern Europe raises huge questions about the future of socialism. We are living in an era of "the transition from socialism to capitalism," but that does not necessarily mean that socialism is dead once and for all. Indeed, I am certain it is not dead, and the reason is because many of the problems of capitalism remain to be solved and in some ways have grown worse (Hobsbawm, 1991). This particular version of socialism, no doubt, is gone. (It will only be a matter of time before Cuba and other less-developed socialist countries abandon socialism; without the Soviet Union's support, they have no future). But socialism will be rethought – indeed, is already being rethought – by socialist opponents of capitalism, who will try to learn from the mistakes of the past. In chapter 9 I shall explore the question of the future of socialism more thoroughly.

270 The Evolution of the Modern World II

STRATIFICATION AND MOBILITY IN THE AGE OF MODERNITY

Stratification in the transition from agrarian to industrial societies

In his elaborate theory of stratification in human societies, Gerhard Lenski (1966) has shown that the extent of stratification is closely related to a society's stage of evolutionary development. Hunting and gathering societies are the least likely to be stratified, and small-scale, low-energy horticultural societies also usually exhibit little stratification. It is among more technologically advanced horticulturalists that stratification tends to emerge in full bloom, and agrarian societies have especially elaborate forms of stratification in which the gap between the top and bottom is typically extreme. However, Lenski says, with the transition to modern industrial societies, the historic pattern of increasing stratification came to be reversed, and industrial societies are less severely stratified than their agrarian predecessors.

To document his assertion, Lenski estimates that in agrarian societies political and economic elites took around 50 percent of the total national income of their societies. By contrast, he argues, it is unlikely that in modern industrial societies elite sections of the population claim more than 25 percent of the total national income. Perhaps the most notable characteristic of modern stratification systems is the enormous diffusion of income throughout the population. In agrarian societies of the past, there was an extreme polarization of wealth between a tiny landed nobility and a very large peasantry, with small classes of merchants and craftsmen existing in between. In modern industrial societies, even though elites enjoy enormous wealth and income compared to the rest of the population, there has nonetheless been a wide diffusion of economic benefits throughout the population so that the average member of society enjoys a very comfortable existence. So it is not difficult to accept Lenski's basic argument about the reduction in the extent of economic inequality in modern industrial societies.

What then is the cause of the "historic reversal" of which Lenski speaks? Lenski suggests several causes, one of which is the magnitude and speed of increases in productivity in the transition to industrial societies. Economic productivity in industrial societies has risen far enough and fast enough, he says, to make it possible for elites to grant concessions to the demands of subordinate classes and still retain a significant fraction of total income for themselves. By granting concessions, elites can "reduce worker hostility and the accompanying losses from strikes, slowdowns, and industrial sabotage" (Lenski, 1966:314). In the long run elites may actually improve their own economic situation by granting concessions. In addition, Lenski claims that sharp reductions in fertility have helped give the masses a greater income share because in agrarian societies the growth of population tended to negate whatever economic gains might be made. A third factor is the growth of human knowledge, and especially its role in the creation of a much more highly skilled work force. Lenski's reasoning is that the more highly skilled workers of industrial societies have greater bargaining power than workers in agrarian societies, most of whom were unskilled. Finally, and most importantly, Lenski points to the rise of democratic ideologies and democratic governments. The fact that a certain degree of power has diffused throughout the population has meant that, to a degree unimaginable in agrarian societies, the many can combine against the few and use their power to effect important changes in the distributive structure of society.

My own view would be that the first and last of Lenski's proposed causes go the farthest in explaining the diffusion of income throughout industrial populations. However, I might put the matter slightly differently. Industrial societies, being capitalist societies, have been driven by the logic of capital accumulation, which of course means by the profitability of industrial activity. What is produced must be sold, and the expansion of productive activity, a *sine qua non* of capitalism, requires the expansion of consumption. Therefore the increasing diffusion of income throughout the population has been absolutely essential to capitalist development. I am not making a functionalist claim to the effect that the "system" has somehow recognized this functional problem and undertaken the means to solve it. I am simply saying that had the capacity for mass consumption not evolved, then capitalism could not have evolved to the extent that it has. The actual mechanism that has led to these powers of mass consumption, or at least the most important mechanism, is the growth of the organizational capacity and power of the working classes, a phenomenon that has been made possible to a large extent because of the rise of parliamentary democratic governments, which incorporated the working classes politically through the granting of universal suffrage. This, of course, is Lenski's final causal factor, and the one he emphasizes most. It has been the struggles of the working classes, through both the ballot box and the trade union, that have made a critical difference.

However, two criticisms of Lenski are in order. First, he does not consider, at least not explicitly, the enormous extent to which modern industrial capitalist society has become an organizational society. This has been a fundamental part of the evolution of industrial capitalism. The basic unit of modern capitalism is the corporation, and its development has meant the enormous expansion of managerial classes. Furthermore, the extraordinary expansion of the size and scope of government has meant the evolution of another form of large organization, and thus of another type of managerial class. The rise of these "middle classes" has been a critical feature of modern stratification systems, one to be discussed shortly.

A second problem with Lenski's argument is that, like most macrosociology, it takes the nation-state as its basic unit of analysis. It is true that at the level of the nation-state the historic reversal of which Lenski speaks is a reality. However, if we take the capitalist world-economy as our unit of analysis, then we see that the extent of stratification has continued to increase. As noted in chapter 6, there has been global polarization between core and periphery from the very beginnings of the capitalist system, and this polarization has actually accelerated over time. In 1750 the ratio of the national income of the richest country to the poorest country was 1.8:1, a ratio that had increased to 29:1 by 1977 (Bairoch, 1981). Relying on a somewhat different set of data, the United Nations reports that in 1960 the ratio of the richest quintile of countries to the poorest quintile was 30:1, and that this ratio had increased to 59:1 by 1989 (United Nations, 1992a). However, in a sense the extent of world inequality is even greater. When inequality is assessed in terms of individuals rather than countries, thus taking into account the inequality that also exists among individuals within countries, the ratio of the richest quintile to the poorest quintile was 140:1 in 1989 (United Nations, 1992a). Thus, economic inequality *on a world scale* has continued the age-old pattern of growing inequality, not reversed it.

Income inequality and class structure in industrial capitalism

Data on income inequality in capitalist societies has become widely available in recent decades, and so we know a good deal about its extent on a comparative basis. A common way of measuring income inequality is to compute the ratio of the income of the top income quintile (as a proportion of total national income) to the income of the bottom quintile. For several major capitalist societies in the late 1970s and early 1980s, the following figures can be reported (these are pre-tax figures) (Phillips, 1990): United States, 12:1; France, 9:1; Canada, 9:1; Britain, 8:1; West Germany, 5:1; Sweden, 5:1; Netherlands, 5:1, and Japan, 4:1. These figures suggest that modern capitalist societies differ significantly in their levels of inequality. However, another way of measuring inequality is to use Gini coefficients. Table 7.1 shows Gini coefficients for 13 industrial capitalist societies. These figures suggest that capitalist societies are rather similar in their levels of inequality. The Gini coefficients (pre-tax) range from .32 to .46, with the average being .387, and most of the countries are extremely close to this average. The post-tax coefficients – and be it noted that they are only very slightly lower than the pre-tax coefficients, thus indicating the extremely limited effect of taxation on income distribution – are even more similar. The range is from .30 to .41 and the average is .352. My

Table 7.1 *Income inequality in selected industrial capitalist societies*

Country	Pre-tax Gini coefficient	Post-tax Gini coefficient
United States	.38	.38
Canada	.38	.35
Australia	.32	.31
Japan	.38	.32
Denmark	.37	.38
Finland	.46	.37
France	.45	.41
West Germany	.41	.38
Italy	.40	.40
Netherlands	.40	.35
Norway	.36	.31
Sweden	.36	.30
United Kingdom	.36	.32

The pre-tax Gini coefficient reported represents an average of three indexes. Data are mostly from the 1960s and 1970s.
Source: Lane, McKay, and Newton (1991), table 2.4

conclusion is that industrial capitalist societies are remarkably similar to one another in their levels of inequality, although of course differences exist and should not be overlooked. There is thus something of a "logic of capitalism" operating to produce similar income distributions, but at the same time this logic isn't everything, for there are particular characteristics of individual countries that make a difference.

How has the distribution of income changed over time? Comparative data looking at changes in income distributions over time are very difficult to come by, but we can explore this matter for the United States. Gabriel Kolko (1962) calculated the US income distribution from 1910 to 1959 using income deciles, a more precise measure than quintiles. A synopsis of his findings is reported in table 7.2. These data are extremely important because they show the extent to which the introduction of progressive income taxation in the 1930s has altered the income distribution in a more egalitarian direction. The data show a significant reduction in the income share of the top income decile, from 39 percent in 1929 (when the top decile's income share peaked) to 28.9 percent in 1959. However, overall there was no real redistribution of income to the bottom segments of the population. The income shares of the bottom three deciles, in fact, went down, from 13.8 percent in 1910 to 8.6 percent in 1959. In 1929, the ratio of the top decile to the bottom decile was 22:1, and by 1959 that ratio had actually increased to 26:1. Who benefited from the declining income share of the top decile? The answer is, the second and third deciles, which increased their income share moderately from 22.5 percent in 1910 to 28.5 percent in 1959. Income was redistributed, in other words, from the rich to the near rich or moderately rich rather than from the rich to the poor.

Table 7.2 *Income inequality in the United States, 1910–59*

Year	Income decile									
	Highest	*2nd*	*3rd*	*4th*	*5th*	*6th*	*7th*	*8th*	*9th*	*Lowest*
1910	33.9	12.3	10.2	8.8	8.0	7.0	6.0	5.5	4.9	3.4
1921	38.2	12.8	10.5	8.9	7.4	6.5	5.9	4.6	3.2	2.0
1929	39.0	12.3	9.8	9.0	7.9	6.5	5.5	4.6	3.6	1.8
1941	34.0	16.0	12.0	10.0	9.0	7.0	5.0	4.0	2.0	1.0
1951	30.9	15.0	12.3	10.6	8.9	7.6	6.3	4.7	2.9	0.8
1959	28.9	15.8	12.7	10.7	9.2	7.8	6.3	4.6	2.9	1.1

Source: Kolko (1962), table I

The changes that we have been discussing have been referred to by Randall Collins (1979) as the "twentieth-century income revolution." Collins explains further (1979:188–9):

> The height of the income shift came during the New Deal period when government employment substantially took off. This was a period of liberal reform as well as of consciously Keynesian employment policies. Substantial bureaucratization occurred during that period, but not only within government: This is the period of the massive bureaucratization of the private corporations as well. This bureaucratization, I would suggest, was responsible for the income revolution. . . . [T]he beneficiaries of the income revolution have been the bureaucratic middle class themselves and particularly favored craft-union enclaves of the upper working class.

To understand just who has benefited and why from this income revolution, we need to try to translate data on income distribution into a conception of class structure. Much of what has happened in the United States has also happened along many of the same lines in other industrial capitalist societies, and so this discussion is intended to apply to industrial capitalism generally.

Conceptualizing the class structure of contemporary capitalism has not been an easy task. Most sociologists have conceptualized the class structure largely as a *socioeconomic* structure, or one in which there is a hierarchy of social strata that differ in occupational prestige and economic privilege. In this conventional conception of class structure, occupation is the criterion for placing individuals in a location within the class structure. A textbook example of this notion of class structure, based on the United States, has been provided by Daniel Rossides (1976). He conceives of five basic social classes. At the top is an upper class (1–3 percent of the population), which consists of families who possess great wealth, much of which is inherited. Included here are the propertied rich and highest-echelon corporate managers. Next is an upper-middle class (10–15 percent of the population), which consists largely of medium- to high-level business managers, moderately well-off business owners, and learned professionals. The lower-middle class (30–35 percent) includes small businessmen and lower-level business managers, such lower-level professionals as public school teachers and social workers, and sales and clerical personnel. The working class (40–45 percent) consists of skilled, semiskilled, and unskilled manual and service workers. Finally, the lower class (20–25 percent) consists of persons living in or at the edges of poverty.

A similar but perhaps slightly more useful and informative conception of class structure has been presented by Robert Erikson and John Goldthorpe (1993). Schematically, their conceptualization is as follows:

I   Higher-grade professionals, administrators, and officials; managers in large industrial establishments; large proprietors.

II   Lower-grade professionals, administrators, and officials; higher-grade technicians; managers in small industrial establishments; supervisors of nonmanual employees.

IIIa Routine nonmanual employees, higher grade (administration and commerce).

IIIb Routine nonmanual employees, lower grade (sales and services).

IVa Small proprietors, artisans, etc., with employees.

IVb Small proprietors, artisans, etc., without employees.

IVc Farmers and smallholders; other self-employed workers in primary production.

V   Lower-grade technicians; supervisors of manual workers.

VI   Skilled manual workers.

VIIa Semiskilled and unskilled manual workers (not in agriculture, etc.).

VIIb Agricultural and other workers in primary production.

A different approach to class structure has been taken by Marxists, who have objected to conventional conceptions because of their alleged failure to treat class in terms of relations of production rather than hierarchies of prestige and privilege. Numerous Marxian approaches to class have been taken, but most have not been very successful because Marx's conception of the key productive relation in capitalist society, bourgeoisie vs proletariat, was formulated in the mid-nineteenth century and is highly unsuitable for the complexities of stratification in the late twentieth century. Relying on it too closely yields such absurdities as placing most of the population in the proletariat, since most of the population does not own any means of production.

To my mind, the most successful of the Marxian approaches to the capitalist class structure is that of Erik Wright (1979, 1985), although, as we shall see, his formulations have problems. To complicate matters, Wright has actually produced more than one conceptualization. His original formulation involved adding the notion of authority to Marx's notion of property ownership. Classes could then be conceptualized according to the way individuals stood with respect to ownership of the means of production *and* the exercise of authority. Wright generated six classes, three built around what he called *basic class locations*, and three more displaying *contradictory class locations.* Basic class relations are those that exhibit consistency on the dimensions of ownership and authority, whereas contradictory class locations are those which contain elements of two different basic class locations. Schematically, they look approximately as follows (Wright, 1979):

I   Basic class locations
  1   Bourgeoisie (1–2 percent): owners of vast amounts of capital and the ultimate exercisers of authority.
  2   Proletariat (41–54 percent): owners of no means of production and exercisers of no authority within the capitalist work place.
  3   Petty bourgeoisie (4.5 percent): owners of small means of production who employ no workers and who neither exert nor are subjected to authority.
II Contradictory class locations
  4   Managers and supervisors (30–35 percent): owners of no means of production who exert authority within the capitalist workplace; includes top and middle managers (12 percent) who exert considerable authority, and bottom managers, foremen, and line supervisors (18–23 percent) who exert moderate authority. This class contains elements of the bourgeoisie (exercise of authority) and elements of the the proletariat (no ownership of means of production).
  5   Small employers (6–7 percent): owners of moderate amounts of capital who, in contrast to the petty bourgeoisie, employ at least one worker and exercise authority. This class contains elements of the bourgeoisie (ownership of capital, exercise of authority) and elements of the petty bourgeoisie (small scale of capital ownership).
  6   Semiautonomous employees: learned professionals working in large, bureaucratic organizations, such as lawyers, physicians, and professors. This class contains elements of the proletariat (no property ownership) and elements of the petty bourgeoisie (neither exerting nor subjected to authority).

Wright (1979) carried out research showing that his class scheme predicted income levels better than a conventional conception of class. Although he had no members of the true bourgeoisie in his sample, he found that small employers had the highest incomes, whereas the proletariat had the lowest incomes. This led him to conclude that one's relation to the means of production was a critical factor in income determination, just as Marxian theory argues. However, Wright eventually became dissatisfied with his scheme because of its failure to make the concept of exploitation as central as he felt a Marxian conception of class should. He then reformulated his scheme significantly and tested its ability to predict income levels. This scheme is presented in table 7.3 along with its relationship to income distribution in two countries, the United States and

Sweden. Classes are now defined according to three factors, each of which is a type of asset: assets in means of production, assets in organizational positions, and assets in credentials. Assets in means of production are, of course, ownership of capital; assets in organizational positions involve coordinating the workplace and directing

Table 7.3 *Classes in contemporary capitalist society and their relation to income*

Owners		Nonowners	
	Expert	Semicredentialed	Uncredentialed
Bourgeoisie	managers	managers	managers
(1.8, 0.7)	(3.9, 4.4)	(6.2, 4.0)	(2.3, 2.5)
US: $52,621	US: $28,665	US: $20,701	US: $12,276
SW: $28,333	SW: $29,952	SW: $20,820	SW: $15,475
	Expert	Semicredentialed	Uncredentialed
Small employers	supervisors	supervisors	supervisors
(6.0, 4.8)	(3.7, 3.8)	(6.8, 3.2)	(6.9, 3.1)
US: $24,828	US: $23,057	US: $18,023	US: $13,045
SW: $17,237	SW: $18,859	SW: $19,711	SW: $15,411
	Expert	Semicredentialed	
Petty bourgeoisie	nonmanagers	workers	Proletarians
(6.9, 5.4)	(3.4, 6.8)	(12.2, 17.8)	(39.9, 43.5)
US: $14,496	US: $15,251	US: $16,034	US: $11,161
SW: $13,503	SW: $14,890	SW: $14,879	SW: $11,876

The numbers in parentheses refer to the percentage of the total population represented by each particular class; the first number is for the United States, the second for Sweden. There were 1,282 American respondents and 1,049 Swedish respondents. The bourgeoisie is operationalized as owners who employ ten or more workers, small employers as owners employing between two and nine workers, and the petty bourgeoisie as owners employing no workers or only one worker. All data are for 1980.
Source: Wright (1985), tables 6.1, 6.17

and supervising others (it is apparently a refurbished version of the old concept of "authority"); and assets in credentials involve the possession of educational degrees. Wright insists that each of these factors is to be understood in terms of exploitative relations. People can exploit others in three ways: by owning capital, by possessing organizational positions, and by possessing educational degrees. Thus, nonowners can exploit other nonowners just as owners can exploit nonowners; it is just that they draw on the control of different resources in doing so.

As table 7.3 reveals, when the three class variables are combined, they yield 12 social classes. The nature of each class should be clear enough. The three owning classes in the left-hand column are carried over from the earlier scheme. The nonowning classes are simply combinations of organizational positions and credentials. Moving from left to right we move through three levels of credentials, and moving from top to bottom we move through three levels of organizational positions. Of the nonowners, expert managers possess the greatest number of resources, proletarians the fewest. The table reveals that Wright's new scheme predicts income inequality very nicely. As individuals gain control over each of the resources, their income level improves. There is also an important new finding. Whereas small employers received the second highest income using Wright's original scheme, they fall below the income level of expert managers in the United States, and in Sweden they fall below the income level of four classes: expert managers, semicredentialed managers, expert supervisors, and semicredentialed supervisors.

Despite the success of his class scheme in predicting income inequality, it is most surprising that Wright never asks about the relative contribution of each of his three class variables. But we can do it for him, and thus I have generated table 7.4. The calculations in this table were carried out by looking at the increment in income received as we moved from less of an asset to more of it. For example, in the case of the United States, as we moved from the petty bourgeoisie to the small employers the increment in income

Table 7.4 *Relative contribution of ownership of the means of production, organizational assets, and credential assets to income determination*

Type of resource	Country	
	United States	Sweden
Means of production		
Total contribution	$38,125	$14,830
Per comparison contribution	$19,063	$7,415
Credential assets		
Total contribution	$30,491	$20,939
Per comparison contribution	$5,082	$3,490
Organizational assets		
Total contribution	$19,196	$24,602
Per comparison contribution	$3,199	$4,100

Source: Data on which these calculations were based come from Wright (1985), table 6.17

was $10,332, and as we moved from the small employers to the bourgeoisie the income increment was $27,793. The average increment in income from one level to the next was thus $19,063.

Table 7.4 shows that, for both the United States and Sweden, ownership of the means of production makes the greatest contribution to income inequality (an average of $19,063 for the United States, $7,415 for Sweden). For the United States, credential assets make the next-greatest impact on income inequality (an average of $5,082) and organizational assets make the least impact ($3,199). For Sweden, the relative positions of credential assets and organizational assets are reversed (credential assets average $3,490 and organizational assets average $4,100).

In a sense, then, Wright's Marxist position is vindicated: ownership of the means of production, just as Marxism predicts, is the most critical factor in income determination. (Actually, its effect is undoubtedly much larger than Wright's data are able to show, because he operationalizes the bourgeoisie as owners employing ten or more workers – a pretty poor bourgeoisie!) Yet in another sense his Marxian position gets in the way of understanding; this involves Wright's insistence that his overall scheme is a *Marxian* scheme that is centered around the concept of *exploitation*. Apparently the only reason Wright insists on talking about exploitation is because he is a Marxist and, as such, wants exploitation to be the central dynamic in the class structure. My own view is that Wright stretches the concept of exploitation beyond its breaking point. Exploitation can be a troublesome enough concept just when we are dealing with ownership, but it loses all coherence when we move into other realms. Elsewhere I have defined exploitation as occurring when one party compels another party to give up more than it receives in return (Sanderson, 1995). How are the possessors of organizational assets or educational credentials doing any thing like that?

Fortunately, there is an easy way out for those of us who do not feel compelled to force everything into a Marxian mold. It seems to me that there is great value in what Wright has done, but we should recognize it for what it is: a Weberian supplementation of Marx, not a new Marxian scheme.[2] The key to stratification is control over resources, and there are several important types of resources to be controlled. In a capitalist society the most important resource to be controlled is the means of production, but if we limit ourselves to that we will be considering only a small segment of the population.

(Wright's data show that all types of owners combined comprise only about 15 percent of the population in the United States and only 11 percent of the population in Sweden.) For the great bulk of the population, it is organizational assets and educational credentials that are vital to economic success, and it is extremely difficult for me to see how someone can be exploiting someone else merely by pursuing educational credentials or gaining managerial authority. The proper phrase is "struggle for resources," not "exploitation."

This brings us back to Collins's point about the twentieth-century income revolution, which is an inextricable part of the emergence of what he calls "the sinecure society." This is a type of society far different from the one familiar to Marx in the middle of the nineteenth century. For most people, what is critical now is not the possession of capital, because most people do not possess any capital and most of those who do don't possess very much. The "class struggle" of the late twentieth century is very different from that of the nineteenth century, as Collins (1979:53–4) explains:

Social classes may be distinguished by the amount of property they possess, but the most important form of such "property" is not limited to the traditional notion of material and financial possessions. Rather it is how "positions" are shaped that constitutes the most immediate form of property in the labor market, and it is by the shaping of such positions that income is distributed. The term *position* is only a metaphor (although it is widely accepted and taken for granted) for the seemingly object-like immutability of a collection of behavioral patterns that are reserved for particular individuals under particular conditions of tenure. Indeed, material and financial *property* is a similar metaphor, for the property relation is a behavioral one, a particular degree of tenure of action toward certain objects and persons, not a physical relationship of owner to thing. It is *property in positions* that is crucial in determining most of class organization and class struggle in everyday life. For material and financial property . . . is concentrated in a quite small group, but property in positions shapes class relations throughout the population and has a wide range of variations. The actual details of economic conflict are carried out on this level.

Social mobility in industrial societies

The issue of social mobility has been a central one in the sociological analysis of the transition to modern industrial societies. Perhaps the most important guiding theory in the contemporary analysis of mobility is what has been called the *liberal theory of industrialism* (Erikson and Goldthorpe, 1993), a theory closely associated with the functionalist view of social evolution developed by Talcott Parsons (1960, 1967, 1971) and Clark Kerr and his colleagues (Kerr, Dunlop, Harbison, and Myers, 1960). This theory assumes, first, that industrial societies exhibit much higher levels of mobility than are found in preindustrial societies, and that most of this mobility is upward rather than downward. These high rates of social mobility are said to spring from the rapid pace of technological change, and thus change in occupational structures. In addition, in an industrial society the basis for the allocation of individuals to social positions shifts from ascription, which prevailed in preindustrial societies, to achievement. As societies industrialize, achievement gradually replaces ascription and societies display increasing levels of social mobility, and thus become more open. As Erikson and Goldthorpe (1993:8) point out, in the liberal theory "high and rising levels of mobility are represented as functional imperatives of industrial development."

Vast quantities of research on social mobility have been produced by sociologists, and there is space here only to summarize some of the most important findings of the major studies. One of the earliest comprehensive studies of mobility was that of Peter Blau and Otis Dudley Duncan (1967), who studied American society. Some of their most important findings were that there has been considerable mobility in American society; that upward mobility has been much more common than downward mobility; that most mobility has occurred over relatively short distances (for example, from the upper reaches of the working class to the lower reaches of the middle class, or from the lower-middle class to the upper-middle class); and that mobility rates increased only very little in the half-century between the 1910s and the 1960s.

Blau and Duncan's finding that there is considerable mobility in the United States seems to confirm one aspect of the liberal theory. Hard data on mobility in preindustrial societies are difficult to come by, but what we know of such societies strongly suggests that mobility rates are low, except possibly during major periods of economic transformation. However, the fact that Blau and Duncan found most mobility to occur over very short distances is not particularly supportive of the liberal theory. Moreover, the finding that mobility increased only very slightly between the 1910s and the 1960s directly contradicts the liberal theory, which predicts increasing mobility with increasing industrialization.

Blau and Duncan limited their analysis to one industrial society, and the liberal theory of industrialism can be properly evaluated only with extensive comparative data. There have been a number of comparative studies of mobility (e.g., Lipset and Bendix, 1959), but most of these have suffered from one or another methodological defect (Erikson and Goldthorpe, 1993). The most comprehensive and methodologically sophisticated comparative study of mobility has been carried out by Robert Erikson and John Goldthorpe (1993), who studied 12 industrial nations, and who were especially interested in directly testing the liberal theory. In looking at mobility trends, they found that in all the societies they studied there was nothing that could be identified as a general trend toward increasing mobility. Instead, their findings supported Pitirim Sorokin's (1927) argument made earlier in this century that mobility trends in industrial societies display "trendless fluctuation," rising during periods of social upheaval (e.g., war, revolution, rapid commercial or techno-logical change) and then falling back again and remaining relatively stable the rest of the time. Sorokin based his argument on the view that barriers to mobility can usually be taken as a constant in all stratification systems. Thus, although they may permit somewhat greater mobility than preindustrial societies, industrial societies sub-stitute new barriers to mobility (e.g., educational qualifications) for old ones, and the class structure tends to rigidify around these new barriers.

Erikson and Goldthorpe also calculated absolute rates of mobility for the 12 industrial nations they studied. Their findings are pre-sented in table 7.5. These findings confirm earlier studies that show relatively high levels of mobility in industrial societies. They also show that the differences among industrial societies are relatively modest. The range of variation in upward mobility is 30–42 percent, in downward mobility 8–18 percent, and in net mobility 15–29 percent. The societies with the highest levels of upward mobility are Sweden, the United States, Australia, and Japan, whereas the societies with the lowest levels of downward mobility are Hungary, Ireland, and Poland (which is not surprising since these are the least industrialized societies in the sample). If we calculate mobility levels in terms of net mobility, then the societies with the highest net mobility rates are Sweden, Poland, and Japan, whereas the societies with the lowest net mobility rates are England, Scotland, and West Germany. The question of just how different something has to be

Table 7.5 *Rates of absolute mobility in 12 industrial nations*

Nation	Total upward mobility (%)	Total downward mobility (%)	Net mobility (%)	Immobility & downward mobility combined (%)
England	32	17	15	68
France	32	12	20	68
West Germany	33	14	19	67
Hungary	35	9	26	65
Ireland	30	9	21	70
Northern Ireland	34	11	23	66
Poland	35	8	27	65
Scotland	33	18	15	67
Sweden	42	13	29	58
United States	40	15	25	60
Australia	39	13	26	61
Japan	39	12	27	61

Source: Erikson and Goldthorpe (1993), tables 6.3, 9.4, 10.5

to be called different (rather than similar or the same) is always a difficult one to answer. My own conclusion in this case is that, while industrial societies certainly cannot be said to have identical rates of mobility, the rates they display are reasonably similar.

What goes unsaid in Erikson and Goldthorpe's analysis is anything concerning the fact that the most prevalent feature of modern industrial societies is intergenerational *immobility* from one generation to the next. When the rate of immobility is added to the rate of downward mobility, it is seen immediately that industrial societies are strikingly alike, and that approximately two-thirds of the families in industrial populations are either no better off or actually worse off from one generation to the next. This finding is clearly not what the liberal theory of industrialism predicts and supports instead Sorokin's view that stratification systems always tend to rigidify. And we saw earlier just what criteria are the primary bases in industrial societies for the intergenerational transmission of social and economic advantages: ownership of the means of production, educational credentials, and organizational positions. Industrial societies certainly permit more mobility than agrarian societies of the past, but they are actually more notable for their "closed" than for their "open" features, a point largely lost in the mad rush to apply the latest forms of methodological and statistical sophistication to the study of mobility.

THE EVOLUTION OF THE MODERN STATE

The rise of national states in early modern Europe

In the centuries before the early modern era, Europe was home to a large number of relatively small states, many of which were highly decentralized feudal states characterized by what Perry Anderson (1974b) has called the "parcellization of sovereignty." There were approximately 500 sovereign states throughout all of Europe, some 200 to 300 of which were found in the Italian peninsula alone (Tilly, 1990). Beginning in the late fifteenth century, the European political scene began to change dramatically with the emergence of much larger and more highly centralized national states, what many historians have referred to as *absolute monarchies*. These states were not only much larger and more highly centralized than their predecessors, but also played a much greater role in the direction of economic and social life. Among their most prominent characteristics were "a standing army, a permanent bureaucracy, expanded national legal codes and judicatures, national taxation, political unification or domestication of religion and other political and economic jurisdictions, the nationalization of markets, and the generally accepted claim of royal (read 'central') preeminence in all of these areas" (J.W. White, 1988:5).

The earliest of the absolutisms emerged in Spain and England in the late fifteenth century. Spanish absolutism emerged with the Hapsburg Dynasty that formed through the marriage of Ferdinand and Isabella. English absolutism began with the rise to power of the Tudors, who were followed by the Stuarts in the early seventeenth century. Sweden also developed an absolutist state in the early sixteenth century, and it was one of the most rapid to develop in western Europe. The grandest and most exemplary of the western European absolutisms was unquestionably that of France, which reached its pinnacle during the reign of Louis XIV, the "sun king," in the late seventeenth century. Louis, of course, is alleged to have uttered the famous expression *l'État, c'est moi* (P. Anderson, 1974b).

Several absolutisms also developed at about the same time in eastern Europe, especially in Prussia, Austria, Poland, and Russia (P. Anderson, 1974b). There has been considerable dispute concerning whether or not Tokugawa Japan was a type of absolute state. Perry Anderson (1974b) has claimed that Tokugawa Japan was not absolutist, whereas others (e.g., Vlastos, 1986; J.W. White, 1988) have claimed that it was, or at least that it had many of the earmarks of absolutism. James White (1988) has shown that there were many parallels between western European and Tokugawa Japanese political institutions. If Tokugawa Japan was not an absolutism, then it was certainly close to it.

What was behind the formation of these national states? Perhaps the best-known explanation is the Marxist argument that absolutism emerged to protect the economic interests of the feudal nobility in the period of the transition from feudalism to capitalism (Takahashi, 1952; Hill, 1953; Kiernan, 1965, 1980; P. Anderson, 1974b). Perry Anderson (1974b) has developed the most extensive version of this argument. Anderson's interpretation is that the era of the rise of absolutism was a period during which the rise of capitalism and the growing economic power of the bourgeoisie had severely undercut the class interests of the old feudal nobility. The nobility was unable to exercise the power over the peasantry that it once had, and therefore it looked to a new form of state to exercise this power for them. As Anderson (1974b:18) has remarked:

Absolutism was essentially just this: *a redeployed and recharged apparatus of feudal domination*, designed to clamp the peasant masses back into their traditional social position – despite and against the gains they had won by the widespread commutation of dues. . . . [The absolutist state] was the new political carapace of a threatened nobility.

But, although Marxists have agreed that the absolutist state represented a form of class power, they have disagreed among themselves about which social class the absolutist state represented. Friedrich Engels (1970[1884]) viewed absolutism as mediating the economic interests of capitalists and nobles in a transitional era. Absolutism was a balancing mechanism that attempted to achieve a sort of equilibrium between these two classes. In the early stages of his work, Wallerstein (1974b) appeared to take a similar view, holding that absolutism was "the best choice between difficult alternatives for the two groups that [were] strongest in political, economic, and military terms" (1974b:355). However, later on he seems to slide toward the view that the absolutist state was by and large a state that promoted the economic interests of capitalists. A significant part of the problem here, as Wallerstein notes, has to do with just what is meant by the terms "nobility" and "capitalists." Especially in England, by the time of the emergence of absolutism the nobility had become essentially capitalist farmers and were thus not nobles in the traditional sense at all. Indeed, Wallerstein (1980a:32) says that he

could accept Anderson's entire statement if the adjective *feudal* were dropped. To me, the redeployment precisely involved substituting capitalist domination for feudal domination, whatever the outer shell of public terminology. Even Anderson himself admits that there is an "apparent paradox of Absolutism"; he states that while absolutism was protecting "aristocratic property and privileges," it "could *simultaneously* ensure the basic interests of the nascent mercantile and manufacturing classes."

Michael Hechter and William Brustein (1980) have tried to reconcile this disagreement by claiming that each position represents a significant portion of the truth. They argue that the absolutist states emerged originally for the reasons suggested by Anderson, but that in due time the state came to be increasingly aligned with the interests of capitalists. Some of the evidence does indeed seem to support Anderson's argument. The earliest of the absolutisms was that in Spain and, as we saw in chapter 6, Spain failed to achieve core status in the world-economy because of the nature of its overgrown and highly parasitic state. This was not a state at all suited to advancing capitalist interests and was much more a "feudal state." Moreover, the weakest and most short-lived of all the absolutisms was that of England, and yet England was clearly in the forefront of capitalist advance. Nobles had become capitalist farmers here more than in any other early modern nation. Consider also the fact that Holland never experienced an absolutism at all, but was instead characterized by a highly decentralized federation. And yet the United Provinces was the leading capitalist power in the age of absolutism.

A more Weberian interpretation of the rise of national states has been presented by Charles Tilly (1990). Tilly has shown that in the half-millennium before 1500 there were two major kinds of states in Europe: small city-states or urban federations, and large territorial states. The former prevailed where the economy was dominated by merchants, whereas the latter was found where mercantile interests were weak and the landlord class held sway. The city-states and urban federations rested on the concentration of the economic power of capitalists, whereas the large territorial states rested on the concentration of coercive (i.e., military) power. The new national states after 1500, Tilly argues, emerged as the result of the combination of both forms of power and, once in existence, these new national states were so effective in the interstate system, especially as war machines, that other states were compelled to imitate them or suffer severe consequences. And what made these new national states so effective at this particular time? The answer, Tilly says, is that the extensive capital accumulation going on in the larger states (such as England and France) reduced the military advantages of the small, merchant-oriented states. As a result, "war expanded in scale and cost, partly as a function of the increased ability of the larger states to milk their economies, or their colonies, to pay for armed force. They won at war. The efforts of the smaller states to defend themselves either transformed, absorbed, or combined them into national states" (Tilly, 1990:190).

In my view, explaining the rise of the new national states is one of the most difficult problems in modern macrosociology. I am not completely satisfied with any of the explanations, but I would tentatively combine Hechter and Brustein's argument with Tilly's. Absolutism emerged, as Hechter and Brustein argue, "at the behest of the landed aristocracy," but increasingly became a capitalist state over time (indeed, just as nobles were increasingly becoming capitalist farmers). Yet we must not forget the role of the interstate system. Once in existence, large bureaucratic states able to draw extensively on concentrated capital to increase their concentration of the means of coercion were extremely formidable foes (note the tremendous military effectiveness of the Spanish Hapsburg state). This new type of state became the model for others, and thus that form of the state spread throughout Europe. Anderson relies on this very argument to explain the rise of eastern European absolutisms – they were, he says, merely reactive to what was happening in western Europe, which dominated the interstate system – but there is no reason to limit the argument to eastern Europe. The new national state was a striking evolutionary adaptation throughout Europe, and it was clearly recognized as such by both its creators and its imitators.

The increasing size and scope of the state

One of the most striking trends in the evolution of the modern world is the enormous increase in the size of the state and the scope of its functions. Michael Mann (1993) has examined the growth of the state from a quantitative standpoint from 1760 to 1910, and I have provided quantitative data on state growth from 1910 to the present. Table 7.6 summarizes the gross size of government expenditures throughout this period for four Western nations. These data show an enormous increase in state spending. In France, state spending increased eight-fold from 1760 to 1910, another 53-fold from 1910 to 1940, and then another 21-fold between 1960 and 1988. In Germany, there was a 44-fold increase in state expenditures between 1760 and 1910, another 104-fold increase from 1910 to 1988, and over the entire period between 1760 and 1988 Germany's state expenditures multiplied by a factor of 4,557. In the United Kingdom and the United States state spending increased even more dramatically. In the United Kingdom, there was only a nine-fold increase in expenditures between 1760 and 1910, but from 1910 to 1988 spending increased by a factor of 809, and over the entire period from 1760 to 1988 spending multiplied 7,056 times. Finally, in the United States state expenditures increased 89–fold from 1800 to

Table 7.6 *Central government expenditures of advanced industrial societies, 1760–1988*

Year	United States	United Kingdom	France	Germany
1760	——	18	506	61
1800	11	51	726	106
1850	45	56	1,473	252
1900	607	144	3,557	1,494
1910	977	157	3,878	2,673
1920	6,358	1,188	39,644	145,255
1930	3,320	814	55,712	8,392
1940	9,055	3,954	204,000	——
1950	40,000	3,417	——	11,613
1960	92,000	6,157	60,034	30,820
			(new francs)	
1970	196,000	14,086	162,233	87,602
1980	591,000	76,200	624,000	218,000
1988	1,064,000	127,000	1,231,000	278,000

Figures are given in millions of units of national currency.
Sources: Mann (1993), table 11.1; Mitchell (1992), table G5; Mitchell (1993), table G5

1910, another 1,089–fold between 1910 and 1988, and during the entire period between 1760 and 1988 state spending increased by the huge factor of 96,727!

Mann (1993) has suggested that these data may be misleading because they do not control for price inflation and population growth. He therefore examined state spending as a percentage of national income from 1760 to 1910, and I have extended the data to 1985 (table 7.7). As we can clearly see from these data, growth in the size of the state does not appear so dramatic. In fact, between 1760 and 1910 state spending actually *declined* as a percentage of national income: in France from 12 to 11 percent, in Germany from 35 to 6 percent, and in the United Kingdom from 22 to 7 percent. In the United States state spending increased only very slightly, from 2.4 percent of national income in 1800 to 2.5 percent in 1910. So, although the state was growing in absolute terms during this period, it was shrinking relative to the size of national income. However, in the second period we are considering (1910–85), state spending clearly increased in size even in relative terms: in the United States from 2.5 percent of national income to 18.4 percent, in the United Kingdom from 7 percent to 33.5 percent, in France from 11 percent to 23.6 percent, and in Germany from 6 percent to 14.1 percent. After 1960 data are available for another country, Japan, and we can see that state spending grew considerably there in a very short period, from 5.9 percent of national income in 1960 to 15 percent in 1985. Although these numbers do not look all that dramatic, if we remember that national income increased greatly from 1910 to the present then it is quite clear that the state has grown enormously. State spending took an increasing proportion of a quantity of funds that was itself increasing dramatically.

The figures we have been discussing refer only to central or federal government expenditures. If we add to these figures expenditures from local, state, or provincial governments, then we can see that total government spending currently takes a large bite out of national income and that this bite increased significantly just in the short period between 1950 and 1985 (table 7.8). During this period, total state expenditures increased from 20 percent of national income to 35.3 percent in the United States, from 14.6 percent to 26.9 percent in Japan, from 30.1 percent to 44.9 percent in the United Kingdom, from 26.7 percent to 49.4 in France, and from 28.3 percent to 43.4 percent in West Germany. In three of these countries

Table 7.7 *Central government expenditures as a proportion of Gross Domestic Product, 1760–1985*

Year	United States	Japan	United Kingdom	France	Germany
1760	——	——	22	12	35
1800	2.4	——	27	9	23
1850	1.7	——	10	9	9
1900	2.8	——	8	12	5
1910	2.5	——	7	11	6
1920	5.5	——	19.1	25.5	——
1930	4.0	——	16.6	14.3	10.2
1940	11.1	——	66.1	——	——
1950	12.3	——	25.6	——	10.2
1960	15.0	5.9	22.9	18.2	10.8
1970	16.5	8.7	24.1	19.0	11.5
1980	16.3	15.1	31.9	20.8	14.1
1985	18.4	15.0	33.5	23.6	14.1

Sources: Mann (1993), table 11.3; Mitchell (1992), table G5; United Nations (1948), table 139; Webber and Wildavsky (1986), table 13; Lane, McKay, and Newton (1991), table 5.9

Table 7.8 *General government expenditures as a proportion of Gross Domestic Product, 1950–85*

Year	United States	Japan	United Kingdom	France	West Germany
1950	20.0	14.6	30.1	26.7	28.3
1960	25.0	13.6	29.3	30.2	28.2
1970	30.3	14.0	33.2	34.7	32.6
1980	33.5	25.4	42.3	43.1	42.8
1985	35.3	26.9	44.9	49.4	43.4

Source: Lane, McKay, and Newton (1991), table 5.6

total government expenditures amount to nearly half of national income.

Michael Mann (1993) argues that many social scientists, even those of quite different theoretical persuasions, have treated the development of the modern state as an evolutionary "onward-and-upward" story, and that this story is quite mistaken. There is some justification for Mann's view in the period he is considering (1760–1910) because, although the state was increasing in absolute size it claimed a decreasing proportion of national income and therefore was smaller relative to the size of civil society. But Mann's view cannot be extended into the twentieth century at all. During this time the absolute size of the state increased enormously and grew ever larger in relation to civil society.

The question arises, though, as to why relative state spending declined between 1760 and 1910. The reason seems to be a decline in the frequency of war. In this period the bulk of state expenditures was for military purposes, and with the decline of war relative state expenditure declined (Mann, 1993). Mann asks why relative state expenditures did not decline even more, and his answer is that the state was increasing its spending on *civilian* functions. He calculates that in 1760 about 25 percent of government spending was of a civilian nature but that this figure had increased to about 75 percent in 1910. Mann (1993:376) remarks that this marked a political transformation that was unparalleled in world history:

> The broadening of scope was occurring across European states of very diffrent constitutions and levels of economic development. The nineteenth century introduced major nonmilitary government expenditures. In contrast to previous centuries, civil expenditures increased through periods of peace instead of being, as in the past, a by-product of war. In 1846, the civil expenditure of the British state was more or less what it had been in 1820 and in every intervening year. But from 1847 on, a steady increase occurred in almost every year, war or peace. The pattern is confirmed in all available national statistics. War was no longer the only ratchet of state growth.

What, then, were civilian expenses actually devoted to? As Mann shows, education and transportation were the main items, followed closely by welfare spending (T.H. Marshall's [1964] "social citizenship"). Postal and telegraph services were also important. Table 7.9 extends Mann's analysis to 1975. Here we can see that civilian spending has continued to claim a larger and larger portion of all government expenditures. Only in the United States is military spending still about a quarter of total spending. In the United Kingdom, France, and West Germany military spending averages

Table 7.9 *Central government expenditures by type, 1975*

Country	Defense	Education	Health	Social security	Housing	Economic	Other
United States	24.6	3.4	9.3	36.6	2.9	8.7	14.4
United Kingdom	13.7	2.6	12.9	21.7	3.5	12.4	33.3
France	7.6	9.9	15.0	40.8	3.2	9.5	14.0
West Germany	10.5	1.1	19.6	48.9	0.3	8.7	10.9

The numbers are the percentage of total expenditures spent on each government function.
Source: Lane, McKay, and Newton (1991), table 5.35

only 11 percent of total spending. And the particular nature of civilian spending has changed. Education absorbs much less of it than it did a century ago, and much more is being spent on health and welfare items, especially on social security. This, of course, represents the well-known rise of the "welfare state."

So far we have been talking only about the most advanced industrial capitalist societies. But, as John Boli-Bennett (1980) has shown, the state has grown almost as much throughout the capitalist periphery and semiperiphery. Boli-Bennett assessed state growth by looking at increases in government revenue from 1910 to 1970. He found that in core societies government revenue increased from 13 percent of national income in 1910 to 31 percent in 1970. For the periphery, the increase was from 10 to 25 percent, and in the semiperiphery the increase was from 9 to 29 percent. Clearly the increasing size and scope of the state in the twentieth century is a truly global phenomenon. Why should this be so?

As Boli-Bennett points out, theories that focus only on the endogenous or internal development of societies cannot explain the growth of the modern state, because the state has grown almost as much in economically less-developed countries as it has in highly developed countries. Actually, because of global economic polarization, if state growth was simply a matter of economic development then there should be a widening gap in state growth between the developed and the less-developed countries. But of course just the opposite is occurring: states are becoming more equal in relative size and increasingly alike. Boli-Bennett explains this universal growth of state size in terms of what he calls *global integration*. By global integration Boli-Bennett (1980:87) means "the degree to which the local economy is oriented to the world economy, the degree to which local politics reflect developments in world politics, the degree of penetration of 'world culture' . . . into the local culture, and so on." Boli-Bennett's hypothesis is that the higher the level of a state's integration into the modern world-system, the more likely it has grown during the period from 1910 to 1970. Multiple regression analyses that he has carried out generally support his argument. But why, exactly, should states grow more if they are more integrated into the world-system? The answer seems to be that larger and more elaborate states are extremely important, or at least are perceived to be important, for success in the world-economy. As Boli-Bennett (1980:90) expresses it, "Those portions of the peripheral-country elites who are most thoroughly committed to the standards of the world system have been generally aware of the weakness of nonstate power centers and have recognized the importance of taking command of the state both for success in the system and for personal success in the local arena." It thus follows that "the degree of integration into the world system . . . boosts state dominance by implanting the ideology of statism and the organizational forms and techniques needed to implement the ideology; better integrated countries conform to statism more fully. Further, global integration increases the economic resources available to peripheral states to aid their expansion" (1980:95).

Peripheral and semiperipheral states in the twentieth century, then, have tried to use the state as a means of "catching up" economically with the core. And core societies have experienced enormous state growth largely because of the economic benefits of large and complex states. As we shall see in more detail later, core states have created systems of mass education to promote the ideology of statism and ensure ideological conformity of citizens to the state and its goals. Health and welfare systems have been created and have expanded to deal with one of the major contradictions of capitalism: its creation of high levels of economic inequality. The state has also created and expanded the infrastructures of communication and transportation that are vital to economic success. And we should not overlook the Keynesian role of the state as a major economic consumer, a role that it undertook to solve another major contradiction of capitalism: its tendencies toward underconsumption.

I know that this view of the state will be called "economistic" by its detractors, but it seems to me that the state is primarily understandable in terms of its economic functions. This does not mean that the state can be reduced entirely to economics. I agree with the neo-Weberians on that. But the state's autonomy is much less than they think, and as the modern world-system continues to expand and evolve its autonomy is reduced even further. I am not ashamed of the label "economism," but proudly embrace it.

The evolution of parliamentary democracy

Most of the large national states that began to form in Europe after the late fifteenth century initially took the form of absolutist monarchy. However, absolutism was to be short lived, and it, and monarchy itself, gradually gave way to states that took on parliamentary dimensions in which the power of the monarch was checked. Eventually, parliamentary government was combined with the basic principles of democratic government – constitutional liberties and mass suffrage – to create, in the nineteenth and twentieth centuries, the modern form of government that we now know as parliamentary democracy.

I shall understand by parliamentary democracy a form of government having the following characteristics (Reuschemeyer, Stephens, and Stephens, 1992):

1 parliamentary or congressional bodies that constitute power bases separate from the power bases of presidents or prime ministers and to which the remaining segments of government are responsible;
2 regular and fair elections of government officials to office by means of universal suffrage; and
3 the allocation of individual rights and liberties to the mass of the population.

In the actual evolution of parliamentary democracies, the parliamentary dimension was laid down first and was followed by the emergence of constitutional liberties. Mass suffrage appeared last and often much later than the other two dimensions of democracy.

It is important to recognize that in a number of societies the formal apparatus of democracy has evolved without there necessarily being an actual implementation of the content of this apparatus. In many Third World societies, especially in Latin America, the evolution of democracy has been largely limited to purely *formal* democracy. In Western capitalist societies, on the other hand, the formal apparatus of democracy has not been a sham but has been put into actual practice. In contrast to formal democracy, we usually call this *substantive* democracy. We should also distinguish between *restricted* and *unrestricted* democracies. Restricted democracies are those in which certain criteria, usually property qualifications, limit voting rights to those members of the population meeting the criteria. Until the early twentieth century (and much later in some societies) all parliamentary democracies restricted voting rights to the male population. All parliamentary democracies that are today unrestricted (except, of course, by age) began as restricted democracies that gradually eliminated restrictions over the course of time. In the United States, for example, there was a legal racial restriction on voting until 1865, and this restriction prevailed in a de facto manner until 1965. Today, all democracies in Western capitalist societies are unrestricted.

Barrington Moore (1966) was one of the first sociologists to carry out a systematic study of the historical origins of democratic government, concentrating, however, only on its parliamentary aspect. Parliamentary government emerged first in England during the English Civil War of the 1640s. At this time England was still a monarchy, but a major outcome of the war was to increase the power of parliament to the extent that it became more powerful than the king. In the United States parliamentary government can be dated to 1776 with the emergence of that country to sovereign status, although, of course, parliamentary bodies already existed in the American colonies. The American Constitution was written in 1787, thus establishing the second critical element of modern democracy. In France the turn toward parliamentary and constitutional government occurred through the French Revolution of the 1790s. The revolution was an attack on the monarchy and the aristocracy and it attempted to establish basic constitutional rights. *Liberté, Egalité, Fraternité!* was, of course, the famous slogan of the revolution.

Parliamentary and constitutional government, however, normally preceded by a long time the actual granting of voting rights to the population at large. Some scholars see mass suffrage as the critical element of modern democracy, and do not acknowledge these early parliamentary governments as democratic (Rueschemeyer, Stephens, and Stephens, 1992). It was not until well into the nineteenth century that Western capitalist societies began to implement mass suffrage. Table 7.10 presents a chronology of the development of suffrage in Western societies. If we define mass suffrage as universal manhood suffrage, then we can see that the first societies to achieve it were Switzerland, France, Norway, Denmark, Sweden, the United Kingdom, the Netherlands, and Belgium, all of which did so between 1848 and 1919. The British settler colonies – the United States, Canada, Australia, and New Zealand – were also among the earliest democracies, although the situation in the United States was complicated by the de facto racial restriction on voting in the southern states.

Table 7.10 *Chronology of the development of mass suffrage in industrial societies*

Country	Milestones in the development of mass suffrage	
United States	1776:	restricted manhood suffrage (restricted by property or taxpaying qualifications, which varied from state to state; also restricted by race);
	1792–1863:	elimination of property and taxpaying restrictions; by the end of this period all but four states had removed these restrictions; after Mississippi in 1817, no state entered the union with a property or taxpaying qualification;
	1865:	restriction by race eliminated, but not effectively implemented in the southern states;
	1920:	universal suffrage for adult men and women (but a de facto racial restriction still prevailed in the southern states);
	1965:	universal suffrage for adult men and women (de facto racial restriction finally abolished in the southern states).
Japan	1889:	restricted suffrage for males 25 and older (restricted by minimum tax payments);
	1925:	restricted manhood suffrage for citizens 25 and older (exclusion of the indigent);
	1946:	universal and equal suffrage for all men and women 20 and older.
Belgium	1831:	equal but restricted manhood suffrage;
	1894:	universal but unequal manhood suffrage (additional votes for house owners and citizens with higher education);
	1919:	universal and equal manhood suffrage for men over 21;
	1948:	universal and equal suffrage for all men and women over age 21.
Denmark	1849:	equal but restricted suffrage for male citizens age 30 and older (servants and farm laborers without their own household and those receiving public relief excluded);
	1918:	universal and equal suffrage for all men and women 29 and older.
France	1815:	almost universal and equal manhood suffrage;

Table 7.10—*contd.*

	1824:	restricted and unequal suffrage for male citizens 30 and older (general electorate restricted by high direct tax minima);
	1831:	restricted but almost equal manhood suffrage for citizens 25 and older;
	1848:	universal and equal suffrage for all male citizens 21 and older;
	1945:	universal and equal suffrage for all men and women 21 and older.
Germany	1848:	universal and equal suffrage for all male citizens (with minor exceptions);
	1871:	universal and equal suffrage for all male citizens 25 and over;
	1919:	universal and equal suffrage for all men and women 20 and older.
Italy	1861:	equal but restricted manhood suffrage (limited to citizens 25 and older who were literate and who paid minimum taxes);
	1913:	almost universal and equal suffrage for male citizens 30 and over, and for male citizens 21 and over who had completed military service or had one of the following: had finished primary school, had paid a minimum tax, or had exercised official functions;
	1919:	universal and equal manhood suffrage for citizens 21 and older; also, suffrage for all men who had participated in war, regardless of age;
	1946:	universal and equal suffrage for all men and women 21 and older.
Netherlands	1849:	equal but restricted manhood suffrage for citizens 23 and older (restricted by payment of high direct taxes);
	1897:	equal but restricted suffrage for male citizens 25 and older (restricted by property ownership, payment of taxes, income level, savings, or having passed certain occupational examinations);
	1918:	universal and equal suffrage for male citizens 25 and older;
	1922:	universal and equal suffrage for men and women 25 and older.

Table 7.10—*contd.*

Norway	1815:	equal but restricted manhood suffrage (restricted by high occupational and property requirements);
	1900:	almost universal and equal suffrage for male citizens 25 and older (suffrage temporarily suspended in cases of bankruptcy and receipt of public relief);
	1921:	universal and equal adult suffrage for citizens 23 and older.
Sweden	1866:	equal but restricted manhood suffrage for citizens 21 and older (restricted by high economic qualifications);
	1909:	almost universal and equal suffrage for male citizens 24 and older (excluding those receiving public relief);
	1921:	universal and equal suffrage for men and women 23 and older.
Switzerland	1848:	universal and equal suffrage for male citizens 20 and older;
	1971:	universal and equal suffrage for men and women 20 and older.
United Kingdom	1832:	restricted and unequal manhood suffrage for citizens 21 and older (restricted by income and property qualifications);
	1868:	reduction of income and property qualifications (England and Scotland only);
	1885:	reduction and standardization of qualifications throughout UK;
	1918:	universal and almost equal suffrage for male citizens 21 and older, and for women 30 and older who are householders or wives of householders (some citizens allowed two votes);
	1928:	universal and almost equal suffrage for men and women 21 and older (some plural voting still permitted).

Sources: Flora (1983: 100–48); Hane (1992); Porter (1918: 12–13, 110)

There were four other western European countries that established mass suffrage during this period but which suffered democratic breakdowns in the twentieth century: Austria-Hungary, Germany, Italy, and Spain. Germany and Italy, of course, suffered fascist interludes during and around the period of the Second World War. All of these countries have since reestablished democratic institutions, although Spain did so only very recently. In Japan, the evolution of parliamentary democracy closely paralleled its evolution in the West. The development of parliamentary democracy in Japan is quite similar to its development in Germany. It established universal manhood suffrage in 1925 (Hane, 1992) but experienced a fascist democratic breakdown during World War II. As a result of American occupation after the war, Japan reestablished and extended democratic institutions after 1946 (Ishida and Krauss, 1989).

As noted in the last chapter, democracy is today universal in the capitalist core, but seldom found in the periphery and semiperiphery. The largest number of democratic governments in the Third World have been located in Latin America, but for the most part these have been formal democracies involving little implementation of the real content or substance of democracy. A great deal of discussion has taken place in recent years concerning the so-called redemocratization of Latin America after the interlude of military-led bureaucratic-authoritarian states in the 1960s and 1970s. Some observers believe that the replacement of military governments with civilian governments signals a real move toward democracy (Cammack, 1986). However, much caution is in order. The political history of Latin America is strongly marked by a cyclical alternation between more democratic and less democratic periods rather than by a truly linear process of gradual democratic triumph (E. Stephens, 1989), and what is happening now may simply be a democratic phase of the cycle. Moreover, the shift toward democratic government is more aptly described as the move to civilian governments that exhibit the outer shell of democracy but little of its real substance (Cardoso, 1986; Herman and Petras, 1985; Petras, 1987). Latin America is still a very long way from democratic government on the Western model.

What lies behind the evolution of parliamentary democracy? Why is this form of government universal in the capitalist core but infrequently found in the periphery and semiperiphery? The answer surely must have to do with the evolution of capitalism, since parliamentary democracy has evolved in tandem with capitalism (or at least core capitalism) in the West. Marxists such as Barrington Moore (1966) and Albert Szymanski (1978) have argued that parliamentary democracy has evolved in conjunction with capitalism because it is the form of government most suited to the economic interests of the bourgeoisie. Parliamentary democracy works best for capitalists because it allows maximum freedom of economic action and thus permits capitalists a relatively unimpeded search for profits both domestically and around the globe. As Szymanski has put it (1978:147):

> As the commercial class became the dominant class in society, it established republican and parliamentary forms as the instruments of its rule. These forms are best suited to articulate the diverse interests within this class and work out a common class will. . . .
> . . . [B]usiness must have assurances from the state that it will not arbitrarily interfere with the system of contracts and expectations. The best guarantee of moderation and lack of arbitrariness on the part of the state is the parliamentary form.

Moore argues that parliamentary government triumphed in England after the 1640s because of the rise of capitalist farmers to economic dominance. Similarly, Szymanski (1978:150) has said that "parliamentary forms developed further and consolidated themselves earlier in England because England was always a major and eventually *the* leading commercial power in the world. The development and triumph of parliamentarianism in the British Isles must be understood as the natural result of the early development of commercial, and later industrial capitalist forms in that country."

Easily the most comprehensive sociological analysis of the rise of democracy is the very recent work of Dietrich Rueschemeyer, Evelyne Huber Stephens, and John Stephens (1992), who challenge the Marxist interpretation. They claim that the Marxist argument may be correct for the parliamentary dimension of democracy, but that it is completely incapable of explaining the rise of mass suffrage, which they believe is the most important dimension of democracy. Capitalists, they say, have normally been opposed if not downright hostile to mass suffrage for the simple reason that granting the working class a share of political power would promote working-class economic interests against capitalist interests. The rise of mass suffrage was due, instead, to the formation of large, well-organized working classes who struggled mightily to gain the vote. Rueschemeyer, Stephens, and Stephens are able to show that mass suffrage developed earliest and most fully in those capitalist societies that had achieved the highest levels of industrialization, and thus the largest working classes.

Democracy, then, or at least mass suffrage, was a class phenomenon, but it was the product of the struggles of the working classes rather than the aims of capitalists. Although the bourgeoisie generally favored suffrage only for themselves and strongly opposed mass suffrage, the class that was the most hostile to mass suffrage was the landed nobility. This class was normally engaged in what Rueschemeyer, Stephens, and Stephens call *labor-repressive agriculture*, which depended on the economic and political subjection of the peasantry. In societies where this class still retained great economic power – in other words, in societies with low levels of industrialization – little progress toward mass suffrage was made because the politically powerless peasantry was the largest social class and the working class was small and weak. Most notable here are the countries of Austria-Hungary, Germany, Italy, and Spain. These were societies in which democracy emerged later and was highly unstable for certain periods, and they were also societies in which the landed nobility retained a great deal of political power. The last of these societies to democratize, Spain, is the one in which the economy was dominated longest by the landlord–peasant relationship.

In the British settler colonies mass suffrage emerged in a somewhat different way. Although they were still highly agricultural even toward the end of the nineteenth century, the widespread availability of cheap land prevented (except in the US South) the emergence of a wealthy class of landlords engaged in labor-repressive agriculture. Most farmers were free and independent. Moreover, all these colonies inherited the political traditions of Great Britain, which gave them a democratic (or at least parliamentary and constitutional) foundation on which to build. And, in time, the working classes of these societies did grow larger and stronger and were able to exert strong pressures for their political inclusion.

The failure of genuine democracy to emerge in the Third World also seems to confirm Rueschemeyer, Stephens, and Stephens's theory. As we saw in chapter 6, Latin America is the most industrialized part of the Third World, and democracy has developed farther there than in Asia and Africa. But why has it been so limited? In chapter 6 we identified some of the reasons, but we can now add the all-important fact that, compared to the capitalist core, Latin America's level of industrialization is quite low, especially in Central America where the most repressive Latin American governments tend to be found. The landed upper classes still exert enormous economic and political power, and the working classes are relatively small and weak. Democracy has had the best chance of development and consolidation where export expansion has been basic to the economy, where exports have tended to be minerals rather than agricultural goods, where agriculture has tended to be nonlabor-intensive, where considerable industrialization and economic diversification have occurred, where mass political parties are not too radical (in order that they not prompt a feeling of severe threat on the part of the capitalist and landed upper classes), and where possibilities have existed for a political alliance between the middle and working classes. This last factor seems to be especially crucial, for Rueschemeyer, Stephens, and Stephens note that no democratic success has been achieved in Latin America without the political involvement of the middle classes because the working classes are too small and weak by themselves. In addition, political intervention by the core, especially by the United States, has impeded the development of democracy because that country, despite all of its sanctimonious talk of human rights, has generally favored repressive governments because they have been aligned with American capitalist interests.

Rueschemeyer, Stephens, and Stephens's argument seems to work remarkably well in explaining the development of democracy in the modern world. However, one weakness that can be pointed to is their relative neglect of the *constitutional* dimension of modern democracy. This would seem to be a dimension that, if not quite on a par with mass suffrage, nonetheless is of great importance in terms of the nature of government. In many instances, constitutional liberties evolved considerably earlier than mass suffrage. For example, the US Constitution was written in 1787, nearly three-quarters of a century in advance of universal manhood suffrage in the United States, and basic constitutional liberties were established in France in 1791, Sweden in 1809, Norway in 1814, the Netherlands in 1815, and Belgium in 1831 (Peaslee, 1966–70). And, as Anthony Giddens (1982:172) has noted, "The civil rights of individual freedom and equality before the law were fought for and won by the rising bourgeois or capitalist class in pursuit of their quest to destroy feudal obligations and restrictions on trade." This means that the capitalist class has had a greater role in the development of democracy than Rueschemeyer, Stephens, and Stephens wish to acknowledge.

In the final analysis, though, this work is to my mind the finest sociological study and interpretation of the growth of democracy ever undertaken. It is a type of non-Marxian materialist argument that explains the development of democracy largely in terms of the inner tensions of capitalism as an economic system. As the authors put it (1992:302; emphasis added), "In the end our conclusion is simple. It was neither capitalists nor capitalism as such but rather the *contradictions of capitalism* that advanced the cause of political equality. Capitalism contributed to democracy primarily because it changed the balance of class power in favor of the subordinate classes." With the qualifications noted above (i.e., the role of capitalists in promoting parliamentary and constitutional government), this is an argument that is not difficult to accept and that fits nicely within the theoretical framework of evolutionary materialism.

THE EMERGENCE AND EXPANSION OF MASS EDUCATION

One of the more noteworthy aspects of the modern world is the emergence and expansion of systems of mass education. Within the last century and a half, education has been transformed from a tiny social institution that had little relevance to the lives of most individuals to a large-scale, mass institution with a great deal of relevance to the lives of most individuals. This has been especially true in the advanced industrial societies, but it has also been true to a significant degree in less-developed countries.

The emergence and early expansion of primary education is depicted in tables 7.11 and 7.12. Table 7.11 shows the dates at which primary schooling was made compulsory by the governments of industrial societies. Germany was the first society to establish compulsory primary education, having done so in 1763. It was followed in order by Denmark, Sweden, Norway, Italy, Switzerland, England and Wales, and France, all of which established compulsory primary schooling in the nineteenth century, and by the Netherlands, which did so just at the turn of the twentieth century. In the United States the establishment of compulsory education was a matter for individual states rather than the federal government. As table 7.11 shows, Massachussetts was the first state to make primary schooling compulsory, and 32 states had done so by the beginning of the twentieth century. In Japan, compulsory schooling was established as early as 1872.

Table 7.11 *The development of primary education in industrial societies*

Country	Timing of introduction of compulsory education	
United States	1852–1900:	first law establishing compulsory schooling passed by state of Massachusetts in 1852; by 1900 32 states had established compulsory schooling.
Japan	1872:	8 years of compulsory schooling introduced (but frequently not enforced);
	1879:	period of compulsory schooling set at 4 years, with each school year lasting 4 months;
	1880:	period of compulsory schooling reduced to 3 years, but school year extended to 32 weeks;
	1900:	period of compulsory schooling extended to 4 years.
Belgium	1914:	8 years of compulsory schooling introduced (ages 6–14).
Denmark	1814:	7 years of compulsory schooling (ages 7–14) introduced 3 days a week;
	1849:	compulsory schooling extended to 6 days a week.
France	1882:	7 years of compulsory schooling (ages 6–13) introduced; extended to 8 years (6–14) in 1936 and 10 years (6–16) in 1959.
Germany	1763:	in Prussia, 7–8 years of compulsory schooling (ages 6–13/14) introduced;
	1871:	in German Empire, 8 years of compulsory schooling introduced (ages 6–14).
Italy	1859:	in Kingdom of Sardinia, 2–4 years of compulsory education introduced (ages 6–8/10);
	1877:	compulsory schooling extended to all regions of united Italy;
	1904:	compulsory schooling extended to 6 years (ages 6–12);
	1923:	compulsory schooling extended to 8 years (ages 6–14).
Netherlands	1900:	6 years of compulsory education introduced (ages 7–13);
	1920:	compulsory schooling extended to 7 years (ages 7–14);

Table 7.11—*contd.*

	1942:	compulsory schooling extended to 8 years (ages 7–15).
Norway	1848:	7 years of compulsory education introduced (ages 7–14).
Sweden	1842:	compulsory schooling introduced for undefined period of time;
	1878:	length of compulsory schooling fixed at 6 years (ages 7–13).
Switzerland	1874:	compulsory schooling introduced (age of entry and length of time varied by canton).
England and Wales	1880:	8 years of compulsory schooling (ages 5—13) introduced;
	1918:	length of compulsory schooling extended to 9 years (ages 5–14).

Sources: Flora (1983: 561–623); Johansen, Collins, and Johnson (1986: 230); Hane (1992: 102–4)

Table 7.12 displays primary school enrollment figures for the years between 1870 and 1940. As can be seen, primary enrollments were already very high in most industrial countries by 1870, and they expanded considerably between that date and 1940. In the less-developed countries, primary enrollments were weak in 1870, but had increased substantially by 1940. Primary education had obviously become an important aspect of the lives of most individuals in industrial countries, as well as important to the lives of many in the less-developed world.

Table 7.12 *Worldwide primary educational enrollments, 1870–1940*

Country	Enrollment as a percentage of persons aged 5–14	
	1870–5	1935–40
Developed countries		
United States	72	91
Canada	75	103
Australia	70	89
Japan	20	61
Belgium	63	63
Denmark	58	67
France	57	——
Germany	67	72
Italy	29	59

Table 7.12—*contd.*

Netherlands	59	70
Norway	61	76
Sweden	57	65
Switzerland	76	70
England and Wales	49	73
Eastern European countries		
Czechoslovakia	——	65
Hungary	40	59
Poland	——	60
Romania	7	63
Russia (USSR)	4	——
Less-developed countries		
Barbados	33	62
Cuba	——	41
Jamaica	21	55
Martinique	——	59
Costa Rica	——	44
Dominican Republic	5	25
Mexico	16	38
Argentina	21	58
Brazil	6	30
Chile	19	48
Colombia	6	26
China	——	12
India	2	12
Ceylon (Sri Lanka)	7	54
Egypt	——	25
Iran (Persia)	——	8
Ghana	——	10
Mauritius	9	41
Nigeria	——	10

Source: Benavot and Riddle (1988: appendix)

Secondary education, however, lagged considerably behind primary education in the period being considered. Good secondary enrollment data are difficult to come by, but a few are available. As late as 1910, when primary enrollments were very high, a mere 4 percent of the relevant age cohort was enrolled in secondary schools in Britain, and only 12 percent was enrolled in Japan (Dore, 1976). In the United States the percentage was only 11 percent (Collins, 1979). As late as the 1960s, secondary enrollments were relatively strong in the United States and Japan, with, respectively, 75 and 57 percent of the relevant age cohorts completing secondary school; however, throughout much of western Europe secondary education was still of minimal significance, with only 30 percent of the relevant age cohort in France, 12 percent in England, and 11 percent in West Germany completing secondary school (Collins, 1979). Table 7.13 gives more complete data on secondary school enrollments, even though they are not expressed in ideal form. It is clear from the table that secondary education was irrelevant to the lives of most members of Western industrial societies until well into the twentieth century. The average date of the first significant expansion of secondary enrollments was 1938, and the average date at which enrollments began to exceed 20 percent of persons aged 10–19 was 1955.

Table 7.13 *Secondary education in western industrial societies*

Country	Approximate date of beginning of first significant expansion of secondary education[a]	Approximate date at which secondary enrollments reached 20% of 10–19-year olds
United States	1910	1930
Belgium	1947	1957
Denmark	1930	1964
France	1940	1957
Germany	1950	1964
Italy	1950	1962
Netherlands	1937	1957
Norway	1949	1959
Sweden	1938	1958
England and Wales	1925	1941

[a] Before this date secondary enrollments were very low and grew very slowly.
Sources: Flora (1983: 561–628); Collins (1979), table 1.1

Enrollments in higher education have, of course, lagged behind secondary enrollments. As table 7.14 shows, as late as 1965 an average of only 18 percent of the relevant age cohort was enrolled in an institution of higher education in 12 Western industrial countries, and the corresponding figure was a mere 4 percent in 16 less-developed countries. Nevertheless, higher education has expanded considerably in industrial countries in the second half of the twentieth century, and especially from the early 1960s on. By 1989, the 13 industrial countries shown in table 7.14 had achieved an average enrollment percentage of 33 percent (38 percent if the three less-

Table 7.14 *Worldwide enrollments in higher education, 1965–89*

Country	Enrollments as a percentage of relevant age cohort	
	1965	1989
Developed societies		
United Kingdom	12	24
Netherlands	17	32
France	18	37
West Germany	——	32
Denmark	14	32
Sweden	13	31
Canada	26	66
United States	40	63
Australia	16	32
Japan	13	31
Czechoslovakia	14	18
Hungary	13	15
Poland	18	20
Less-developed societies		
Zaire	0	2
Tanzania	0	0
India	5	——
China	0	2
Senegal	1	3
Indonesia	1	——
Nigeria	0	3
Egypt	7	20
Peru	8	32
Turkey	4	13
Colombia	3	14
Chile	6	19
Brazil	2	11
Mexico	4	15
Argentina	14	41
South Korea	6	38

Source: World Bank (1992), table 29

developed eastern European countries are omitted). It has also expanded a great deal in the Third World, the enrollment percentage increasing from an average of 4 percent in 1965 to an average of 15 percent in 1989 for 14 less-developed countries in table 7.14. The two industrial societies that have undergone the greatest expansion of higher education are clearly the United States and Canada, where by 1989 approximately two-thirds of the relevant age cohort was attending an institution of higher education. It might even be argued that these two countries are moving toward the universalization of higher education.

There can be no doubt that education has become an increasingly important part of the lives of the members of industrial societies, and even of less-developed countries, within the last century. Indeed, John Meyer, Francisco Ramirez, Richard Rubinson, and John Boli-Bennett (1977) have spoken of what they call a "world educational revolution" in the middle of the twentieth century, and especially in the years between 1950 and 1970. The tremendous expansion of educational enrollments that they speak of can be seen to be continuing right down to the present time. An important feature of this expansion is that it is occurring not only in the highly industrialized countries, but in much of the less-developed world as well. The less-developed world still lags considerably behind the industrialized world, especially in secondary and tertiary enrollments, but it has expanded considerably nonetheless.

A few figures will establish the point that Meyer et al.'s basic argument about a world educational revolution is no fantasy. By 1950 the industrialized countries had achieved almost universal primary education, but the less-developed half of the world expanded its primary enrollments from an average of 37 percent of the relevant age cohort in 1950 to an average of 80 percent in 1989.[3] Secondary education expanded from an average enrollment figure of 13 percent in 1950 to an average of 50 percent in 1989 for all countries in the world (for the richer half of the world's countries, from 21 percent to 74 percent; for the poorer half, from 5 percent to 26 percent). Enrollments in higher education expanded in all countries from an average of 1.4 percent in 1950 to an average of 15 percent in 1989 (for the richer half of the world's countries, from 3 percent to 23 percent; for the poorer half, from 0.6 percent to 6 percent).

Explaining the expansion of mass education

What accounts for the enormous expansion of education at all levels from the middle of the nineteenth century to the present? Four major theories have been constructed, each of which we need to scrutinize.

The functionalist or meritocratic theory. The oldest and most widely known theory of educational expansion is a type of functionalist theory (Clark, 1962; Trow, 1966). This theory holds that education has expanded in direct conjunction with industrialization and occupational upgrading. As Western societies have industrialized in the nineteenth and twentieth centuries, their occupational structures have changed dramatically. Agricultural work has been replaced by work in factories and offices, but even more importantly there has been a long-term increase in the skill- and knowledge-levels of jobs. Less-skilled jobs have been gradually replaced by jobs requiring higher levels of knowledge and skill, and thus education has expanded to provide these capacities. More and more people have been required to spend longer and longer periods of time in school in order to acquire the things needed to do the increasingly demanding work of an industrial society.

Several serious problems with this theory have been identified (Collins, 1979; Berg, 1971). First, it has become increasingly apparent that students learn few relevant job skills in school. Randall Collins (1979) has argued that what schools convey is far more in the way of a status culture than a set of useful occupational skills. Krishan Kumar (1978:251) has marshalled evidence which strongly suggests that, whatever the extent to which schools once taught useful work-related skills, they seem to be doing an ever poorer job of it in recent decades:

Basic skills in literacy and numeracy seem actually to be falling in the populations of the industrial societies. In Britain, a survey of sixteen-year-old school-leavers in Liverpool revealed an average reading age of nine. Another survey, of employment agencies specifically concerned with school-leavers, found widespread complaints from the agencies of school-leavers barely literate and scarcely able to fill in application forms correctly. The University Grants Committee in its 1974–5 Report, pointed to the disturbing number of students who were entering universities without the basic skills and information needed to pursue their courses.

Kumar points to similar evidence from the United States. Indeed, almost any professor in an American college or university could testify that since the time Kumar wrote things have gotten much worse. And the evidence suggests that students at all educational levels are achieving at lower and lower levels compared to their predecessors. College graduates in the mid-1990s may well know less than high-school graduates knew in 1965. If achievement levels are dropping at the very same time that enrollments are expanding, as almost everyone seems to agree they are, then how is it possible to conclude that educational institutions teach relevant job skills that are becoming increasingly demanding over time? It defies all logic. Where, then, do workers learn their work-related skills if they are not learning them in school? The answer, as Collins points out, is that they learn them on the job. I would argue that the vast majority, probably in excess of 80 percent, of the jobs that people perform in modern industrial societies can easily be learned on the job itself within the first six months.[4]

In addition, there is the matter of the relationship between educational attainment and worker productivity. The assumption of the functionalist theory that this relationship is a close one has not fared well in empirical research (Collins, 1979; Berg, 1971). Ivar Berg (1971) has carried out a number of studies showing that there is no necessary relationship at all between productivity and education. In fact, in numerous situations workers with more education have actually been shown to be *less* productive. Berg reports the results of one study that examined job performance in 125 branches of a major bank in New York. It was found that performance (1971:93–4)

was inversely associated with the educational achievements of these 500 workers. The branches with the worst performance records were those in which a disproportionately (and significantly) high number of employees were attending educational programs after working hours! There was also evidence that performance was worst in precisely those branches in which, besides the educational achievements being higher, the managers stressed education in consultations with tellers concerning their futures with the bank.

The Marxist labor discipline theory. A sharp alternative to the functionalist argument is the notion, represented best by the work of Samuel Bowles and Herbert Gintis (1976), that formal education emerged and expanded in the nineteenth and twentieth centuries as a means of socializing and disciplining the nascent industrial working class. Bowles and Gintis's study is confined to the United States, but the logic of their argument applies (and indeed has been applied) to other industrial capitalist societies. The argument is that public primary education functioned to teach workers respect for authority and for the capitalist system and, in general, to provide them with the habits of mind and behavior that would make them productive workers who would help capitalists maximize their profits. Bowles and Gintis paid special attention to the emergence of primary education in Massachusetts, noting that it arose in conjunction with the American Industrial Revolution. They also tried to show that capitalists were often members of school boards and had a disproportionately strong influence on educational curricula.

Although much of the content of education is closely related in a general sense to the needs of the capitalist system, the specific formulation of Bowles and Gintis leaves much to be desired. For one thing, early primary schooling in the United States was somewhat more characteristic of rural than of urban areas (Meyer, Tyack, Nagel, and Gordon, 1979). In 1870 enrollment figures as a percentage of the relevant age cohort were 76 percent in rural areas and 70 percent in urban areas for northern and western states. By 1910 the rural–urban gap had actually increased, with the respective enrollment figures being 85 percent and 70 percent. Enrollments also grew faster in rural areas than in urban areas in several western European countries (Soysal and Strang, 1989).

Another line of evidence that contradicts Bowles and Gintis's argument is the fact that the overall temporal correspondence between industrialization and the emergence of compulsory primary education is not particularly close (MacDonald, 1988; Rubinson, 1986). For example, England was the first country in the world to industrialize, with its industrial revolution beginning around 1760, and yet it did not introduce compulsory schooling until as late as 1880 (table 7.11). Similarly, Belgium was an early industrializer (after about 1820 or 1830) but did not establish compulsory education until 1914, and France, another early industrializer, did not introduce compulsory schooling until 1882 (table 7.11). Moreover, the first country to establish compulsory education, Germany in 1763, was not one of the earliest European industrializers (table 7.11).

Finally, it is not possible to accept Bowles and Gintis's claim that education was something imposed on workers by capitalists. As Richard Rubinson (1986) has pointed out, education was not imposed on workers at all. Rather, in the United States at least, it was vigorously sought by workers and its expansion was opposed by the capitalist class. As Rubinson (1986:527) explains, this is what is to be expected: "Schooling everywhere has been valued for its prestige or economic and political power. Dominant groups do not impose valued statuses on subordinate groups. . . . [D]ominant groups want more education for themselves and less for others.

Once in power, such groups attempt to establish a monopoly in schooling to control the content of education to favor their own values and to limit access for other groups."

Educational expansion as credential inflation. Randall Collins (1979) has proposed a type of neo-Weberian explanation for the growth of educational enrollments, focusing especially on the United States, the society with by far the largest and most comprehensive educational system in the world. His argument is a relatively simple one. Beyond the level of primary education, education began to expand in the United States in the late nineteenth century and closely coincided with large-scale immigration from eastern and southern Europe. White Anglo-Saxon Protestants, the dominant ethnic group, viewed the education of immigrants as an important means of assimilating them into the dominant traditions of American culture. However, in due time it came to be recognized by ethnic immigrants and others that education had a kind of value as a credential that could be very useful in the struggle for economic success and prestige. There thus began a process whereby educational credentials came to be sought in increasing amounts, and a process of credential inflation, highly analogous to monetary inflation, was set in motion. As a greater number of individuals received educational credentials, the value of any particular credential declined, and thus higher credentials had to be sought in order to keep up in the struggle for economic success. Once set in motion, the process of credential inflation is a self-perpetuating one that feeds on itself. Educational enrollments expand not because more education is needed to perform the work of industrial societies, but because more credentials are needed to achieve the levels of economic success people seek. People are required to spend longer and longer periods of time in school just to keep up. Like Alice in Wonderland, they must run as fast as they can in order to stay in the same place.

Collins assumes that what education provides is not job skills, but what the French sociologist Pierre Bourdieu has termed "cultural capital" (Bourdieu and Passeron, 1977). Why has the search for cultural capital been more intense and taken to higher and higher levels in the United States than in other industrial countries? Collins's answer is twofold. First, the extreme ethnic diversity of the United States set in motion a process whereby ethnic groups, as status groups, competed with each other. In addition, Collins argues that the greater openness of the stratification system has led to the creation of a "contest-mobility" educational system that is much less class segregated and based on widespread competition.

Although Collins applies his theory only to the United States, there is no reason that it cannot apply in principle much more broadly. Indeed, Ronald Dore (1976) has developed a similar argument that he applies to Britain and Japan, and he has tried to show that the credential inflation process has special applicability to the educational situation of Third World countries. According to Dore, less-developed countries suffer from what he calls the "late-development effect": the later development starts, the greater the speed with which educational enrollments increase. In essence, less-developed countries, which have tried to imitate the developed world in many ways, have imitated its educational systems in the hope that education will pay off in economic development. Educational credentials come to be greatly desired in such countries as a means whereby individuals can gain access to such scarce white-collar jobs as civil servants or bus drivers. Under such conditions, the content of education becomes even more irrelevant, and the educational process grows even more ritualized and hollow.

To my mind, the credential inflation theory is far superior to the previous two. For one thing, it is capable of explaining the seeming paradox, completely unapproachable by the functionalist theory, of the simultaneous expansion of educational enrollments and the decline of academic achievement levels. For the credential inflation theory, this is no paradox at all. As more people remain in the educational system at higher levels, it becomes more difficult to maintain high academic standards for an increasing number of less able students. Student pressure for lower standards, well known to professors in the American university system to be intense and of long standing, eventually is capitulated to. Furthermore, the credential inflation theory tells us what it is about education that makes it much more sought after than imposed: its value as cultural capital in the race for success.

Nevertheless, this theory suffers from two problems, one of which is easily handled and one of which is not. The first difficulty is Collins's argument that educational expansion is closely linked to ethnic heterogeneity. This is an argument that empirical research fails to support (Boli, Ramirez, and Meyer, 1985; Rubinson, 1986).

For example, Japan has undergone tremendous educational expansion in the twentieth century, and in the nineteenth century was more advanced in primary enrollments than virtually any other non-Western nation, and yet it is the world's most ethnically homogeneous large-scale society. Moreover, the old Soviet Union, perhaps the world's most ethnically heterogeneous society, has undergone significantly less educational expansion. The second difficulty is the problem of explaining how educational enrollments get going in the first place. After all, before they inflate they have to exist. Collins has, of course, explained this in terms of ethnic heterogeneity, but the empirical unsatisfactoriness of this argument means we have to find another way to explain the beginnings of mass educational systems.

Education as nation building. The theory that seems to provide the key to understanding the beginnings of mass education is the nation-building theory developed by John Meyer, Francisco Ramirez, and their colleagues (Meyer, Tyack, Nagel, and Gordon, 1979; Boli, Ramirez, and Meyer, 1985; Ramirez and Boli, 1987). These authors make a special point of the fact that educational expansion has occurred all over the world (rather than in just the most developed countries), and that the educational systems that have been built have been amazingly uniform. Modern mass educational systems are highly standardized, highly rationalized, and apply in principle to everyone. The nation-building theory asserts that mass educational systems arose in the nineteenth and twentieth centuries in direct conjunction with the process of the building of modern states. Education has been the means whereby individuals have been socialized into the role of the modern citizen, as Boli, Ramirez, and Meyer (1985:159) explain:

In this model, education becomes the vehicle for creating citizens. It instills loyalty to the state and acceptance of the obligations to vote, go to war, pay taxes, and so on. It also equips citizens with the skills and worldview required for them to be able to contribute productively to national success. The state promotes a *mass* educational system in order to transform all individuals into members of the national polity, and it supports a *uniform* system to build devotion to a common set of purposes, symbols, and assumptions about proper conduct in the social arena.

This view of the origins of modern mass education is supported by numerous lines of evidence. Most obvious and perhaps most significant is the fact that education in all modern nations is *compulsory* up to a certain age. In addition, a little reflection will show that much of the content of primary education is highly political, being devoted to the production of citizen loyalty (pledging allegiance to the flag, learning the capitals of countries, etc.) We can also reflect back on our earlier discussion of the evolution of the modern state. As the state shifted from predominantly military to predominantly civil functions during the nineteenth century, its single most important civil function, at least as judged in terms of state expenditures, was the provision of education (Mann, 1993).

But this theory is, by itself, incomplete. I do not believe it can explain at all the expansion of higher education, and it is doubtful that it can explain much of the expansion of secondary education. These two levels of education extend well beyond what is necessary to ensure the development of the individual into a responsible and loyal citizen. Here is where the credential inflation argument is needed. Once primary education (and to some extent secondary education) was already in place as a result of the process of state-building, then education's credential value came to be recognized and it could expand on its own through an inflationary spiral. In sum, then, the development of mass educational systems in the last century and a half has been the product of the interaction between a state-building process and a process of credential inflation. The latter process has been going on for a long time in the advanced industrial societies, but it is a relatively recent phenomenon in the less-developed parts of the world.

THE SCIENTIFIC REVOLUTION AND THE DEVELOPMENT OF MODERN SCIENCE

The development of science in western Europe and Japan

It is generally acknowledged that in the sixteenth and seventeenth centuries a scientific revolution began in Italy and various parts of western Europe. J.D. Bernal (1971) has divided the period of the Scientific Revolution into three phases. The first was associated mainly with Copernicus's substitution of a heliocentric for a geocentric view of the universe. The second phase was marked by the attempts of such thinkers as Tycho Brahe, Kepler, and Galileo to demonstrate the accuracy of the new Copernican view. In the third phase the first scientific societies were formed, and science was well on its way to becoming an institutionalized part of western European society. The great thinker of this period was Isaac Newton.

The great contribution of Copernicus, of course, was his attack on the Aristotelian view of a static, earth-centered universe. Copernicus attempted to replace the Aristotelian geocentric view with a helio-centric, or sun-centered, conception of the universe. In his great work, *On the Revolution of the Celestial Orbs*, published in 1543, he held that the sun was at the center of the universe and that the earth moved around it while simultaneously rotating on its axis. This idea proved to be inspirational to later scientists, such as Tycho Brahe. Tycho made many observations of the positions of stars and planets and used them to develop his own conception of the universe. He modified the Copernican view by claiming that the sun moved around the earth, but that the other planets moved around the sun. As Bernal has pointed out, what Tycho gives us is "the Copernican system relative to a motionless earth" (1971:421). Tycho's results were worked on by his assistant, Johannes Kepler, whose main concern was giving a representation of planetary motion. Kepler eschewed the idea of the circular motion of the planets because it was contradicted by the most recent observations. He was eventually able to show that the orbit of Mars was elliptical rather than circular, a result that allowed him to formulate a law of planetary motion, to which he was eventually able to add two other laws.

Kepler's contributions, however, were surpassed by those of Gali-leo, and it was the contributions of the latter that stand as the greatest achievements of the second phase of the Scientific Revolu-tion (Bernal, 1971). Galileo benefited enormously from the invention of the telescope. When he turned his telescope toward the sky, what he saw had extraordinary implications. As Bernal (1971:427) has noted:

In the first few nights of observation of the heavens he saw enough to shatter the whole of the Aristotelian picture of that serene element. For the moon, instead of being a perfect sphere, was found to be covered with seas and mountains; the planet Venus showed phases like the moon; while the planet Saturn seemed to be divided into three. . . .

. . . He sensed at once the really revolutionary character of the new observations. Here he had for everyone to see the very model of Copernicus's system in the sky.

But Galileo was not content simply with observations that confirmed the heliocentric view, for he also wanted to be able to explain how such a solar system could exist. He was eventually led in the direction of formulating a mathematical description of the motion of bodies, a description that was derived from experimental results.

Most of the achievements of the Scientific Revolution's second phase lay in astronomy and physics, but important contributions were nonetheless made in other areas of science. During this period the microscope was invented, and the Englishman William Harvey was able to conduct experiments that demonstrated the manner of circulation of blood in the body.

During the third phase of the Scientific Revolution science was clearly in the process of becoming an institutionalized feature of several of the societies of western Europe. Two important scientific societies were established during this period, the Royal Society of London and the French Royal Academy. Many of the members of these scientific associations devoted themselves to the most important technical problems of the day. The person who stood out as the greatest scientist of the third phase was indubitably Isaac Newton, whose achievements provided the standard thinking in physics and astronomy for two centuries. Along with Leibniz, Newton was a coinventor of the infinitesimal calculus. This was a major achievement, but Newton's greatest contribution was the formulation of the inverse square law of gravitation. In 1686 he published *De Philosophiae Naturalis Principia Mathematica*, which was the greatest scientific achievement to that point and is still regarded today as one of the greatest works in the entire history of science. The *Principia* set forth and mathematically demonstrated Newton's famous theory of gravitation, his attempt to show how the universe was bound together by gravity. As Bernal has noted, this theory dealt another severe blow to the old Aristotelian conception of the universe as consisting of perfect, crystalline spheres: "For a vision of spheres, operated by a first mover or by angels on God's order, Newton had effectively substituted that of a mechanism operating according to a simple natural law, requiring no continuous application of force, and only needing divine intervention to create it and set it in motion" (Bernal, 1971:487).

Yet despite the importance of science in the Europe of the late seventeenth century, it was miniscule compared to its size and importance today. As Derek de Solla Price (1963) has shown, in the last three centuries science has grown from "little science" to "big science," that is, from a situation in which a few scientists worked away in their private studies and laboratories to one in which thousands of scientists conduct their research in gigantic laboratories housed in large universities or major research institutes. According to Price, in the last two to three centuries science has been growing at an exponential rate, and some 80 to 90 percent of scientists who have ever lived are alive now. As of the time that Price was writing (the early 1960s), the size of science, as calculated by either the number of scientists or the number of scientific publications, was doubling approximately every 10 to 15 years. Price tries to demonstrate the enormous growth of Western science by comparing it to the growth of population (1963:14):

> The immediacy of science needs a comparison of this sort before one can realize that it implies an explosion of science dwarfing that of the population, and indeed all other explosions of nonscientific human growth. Roughly speaking, every doubling of the population has produced at least three doublings of the number of scientists, so that the size of science is eight times what it was and the number of scientists per million population has multiplied by four. Mankind's per capita involvement with science has thus been growing much more rapidly than the population.

Indeed, science has grown so large that today it is a vital component of the infrastructures of modern industrial societies, being absolutely crucial to their economic functioning.

Japan also experienced a major spurt of scientific growth beginning in the seventeenth century (Bartholomew, 1989; Sugimoto and Swain, 1978). The development of science was considerably more limited than in Europe, and it would perhaps be inappropriate to talk about a Japanese "scientific revolution," but there is no question that science was growing in importance. Masayoshi Sugimoto and David Swain (1978) speak of the seventeenth century as marking a genuine renaissance of science and learning in Japan, one that they claim was without parallel in any earlier period of Japanese history. As in Western science, work in astronomy was of great importance, and there were major developments in mathematics (the Japanese developed their own version of mathematics, known as *wasan*). Work in the medical sciences was also of great importance. During the second half of the Tokugawa epoch (approximately 1720 to 1854) scientific developments were even more pronounced. In the eighteenth century there were three important developments in astronomy: the acquisition of better observational instruments, the gradual diffusion of Copernicanism, and the preservation of Newtonianism (Bartholomew, 1989). In the nineteenth century science continued to expand. As James Bartholomew (1989:17) notes:

By 1800 Japanese astronomers were regularly producing telescopes and even grinding lenses. Using a telescope of his own devising, Kunitomo Tobei observed sunspots in 1835 and published a drawing of the surface of the moon; other astronomers began to do systematic observations of the planets. However, the most important development was the arrival (in 1803) of a book in Dutch by the French astronomer J.J.F. de Lalande. Lalande was a preeminent figure in eighteenth-century science, and his work was the first "advanced treatise on contemporary Western astronomy" to make its way to Japan.

Moreover, by the early nineteenth century Western anatomy was in the process of being adopted; several botanical works, based either partially or entirely on the Linnaean classification, had been compiled; at least some Japanese scholars were studying Newtonian physics; the Japanese coastline was being surveyed with the use of the most advanced mathematical techniques available; and Western data had been used to undertake the first complete revision of the national calendar (Bartholomew, 1989).

Japan also created a number of scientific organizations. The first, the Astronomical Bureau and Observatory, was founded in 1684. In 1791 the Shogunate created an academy of medicine. An agency for translating and spreading technical materials was set up in 1811, as was a school for scientific studies in 1856 and a bureau for mathematical studies in 1863 (Bartholomew, 1989).

It would be stretching things to say that science in Japan developed as fully and as vigorously from the seventeenth century on as it did in western Europe. Nevertheless, just as Japan underwent dramatic economic changes in the Tokugawa era, it also experienced a spurt of science without precedent in its own history. Once again we see that the recent social evolution of Japan has remarkably paralleled that of the West.

If we look at the practice of science in the modern world, we see that its global distribution closely approximates the world distribution of wealth and power. Table 7.15 gives some indication of the size and importance of science in selected developed and less-developed countries. As can clearly be seen, the scale of scientific development is far greater in the developed countries. For those developed countries shown in the table, the average number of scientists per 100,000 population is 486. By contrast, the average number of scientists per 100,000 population in the less-developed countries shown in table 7.15 is 40 (24 if South Korea is excluded). Even within the Third World itself we can see that scientific development is directly proportional to economic development. Leaving South Korea aside, we see that the four Latin American countries

Table 7.15 *Number of scientists and engineers engaged in research and development in developed and less-developed countries*

Country	Number of scientists and engineers per 100,000 population
Developed societies	
Denmark	429
Sweden	618
United Kingdom	292
France	500
West Germany	472
Netherlands	434
Canada	326
United States	293[a]
Australia	321
Japan	586
Soviet Union	532[a]
Czechoslovakia	715
East Germany	1,187
Poland	239
Hungary	348
Less-developed societies	
Brazil	37[a]
Venezuela	44
Peru	29[a]
El Salvador	34
Egypt	56
Nigeria	7
Senegal	8
Kenya	3
India	20
Indonesia	17[a]
Iran	5
South Korea	216

[a] This figure excludes technicians, and therefore may be underrepresentative.
Sources: United Nations (1992b), table 121; all data come from the time period 1975–88, but are mostly for the mid- to late-1980s.

in table 7.15 contain more scientists (mean = 36) than either Africa (mean = 19) or Asia (mean = 14). If we include only sub-Saharan African countries, then Africa is clearly the continent with the fewest scientists.

That the global distribution of science and scientists is extremely unequal has been shown even more dramatically in a study by Frame, Narin, and Carpenter (1977). They calculated the Gini coefficient for the world distribution of science and found it to be .908, an extremely high figure. This figure exceeded the coefficients for the world distribution of national land area (.745), the world distribution of national population (.750), and the world distribution of Gross National Product (.847). The same authors also calculated the ten largest producers of science, as measured by the number of scientific publications in 1973, and found them to be the United States (103,780 publications), the United Kingdom (25,005), the Soviet Union (24,418), West Germany (16,408), France (15,102), Japan (14,265), Canada (11,907), India (6,880), Australia (5,341), and Italy (4,691). The United States is far and away the leading producer of science in the world, and nine of the top ten science producers are developed countries. The exception, India, is attributable largely to the enormity of its population. Frame, Narin, and Carpenter also calculated the proportion of world scientific papers published by the countries of western and eastern Europe combined, finding it to be a huge 94 percent. An almost identical figure (93.6 percent) was obtained by Thomas Schott (1991) for a later year (1986).

Despite the enormous differences in the size of science in the developed and less-developed countries, the less-developed countries have nonetheless attempted to adopt the same scientific institutions as those that prevail in the developed world (Schott, 1993; Ramirez and Drori, 1992). As Schott (1993:206) has remarked, "Science has become institutionalized throughout the world, with institutional arrangements that are strikingly similar because they have a common source in world standards, namely models diffusing through the global scientific community from its center to its periphery and doctrines promulgated by the global science policy regime." It seems clear, then, that despite the often tiny size of their scientific infrastructure, less-developed countries are highly motivated to adopt the trappings of Western science. According to Francisco Ramirez and Gili Drori (1992), they do so because they are engaged in a "ritualistic affirmation" of the value of science: they adhere to a Western model of science out of the belief that "science = technology" and "technology = progress." Although unable to afford a large scientific infrastructure, their perception that science is a necessary and useful institution helps legitimate their developmental goals and means. The adoption of the trappings of Western science by less-developed countries thus turns out to be quite similar to their adoption of models of the nation-state and of education established by the developed countries. That is, the adoption of all of these institutions is part of an overall developmental strategy.

Explaining scientific development

What has been responsible for the European Scientific Revolution and for the enormous development of science as a social institution? Why did similar developments occur in Japan? There have been several answers to these questions, none of which, unfortunately, make any reference to Japan.

Undoubtedly the most famous sociological attempt to explain the rise of Western science is Robert Merton's *Science, Technology, and Society in Seventeenth Century England* (1970[1938]). Merton, of course, appropriated Weber's Protestant Ethic thesis linking the Protestant Reformation to the rise of Western capitalism, and reformulated it so that Protestantism was also said to spur the rise of Western science. Actually, as we shall see, this was only part of Merton's argument, for he also gave economic factors an important role in the development of science. But let us stay for the moment with the religious side of his argument.

Merton argued that Protestant religious values, especially those of the Puritan and Pietist sects, provided an intellectual atmosphere that was highly favorable for scientific development. These values, he claims, encouraged the rational and empirical study of nature because such habits were thought to glorify God and all his creations. Merton concentrated much of his effort on trying to show that men of Protestant background played a major role in the leadership of the Royal Society of London in the seventeenth century. Among others, Merton pointed to Theodore Haak, a strong Calvinist; to Denis Papin, a French Calvinist who had been driven out of France; to Thomas Sydenham, an ardent Puritan; and to Sir William Petty, a man who was greatly influenced by Puritanism.

To my mind, the Merton thesis is no more acceptable than its earlier Weberian incarnation. Lotte Mulligan (1973) has shown that only a small number of the members of the Royal Society of London were in fact Puritans, thus casting doubt on Merton's use of evidence from that association. Along similar lines, but perhaps more significantly, it must be noted that science flourished in Catholic countries and that Catholics were often among the leading scientists in the European Scientific Revolution (Rabb, 1965). Italy was in the forefront of the Scientific Revolution in the sixteenth century, and both Italy and France had more vigorous scientific activity in the mid-nineteenth century than did the Netherlands, a country with a large Protestant population (Wuthnow, 1980). And the Merton thesis can be challenged right at its heart, that is, in terms of the extent to which certain Protestant beliefs and values promoted science. Richard Greaves (1969) has concluded that there was nothing about Puritanism that was especially conducive to science. He says (1969:360) that

a careful reading of Puritan tracts does not . . . lead one to believe that Puritans were fundamentally curious people. The curious man is a "doubting Thomas," not a man exhorted at every turn to have faith in the divine providence. Puritans were exhorted to study the Bible, but not to be curious about its teachings – including those touching on scientific matters. Baxter was critical of the scientific spirit – the spirit of curiosity – because he thought it endangered Christianity.

Indeed, some Puritan ministers were concerned about the dangers of science and often cautioned their congregations against it. T.K. Rabb (1965) has similarly argued that Protestant ideas were not especially encouraging of science, claiming that (1965:57) "Calvinist theology could have approved as easily of the outlook of a mystic as of bourgeois or scientific attitudes."

George Becker (1984) has also challenged the Merton thesis in terms of the compatibility of religious and scientific ideas. In dealing with Pietism, he counters Merton's argument that it was strongly proscience, suggesting that in fact it was much more frequently indifferent or even hostile to science and encouraged mysticism and emotionalism over science. Becker gives special attention to the thinking of August Hermann Francke, a major Pietist leader and an individual singled out by Merton as the most important Pietist advocate of science. Becker claims that Francke was just the opposite, and quotes him to the following effect (Becker, 1984:1070):

A small amount of living faith is to be valued more highly than a ton of purely historical knowledge and a drop of true love more highly than an entire ocean of knowledge regarding all sorts of secrets. . . . Alas I say to you, all erudition is vanity and folly. . . . No people are more subject to the fetters of Satan than those who study. For while they extol understanding and search for much knowledge, Satan . . . finds more occasion to lead them into all kinds of corruption.

It seems to me that Merton's thesis is fundamentally wrongheaded and that we will have to look elsewhere to find the forces stimulating the development of modern science. Fortunately, better ideas abound, one of which has even been suggested by Merton himself. However, before considering that idea we first need to look at a theory similar to Merton's. Toby Huff (1993) also presents a culturalist interpretation of the rise of modern science, but without any particular emphasis on religion. Huff begins from the fact that as late as the fourteenth century science was much less developed in Europe than it was in China and, especially, in the Arab world. The Arab world had preserved and extended the ancient Greek scientific contributions and was far ahead of Europe scientifically. China had its own independent tradition of science that was less developed than Arabic science, but its science was nonetheless ahead of Western science. After the fourteenth century, and *a fortiori* after the sixteenth and seventeenth centuries, a complete reversal occurred. Arab and Chinese science stagnated and declined, whereas Western science began to develop by leaps and bounds.

Huff argues that this reversal can only be explained in terms of the dramatic cultural differences between the respective civilizations. The key to European scientific advance, he claims, was a major legal revolution of the twelfth and thirteenth centuries. As a result of this revolution there arose an emphasis on the rational study of nature employing universalistic standards of judgment and criticism. This was extremely conducive to science, and a new and important system of universities was established in which to conduct and teach this science. As Huff puts it (1993:146):

In acknowledging natural law, as well as recognizing reason and conscience as inalienable elements of man's constitution, the legal revolution of the twelfth and thirteenth centuries established new standards for eliminating unjust laws, whether they be customary, royal, or ecclesiastical. This was a major breakthrough in the construction of objective and universal standards for judging the justice and equity of social relations and probably served as a model of such external standards used to evaluate other human constructions in ethics, science, and politics.

Moreover, according to Huff, Arab and Chinese science stagnated and then declined because of the absence of any such legal revolution. The Chinese and the Arabs failed to develop any rationalist concept of man and nature, and their thought remained deeply personalistic and particularistic. In the Arab world in particular, the model of inquiry was based on the personal authority of the inquirer. Neither China nor the Arab world created the legally autonomous corporate bodies needed for the free and objective investigation of nature. In the case of the Arab world, this failure was deeply rooted in Islamic religious commitments. The Arab world also had a strong bias against allowing the masses open access to knowledge. In China, emphasis was placed on a harmonious view of man and nature rather than on critical thought and faith in reason. The university system, which was under the control of the large, highly bureaucratized state, emphasized rote learning rather than free thought.

There may be something to Huff's argument, but I see a number of problems. The most obvious concerns the degree of advancement of Arab and Chinese science by the fourteenth century: if the legal institutions and cultural and intellectual traditions of these civilizations were so inimical to science, then how was it possible for science to have advanced so far? Moreover, to the extent that there were important cultural differences between these civilizations, it could be suggested that the differences are of considerably longer standing than Huff recognizes. After all, the first great burst of science came in the Western world, in ancient Greece. Indeed, it was many of these ideas that were recovered to serve as the basis for the European Scientific Revolution. But then Greek science stagnated and disappeared and was ultimately lost to the West for well more than a millennium. Was it the absence of the right kind of legal and cultural tradition that led to this decline? I doubt it.

What Huff overlooks entirely are the economic differences between the West on the one hand and China and the Arab world on the other. The Scientific Revolution of the sixteenth and seventeenth centuries occurred right in the midst of the dramatic shift from a feudal to a capitalist economy, a shift that was certainly not occurring in China and the Arab world. Moreover, the decline of Chinese science of which Huff speaks corresponded closely to the economic stagnation and decline of China in the fourteenth and fifteenth centuries. A coincidence? Not likely. And furthermore, was the alleged European legal revolution of the twelfth and thirteenth centuries a free-floating phenomenon? I doubt it, for, as Abu-Lughod (1989) and others (e.g., Lopez, 1971) have pointed out, during this time Europe was in the throes of a major economic surge.

What I am suggesting is that economics played a much greater role than cultural factors in the rise of European science. This returns us to Merton. Although it is seldom commented on, Merton regarded economic factors as being essentially on a par with religious ones in the seventeenth-century Scientific Revolution. As have a number of other scholars, Merton gave special emphasis to a major technological problem confronted in early modern England, that of finding the longitude while at sea. This was a problem whose urgency increased as English commercial activity intensified and as an ever greater number of ships put out to sea. The various methods that were proposed for finding the longitude directly contributed to a variety of scientific investigations: computation of lunar distances from the sun or from a fixed star, observations of the moon's transit of the meridian, observations of the eclipses of Jupiter's satellites, and the use of pendulum clocks and other chronometers at sea (Merton, 1957). There were also other pressing technological and economic problems that served as major stimuli to scientific research. Most of these problems involved mining and military technology. Merton has attempted to estimate the degree to which scientific research was shaped by economic concerns. The results of his calculations show that, for the years 1661–2 and 1686–7, somewhat more than half of the scientific research conducted by members of the Royal Society was directly or indirectly related to economic concerns.

J.D. Bernal (1971) has also argued in favor of an economic approach to scientific advance. As a Marxist, Bernal claims that the Scientific Revolution was spurred by the rise of modern capitalism. As he puts it (1971:489–90):

Looking back over the epic movement of the new science in the fifteenth, sixteenth, and seventeenth centuries we are now better placed to see why the birth of science occurred when and where it did. We can see how it followed closely on the great revival of trade and industry that marked the rise of the bourgeoisie in the fifteenth and sixteenth centuries and its political triumph in England and Holland in the seventeenth. The birth of science follows closely after that of capitalism.

An economic explanation for the development of science in early modern Europe is also strongly supported by the parallel case of Japan. The most fundamental thing that seventeenth-century Japan had in common with seventeenth-century Europe lay in the kind of economic transition it was making. As we have already seen in some detail, Japan of the seventeenth century was undergoing major changes involving the emergence of a capitalist economy, and science closely accompanied this economic transition. The Tokugawa Shogunate could increasingly afford science, and science was, or at least was thought to be, of practical economic benefit.

Exactly how and why economic forces exert their influence on the advance of science is a question of considerable importance. Neither Merton nor Bernal means to suggest that all scientific activity is spurred by considerations of practical economic benefit, or that scientists only regard scientific ideas as valuable to the extent that they have technological applications. Indeed, many individual scientists care nothing for the practical benefits of science and are concerned with ideas only at a purely intellectual level, being driven by an intense intellectual curiosity that must be satisfied. Merton captures almost perfectly the double way in which economic and technical forces stimulate scientific research (1957:609):

It is important to distinguish the personal attitudes of individual men of science from the social role played by their research. Clearly, some scientists were sufficiently enamored of their subject to pursue it for its own sake, at times with little consideration of its practical bearings. Nor need we assume that *all* individual researches are directly linked to technical tasks. The relation between science and social needs is two-fold: direct, in the sense that some research is advisedly and deliberately pursued for utilitarian purposes and indirect, in so far as certain problems and materials for their solution come to the attention of scientists although they need not be cognizant of the practical exigencies from which they derive.

J. Davidson Frame (1979) has pointed out that science, especially modern twentieth-century science, is expensive, and thus to a certain extent constitutes a luxury item in the budgets of states. It thrives, therefore, not only under conditions in which it is needed or perceived to be economically useful, but in situations in which a great deal of economic surplus is available. This allows us to see why science is so unevenly distributed throughout the world in the late twentieth century: most less-developed countries have more of the trappings of science than its practice because scientific practice at high levels involves greater expenses than these countries can afford. It also allows us to understand patterns of scientific development in early modern Europe. Robert Wuthnow (1980) has graphed the relationship between economic and scientific development in western Europe between 1500 and 1850 (figure 7.1). This graph shows the following: the dramatic economic decline of Spain in the sixteenth and seventeenth centuries was associated with a sharp decline in its number of scientists; Italy's transition to semiperipheral status in the sixteenth and seventeenth centuries was accompanied by a decline in its scientific activity; Dutch science grew markedly from 1500 to 1650, which was a period of economic vitality and growth, but declined after its loss of hegemony in the second half of the seventeenth century; by the beginning of the eighteenth century France and England had more scientists than any other country in Europe, and this was precisely the time by which they had become the leading European economic powers; and as France and England continued to develop economically throughout the eighteenth and nineteenth centuries, their economic expansion was closely associated with an expansion of science. These patterns can be explained not only by the economic need for science, but also by the ability to pay for it. As countries expand economically the funds available to governments increase, and science becomes more affordable; conversely, as countries decline, decreasing revenues mean that states may no longer be able to afford the scientists and scientific institutions they once supported.

Harold Dorn (1991) has made the point that the practical benefits of science were meager until approximately the middle of the nineteenth century. Before that date, he says, most technological innovations came from the work of inventors and tinkerers rather than scientific researchers. The problem of finding the longitude at sea, for example, was solved not by a scientist, but by a clockmaker. Nevertheless, governments generally held to the *perception* that science could be beneficial, and therefore were willing to support it.[5]

Scientific advance in Europe may also have benefited significantly from the fact that the European world-system was highly politically decentralized. Robert Wuthnow (1980) has argued that Europe's division into many competing states created an atmosphere that was highly conducive to scientific development, and for three reasons. First, political decentralization helped promote scientific freedom.

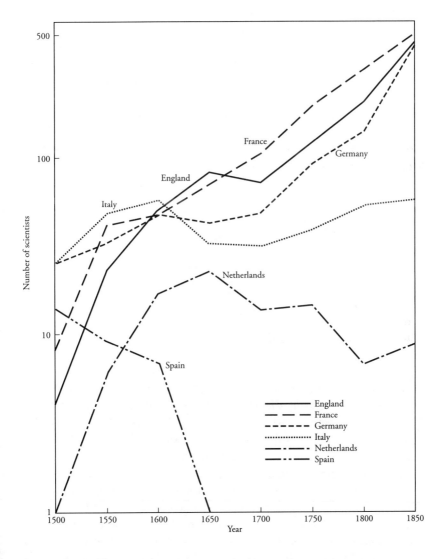

Figure 7.1 *Scientific activity in western Europe, 1500–1850*
Source: Wuthnow (1980:48)

Scientists who were confronted in their own countries with an atmosphere that was hostile to the pursuit of their scientific work could continue to pursue this work by fleeing to a country more supportive of it. As Wuthnow points out, there is considerable evidence pointing to the frequency with which scientists often left their homelands to pursue research elsewhere. In addition, because the world-system was a highly decentralized world-economy, the nations of Europe were put into direct economic, political, and military competition. Science had a major role to play in this competition because, by promoting science and its potential practical benefits, states were hopeful of enhancing their ability to compete. Finally, political decentralization was conducive to the formation of different national scientific communities throughout Europe. Because these communities both competed and shared information, scientific knowledge as a whole was increased, and increased more rapidly.

Wuthnow's emphasis on the role of the world-system in the development of European science should not be seen as in any particular way antagonistic to an economic explanation. My argument is simply that it may have further enhanced the operation of the economic stimuli at work.

THE EMERGENCE OF A POSTINDUSTRIAL SOCIETY?

Within the last 20 years the notion has become popular among numerous social scientists that Western industrial societies are in the process of making the transition to a "postindustrial society." This idea has been put forth by several scholars, but most forcefully and elaborately by Daniel Bell in his book *The Coming of Post-Industrial Society* (1973). Bell's argument is that by the early 1970s a new type of society, the postindustrial society, had begun to emerge in the West, and especially in the United States. Bell argued that this type of society has a number of characteristics that distinguish it from industrial society. Most importantly, it is characterized by a shift in emphasis from the production of goods to the production of services. Moreover, in contrast to industrial society, whose services were mainly in the areas of transportation, utilities, and telecommunications, the postindustrial society emphasizes services in the areas of health, science, and education. Bell also pointed to what he thought was a major change occurring in the class structure. The old capitalist class of industrial society was withering and being replaced by a new dominant class whose control rested on knowledge rather than property ownership. The new dominant class was a kind of "intelligentsia," and consisted primarily of teachers, physicians, lawyers, scientists, and engineers. Bell also thought that the post-industrial society was in the process of eliminating the profit motive as the driving engine of society and replacing it with an emphasis on the accumulation of knowledge for human betterment. Corporations were coming to emphasize the provision of benefits for their employees and "social responsibility," and thus were no longer driven simply by the pursuit of profits.

Although the notion of postindustrial society has been highly influential and won widespread support in the social sciences, a number of serious criticisms of it can be offered. First, the transformation of which Bell speaks seems to be somewhat different from what he assumes. Krishan Kumar (1978) points out that there has not been so much a shift from manufacturing to services as one in which agriculture has declined greatly and services have grown in importance. Manufacturing is still an important part of "postindustrial" society. For example, Kumar shows that, in the United States in 1900, 38 percent of the workforce was employed in agriculture, 38 percent in manufacturing, and 24 percent in services. By 1970 the percentage employed in manufacturing had stayed about the same (35 percent), but the percentage employed in agriculture had declined to 4 percent and the percentage working in services had increased to 61 percent.

In addition, Bell's notion that postindustrial society is characterized by a new dominant class is extremely dubious. There is no evidence that the individuals who work as teachers, scientists, or engineers have any real control over the functioning of the economy. They seem to be largely mere functionaries, or simply paid employees of those who really do control the economy. There is no real evidence to suggest that capitalists are any less in control of the economic system now than they were decades ago. Moreover, we can also question the extent to which the "intelligentsia" of which Bell speaks is in any way a homogeneous class that has the characteristics he imagines. While some members of this group may have a great deal of autonomy, responsibility, and self-direction in their work, the work of many others is very different from what it is often imagined to be. Kumar (1978:209) points out that "for the great majority of white-collar workers, the work environment, work activities, and work relationships will be remote indeed from the humanized, personalized, and self-fulfilling pattern envisaged in the post-industrial scenario." The majority of work performed in the service sector is routine and repetitive work that bears little resemblance to the kind of work done by traditional professionals. And it is jobs emphasizing this kind of work, Kumar argues, that have accounted for most of the expansion of the service sector in recent decades. "It has become quite clear," he says, "that 'pure' or 'basic' research – a central component of Bell's 'theoretical knowledge' – forms only a tiny fraction of the overall R. & D. effort in all industrial countries" (1978:226).

Finally, Bell's claim that the new postindustrial society represents some sort of radical shift can be seriously challenged (Kumar, 1978; S. Berger, 1974). It seems much more plausible to conceive of the changes that Bell is concerned with as a fundamental part of the evolution of the capitalist system. The enormous expansion of government services in this century, and especially after the Second World War, makes sense only in the context of the political management of the contradictions of capitalism. As Stephen Berger (1974) has pointed out, most of the recent expansion of science has resulted from government involvement in military defense and in the exploration of space. As for the expansion of services in the private sector, this represents simply the extension of the logic of capitalist commodification to wider and wider areas, which of course is a fundamental and long-term trend within the capitalist world-system as a whole. Kumar (1978) notes that many of the allegedly "new" developments that Bell speaks of can be located well back into the nineteenth century. England in 1850 already had a substantial service sector, a "new middle class" was already emerging, and there was significant development in the formation of new professions. Kumar concludes that what we have here is the old story of *plus ça change, plus c'est la meme chose* (1978:232):

Far from being departures from the main tendencies of industrialism, however, these developments only too clearly fall within them. The post-industrial theory assumes that the structural features of the new society mark actual discontinuities with the patterns of the old industrial society: novel and to a large extent unexpected directions in the nature of economic activities, the quality of work, the shape of the occupational structure, the future of class conflict, and so on. The theory postulates a "system break" in the transition to post-industrialism. Such a break is largely illusory. What are projected as novel patterns of development turn out on examination to be massive *continuities* within the basic system of the developing industrial society. Essentially, and insofar as they are actually occurring, the trends singled out by the post-industrial theorists are extrapolations, intensifications, and clarifications of tendencies which were apparent from the very birth of industrialism.

NOTES

1 Of course, the Soviet Union no longer exists as a state, and the eastern European countries have largely abandoned Marxism–Leninism. My use of the present tense here and elsewhere is the anthropologists' "ethnographic present."

2 I am reminded here of Frank Parkin's (1979:25) pithy comment: "Inside every neo-Marxist there seems to be a Weberian struggling to get out."

3 These and the following figures for 1950 come from Meyer et al. (1977). All figures for 1989 come from World Bank (1992).

4 Think for a moment about an occupation that really does require demanding skills that cannot be learned quickly, that of airline pilot. Everyone would agree that such individuals possess enormous skills, and yet are such skills taught in any sort of conventional school at any level? Not at all. These skills are learned entirely outside the context of the traditional educational system.

5 In general states had little interest in pure science and were unwilling to support research that had no apparent utility. The same situation prevails today. In the United States, for example, only about 12 percent of government funding of science is devoted to pure research (Dorn, 1991).

8

The Question of Progress

The concept of progress has been closely associated with that of social evolution ever since the emergence of evolutionary theories of society in the eighteenth and nineteenth centuries. As I showed in *Social Evolutionism* (Sanderson, 1990), most theories of social evolution have been progressivist, many of them strongly so. These theories have generally assumed that social evolution has brought a variety of improvements in the human condition, especially with respect to the standard of living and the overall quality of human life. Nevertheless, in recent years the assumption that social evolution is generally progressive has been challenged by a number of social scientists, most particularly by Marvin Harris (1968, 1977, 1979), and Mark Nathan Cohen (1977, 1989). My view is that social evolution has led to both progressive and regressive outcomes, but that throughout most of world history social evolution has been largely regressive. At least this has been so for most members of society, for a small minority has often been the recipient of various improvements.

In order to simplify our task, I propose to ascertain the progressive or nonprogressive character of social evolution by looking at four major areas of human life: the material standard of living, the nature of work and the human workload, the degree of social and economic equality, and the extent of democracy and freedom. Not only would there likely be widespread agreement about the salience of these areas of human life, but they also have a very high degree of cross-cultural relevance. Humans everywhere seek to enjoy life and an adequate material standard of living is vital to such enjoyment. At a minimum, they prefer to enjoy good health and to live a longer rather than a shorter time. They also, I assume, prefer to minimize the amount of time and energy spent in doing work that is either unpleasant or, at least, not especially rewarding, although certain other kinds of work that provide psychological gratification may consume time and energy that are quite readily given. The extent of social and economic equality is also an important area of human concern in the sense that those who are given less than what they perceive to be their fair share harbor resentments as a result and often try to rectify the situation. Inequalities produce bitterness and social tensions that interfere significantly with the quality of life. Finally, despite the remarkable tendency of humans to try to dominate one another, humans strongly resist domination and control by others, and they regard their freedom to act in their own self-chosen ways as something that contributes in a vital way to the quality of life.

In order to evaluate the question of progress, I believe it is essential to regard the evolution of modern capitalism after the sixteenth century as providing a kind of watershed. Outcomes before the rise of modern capitalism may be quite different from those after the rise of capitalism. Let us look first at what impact social evolution has had on the quality of human life before the sixteenth century AD.

BEFORE THE RISE OF MODERN CAPITALISM

The standard of living

Assessing the standard of living in a fully cross-cultural way requires us to focus on those things that all humans everywhere, regardless of culturally induced preferences and tastes, would regard as fundamental to the quality of human life. I suggest that we can focus on three basic dimensions of the standard of living: the quality of the human diet and overall nutrition, the level of human health, and the extent of human longevity.

How adequate was the standard of living before the rise of agriculture, and how has the rise and intensification of agricultural production affected it? The usual answer to this question, of course, is that the standard of living was extremely low among hunter-gatherers and that it has steadily risen with the advent of agriculture and improvements in agricultural methods. Until the late 1960s it was generally thought that hunter-gatherer societies were the most poverty stricken of all societies. It was assumed that hunter-gatherers were barely able to eke out a living, and that they lived constantly on the brink of starvation. We know now that this picture is highly inaccurate. Beginning in the 1960s a number of anthropologists began to challenge the conventional wisdom, the most important of whom was Marshall Sahlins (1972). Sahlins argued that the conventional wisdom was not only wrong, but that it was almost the reverse of the true situation. Hunter-gatherers, he claimed, constituted a kind of "original affluent society." They enjoyed remarkably good diets and were seldom threatened by starvation, and they did not have to work particularly long or hard to obtain what they needed. How accurate is this picture of hunter-gatherers? My own view is that it is fairly close to the mark. Studies of contemporary hunter-gatherers, such as the !Kung San and Hadza of Africa (Lee, 1968, 1972; Woodburn, 1968) or the Aché of South America (Hill, Kaplan, Hawkes, and Hurtado, 1985) suggest that such groups are remarkably well nourished. They usually enjoy diets that are rich in animal proteins and in basic nutrients. Some groups, such as the !Kung San, may only barely obtain enough calories per day, and bouts of hunger and starvation may occur. However, the !Kung San seem to be a relatively impoverished group of hunter-gatherers compared to other contemporary groups (M. Cohen, 1989). As for bouts of hunger and starvation, these occur also among agricultural peoples, and are in fact more common in such groups. And it is likely that prehistoric hunter-gatherer populations were just as well off if not better off, because contemporary groups represent the last vestiges of the hunting and gathering way of life and have generally been pushed into the least favorable environments that no one else wants (M. Cohen, 1989).

Mark Cohen and his associates (M. Cohen, 1989; Cohen and Armelagos, 1984) have presented some extremely persuasive evidence to the effect that the quality of the diet and nutrition worsened rather than improved after the advent of agriculture. These researchers have reviewed a large number of paleopathological studies, or studies of ancient bones and teeth for evidence of biological stress and poor nutrition. The studies, which have used bone and teeth samples collected throughout the world, consistently show that ancient hunter-gatherer populations were better nourished and freer from disease than later agricultural populations. Infection was shown to be a more severe problem for agricultural populations, and the same is true for chronic malnutrition. Researchers have looked in particular for evidence of porotic hyperostosis and cribia orbitalia, bone diseases that are generally thought to be good indicators of anemia. Most studies have shown these to be primarily diseases of agricultural rather than hunting and gathering populations. The remains of agricultural populations have also shown that agricultural groups had a higher incidence of biological stresses leading to the disruption of childhood growth.

Why did the quality of the diet and nutrition decline with agricultural development? At the root of the problem is population pressure. As we saw in chapter 2, this is the basic cause of the origin of agriculture itself. Under the pressure of greater numbers, a new mode of production (agriculture rather than hunting and gathering) may temporarily relieve that pressure, but the pressure is relentless and returns and intensifies. As a result, people consume fewer animal foods and an ever greater number of plant foods is added to the diet. Animal foods are the best sources of complete protein, as well as the best sources of vitamins B_{12}, A, and D (M. Cohen, 1989). Meat is an excellent source of various minerals. The reliance on grains and tubers as dietary staples has had a negative effect on nutrition because such foods, though high in energy, are not particularly good sources of nutrients. As Cohen (1989:59) has remarked, these foods "are poor sources of protein, vitamins, and minerals when compared to meat and to the variety of wild vegetable foods eaten by modern hunter-gatherers." Moreover, famine is considerably more common in agricultural populations and this, of course, would contribute in a major way to poor nutrition for those who survived. People often have difficulty not only getting the right things to eat, but in getting enough of anything to eat.

Health problems other than those related to poor nutrition are also much more characteristic of agricultural populations. Sedentism directly encourages the spread of a number of diseases, for reasons explained by Cohen (1989:39–40):

More substantial shelters provide better protection against the elements – precipitation and extremes of temperature – but they probably encourage disease transmission. Permanent houses tend to attract vermin, including insects and rats, so that the diseases carried by these vectors may become constant rather than occasional threats to health.

Several species of mosquitoes (culicine mosquitoes carrying a variety of infections including encephalitis and aedine mosquitoes carrying both yellow fever and dengue fever) like to live near human houses and are encouraged by the construction of permanent dwellings. . . .

Moreover, sunlight is one of the best disinfectants known, and conducting one's activities out of doors reduces the transmission of many diseases. Conversely, substantial, permanent houses also provide enclosed air circulation that facilitates transmission of airborne disease. . . .

Refuse associated with sedentary communities can also increase the disease load by attracting wild animals to human settlements. This attraction is the major means by which rat-borne bubonic plague is brought into human communities. . . .

Sedentism also results in the accumulation of human wastes.

And it is well known that many contagious diseases have resulted from the high-density urban populations that have been an accompaniment of complex agrarian societies, and these diseases have been spread throughout wider territories with the expansion of trade (McNeill, 1976; M. Cohen, 1989)

What about the length of the human lifespan? Has it been increasing, as is commonly assumed? The answer is generally negative. On the basis of detailed paleopathological analysis, J. Lawrence Angel (1975) estimated that the average lifespan of ancient hunter-gatherers (30,000 BP) was about 31 years. By 5000 BP it had changed little, and by Roman times it had only increased to about 37 years. Moreover, by late medieval times the average lifespan had actually dropped to about 34 years. Evidence drawn from a variety of other studies is highly consistent with Angel's results (M. Cohen, 1989). Hunter-gatherers had a short lifespan, but it was not that much shorter than the lifespan of later agricultural populations. Most of the real increase in the human lifespan to the point it has reached in industrial societies today has occurred only within the last century.

The conclusion I reach, then, is that the standard of living declined with the advent of agriculture, and probably continued to decline as agriculture was intensified and more high-density societies emerged. However, this conclusion does not necessarily apply to all members of the societies in question. It applies to all members of unstratified societies, but in stratified societies the upper classes did not suffer the dietary deprivations and nutritional inadequacies placed on most of the population. This has led Cohen (1989:127) to say that "what we seem to be seeing is not an improvement in human health and nutrition but rather a partitioning of stress such that some privileged classes or successful communities enjoyed good health and nutrition but others suffered unprecedented degrees of stress associated with low social status, unfavorable trade balance, and the parasite loads of dense settled communities engaged in trade."

Why has the standard of living dropped with the development and intensification of agriculture? I have already indicated the major reason: population pressure. However, to this we must add a second reason: the emergence of class stratification in more advanced horticultural and agrarian societies. It is probably the peasants of agrarian societies who have enjoyed the lowest standard of living in all of world history, and the reason is not population pressure alone, although that is surely one of the reasons. Landlords lived far better, and did so because of their often ruthless exploitation of the peasant masses. Had the system of land ownership been different, then peasants could have enjoyed a significantly higher standard of living.

Work and the workload

The conventional wisdom regarding hunter-gatherers has been not only that they lived at the edge of starvation, but also that they had to work day in and day out just to survive. This notion has also been exploded with the development of Sahlins's original affluent society thesis. One of the first major studies of work in hunting and gathering societies was carried out by Richard Lee (1979), who showed that the !Kung San were spending an average of only about 17 hours per week in food-getting activities. In his study of the Hadza of Tanzania, James Woodburn (1968) generated no quantitative data, but his observations suggested to him that the members of this group obtained subsistence with relative ease and that they spent less time and energy in food-getting than their agricultural neighbors. Sahlins (1972) himself drew on studies of hunter-gatherers of Arnhem land in northern Australia that suggested to him that the hunting and gathering workload was relatively modest. In recent years this conclusion has had to be qualified by other research findings showing that some hunting and gathering groups, or the same groups in different circumstances or at different times of the year, worked considerably harder. For example, John Yellen (1977) studied a group of !Kung during the wet season (Lee had based his calculations on their work during the dry season) and found that they worked more hours than the number reported by Lee. In addition, male members of the Aché of Paraguay have been shown to spend as many as 40 to 50 hours a week in hunting (Hill, Kaplan, Hawkes, and Hurtado, 1985). These findings do not, however, overturn the notion that the hunting and gathering workload is quite modest. Throughout the year the !Kung San still average no more than 25 hours a week in food-getting and, because of their tropical forest location, the Aché of Paraguay are an atypical hunter-gatherer society. Game is notoriously scarce in such an environment, and thus much more time must be spent searching for it. Most contemporary hunter-gatherers still do not work particularly long or hard, and it is likely that most ancient hunter-gatherers worked even less.

Although detailed quantitative data are few, ethnographic studies generally give the impression that hunter-gatherers work less than the members of other preindustrial societies (Boserup, 1965; Sahlins, 1972; Minge-Klevana, 1980; Johnson and Earle, 1987). In her classic work *The Conditions of Agricultural Growth* (1965), as well as in a later work (Boserup, 1981), Ester Boserup has convincingly demonstrated that the workload increased with the transition from hunting and gathering to agriculture, and that as agricultural production was intensified the workload continued to increase. The peasants of agrarian societies in general work harder and longer than do the members of all other preindustrial societies. In these societies a great deal of time must be spent plowing, spreading fertilizers, harvesting, tending animals, and performing the countless other activities that normally occupy peasants.

I conclude, then, that the workload increased rather than decreased with the emergence and intensification of agriculture. I regard this as a regressive development in social evolution because I accept the notion that humans everywhere are psychobiologically constructed so as to follow a Law of Least Effort (Zipf, 1965; Harris, 1979). This law holds that, other things being equal, people prefer to carry out activities with a minimum expenditure of time and energy. As natural time and energy savers, humans regard with various degrees of unpleasantness any increase in work time and work difficulty. There are, of course, circumstances under which the law does not hold. I envision three. First, people will be willing to work harder and longer if they need to do so in order to prevent any significant deterioration in their standard of living. Second, people can be politically compelled by other groups to work harder and longer than they desire. And, third, people can be psychologically conditioned, through such devices as the Protestant work ethic, to regard work as a virtue and as necessary for self-respect and social approval. So people do not always behave in accordance with the law, but for the most part people do regard it as a decline in their well-being if they are compelled by circumstances or by other people to work harder and longer. It should also be pointed out that this law applies only to work that people regard either as unrewarding psychologically or as onerous. A great deal of subsistence work falls into this category. However, there are other forms of work that may be intrinsically rewarding – craftsmanship or creative artistry, for example – and the Law of Least Effort is not meant to apply to this type of work.

Social and economic inequality

Hunting and gathering societies are far and away the most egalitarian societies that have ever existed. They are seldom class divided, normally being characterized by mild prestige differences at most. It is common for them to place great emphasis on generalized reciprocity and compulsory sharing, and competitiveness, boastfulness, and selfishness are highly disdained. Gerhard Lenski (1966) has used ethnographic and historical data to show in great detail how social and economic inequality are evolutionary phenomena. Small-scale horticultural societies with low population densities are also commonly quite egalitarian, although a number have developed what Morton Fried (1967) has called "social ranking," which involves the assignment of high levels of prestige to certain individuals because of their capabilities as organizers of economic production or as war leaders. In horticultural societies throughout Melanesia, for example, men often compete for the status of "big man" (Oliver, 1955; Hogbin, 1964; M. Harris, 1974, 1977). However, small-scale horticultural societies are seldom characterized by genuine class stratification in which there are differences in economic privilege between different groups. Large-scale horticultural societies, on the other hand, often convert "big men" into "chiefs" and turn mere prestige or rank differences into economic inequalities. But it is in

344   *The Question of Progress*

agrarian societies that stratification reaches its highest level. Here we find an extreme polarization between a small landowning nobility and a large, often landless, peasantry, with the few ruthlessly exploiting the many. Agrarian societies stand at the opposite extreme from hunter-gatherer societies, and the former are characterized by social and political tensions that are unimaginable in the latter. It is clear, then, that social and economic inequalities are products of social evolution, and that these inequalities are exacerbated with continuing evolution. Because of the conflicts and tensions engendered by these inequalities, and because of the various burdens that are placed on subordinate groups, it is difficult not to regard such occurrences as regressive in nature.

Democracy and freedom

Discussion of the fate of democracy and freedom is hampered by the various meanings that have been given to these terms. With respect to the discussion of preindustrial societies, I shall think of democracy as a political condition in which the members of a society are free to make decisions by way of open and relatively equal discussion and thus do not have their actions dictated by elite groups. Given this conception of democracy, only one conclusion can be reached: social evolution has increasingly undermined democracy. Hunter-gatherer bands and horticultural tribes are strongly characterized by forms of political leadership in which leaders have no real power or authority over others. Headmen in hunter-gatherer societies usually attain their position simply by group consent, with the group choosing leaders whom they believe to be wise, thoughtful, and considerate. This position confers no right to command anyone to do anything, and to the extent that a headman tries to exert authority he is simply ignored, or perhaps removed from his position. The headmen and "big men" of horticultural societies may enjoy more prestige and renown than the headmen of hunting and gathering societies, but they, too, have no real power or authority, and they, too, enjoy their position only by virtue of community consent. It is normally in the more advanced and intensive horticultural societies that the machinery of government begins to be created. In chapter 3 we discussed the formation of chiefdoms, a common political form in advanced horticultural societies. These political forms are hierarchically organized structures in which a paramount chief, along with his various subchiefs and a variety of other administrative officials, exercises a type of political leadership in which they do have genuine power, sometimes life-and-death power, over others. The major limitation of chiefdoms, at least from the point of view of leaders, is that leaders lack a true monopoly of force, which means that popular rebellions can depose them. Chiefdoms evolve into states when that monopoly of force comes to exist. States have been found in some highly advanced horticultural societies, such as those of Mesoamerica, but they have been most commonly associated with agrarian civilizations. Here the rule of the many by the few reaches extreme proportions, and even vestiges of democracy no longer exist.

We see once again, then, that social evolution has been associated with a major regressive trend: the primitive democracy of bands and tribes was eventually undermined by the formation of increasingly powerful and autocratic political elites. But then there is the question of freedom, a concept that has been subject to several meanings. I shall distinguish three. First, there is what might be called *individual autonomy*. This essentially involves the absence of external constraints on individual action. In this usage of the concept of freedom, individuals are free to the extent that they are not being dictated to by other individuals, such as family members or those with greater power. (This notion blends considerably with the notion of democracy as used above.) Alexandra Maryanski and Jonathan Turner (1992) have employed such a conceptualization in order to assess freedom's evolutionary fate. They claim that, among preindustrial societies, hunter-gatherers have the most individual autonomy, a conclusion that is borne out by other studies (Gardner, 1991). A great deal of individual autonomy was lost, they claim, in the transition to horticultural societies, where individuals came to be constrained by what they call the "cage of kinship." In the transition to agrarian societies, the cage of kinship was replaced by the "cage of power," and individuals came to be controlled by powerful elites of various types. Maryanski and Turner nominate horticultural societies for the dubious honor of being the most unfree of all societies, apparently arguing that kinship is more constraining than power. I would dispute this claim and nominate instead agrarian societies for the status of the most unfree societies, because I regard power as more constraining, at least in more unpleasant ways, than kinship. Moreover, the cage of kinship does not really disappear in agrarian societies, but remains to a large extent along with the cage of power.

A second conception of freedom, closely related to the first, is what might be called *individuality*. I use this term to mean the capacity of individuals to think and act apart from the normative standards of the group, or to engage in what we usually call self-expression. Although individual autonomy and individuality are closely related, it is possible to have one without the other. In fact, this is precisely what prevails in hunter-gatherer societies. Although individuals in such societies are relatively free from the constraints of kinship and power, they are not free from the constraints imposed by the standards of the group itself, that is, by the power of custom and tradition. However, hunter-gatherer societies are not unique in their lack of individuality, for all preindustrial societies must be regarded as being extemely low on this dimension of freedom. In terms of individuality, then, there has probably been little change in freedom throughout the entire preindustrial era.

A third meaning of freedom is what might be called *self-realization*. However, since this has little relevance to preindustrial societies, I shall leave discussion of it until the next section.

AFTER THE RISE OF MODERN CAPITALISM

The standard of living

There is little question but that the rise of capitalism has contributed to an enormous increase in the standard of living for the members of modern industrial societies. The facts are indisputable. The quality of the diet and of nutrition is the highest in world history. The revolution in health and medical care that took place in the twentieth century has reduced infant mortality rates[1] to a tiny fraction of what they were in all preindustrial societies, and of course they were extremely high in those societies. The average infant mortality rate for industrial societies today is 7.4 (World Bank, 1992). As recently as 1900 the countries of western Europe had an average infant mortality rate of 148, the United States had a rate of 162, and Japan had a rate of 151 (Cipolla, 1978). Earlier European infant mortality rates were considerably higher. For example, York, England in the sixteenth century had a rate of 480; Geneva, Switzerland in the seventeenth century a rate between 289 and 358; several German communities in the eighteenth century rates of 350 or more; Amsterdam in the eighteenth century a rate of 290; and Berlin in 1880 a rate of over 300 (M. Cohen, 1989). Life expectancies tell the same story. Longevity at birth in the United States in 1900 was 49 years, which is a considerable improvement over preindustrial populations but still well short of the average for today's industrial societies, slightly more than 76 years (United Nations, 1992a). Compare these figures to some longevity rates for European preindustrial cities: Stockholm between 1725 and 1830, below 20; Geneva before 1725, less than 30; Amsterdam in the early seventeenth century, in the 20s; London in 1604, 18; Sheffield, England in the 1860s, 32 (men) and 35 (women); Manchester, England in the 1840s, 38 (gentlemen), 20 (traders), and 17 (unskilled laborers); Irish cities in the 1830s, 24 (M. Cohen, 1989).

The question of progress with respect to the less-developed countries of the modern world is much more difficult. The most pessimistic position is taken by Immanuel Wallerstein (1983). Everyone acknowledges that the gap between the developed and the less-developed countries has been steadily widening, but Wallerstein argues that this is indicative of an actual *absolute* deterioration in the standard of living for most people in the Third World. It is not merely that the Third World is falling ever farther behind the developed world; the Third World is falling ever farther behind as well *relative to its own past*. Wallerstein puts it this way (1983:100–1):

I wish to defend the one Marxist proposition which even orthodox Marxists tend to bury in shame, the thesis of the absolute (not relative) immiseration of the proletariat.

I hear the friendly whispers. Surely you can't be serious; surely you mean relative immiseration? Is not the industrial worker strikingly better off today than in 1800? The industrial worker, yes, or at least many industrial workers. But industrial workers still comprise a relatively small part of the world's population. The overwhelming proportion of the world's work-forces, who live in rural zones or move between them and urban slums, are worse off than their ancestors five hundred years ago. They eat less well, and certainly have a less balanced diet. Although they are more likely to survive the first year of life (because of the effect of social hygiene undertaken to protect the privileged), I doubt that the life prospects of the majority of the world's population *as of age one* are greater than previously; I suspect the opposite is true. They unquestionably work harder – more hours per day, per year, per lifetime. And since they do this for less total reward, the rate of exploitation has escalated very sharply.

Christopher Chase-Dunn (1989) has interpreted the widening gap between the developed and less-developed worlds to mean only that there has been relative immiseration and that, in fact, there has been a certain amount of improvement in less-developed countries. Even in the periphery, he claims, there has been at least a slight improvement in living standards in recent decades. Quantitative evidence bears Chase-Dunn out. Table 8.1 presents data on the most important indicators of the physical quality of life in the less-developed countries between 1960 and 1990. During just this 30-year time span we can see that considerable improvement has taken place. Life expectancy increased from 46 years to 63 years, infant mortality dropped from 106 to 56 (1965–90), under-five mortality dropped from 233 to 112, adult literacy increased from 46 percent to 64 percent (1970–90), and Gross Domestic Product (in real dollars) increased from $784 to $2,296. In only a 30-year period or less, these represent substantial gains. The decline in the infant mortality rate is especially important, because this is considered perhaps the best single indicator of the quality of health care, and because it has such an important impact on longevity. An average infant mortality rate of 56 represents a dramatic improvement over the infant mortality rates of preindustrial European populations of the recent past, which, as noted earlier, were often in the 300 range.

Table 8.2 provides a summary statement of the improvement we are discussing, using the Human Development Index (HDI) constructed by the United Nations (1992a). This index is based on a weighted average of life expectancy, educational attainment, and Gross Domestic Product. The 33 countries shown in the table are a representative sample of a larger group of 110 countries for which the HDI has been calculated. In the larger sample, 99 countries experienced an increase in the HDI, 10 experienced a decrease, and one experienced no change. In the 33 countries shown here, 30 experienced an increase in their HDI, whereas only 3 suffered a decrease. The average change in the HDI in the larger sample was .082, and in the societies shown in table 8.2, .088. If we limit ourselves to the 25 less-developed countries in table 8.2, then the average increase in the HDI was .080. This is a relatively modest improvement, but it is an improvement nonetheless, and it can be seen that the level of improvement in a number of less-developed countries is considerable.

Table 8.1 *Trends in development indicators in less-developed countries*

Indicator	Year				
	1960	1965	1970	1989	1990
Life expectancy					
High human development nations	59				71
Medium human development nations	49				69
Low human development nations	42				57
Total all less-developed nations	46				63
Infant mortality rate					
High human development nations		84			45
Medium human development nations		94			48
Low human development nations		124			69
Total all less-developed nations		106			56
Under-five mortality rate					
High human development nations	119				40
Medium human development nations	195				55
Low human development nations	278				152
Total all less-developed nations	233				112
Adult literacy rate					
High human development nations			82%		90%
Medium human development nations			56%		75%
Low human development nations			35%		51%
Total all less-developed nations			46%		64%
Gross Domestic Product per capita					
High human development nations	$2,325			$6,025	
Medium human development nations	$885			$3,146	
Low human development nations	$515			$1,115	
Total all less-developed nations	$784			$2,296	

Life expectancy is expressed in years from birth. Infant mortality is the number of babies who die in the first year of life per 1,000 live births. Under five mortality is the number of children who die in the first five years of life per 1,000 children born. The numbers for adult literacy express the percentage of the adult population that is literate. Gross Domestic Product per capita is the total value (in constant US dollars) of goods and services produced within the national boundaries of a country divided by the population.

Sources: (World Bank, 1992), table 28; United Nations (1992: 134–5)

Table 8.2　*Changes in the Human Development Index, 1970–90*

Country	1970 HDI	1990 HDI	1970/1990 Change
Developed countries			
United States	.848	.976	.128
Japan	.853	.981	.128
Australia	.849	.971	.122
France	.854	.969	.116
United Kingdom	.850	.962	.113
Sweden	.873	.976	.103
Netherlands	.866	.968	.101
Italy	.830	.922	.092
Less-developed countries			
South Korea	.589	.871	.282
Indonesia	.316	.491	.176
Brazil	.569	.739	.170
Hong Kong	.762	.913	.151
Thailand	.535	.685	.150
Mexico	.675	.804	.129
Singapore	.730	.848	.119
Venezuela	.715	.824	.109
Iraq	.489	.589	.100
Ecuador	.542	.641	.100
Trinidad and Tobago	.784	.876	.093
Honduras	.385	.473	.088
Iran	.464	.547	.083
Ivory Coast	.212	.289	.077
Guatemala	.416	.485	.069
Philippines	.542	.600	.058
Argentina	.784	.833	.049
India	.258	.297	.039
Zaire	.232	.262	.030
Somalia	.061	.088	.027
Bangladesh	.174	.185	.011
Rwanda	.184	.186	.002
Zambia	.320	.315	−.006
Uganda	.241	.192	−.049
Nicaragua	.549	.496	−.053

Source: United Nations (1992a), technical note table 1.3

It appears, then, that immiseration in the world-system is only relative, and that real gains have been made by less-developed countries in recent decades. And yet can we be so sure about these gains? Could they be to some extent illusory, an artifact of our measurement indices? It is entirely possible. We know that longevity at birth is not independent of infant mortality, and that the main reason for increasing longevity in the less-developed world in the last few decades is falling infant mortality. It is probably not the case that those who make it to age five are living any longer than was previously the case. The data presented also ignore the internal stratification systems of less-developed countries and the fact that internal inequalities have increased in some of these countries in recent years. It is possible that the physical quality of life has improved for only a minority, perhaps even a small minority, of the population, and that most people's lives have been relatively unchanged, or in some cases have even gotten worse. It can also be pointed out that, even if it is true that a smaller percentage of the populations of less-developed countries are living in abject poverty and misery, nevertheless the *absolute number* of such people on a world scale has increased. We therefore have to be extremely cautious in our assessment of developmental trends in the quality of life in the Third World. More precise measures will be needed to settle the matter.[2]

The workload and the quality of work

There is a widespread perception that the transition from agrarian to industrial societies has led to a dramatic decline in the amount of time people spend working. This notion is usually coupled with the idea that modern industrial societies are "leisure societies." However, caution is in order. Wanda Minge-Klevana (1980) has surveyed time-allocation studies that seem to suggest that, while the amount of time people spend working outside the home has declined somewhat, the amount of time people spend working *inside* the home on various tasks of household maintenance has increased. As a result, total labor time in industrial societies remains high. Results from studies in the United States and several western and eastern European societies show that men spend a total of between 6.5 and 8.1 hours per day (in a seven-day week) working both outside and inside the home. Employed women average between 8 and 11.2 hours working both inside and outside the home, and women who are strictly housewives still work between 5.8 and 9.5 hours on inside work only. These data translate into work weeks of between 45.5 and 56.7 hours for men, between 56 and 78.4 hours for employed women, and between 40.6 and 66.5 hours for housewives. Minge-Klevana compared these figures with average work weeks for several contemporary agricultural (Third World) societies, some of which are primarily engaged in horticulture and some of which are engaged in plow agriculture. Total work time both inside and outside the home for both sexes was 41.3 hours a week in the horticultural societies and 72.1 hours a week in the agrarian societies. It is obvious, then, that people in modern industrial societies are working harder than the members of horticultural societies and not all that much less than the members of agrarian societies. Modern industrial societies are thus not quite the "leisure societies" that we have thought them to be.

In addition to the quantity of work, there is of course the question of its quality, or the level of gratification it brings those who perform it. The Marxian conception of the human individual has made the need to work a central part of human nature, for work – by which Marx meant the manipulation of nature according to some conceptual formulation – was seen as the primary means of human satisfaction and well-being (Marx, 1963[1844]). Marx, of course, was particularly concerned with those conditions that blocked the human capacity to achieve meaning and gratification through work – that produced alienation instead of satisfaction – and he identified the capitalist division of labor as the form of work organization most conducive to alienated labor. It was the extreme specialization of work, the separation of conceptualization from execution, and the appropriation of the final product that made it impossible for work within the capitalist system to be meaningful work.

Sociologists have argued for decades about whether Marx was right. My own view is that he may have overstated the case somewhat, but that nonetheless a great deal of work within the industrial capitalist system produces high levels of alienation. Most work in preindustrial societies has a very different character from work in modern capitalism. In preindustrial settings, labor specialization is usually limited or nonexistent and workers have a great deal of control over the work process. The line between work and play is often blurry or even nonexistent (Thomas, 1964). Much work in agrarian societies is physically demanding, and slave labor is oppressive and doubtless highly alienating, but even in these societies a great deal of work does not have the alienating quality it does under modern capitalism. Harry Braverman (1974) has argued that the introduction of the techniques of scientific management created by Frederick Winslow Taylor at the end of the nineteenth century has had a devastating effect on work. It has destroyed craftsmanship and degraded the worker, making him or her an automaton who blindly executes work designed by others. Braverman may overstate his case somewhat, but his basic point is essentially valid. One of the most important studies of alienation ever carried out is that of Robert Blauner (1964). Blauner studied several different types of work organization in different industries and showed that the type of work that had been most thoroughly penetrated by Taylorist principles, the automobile industry, led to much higher levels of alienation than that which was organized along more traditional lines and that involved the workers' retention of genuine craftsmanship, a printing shop. In the printing shop studied by Blauner, workers retained a great deal of personal control over their work and were directly involved in the design and conceptualization of their tasks. They also had a good deal of variety in work tasks, especially when compared to the deadening repetition and monotony of automobile assembly line work. The conclusion seems to be that alienation has increased in proportion to the spread of Taylorist principles.

However, what we seem to find in modern industrial societies is not simply an increase in alienated labor, but a bifurcation in which some workers receive remarkably high levels of gratification from their work. I speak, of course, of the types of work that involve considerable creativity and independence, which would include mostly the work of the modern professions and that performed by high-level managers in business organizations and top administrators in government. Thus, modern industrial societies produce very high levels of alienation for some, but remarkably high levels of satisfaction for others. This has been a major outcome of many aspects of social evolution: improvement for a minority coupled with worsening conditions for the majority.

Although I have been discussing only modern industrial societies, what I have been saying applies to less-developed countries to the extent that these societies have been penetrated by modern capitalist principles of workplace organization. Although we lack any good quantitative data, it is likely that workers in these societies work even longer and harder than workers in industrial societies. In some ways, less-developed countries combine the worst features of agrarian societies with the worst features of industrial societies.

Social and economic equality

There is little more that need be said about the impact of the evolution of the modern world on patterns of social and economic equality. As noted in chapter 7, although industrial capitalist societies display high levels of economic inequality, there has nonetheless been a diffusion of economic benefits throughout the population to an extent unimaginable in an agrarian society. The mass of the population is well off economically. However, as also noted earlier, economic inequality at a world level has been increasing rather than declining over the past few centuries through the polarization between core and periphery. An ever larger proportion of the world's total wealth is increasingly concentrated in the hands of an ever smaller proportion of the world's population. This has exacerbated world political and military tensions considerably, and the process can be expected to continue indefinitely.

Democracy and freedom

The hunting and gathering bands and horticultural tribes that were the only forms of human social life at one time were, as we have seen, the truest of democracies. Their primitive democracy was gradually undermined and eroded by the growth of chiefdoms and states throughout world history and prehistory, as true governments arose and became increasingly autocratic. Although modern industrial capitalist societies are hardly democracies along the extremely egalitarian and participatory lines of bands and tribes, they have brought into existence another form of democracy, parliamentary democracy. This still involves a rule by elites rather than by "the people," but its significance should not be overlooked or demeaned, as it often is by Marxists and certain other thinkers. Parliamentary democracies resting on legislative bodies that check the power of executives, constitutional rights and liberties, and universal suffrage have brought real gains for the large mass of the population, especially compared to the situation of the usually despotic agrarian societies of the past several thousand years. It is a myth to think that in modern capitalist democracies the people rule, but it is also a myth to think that parliamentary democracy accomplishes nothing as long as the means of production are still privately owned.

Freedom in modern capitalist societies, in all three of its senses, has undoubtedly expanded. Compared to all preindustrial societies except hunter-gatherers, there is much greater individual autonomy (at least outside the world of work), and individual autonomy is sanctioned by the state. There is also much greater individuality. In modern industrial societies the power of custom and tradition has receded greatly, and the desire for individual self-expression is given much freer rein. Indeed, Durkheim (1933[1893]; cf. Lukes, 1972) argued that the rise of individualism was the single most important trend in the transition to industrial societies. Maryanski and Turner (1992) have argued that the relationship between freedom (conceived primarily as individual autonomy) and social evolution is curvilinear: individual autonomy was high in hunter-gatherer societies, declined with the evolution of horticultural and agrarian societies (with, respectively, their cages of power and kinship), but returned with modern industrialism. They are highly critical of those sociologists (and they mean to include most sociologists) who have viewed the rise of industrialism negatively – as leading to an increasingly impersonal, fragmented, dehumanizing, and unsatisfying society (1992:162):

Industrialization has often been a brutal, ruthless process, destroying old forms of social control and forcing the exploited masses to endure such hardships as the factory system. But in its brutality, industrialization allows people to tear down at least some of the cage of power. . . . Moreover, large and highly differentiated structures, operating in monied markets, provide options and choices never available in agrarian systems. For all the early sociologists' deep concern with the "loss of community," in truth ordinary people embrace the chance to live and participate in a system relatively well attuned to their primate heritage. Thus, despite all the abuses and indignities that industrial society fosters on humans, it has allowed them to tear down, at least partially, the cages of their confinement. And if post-industrialism has indeed ushered in a new "post-modern" stage of evolution, it should further reduce humans' sociocultural cages.

There is still a third form of freedom that thus far we have only mentioned. It is closely related to the other two forms, especially to individuality, but it nonetheless has distinct features of its own. This is what might be called freedom as *self-realization*. It is essentially what Marx (1963[1844]) meant when he talked about *human freedom* and opposed it to the political freedom of modern parliamentary democracies (cf. Elster, 1985), and is close to what Abraham Maslow (1971) meant by his concept of self-actualization. Self-realization involves the capacity of individuals to fulfill their potentialities as human individuals. Self-realization requires freedom from physical want as well as the possession of a sizable amount of time free from the process of getting a living. Marx thought that the conditions had been created in modern capitalist society for some individuals to engage in self-realization, but that they were only a small minority. The working classes were in no position to engage in self-realization, or even to think about it. Complete human freedom for Marx would be present only when all members of society could become involved in projects of self-realization, and for him this was possible only in a socialist society. Nonetheless, it is still possible to argue, I believe, that the possibilities for self-realization have become in late twenti-eth-century capitalism a good deal more widespread than Marx ever imagined. This form of freedom, too, has been a major creation of modern capitalism, and to the extent that we evaluate such a thing positively then it can only be concluded that it represents a progress-ive aspect of social evolution.

Freedom in all of its senses has obviously been a much less prominent feature of life in less-developed countries. Parliamentary democracy is the exception rather than the rule as the form of government, and most individuals are too concerned with physical want and too busy scratching out a living to formulate projects of individuality and self-realization. The uneven development of capitalism has meant the uneven spread of freedom.

CONCLUSIONS

In terms of the question of human progress, social evolution has presented us with a mixed bag, leading to certain forms of progress at certain stages and times, but generating just as often, if not more often, regressive trends. Although most social evolutionists have been progressivists, there is nothing inherent in the concept of evolution that requires anyone to assume that it must be linked with progress. Whether processes of social evolution are progressive or regressive (or neutral) is always a question to be decided empirically, which is what I have tried to accomplish in this chapter. My overall conclusion is that, except for the modern world in approximately the past century, most social evolution has led to regression along the most important dimensions of human material well-being. I cannot improve on the way the matter has been formulated by Mark Cohen, whose words I shall let stand as the grand conclusion of this chapter (1989:141):

I think we must substantially rethink our traditional sense that civilization represents progress in human well-being – or at least that it did so for most people for most of history prior to the twentieth century. The comparative data simply do not support that image. At best, we see what might be called a partitioning of stress by class and location, in which the well-to-do are progressively freed from nutritional stress (although even they did not escape the ravages of epidemics until recently) but under which the poor and urban populations, particularly the urban poor, are subjected to levels of biological stress that are rarely matched in the most primitive of human societies. The undeniable successes of the late nineteenth and twentieth centuries have been of briefer duration, and are perhaps more fragile, than we usually assume. In fact, some of our sense of progress comes from comparing ourselves not to primitives but to urban European populations of the fourteenth to eighteenth centuries. We measure the progress that has occurred since then and extrapolate the trend back into history. But a good case can be made that urban populations of that period may have been among the nutritionally most impoverished, the most disease-ridden, and the shortest-lived populations in human history. A Hobbesian view of primitive life makes sense from the perspective of the affluent twentieth century. But Hobbes was probably wrong, by almost any measure, when he characterized primitive life as ". . . poor, nasty, brutish, and short" while speaking from the perspective of urban centers of seventeenth-century Europe. At best, he was speaking only for his own social class.

NOTES

1 The infant mortality rate is the number of infants who die in the first year of life for every 1,000 babies born.
2 However, a recent study by Glenn Firebaugh and Frank Beck (1994) examines changes in calorie consumption per capita, infant survival probability, and life expectancy at age one for 62 less-developed countries between 1965 and 1988. On the basis of regression analyses they claim that these changes have produced real benefits for the masses, not just benefits for an already well-off minority. If their results can be accepted as valid, they support the argument that a generalized form of social progress has been occurring throughout the less-developed world in recent decades.

9

The Evolving Future

This chapter attempts to draw on our understanding of the great
evolutionary trends of the modern era to make intelligent projections
about the near- to medium-term future. But first a caveat is in order.
Social scientists in general, and sociologists in particular, have never
had a good record at prediction. Even economists, whose science is
the most mathematically sophisticated of the social sciences, do not
have a particularly good record on this score. But there is a good
reason for this, and it has nothing to do with the youthfulness of
the social sciences. That reason is the extraordinary complexity
of the phenomena that social scientists study. In recent years the
perspective known as *chaos theory* has become extremely popular in
mathematics and the natural sciences (Gleick, 1987; Stewart, 1989;
Prigogene and Stengers, 1984). The basic idea of chaos theory is
that it is extremely difficult if not impossible to make sound predictions about the behavior of complex systems because even a slight
change in just one of the system's variables will produce a very
different outcome. A good example of the action of chaos in complex
natural systems is the weather. Everyone has always known that
weather forecasting is a hazardous activity, and now we know the
reason: weather is a complex system composed of many variables.
Weather forecasts presume that all variables will act as anticipated;
if any variable fails to do so, then the prediction goes awry.

Chaos theory is, in a very real sense, the best thing that has ever
happened to sociology and the social sciences. It allows us to see that
the reason for our many predictive failures is not the youthfulness
of the social sciences, or the intellectual inferiority of the social to
the natural sciences. In fact, according to chaos theory, because

of the very nature of the phenomena that the social sciences study – the most complex systems that exist – they can never have much predictive success. Why, then, do I write this chapter? Because speculating about the future is such an exciting intellectual game, as well as because some of the variables to be analyzed can be predicted with more than average success. Most importantly, however, is the fact that thinking about the future is so critically important to the possible fate of humankind that it would be shirking our responsibility not to contemplate at least the near-term future. To be able to say what might very well happen if certain measures are not taken may be critical to the survival of humankind, or at least to its survival under conditions that humans would deem acceptable.

A FUTURISTIC SCENARIO: W. WARREN WAGAR

The most extraordinary image of the future I have seen, and the one most strongly rooted in the evolutionary assumptions of this book, is that of W. Warren Wagar in his remarkable book *A Short History of the Future* (1992). Wagar is a historian who has drawn on world-system theory to write an imaginary future that covers the twenty-first and twenty-second centuries. His book is fiction, but it is rooted in good social science theory.

Wagar's literary device is to have a historian living at the beginning of the twenty-third century narrate the history of the world from 1990 to 2200 in the form of a "holofilm" for his granddaughter. In the year 2001 began the last of the great Kondratieff upswings of the capitalist world-economy. That economy had come to be increasingly dominated by a few giant corporations, and by 2015 12 giant "megacorps" were in control of the world-economy and the governments of the major capitalist powers. The world had fallen increasingly under the sway of a world culture that was based heavily on electronic news and entertainment. The Kondratieff upswing ran its course by the early 2030s and then a devastating worldwide depression set in, the lowest points of which were reached in 2038 and 2043. Half of the work force in the richer countries was unemployed, and more than half was unemployed in the rest of the world.

The world of the early twenty-first century was rife with massive social problems. World population had grown to 8 billion by 2025, and many of the cities of the less-developed part of the world

360 The Evolving Future

suffered from massive overpopulation. For example, Mexico City had reached a population of 52 million, Calcutta of 38 million, and Cairo of 32 million. By 2010 there were deep holes in the ozone layer and massive soil erosion, and a global warming trend between 1980 and 2040 produced a rise in mean world temperature of 4.2° C. Ice caps and glaciers melted and the sea level rose by some two meters, causing shorelines and lowlands to be inundated. In addition to these major ecological problems, there was continued increase in world poverty, urban unrest, violent crime, and drug use.

The most catastrophic event of the twenty-first century, though, was the nuclear holocaust of 2044. Most of North America and Europe were destroyed, as was the Indian subcontinent, and within one year of the catastrophe approximately 70 percent of the earth's population had died, either from the direct effects of the holocaust or from the ecological devastation that followed (a "nuclear autumn" gripped agriculture). Most of the survivors were in the Southern hemisphere.

Prior to the holocaust a political party known as the World Party had formed, and it became especially active after 2044. Members of this party pressed for the creation of a world socialist common-wealth, and eventually such a form of government was created in 2062. The main aims of the new world government were to end capitalism, sexism, and "tribalism." The economy was converted into a form of socialism that was devoted to the production of use-values rather than exchange-values. Everyone had a guaranteed minimum income as long as they worked, and those who chose not to work received a guaranteed income of half this amount. The work specialization and work hierarchies that prevailed under capitalism were abolished, and workers were required to learn a variety of work skills. The class system eventually disappeared, and national boundaries were also abolished.

Despite its accomplishments, the new world socialist government was plagued by one major drawback: the absence of individual liberty. A massive state bureaucracy had been created, and the state engaged in very sophisticated forms of surveillance of individuals. Dissent against the state grew over time. New political parties formed, the most important of which were the Free Trade Party and the Small Party. The Free Trade Party wanted to reform the personal income laws to allow some individuals higher income shares, and it favored the introduction of forms of capitalist enterprise. The Small Party wanted to abolish the world state and to set up a highly decentralized political system that permitted the existence of many small political communities. It also wanted each state to have the freedom to choose its own form of government, economy, and religion. In 2124 these two parties entered into a coalition and won 31 percent of the votes in the election of that year. The Small Party's political fortunes grew over time, and in 2147 it won 67 percent of the vote. This marked the end of the socialist world commonwealth, and massive centralization gave way to widespread decentralization. By 2157 41,525 autonomous political communities had formed out of the ashes of the old system. Each political community could choose its own form of government, economy, and social system, and many of the new communities introduced a small-scale form of capitalism. The final act of the Small Party was to put itself out of existence, which it did in 2159. It had, essentially, no reason for any continued existence, for it had achieved its fundamental goal.

This account of Wagar's futuristic scenario has been somewhat selective, but it has focused on those dimensions of human life that are, in my view, most critical to human well-being in the decades ahead. How realistic is this scenario?

THE CHALLENGES: POPULATION GROWTH AND ECOLOGICAL DEGRADATION

Who would deny that the biggest challenge for humankind in the near future is the control of population growth and of the enormous degradation of the environment that has been generated by modern industrial capitalism? Since the early 1970s these issues have become a major focus of attention. Numerous scholars have written about the potentially devastating effects of continued population growth, especially in the Third World, and of continued exhaustion of the earth's resources (Heilbroner, 1980; Meadows, Meadows, and Randers, 1992; Kennedy, 1993).

In 1972 what quickly became an extremely famous analysis and set of predictions concerning the future effects of current rates of population growth and resource use, the so-called Club of Rome Report (Meadows, Meadows, Randers, and Behrens, 1974), was made public. The authors of this report generated many computer simulations that showed ominous consequences for humankind of a failure to place sharp restrictions on population growth and resource use within the next two decades. The authors drew three conclusions from their research (1974:24):

1 If the present growth trends in world population, industrialization, pollution, food production, and resource depletion continue unchanged, the limits to growth on this planet will be reached sometime within the next one hundred years. The most probable result will be a rather sudden and uncontrollable decline in both population and industrial capacity.
2 It is possible to alter these growth trends and to establish a condition of ecological and economic stability that is sustainable far into the future. The state of global equilibrium could be designed so that the basic material needs of each person on earth are satisfied and each person has an equal opportunity to realize his individual human potential.
3 If the world's people decide to strive for this second outcome rather than the first, the sooner they begin working to attain it, the greater will be their chances of success.

When this report appeared there was a very severe reaction on the part of some, and the authors were accused of excessive alarmism and of exaggerating the extent of the problem. The authors later admitted they were talking about a worst-case scenario, but they acknowledged that they did so in order to get the attention of the important individuals and groups who could start to do something about the problem.

How much has been done in the twenty years since the Club of Rome report appeared? The only realistic answer is, not very much. Although population growth in the Third World has slowed some-what, it is still very high. Moreover, the rate of resource use has actually grown as a result of increasing industrial activity. Taking these facts into account, in 1992 three of the authors of the original report carried out a new set of computer simulations and reported them in their book *Beyond the Limits* (Meadows, Meadows, and Randers, 1992). The authors ran computer simulations for 13 hypo-thetical scenarios involving four basic physical and biological limits: the amount of cultivable land, the yield achievable on each unit of land, the amount of nonrenewable resources, and the capacity of the earth to absorb pollution. Each scenario could produce one of four possible outcomes: continuous growth, sigmoid growth (i.e., "S-shaped" growth, or growth up to a point and then a leveling off), overshoot and oscillation, and overshoot and collapse. Scenario 1 involved letting current trends continue unchanged. This led to overshoot and collapse occurring in the early part of the next century (figure 9.1). Overshoot means that the earth's environment has been degraded to the extent that it can no longer support human populations at the level it once had. Collapse means a marked deterioration in life expectancy, the amount of consumer goods and services available per person, and the amount of food available per person. Scenario 2 assumed the availability of twice as many resources. It also led to overshoot and collapse, although at a somewhat later date. Scenarios 3 through 7 were the same as scenario 2, but a new condition was added each time. In scenario 3 it was pollution control; in scenario 4 it was all of the preceding plus land yield enhancement; in scenario 5 it was all of the preceding plus land erosion protection; in scenario 6 it was all of the preceding plus a more resource-efficient technology; and in scenario 7 it was all of the preceding plus faster development of new technology. In every scenario the outcome was overshoot and collapse, although with the addition of each restriction the collapse tended to come later and more gradually.

In scenarios 2 through 7, no restrictions were placed on population growth and industrial output and, as we saw, overshoot and collapse was the inevitable result. In the remaining scenarios, population growth, industrial output, or both, are restricted. Scenario 8 assumes that every couple in the world limits itself to two children. The result is overshoot and collapse by the middle of the twenty-first century or earlier. Scenario 9 is the same as scenario 8 but involves a further restriction: industrial output per capita is reduced to approximately the level of contemporary South Korea. Overshoot and collapse are again the result, but they do not occur so abruptly. In scenario 10, the restrictions of scenario 7 – pollution control, land yield enhancement, land erosion protection, a more resource-efficient technology, and faster development of new technology – are added to the population and output restrictions of scenario 9. The result is a sustainable world at a high standard of living (figure 9.2). Scenario 11 is the same as scenario 10, except it assumes that the necessary changes start in 1975 rather than in 1995. This produces a sustainable outcome at a slightly higher standard of living. Scenario 12 is the same as scenarios 10 and 11, except that the restrictions begin in 2015. This leads to overshoot and collapse, but one that permits recovery by the end of the twenty-first century.

State of the world

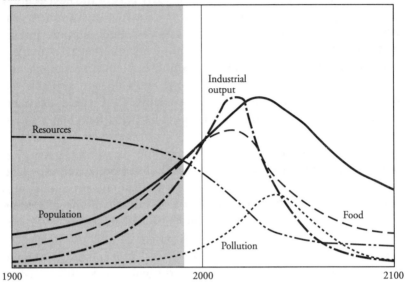

1900   2000   2100

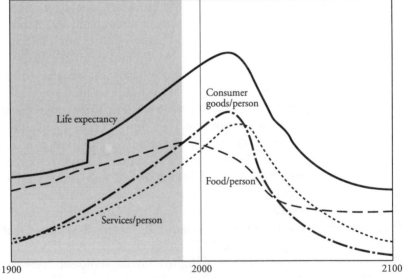

1900   2000   2100

Figure 9.1 *Ecological and economic overshoot and collapse through human inaction.*
Source: Meadows, Meadows, and Randers (1992:133)

State of the world

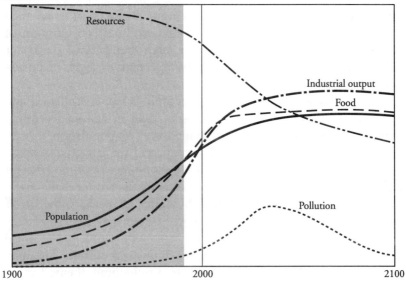

Resources

Industrial output

Food

Population

Pollution

1900   2000   2100

Material standard of living

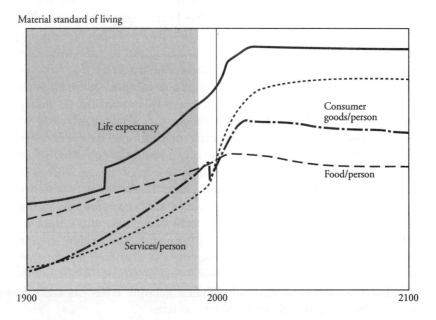

Life expectancy

Consumer
goods/person

Food/person

Services/person

1900   2000   2100

Figure 9.2 *A sustainable world through concerted human action.*
Source: Meadows, Meadows, and Randers (1992:199)

However, the recovery is associated with a standard of living that is notably lower than the standard of living in scenarios 10 and 11. Finally, scenario 13 is the same as scenario 11, except it is assumed that there are greater demands for food and the consumption of goods and services. This produces a high standard of living for awhile, but by the end of the twenty-first century signs of unsustainability emerge.

The results seem clear. In order to avoid a major ecological and economic collapse at a world level sometime in the next century, sharp restrictions must be placed immediately on population growth, industrial output, pollution, land erosion, and the use of nonrenewable resources. It is also necessary to develop more resource-efficient technologies and an agricultural system with greater land yield. Anything short of this fails. Can it be done? Or perhaps the better question is, will it be done? I doubt it. Scenarios 10 and 11 assume two highly unrealistic conditions: limiting every couple in the world to two children, and sharply reducing industrial output. The only way couples in Third World countries would limit themselves to two children or fewer is through the implementation of strict fertility policies by highly authoritarian and repressive governments, something along the lines of what China has been doing since the 1970s. It can be done, but it is difficult to imagine that it is likely to be done. As for the voluntary reduction of industrial output by capitalists, this is almost impossible to imagine. Robert Heilbroner (1980) believes that private individuals and groups will not voluntarily accept such restrictions but will have to be coerced, and this means the necessary rise of highly authoritarian governments that could easily lead to the collapse of our basic democratic institutions. As Heilbroner (1980:106) says, "I do not see how one can avoid the conclusion that the required transformation will be likely to exceed the capabilities of representative democracy." However, I have my doubts as to whether governments themselves would engage in such coercion, given the enormous control that capitalists normally have over the actions of states. The expanded accumulation of capital is the driving engine of the modern world, and I can imagine the abandonment of that principle only under the most extreme circumstances. To my mind, it is likely to be abandoned only when a genuine crisis has ensued, and by that time it will probably be too late.

My pessimism is reinforced by the fact that the 13 scenarios we have examined are even more unrealistic than we have so far indicated. The computer simulations, as all such simulations must, simplify greatly. They deal with only a few variables and take no account at all of such things as military drains on resources and civil strife. Indeed, Meadows, Meadows, and Randers (1992) openly admit that their models are "wildly optimistic." Military drains on resources and civil strife are not only rampant in the world today, but may be expected to increase with each passing year. As Heilbroner (1980) has suggested, the future looks very grim indeed.

THE CHALLENGES: NUCLEAR WAR

The other great worry of humankind in the late twentieth century is the possibility of nuclear war. To get some idea of the probability of a nuclear catastrophe, it will be helpful to understand the conditions under which war has occurred in recent centuries.

Joshua Goldstein (1988) has explored the relationship between the outbreak of war and Kondratieff cycles in the world-economy during the period between 1495 and the present. Looking at ten Kondratieff cycles over this 500-year period, and considering only the truly major wars that have involved a large number of casualties, Goldstein has found that large wars have occurred almost always toward the end of the upturn phase of the Kondratieff cycle. The only possible exception is the Second World War, which occurs right before the beginning of an upturn phase. However, it is not clear whether or not this is a true exception. World Wars I and II are often regarded not as two distinct wars, but as two phases of one great war. If we assume the correctness of this view, then there is no exception: major wars in the last 500 years have always occurred near the end of the upturn phase of the cycle. Regardless, the relationship of war to the Kondratieff cycle is very strong. Exactly why major wars should occur in the second half of the upturn phase is not clear. Goldstein himself believes that major wars occur when they do because it is during the second half of the upturn phase that states can most afford them.

Goldstein uses these data to try to predict the occurrence of the next major war. We know that the world-economy entered a downturn phase about 1970 and that this downturn phase has not yet run its course. Wallerstein and other world-system theorists have suggested that this phase should bottom out around 2000. This would give us a new upturn phase from about 2000 to 2025, which would place the next major war roughly in the time period between 2015 and 2025. Goldstein actually suggests that the longer period between 2000 and 2030 is a time of serious possibility for the next major war, although he thinks such a war would be more likely to occur near the end of this period.

Is it likely that the next major war will be a nuclear war? It is widely assumed that this would inevitably be the case, but not everyone agrees. Immanuel Wallerstein (1982) and Giovanni Arrighi (1982) argue that the presence of nuclear weapons alters everything. Inasmuch as several core states have nuclear weapons, war becomes unthinkable because all parties recognize the potentially catastrophic results, and the virtual "unwinnability," of a nuclear war. Wallerstein has said that the fact that nuclear weapons have been available for so long without being used demonstrates the strong commitment of world powers to avoid nuclear war.

Christopher Chase-Dunn and Kenneth O'Reilly (1989) take a different view. They have examined a variety of factors they believe have a strong bearing on the likelihood of a major war, or what they call a "core war," in the near future. These factors include the phase of the Kondratieff cycle, increasing ecological degradation, the deteriorating position of the United States in the world-economy, efforts at nuclear disarmament, and the emergence of new international organizations with the explicit intent of reducing the threat of war. They conclude as follows (1989:61):

After reviewing the factors that might increase or decrease the chance of core wars, we can only estimate its likelihood. Nevertheless, it is our best guess that the developments that lower the probability of core war are not great enough to offset those factors that will increase the chance of war in the coming decades. The probability of a serious war among core states over the next four decades may be as much as fifty-fifty.

And Chase-Dunn and O'Reilly expect that any such war would likely involve the use of nuclear weapons.

It need not be assumed, however, that a nuclear war would have to be initiated by a core state. In the future several Third World states will have acquired nuclear weapons, and it is these states, I suspect, that are the ones that are most likely to use them. A major reason for this is the world maldistribution of economic resources, and the growing resentment that can be expected to result in the near future from increasing global polarization. Failure to cut back on population growth and resource use will only compound the problem. As Robert Heilbroner (1980) has suggested, deterioration in living standards in the Third World would lead to enormous increases in social unrest as well. If things get bad enough, "The possibility must then be faced that the underdeveloped nations which have 'nothing' to lose will point their nuclear pistols at the heads of the passengers in the first-class coaches who have everything to lose" (Heilbroner, 1980:44).

THE CHALLENGES: A WORLD STATE

It is, of course, impossible to say with any assurance just what would be the probability of a nuclear war in the near future. Nonetheless, because of the horrendous suffering and misery that such a war would produce, even the existence of a slight probability gives us reason to take steps to avoid such an outcome. A number of social scientists, one of the most vocal of which has been Christopher Chase-Dunn (1990), favor the establishment of a world state as the only real hope of avoiding an eventual nuclear holocaust. What Chase-Dunn has in mind is not a single state that would completely eliminate the sovereignty of all other states, but a kind of "world confederation of states with the power to inspect the military forces of single states and to overcome by force any force which might be brought against it" (Chase-Dunn, 1990:120). Moreover, such a world federation need not impose cultural uniformity, and it could try to combine the best features of both capitalism and socialism while minimizing their weaknesses. Individual nation-states within the federation would still retain considerable control over investment decisions, although the federation itself would deliberately try to create a much more even distribution of world resources and world wealth. Chase-Dunn says that his vision of a world state is that of a "multilevel, self-reliant, culturally pluralistic, minimally centralized system with a world level of government to guarantee the peace and to facilitate more balanced development. This would not be the end of history, but continuing struggles among interest groups would be carried out in ways that do not threaten the survival of the species" (1990:124). Chase-Dunn explicitly recognizes the potential threat to human freedoms posed by such a megastate, but he believes that, because there is so much at stake, the risk is worth taking. It is difficult not to agree. As he says (1990:121), "Let us hope that we have the opportunity to campaign for civil liberties in a future world state."

Several scholars have tried to estimate the timing of world state formation as a result of the natural process of political evolution. Extrapolating from the long-term trend in the reduction in the number of political units in the world, Robert Carneiro (1978) has estimated that the world will be unified under a single state no later than the year 2300. Raoul Naroll (1967), also extrapolating from political history, estimates that the probability of the formation of a world state will finally reach 50 percent by approximately the year 2175. Rein Taagepera (1990) has also tried to estimate the timing of the emergence of a global polity, basing his conclusions on the history of empire formation over the past 5,000 years. He sees a world state occurring much farther in the future, with a 50 percent probability of a world state forming only being reached in the year 3800.

All of these estimates, even Naroll's, put the world state much too far in the future to save humankind from nuclear devastation. But the analyses of Carneiro, Naroll, and Taagepera assume a process of natural political evolution that is not helped along in any particular way by a deliberate human intent to create a world state. Certainly a world state can be created in the very near future if humans so desire. But do they now, or will they do so? I have my doubts, which rest most prominently on the intense nationalistic tendencies that humans everywhere seem to display, as well as on the fairly well established fact that humans do not take major steps toward a new form of social organization until they are forced into doing so by dire circumstances. I do not foresee a world state forming until it is already, in a sense, too late – until the holocaust has already happened. This is exactly how a world state came to be formed in Wagar's futuristic scenario, and I think he has imagined things correctly. It is not an attractive conclusion, but it seems to me appropriately realistic and almost impossible to avoid.

THE CHALLENGES: CAPITALISM, SOCIALISM, OR BARBARISM?

Assuming that the world is capable of avoiding nuclear war and ecological and economic collapse, what is the future likely to hold in terms of the form of social, economic, and political organization? Marx's prediction of a transition from capitalism to socialism has, of course, been falsified in various ways, and in many ways the world is witnessing now a reverse transition from socialism to capitalism. However, Immanuel Wallerstein (1984) has claimed that, although Marx's specific predictions have not worked out, Marx may still turn out to be right in the long run. Capitalism has more life in it than Marx ever expected, and it has shown itself to be amazingly resilient and adaptable. Nevertheless, Wallerstein argues, the capitalist system contains fatal contradictions that will eventually explode it, and there will be a worldwide transition, probably in about 100 to 150 years, to some other mode of production, most likely a world socialist system with a world government. Wallerstein (1984:111) puts it this way:

Both the structural contradictions of capitalism and the antisystemic movements it has bred in such force will continue to eat away at the entrails of the system. The details are impossible to predict, but the broad pattern is clear. We are living in the historic world transition from capitalism to socialism. It will undoubtedly take a good 100–150 years to complete it, and of course the outcome is not inevitable. The system may yet see several periods of remission. There may come again moments where capitalism will seem to be in bloom. But in a comparison of life-cycles of social systems, the modern world-system can be seen to be in a late phase. What will replace it will surely not be utopia.

And what will the new socialist world-system, when it arrives, be like? Wallerstein conceives of it in a manner strikingly similar to Marx's notion of the content of socialism (1984:157):

The idea is that on the basis of an advanced technology, capable of providing a rate of global production adequate to meet the total needs of all the world's population, the rate and forms of production will be the result of collective decisions made in virtue of these needs. Furthermore, it is believed that the amount of new labor-time to maintain such a level of productivity will be sufficiently low as to permit each individual the time and resources to engage in activities aimed at fulfilling his potential.

The global production required will be attained, not merely because of the technological base, but because the egalitarian collectivity will be interested in realizing the full "potential surplus." This being the case, the social motivations for collective aggressive behavior will have disappeared, even if, in the beginning phases, not all the psychological motivations will have done so. Since collective decisions will be pursued in the common interest, then worldwide ecological balance will follow as an inherent objective.

In short, the socialist mode of production seeks to fulfill the objective of the rational and free society which was the ideological mask of the capitalist world-economy. In such a situation, repressive state machinery will have no function and will over time transform itself into routine administration.

Like Wallerstein, Walter Goldfrank (1987) sees capitalism rife with fatal contradictions that will eventually destroy it. As he says, nothing is forever. He has also suggested that socialism has a reasonable probability of appearance within the medium-term future, but he sees other possibilities as well. Goldfrank imagines four possible futures: Barbarism I, Barbarism II, Socialism I, and Socialism II. Barbarism I is a nuclear holocaust, and he sees the period from about 2015 to 2050 as the greatest danger period for this outcome. Barbarism II is global fascism, which would be a kind of world order built along the lines of Hitler's Germany or Stalin's Soviet Union. A giant centralized bureaucracy would supersede the interstate system, and it would maintain a monopoly over the means of production, the means of violence, and the means of communication. The state would confiscate and expropriate private property, and labor would be tightly controlled through such means as police repression, corporatist inclusion, and possibly even extermination and eugenics.

Socialism I is a world welfare state that would be organized roughly along the lines of present-day Sweden. The system would still be largely capitalist, but a left-leaning "world populist party" would seek to make "inroads on the prerogatives of the world capitalist class to make investment decisions and to distribute profits as it sees fit. The children of capitalists would tend to become technocrats, and a gradual socialization of the world economy would occur" (1987:88–9). Socialism II is a democratic socialist world state. This state would engage in democratic investment planning on a global scale for major sectors of industrial and foodstuff production, while at the same time allowing market forms of production for many consumer goods. The power of capitalists would be eliminated by worker control of enterprises and popular control of communities. Economic decisions would be motivated by a rational assessment of human needs rather than by the profit motive.

Goldfrank has gone so far as to try to estimate how likely each of these future scenarios is, as well as when, if it is to occur, it might occur. He estimates that Barbarism I and Barbarism II each have a probability of occurrence of 15 percent, or a 30 percent chance of one or the other occurring. Socialism I is estimated to have a 50 percent chance of occurrence, Socialism II a 20 percent chance. The chances, therefore, of some version of socialism occurring is a remarkably high 70 percent. As to when these outcomes might be realized, Goldfrank suggests the period between 2015 and 2050 for the two barbarisms, and a significantly later date for the two socialisms, roughly 80 to 140 years from now (a dating quite similar to Wallerstein's). As Goldfrank explains, for some form of socialism to occur the time must be ripe, and that means that such basic capitalist processes as commodification and proletarianization have to run their course. We still have some time before these processes begin to run up against their limits, perhaps even longer with the reopening of the old Soviet Union and eastern Europe to capitalist enterprise on the Western model.

Although Goldfrank seems to prefer Socialism II to the other outcomes, as would Wallerstein, my own preference would tend to be for Socialism I. My political outlook in the abstract is that of democratic socialism, but I have always parted company with Marxists in two major ways. I do not judge capitalism quite as harshly as they do, nor do I take as sanguine a view of a socialist mode of economic production. Both capitalism and socialism have strengths and weaknesses. As I see it, the major strengths of capitalism are:

1 It promotes enormous scientific and technological development (which, of course, does have its negative side).
2 It promotes enormous increases in economic productivity and the creation of wealth.
3 It has led to the formation of parliamentary democratic forms of government that have been a vast improvement over the various despotisms of the past.
4 It has created enormous opportunities for the realization of human potential even if these have been limited to a minority of the population.

Its main weaknesses I would summarize as follows:

1 It has produced very high levels of economic inequality both within, and, especially, between and among societies.
2 It has generated forms of work that have been associated with very high levels of boredom and alienation.
3 It has promoted an intense commercialization of human life that has increasingly pushed other human values, especially those related to aesthetic and intellectual endeavors, into the background.
4 As a result of this commercialization, it has promoted a consumerist mentality and culture that has, in the late twentieth century, been carried almost to bizarre extremes.

5   Because of the enormous emphasis on commercialism and consumerism, it seems
to have dragged the level of modern culture (using the term in its more narrow
sense) down to the lowest common denominator.
6   A byproduct of its promotion of science and technology has been, as we have seen,
an enormously detrimental impact on the environment.

What then are the strengths and weaknesses of socialism? Its main
strengths lie in its much more humane concern for the welfare of
all individuals in society and for a more egalitarian and economically
democratic form of social life. Its main weaknesses are well known.
These are its tendency to centralize economic planning to an extent
that produces a range of inefficiences and other economic problems that lead to serious difficulties in the long run, and its tendency
to concentrate political power in a huge bureaucracy that limits
human freedom. Because of these difficulties, I am much less optimistic than either Wallerstein or Goldfrank concerning a world
socialist system's capacity to produce a mode of human existence
truly superior in all respects to capitalism as we know it. I have
gradually come to the conclusion that perhaps the best we can do,
at least for the foreseeable future, is to extend to as much of the
world as possible something like the Swedish model of social democracy. This means a capitalist system that has a large number of
built-in protections in terms of minimum standards of income,
health care, education, and other aspects of the modern welfare
state, but at the same time a great deal of economic planning. A
world state that would seek to combine the best elements of the
plan and the market, while at the same time eliminating or neutraliz-
ing their worst elements, seems to me to be the most appropriate
path to follow. Such a system should seek to promote a level of
economic productivity commensurate with environmental protection; to eliminate through robotization and other advanced technologies the dullest and most repetitive forms of work (thus keeping
worker alienation to the lowest level possible commensurate with a
high standard of living); to promote the arts, sciences, and intellectual life in general as a realm of human activity at least equal in
importance to the creation and consumption of wealth, and do so
by providing universal and free (or at least very low-cost) lifetime
education; and, in general, to allow all individuals the time and
resources necessary for the achievement of their potential as members of the human species. It goes without saying that such a social

system should be as democratically organized as possible, and that it should seek to avoid excess centralized economic planning on the one hand as well as too much attention given to the market on the other. Such a system does not have to be rigidly egalitarian – the Marxists overemphasize this, I think – but it should avoid serious inequalities, or those that produce high levels of envy and social tension and that deny those at the bottom the opportunities that others have for self-realization. As John Rawls (1971) has said, inequalities are acceptable to the extent that they thereby enhance the situation of the worst-off members of society. The task of creating such a social system, or even approximating it, is daunting, but it is not impossible and is certainly worth a try.

THE CRISIS AND COLLAPSE OF CAPITALIST-SENSATE CULTURE

Much earlier in this century the historical sociologist Pitirim Sorokin (1957) formulated a theory of historical change that emphasized a cyclical alternation between two great types of cultural mentalities that he called *Ideational* and *Sensate*. Ideational culture is character-ized by an emphasis on things nonsensate and nonmaterial, and thus emphasizes spiritual aims as against those relating to the body. It is also characterized by an attitude of self-renunciation or asceticism. Sensate culture is just the opposite. It emphasizes the material world and the body, and seeks the maximum satisfaction of bodily needs. Mottos such as "Eat, drink, and be merry," "Life is short," and "Wine, women, and song" are the leading mottos of this type of cultural mentality. Sensate culture is also notable for its attempts to interpret, actively control, and master both the world of nature and that of human society. Sorokin also identified a third type of cul-ture that he referred to as *Idealistic*, which represented a kind of balanced mixture of Ideational and Sensate elements. For Sorokin, each cultural mentality evolved over a long period of time and eventually ran its course, going as far as it could. It then began to die out and give way to its opposite, although possibly passing through the Idealistic or Mixed mentality in the process. A cultural mentality changed immanently, or by working out all of its internal logical possibilities, and then gave way to a new one. History, for

Sorokin, was a long story of the rise and fall of cultural mentalities over hundreds and thousands of years.

As can clearly be seen, Sorokin's conception of human culture and civilization was distinctly idealist or mentalist. However, he did not see cultural mentalities as entirely free-floating but as linked to some extent to economic realities. He conceived of Ideational culture as characteristic of periods of economic stagnation or decline, whereas Sensate culture was likely to be associated with periods of economic vitality and growth. Each mentality also has its characteristic bearers. The main bearers of Ideational culture are priests and other religious leaders, as well as the religious landed aristocracy. The bearers of Sensate culture, on the other hand, are capitalists, secular governments, and secularized intellectuals.

Sorokin regarded modern Western capitalist civilization as strongly embodying the Sensate mentality and as having become progressively more Sensate over the last several hundred years. An independent test of this idea has shown Sorokin's point to be quite valid (Eckhardt, 1992). Western culture, however, had in the twentieth century entered a period of cultural crisis that Sorokin thought would soon lead to the collapse of Sensate culture and the transition to a much more appropriate Idealistic culture. Sensate culture had come near the end of its immanent development and was in the process of burning itself out. Writing originally in the 1930s, Sorokin attempted to predict the main trends of Western civilization in the coming decades. I quote at length (1957:699–701):

The present status of Western culture and society gives a tragic spectrum of the beginning of the disintegration of their Sensate supersystem. . . . In a terse delineation the following trends will prevail in this period.

1   Sensate values will become still more relative and atomistic. . . . The boundary line between the true and false, the right and wrong, the beautiful and ugly, positive and negative values, will be obliterated increasingly until mental, moral, aesthetic and social anarchy reigns supreme.

2   These progressively atomized Sensate values, including man himself, will be made still more debased, sensual and material, stripped of anything divine, sacred, and absolute. . . .

3   With all values atomized, any genuine, authoritative and binding "public opinion" and "world's conscience" will disappear. Their place will be taken by a multitude of opposite "opinions" of unscrupulous factions and by the "pseudo consciences" of pressure groups.

4   Contracts and covenants will lose the remnants of their binding power. . . .

5 Rude force and cynical fraud will become the only arbiters of all values and of all interindividual and intergroup relationships. . . .
6 Freedom will become a mere myth for the majority and will be turned into an unbridled licentiousness by the dominant minority.
7 Governments will become more and more hoary, fraudulent, and tyrannical, giving bombs instead of bread; death instead of freedom; violence instead of law; destruction instead of creation.
8 The family as a sacred union of husband and wife, or parents and children will continue to disintegrate. Divorces and separations will increase until any profound difference between socially sanctioned marriages and illict sex-relationships disappears. . . . The main sociocultural function of the family will further decrease until the family becomes a mere incidental cohabitation of male and female while the home will become a mere overnight parking place mainly for sex-relationship.
9 The Sensate supersystem of our culture will become increasingly a shapeless "cultural dumping place," pervaded by syncretism of undigested cultural elements, devoid of any unity and individuality. . . .
10 Its creativeness will continue to wane and wither. The place of Galileos and Newtons, Leibnitzes and Darwins, Kants and Hegels, Bachs and Beethovens, Shakespeares and Dantes, Raphaels and Rembrandts will be increasingly taken by a multitude of pseudo thinkers. . . . The place of moral categoric imperatives will be occupied by progressively atomistic and hedonistic devices of egoistic expediency, bigotry, fraud, and compulsion. . . . More specifically:
   (a) Quantitative colossalism will substitute for qualitative refinement; "the biggest for the best"; a best-seller for a classic; glittering externality for inner value; technique for genius; imitation for creation; a sensational hit for a lasting value. . . .
   (b) Thought will be replaced by "Information, please"; sages by smart Alecs; real criteria by counterfeit criteria; great leaders by frauds.
   (c) Even the greatest cultural values of the past will be degraded.
11 In the increasing moral, mental, and social anarchy and decreasing creativeness of Sensate mentality, the production of the material values will decline, depressions will grow worse, and the material standard of living will go down.
12 For the same reasons, security of life and possessions will fade. With these, peace of mind and happiness. Suicide, mental disease, and crime will grow. Weariness will spread over larger and larger numbers of the population.
13 Population will increasingly split into two types: the Sensate hedonists with their "eat, drink and love, for tomorrow we die"; and, eventually, into ascetics and stoics indifferent and antagonistic to Sensate values.

I have quoted at such length because of the extraordinary perceptiveness of Sorokin's vision from the vantage point of some 60 years ago. Virtually every single prediction made by Sorokin has come about, an extraordinary accomplishment for a social scientist. My only real disagreement with Sorokin concerns his idealist view that it is a culture's mentality that shapes it, and that mentalities may become relatively free-floating. For me, modern Sensate culture, by far the most Sensate culture the world has ever seen, has been driven along by the expansion and intensification of world capitalism rather than by its own internal logic (although I wouldn't deny some degree of autonomy to the Sensate mentality). Capitalism is Sensate by its very nature, inasmuch as it promotes the consumption of goods that give material well-being and pleasure. (I therefore prefer to speak of "Capitalist–Sensate" culture, rather than simply Sensate culture.) As Western capitalism expanded and evolved, it finally reached the point, sometime in the middle of the twentieth century, at which the mass consumption of luxury goods became possible for the majority of the population in the most developed societies. This brought a new burst of Sensate culture, which is now threatening to run completely out of control, and which has very possibly gained a larger measure of autonomy. I agree with Sorokin that we are witnessing a cultural crisis, and I agree that this crisis will lead to a cultural collapse. However, to me this will be more of an accompaniment of the ecological and economic collapse than an independent reality. And the collapse will not be complete in the sense that Sorokin visualizes, but will represent more of a toning down of Sensate culture than its genuine transcendence. If the standard of living, for example, would regress to the level it had attained in 1900, then it is reasonable to expect that the accompanying cultural worldview would shift itself back to that level.

Johan Galtung, Tore Heiestad, and Erik Rudeng (1980) have drawn an explicit comparison between the condition of modern Western civilization today (which they call Western imperialism) and the situation of Rome during its period of economic and cultural decline. They argue that decline and fall are built into the very nature of civilizations, and that Western civilization cannot escape this fate. They see in contemporary Western civilization the very same symptoms of crisis that were present in Rome during its long period of crisis. These symptoms include such things as increased rejection of the dominant cosmology and lifestyle, as expressed in the contemporary West, for instance, by increasing interest in Eastern religion and mysticism, as well as by increased interest in parapsychology, astrology, and occultist traditions; increasing anomie, as expressed by increases in crime and other deviance, drug use, alcoholism, and mental disorder; alienation, as expressed in such things as the increasing loss of confidence in governments and politicians; the promotion of "leisurism" as a new lifestyle; increasing social fragmentation; and ecological breakdown. To these symptoms I would add several others: the extraordinary decline in the Protestant ethic and a sense of pride in workmanship; a major decline in the quality of education, especially in the United States; the increased passivity and lethargy of students and other young people; the emergence of "decivilizing" (or "retribalizing") processes, as indicated, for example, by major shifts in manners, morals, dress, and the increasing practice of bodily adornment through tatooing and the wearing of ever more jewelry on ever more parts of the body; and the rise of "postmodernism" as a cultural sensibility (Harvey, 1989; Wagar, 1992). The list could no doubt be extended.

The decline and fall of civilizations is almost universally thought of in negative terms, but this does not have to be the case. Joseph Tainter (1988) has suggested that the collapse of complex societies is in a sense to be welcomed because it is a solution to a growing problem, that of the increased inability of societies and governments to maintain the vast material and social infrastructure they have created. Along similar lines, Galtung, Heiestad, and Rudeng (1980:146–8) make the following points:

Does that mean that we are entering the Dark Ages? And would that not be a pessimistic view? The question is, of course, whether the Dark Ages were that dark, or only appear dark in the light of generations (historians among them) for whom expansionist, centrifugal cosmology is taken for granted, and who define life in that earlier period as highly abnormal, highly unnatural. The metaphors that are used reflect this. One talks about the "rise" and "fall" of imperialism, but not about the "rise" and "fall" of the Middle Ages. . . .

. . . In terms of the organic analogy, if the patient is very, very old and quite ill, shall we prolong life artificially by inserting synthetic body pieces? Or shall we let nature run her course, and opt for a death in beauty? Shall we perhaps speed up the process through euthanasia? Or shall we focus on the children, see to it that they become healthy, thriving, and strong, autonomous, neither flattering the big, nor trampling on the small? Our personal inclination would be for "death in beauty" and "focus on the children". . . . To learn from history should not only mean to learn how to preserve something old, but also how to give easier birth to something new – otherwise the entire exercise would be of very limited value.

I am completely sympathetic to these authors' views, but a willful renunciation of Western civilization and a gradual, peaceful transition to a different, less complex and less Sensate form of society is not in the cards. Not enough people are paying attention, and a variety of vested interests would strongly oppose any such outcome. My prediction is that population growth will continue to be rapid (although perhaps slightly less rapid) throughout most of the Third World, that the rate of industrial output will grow rather than shrink, and that we will continue to use the earth's resources at an alarming rate. The Capitalist–Sensate culture will continue along its evolutionary path for at least a few more decades. When solutions are finally attempted, they will come too late, and a major economic, demographic, and ecological crisis, or possibly even a nuclear holocaust, will not be avoided. It does not have to happen, but it will happen. Nothing is forever, and Western capitalist civilization is rapidly running out of time. When the collapse comes, the only questions will be ones concerning how devastating it will be and what will follow. We are on the brink of a great historical shift that will be studied carefully by historians and social scientists of the future to see what they can learn in order to avoid repeating our mistakes. This shift will probably not come in my lifetime, or possibly even in my children's lifetime, but it will come, and sooner rather than later. The forces are too great, and the human will to respond too weak. It is our fate. It is our destiny.

10

Theoretical Reprise

Our survey and analysis of worldwide social evolution over the past 10,000 years is now complete, and at this point it may be appropriate to return to the basic theory outlined in chapter 1 and assess it in light of the evidence presented in chapters 2 through 9. As will be obvious, the general theory holds up remarkably well in the light of anthropological, archaeological, historical, and sociological data.

I.1 *World history reveals social transformations and directional trends of sufficient generality such that an evolutionary interpretation of world history is both possible and necessary.* The first great evolutionary transformation in world history was the Neolithic Revolution, which ushered in agriculture and settled village life. This was the first great instance of parallel evolution in world history. The Neolithic Revolution occurred independently in at least eight major regions of the world – southwest Asia, southeast Asia, China, Africa, Europe, Mesoamerica, South America, and North America – and also in many different subregions within each of these regions. The fact that the transition to agriculture and settled village life was made independently in region after region all over the world, and the fact that these transitions occurred at remarkably similar times, is extremely strong evidence for parallel evolution. Such a dramatic worldwide directional trend can only be accounted for in evolutionary terms. Within a few thousand years most of those regions of the world where the Neolithic occurred evolved the much more complex and elaborate forms of human society that we know as civilization and the state. Once again we have a major example of parallel evolutionary trends from many different world regions and subregions, and a phenomenon that can only be explained in evolutionary terms.

The agrarian civilizations that evolved after 3000 BC became the dominant form of society of their time. After the evolution of this kind of society, social evolution essentially slowed its pace, and no fundamental evolutionary transformations out of the agrarian stage occurred until just the last few centuries. However, a careful scrutiny of the "evolutionary logic" of agrarian civilizations reveals some surprises. The great agrarian societies were not simply characterized by a kind of "stagnation" associated with a cyclical process of dynastic rise and fall. They underwent various forms of social growth in terms of technological advancement, growth in the size and scope of political empires, and increasing commercialization and urbanization. These processes of social growth over several millennia provided an important foundation for the emergence of the modern world in the last few centuries. In other words, there were definite directional trends even in an epoch of world history normally regarded as primarily one of stasis.

I regard the third great evolutionary transformation in world history as the rise of modern capitalism after the sixteenth century. It is usually assumed that this was an occurrence unique to Europe but, as we saw in detail in chapter 5, a remarkably similar transition to capitalism occurred as well at approximately the same time in Japan. The rise of capitalism is the whole context for understanding the evolutionary dynamics of the modern world. The evolutionary logic inherent in capitalism – the ceaseless accumulation of capital – has brought into existence the major features of the modern world, and so we find a remarkable parallel evolution of the basic institutional characteristics of modernity: industrialism, the nation-state, parliamentary democracy (although totalitarianism for awhile in socialist states), class stratification with substantial mobility levels, mass education, and advanced science and technology.

1.2   *Stasis, devolution, and extinction are important processes to be explained by the same evolutionary principles as parallel, convergent, and divergent evolution.* Social stasis is abundant. Many societies of a preindustrial and precapitalist character have survived into the twentieth century, and some still remain. The record of extinction, of course, is well known, and has been assembled by archaeologists, anthropologists, historians, and other social scientists. Devolution is a less common feature of world history, but the agrarian epoch reveals much of it. The great agrarian civilizations and states had a remarkable tendency to spectacular collapse. This phenomenon has been carefully studied by Tainter, whose theory of collapse was discussed in chapter 4. This theory – which fits very well within the overall framework of evolutionary materialism – holds that the collapse of agrarian civilizations results from the enormous investment in technological, economic, and political infrastructure. The massive infrastructure that is created leads to costs that eventually can no longer be met, and the whole system ultimately fails.

I.3   *The directional trends of world history and prehistory are not teleological processes.* This proposition is a type of foundational statement that cannot be tested empirically, at least not directly. However, it can be made highly plausible through the demonstration of the range of basic causal mechanisms that drive social evolution. For this, see the discussion regarding Propositions III.1 to III.5.

II.1   *Social evolution occurs at all levels of social organization, but macroevolutionary phenomena are only the aggregation of microevolutionary phenomena.* It is clear enough that, when societies evolve, all of their basic features undergo modification, usually as "packages" of institutions and organizations. This is not likely to be in dispute. However, the additional claim that macroevolution is aggregated microevolution is difficult to demonstrate empirically, but a plausible case can at least be made. We can take as one example the prevalence of intense forms of reciprocity and sharing in hunter-gatherer societies. This social practice has been interpreted as resulting from the severe temporal and spatial fluctuation of resources commonly found in hunter-gatherer environments. People establish and follow strong norms of giving and sharing because it is in their long-run self-interest to do so, that is, because they must depend intimately on one another during times when they have little. This is a social pattern that involves the entire society, but it evolved as a result of selection at the level of individual benefit.

Another good example is the origin of agriculture. This important shift in subsistence technology was motivated by everyone's self-interest in the sense that individuals were striving to prevent living standards from dropping any lower. It was, quite literally, the "gut-level" interests of each individual acting in concert with other individuals that brought about this evolutionary transformation in the structure of society. Or consider the evolution of the state. It is my view that the state arose as a result of the long-term accumulation of changes in political behavior, especially the political relations between leaders and followers. These changes in the behavior of individuals toward one another were probably so small from one generation to the next that people were only dimly aware of what was happening (M. Harris, 1977). We describe the evolution of the state as a long-term historical process with dramatic consequences for political life, but this process could only have occurred as the result of changes in individual behavior from generation to generation. The evolution of the state over thousands of years was but the temporal aggregation of small changes in the behavior of millions of individuals.

The expansion of modern systems of mass education is perhaps a classic example of how the aggregation of individual behavior produces large-scale macrosocial effects. As argued earlier, much of the expansion of systems of mass education in the modern era has resulted from the competition among individuals for places in the system of privilege and prestige. It is simply individuals striving to satisfy their economic self-interest that drives the process forward. The rise of modern parliamentary democratic governments affords another good example. Parliamentary government, and to some degree constitutional liberties, favored the interests of individual capitalists, whereas mass suffrage was in the economic and political interests of members of the working class. Thousands or millions of individuals acting collectively in order to satisfy their individual desires brought these things about. We can even say that the evolution of the modern world-system itself, as discussed in detail in chapter 6, was the result of the actions of billions of individuals over a long expanse of time. Of course individuals acted as members of classes, interest groups, governments, and various other social groups, but these collectivities were the result of the aggregation of individual interests. One of the ways in which social evolution is very much like biological evolution is that both are driven by the behavior of individual organisms acting in their interests. Long-term outcomes result from the long-term aggregation of individual behavior. Neither evolutionary process must be reified.

II.2.   *Increasing social complexity is an important evolutionary process, but social evolution is much more than just increases in the level of complexity.* It has become very clear that considerable social evolution can be described as a process of growing complexity and the differentiation of institutions. However, there are important evolutionary events that have nothing to do with complexity. For example, the transition from feudalism to capitalism cannot be meaningfully described as a process of growing complexity. This transition represented a shift from one qualitative mode of economic organization to another. Even if we admit that capitalism did ultimately inaugurate a much more complex mode of social life, the transition from feudalism to capitalism in itself is not a matter of growing complexity. By concentrating only on complexity, we lose much information about the process of social evolution.

The evolution of the modern state was, in a very real sense, a process in which the state grew enormously in size, scale, and complexity. This is one of the most striking aspects of the evolution of the modern world. However, some aspects of recent political evolution do not involve increasing complexity in any particularly significant way. The evolution of modern democracy, for example, represented the emergence of a new *form* of government that contrasted markedly with the monarchies and other despotisms of the long agrarian era. In many ways the most important evolutionary transformations are those that involve *qualitative* shifts, rather than quantitative shifts in the direction of greater complexity.

II.3   *There are important similarities between biological and social evolution.* The fact that social and biological evolution both exhibit parallel, convergent, and divergent processes is readily seen and probably not seriously disputed. The claim that both are adaptational processes, as well as the claim that both represent the large-scale and long-term aggregation of individual behavior, is more contentious. However, for discussion of the point that social evolution is an adaptational process, see Propositions IV.1 through IV.10.

II.4   *There are also important differences between biological and social evolution.*

(a) *Biological evolution mainly involves divergence, whereas social evolution mainly involves parallelism and convergence.* The divergent character of biological evolution has been well established by evolutionary biologists. That parallelism and convergence dominate social evolution is a highly contentious statement about which social scientists will vehemently disagree. The problem is to a large extent a matter of just what is counted as parallelism, convergence, or divergence. For example, Michael Mann (1986) has claimed that the origin of the state cannot have been an evolutionary process because it occurred in only half a dozen or so instances. For Mann half a dozen instances is not impressive, but for many anthropologists and archaeologists, such as Marvin Harris and Robert Carneiro, half a dozen instances is a striking parallelism. Mann (1993) also claims that the development of the modern state is not a simple "onward-and-upward" story of the increasing size and scale of the state. Yet as I sketched the development of the modern state in chapter 7 that is exactly what it looked like to me, as it has to numerous others.

To some degree this is a "beauty-is-in-the-eye-of-the-beholder" phenomenon. This point is not easily settled, but I would claim that, at a minimum, there is enough parallelism and convergence in social evolution to show that it is indeed different in fundamental respects from biological evolution. Demonstration of the amount of parallelism was given in regard to Proposition I.1.

(b) *Random genetic variations provide the basis for biological evolution, but no such process is involved in social evolution.* The randomness of genetic variations has been conclusively established by evolutionary biologists and geneticists. There is obviously no strictly equivalent process in social evolution. However, the issue arises as to whether sociocultural variations are random or deliberate and purposive. That many of them are the latter is beyond doubt. This is especially the case with respect to the evolution of technology, but the same point also holds for the evolution of the basic institutional sectors of human societies. However, there is an important difference between saying something is deliberate and purposive and saying it is clearly recognized by the individuals who are carrying it out. A good example concerns the process of industrialization. What we now call the Industrial Revolution could only be named, and thus clearly recognized, long after the fact. People were only dimly aware of just how dramatic were the changes that were occurring, and could only see that in retrospect. Nevertheless, the actions of various individuals – capitalists, inventors, workers, etc. – were certainly not random in any meaningful sense. People knew what they were doing, and they were doing it deliberately, but the process as a whole was not intended or deliberate. Anthony Giddens (1981, 1984) argues that society is the result of human intention but is not an intended project. That is precisely the point I am making, and that makes social evolution different in one crucial respect from biological evolution.

(c) *If we started biological evolution all over again we would get different results, but if we started social evolution over again we would get very similar results.* The first part of this statement is established biological knowledge. The second part has not been conclusively established by social scientists, but it follows logically from point (b) above. Moreover, the frequency of parallelism and convergence in social evolution, and the infrequency of such processes in biological evolution, are evidence in support of this part of Proposition II.4.

(d) *Social evolution occurs at a much faster pace than biological evolution.* This is exceptionally easy to document. The earth is about 5 billion years old, and life apparently originated on it approximately $3^{1}/_{2}$ billion years ago. From that point until about 600 million years ago, not much biological evolution occurred. After that point, with the so-called Cambrian explosion (Gould, 1989), life began to proliferate, diversify, and evolve in earnest. By almost anyone's standards, this process of evolution has been extremely slow. By contrast, the bulk of social evolution has been compressed into a period of about 10,000 years. Within this period of time we see the shift from nomadic hunting and gathering bands to settled, autonomous agricultural villages; the shift from autonomous agricultural villages to centrally organized chiefdoms; the shift from chiefdoms to agrarian states; and the shift from states to multistate empires. We also see during the long era of the agrarian civilizations, as mentioned earlier, a process of technological change, growth in the size of empires, expansion of the size and density of trade networks, and large-scale urbanization. In the last 500 years the world has been radically transformed by the rise of modern capitalism and the emergence of a highly industrialized, global order. This should be sufficient to show how much faster social evolution is than biological evolution, and how it undoubtedly must operate on the basis of different mechanisms.

(e) *There is no counterpart in biological evolution to the social evolutionary process of diffusion.* Self-evident.

(f) *The concept of natural selection is, by itself, inadequate as an explanation of social evolution.* Much of social evolution may work, in a general way, as a process of natural selection. For example, in chapter 7 we examined Charles Tilly's argument that the evolution of national states in Europe after the fifteenth century was a kind of selection process. Once one society had adopted such a political form, its advantages were such that other societies had to adopt it or suffer enormous consequences, possibly including extinction. Tilly's argument seems eminently reasonable, but if we were to stop there – to his credit Tilly doesn't – we would fail to learn what we really need to know: why the very first national state was created when and where it was. It is only by knowing this that we can actually understand the basic *causes* of the evolution of the national state.

II.5   *Social evolution must be studied as a process in its own right, not simply in terms of an analogy with biological evolution.* This proposition logically follows from the basic differences between biological and social evolution stated above.

II.6   *Coevolution is an important evolutionary process, but most social evolution has nothing to do with changes in gene frequencies.* We have not discussed coevolution in this book, but excellent examples have been provided by Robert Boyd and Peter Richerson (1985), by Marvin Harris (1985) and William Durham (1991) concerning the evolution of dairying and milk drinking in prehistoric northern Europe, and by Pierre van den Berghe and Peter Frost (1986) in regard to the fact that upper social strata all over the world tend to be lighter in skin color than subordinate classes. Coevolution is certainly a real phenomenon. However, it constitutes only a small portion of social evolution, and there is little evidence that social evolution is associated with dramatic changes in gene frequencies. Indeed, most social evolution has been far too rapid for this to be possible. As noted earlier, most social evolution has occurred within the past 10,000 years, and this is much too brief a time for any major biological evolution to have occurred.

II.7   *Social evolution is a process entirely separate from the processes involved in the psychological development of individuals.* There really should be no need in the late twentieth century for this proposition, which few social scientists would dispute any longer, but Giddens (1984) has made the assertion that theories of social evolution tend to see social evolution as a process intertwined with the psychological development of the person. I think Giddens is beating a dead horse and that few social evolutionists would any longer accept such a notion. Indeed, I know of no social evolutionist who would. On the other hand, there can sometimes be a problem because scholars looking at the two processes from the other direction – that is, psychologists making inferences about social evolution – sometimes do see the two processes as intertwined. The developmental psychologist Lawrence Kohlberg (1981), for example, asserts that stages of moral development are intertwined with stages of social evolution, and that the former have been driving the latter. However, I know of no evidence to support this notion.

III.1   *The principal causal factors in social evolution are the material conditions of human existence, i.e., the demographic, ecological, technological, and economic forces at work in social life.* The evidence for this proposition is enormous, but to conserve space I shall provide only three illustrations. The first great social transformation in world prehistory, the Neolithic Revolution, seems most clearly linked to population growth and subsequent population pressure. This type of argument has been favored by numerous scholars but, as we saw in chapter 2, has been developed most thoroughly and carefully by Mark Cohen. Cohen argues that a general theory of the Neolithic is demanded by the striking parallelism it displays. Cohen's argument, of course, is that prehistoric hunter-gatherers had long understood the basics of agriculture but had failed to implement it because their food supply was sufficient to satisfy their basic needs. Over time, however, with the growth of population a disequilibrium between hunter-gatherers and their environments emerged, and they had to begin the shift to agriculture to produce the greater amounts of food needed to feed larger and denser populations.

Population pressure is also involved in the rise of civilization and the state. Perhaps the most widely favored theory is that of Robert Carneiro, which makes population pressure, warfare, and environmental circumscription the basic causal factors. Carneiro argues that the first states arose in environments that were highly circumscribed, or that prevented the movement of people beyond their borders. Circumscribed regions would not pose a problem for human adaptation so long as populations were sparse. When one group attacked another, the second could simply move elsewhere. But as population density grew this would become more difficult and eventually there would be no escape from invading groups. Warfare would then lead to political conquest, and increasingly complex and powerful political systems would be created, the culmination of which would be states and multistate empires.

As for the rise of modern capitalism, material factors have been crucial here too. Capitalism as a mode of production arose first in northwest Europe and Japan around the sixteenth century. I believe that capitalism arose first in these regions because they had the most suitable preconditions for capitalist development. As I argued in chapter 5, five factors were critical. First, Japan and the major

European capitalist countries (especially England and the Netherlands) were small in size and thus avoided the large costs of systems of transportation and communication that large centralized empires, such as those of China and India, incurred. Second, Japan and the European countries were located on large bodies of water and thus could concentrate on maritime rather than overland trade. Maritime trade is much more efficient and permits a much greater volume of trade, and hence high levels of commercialization. Third, the temperate climates of Japan and Europe meant that these regions were not suitable for an economy based on raw materials production for export of the type that Europe was to develop in its colonies. One of the secrets to Japan's capitalist development has undoubtedly been that it never became a colony of Europe and thus could harness its resources for its own development. Fourth, there is the factor of population growth. Both Europe and Japan experienced major increases in population during the periods in which they were shifting toward capitalism, and such growth led to increased urbanization and an expansion in the potential size of the labor force. Finally, and most importantly, Europe and Japan both had feudal politico-economic systems. The importance of these is that they were highly decentralized systems of political economy that permitted enormous freedom to the merchant classes. Mercantile activity could get a much firmer foothold in these regions than in such large bureaucratic empires as China and India, where merchants were held on a much tighter rein.

I have argued, of course, that these five factors operated within the context of a major world-historical trend, that of expanding world commercialization. For some 4,500 years prior to the sixteenth century AD world trade had grown in size, complexity, and density. Trade was first local, then regional, then extended throughout large portions of the globe. By about the period AD 1000–1500 the level of world commercialization had built up sufficiently to trigger a capitalist explosion in those regions that had the most suitable preconditions. A kind of "critical mass" of commercialism had been reached.

III.2   *Material conditions operate probabilistically, and allowance is made for "superstructural feedback."* No assertion is being made that the material conditions of human existence determine, by themselves, all social evolution. It is only claimed that the bulk of long-term evolution, and especially the most significant transformations, are rooted in material factors. However, plenty of allowance is made for nonmaterial conditions to operate causally. For example, parliamentary democracies began to emerge in conjunction with the rise of capitalism in the seventeenth and eighteenth centuries, and after the middle of the nineteenth century much of the Western world began to adopt systems of universal suffrage to go with their parliamentary regimes. The rise of democracy seems to have been rooted in changing material conditions, but who would deny the force it has been in the world after it truly began to bloom? If we look at the emergence of systems of mass education, then we see that in chapter 7 I put emphasis on the nation-building process rather than on economic development. Mass education seems to have been a product of the desire of rapidly growing nation-states to socialize the individual into the role of citizen. In addition, I am willing to give some credence to the argument made by Toby Huff (1993) that cultural differences between western Europe on the one hand and China and the Arab world on the other accounted for the tremendous spurt in Western science in the sixteenth and seventeenth centuries and the relative stagnation and decline of science in the other two civilizations. I would not go as far as Toby does with this argument, for economics undoubtedly played a major role in Western scientific advance, a role that Toby entirely fails to acknowledge. Nonetheless, the West possessed a cultural distinctiveness that is perhaps traceable all the way back to the ancient Greeks.

III.3 *Material conditions have the significance they do because they relate to basic human needs concerning production and reproduction.* This is a nonempirical, ontological proposition that is used as a grounding assumption. It cannot really be empirically evaluated.

III.4 *The causal importance of any particular material condition varies from one historical period and evolutionary stage to another.* We can use the examples given with respect to Proposition III.1 to illustrate this point. The Neolithic Revolution seems to have been rooted fundamentally in changing demographic conditions. The rise of civilization and the state was also rooted in demographic change, but other factors, such as environmental conditions and warfare (the latter a nonmaterial condition) were also involved in an important way. Moreover, it is likely that changing economic conditions and the emergence of more intensive forms of class stratification, even though Carneiro's theory does not employ these factors, played a significant role in the rise of the state. As for the rise of capitalism,

I have conceptualized this phenomenon as being driven by a great historical economic process, expanding world commercialization, working in conjunction with such conditions as size, geography, climate, population growth, and feudal politico-economic arrangements. The large-scale industrialization process that is such a dramatic feature of modernity was driven primarily by the logic of capital accumulation, and not by population pressure as thinkers like Wilkinson and Boserup have argued.

Different evolutionary events require different theories, and it is always an empirical question which of the four major material conditions, or which combination or permutation of conditions, may be operative in a particular instance.

III.5   *Different types of social systems and different historical epochs embody different "evolutionary logics."* A few brief examples should suffice. Hunter-gatherer and horticultural systems seem to have a strong aversion to basic change, a kind of "evolutionary inertia." They change only by disruption from the outside, or from factors such as population growth or ecological degradation that disequilibriate them. Their evolutionary logic is a deeply conservative one. The long agrarian epoch that ranged from about 3000 BC until the last few centuries also had a kind of inertia based on the dominance of the economy by landlords. Perhaps the dominant tendency in agrarian societies was that of dynastic cycles – the continuous rise and fall of empires. However, agrarian societies were changing, and in ways that we have come to appreciate only recently. But they were changing slowly, and much more so than would have been anticipated on the basis of the pace of social evolution between the Neolithic and the rise of the state. Finally, let us note that with the rise of modern capitalism after the sixteenth century a whole new evolutionary dynamic was introduced into the world. Capitalism has been by far the most fast-paced mode of production in history. Its evolutionary logic is not demographic or ecological or even technological, but primarily economic: it is premised on the ceaseless accumulation of capital. This evolutionary logic is such that the pace of social evolution is accelerating by leaps and bounds, and so much so that contemporary humanity has become dizzyingly disoriented by it.

IV.1   *Much social evolution results from adaptational processes.* This is a grounding assumption used to orient evolutionary analyses. It assumes that much social evolution arises from the efforts made by individuals to meet particular sets of needs and desires. Although not all social evolution is necessarily adaptational, starting from an adaptational assumption has heuristic value because it allows us to determine whether an evolutionary phenomenon is an adaptational product and, if it is, how it is. The grounding assumption also allows us to determine which evolutionary phenomena are not adaptational products and therefore must be explained in other terms.

IV.2 *Adaptation must be distinguished from adaptedness.* This is a definitional statement rather than a causal proposition.

IV.3 *Many adaptations lead to adaptedness in the short run but may become nonadaptive or maladaptive in the long run.* The whole process of the intensification of economic production that is such a major part of long-term social evolution illustrates this notion perfectly. We have argued that ancient hunter-gatherers gradually gave up the foraging way of life as a result of population pressure, ecological degradation, and declining standards of living. The shift to agriculture was highly adaptive for them. However, the adaptation was short-lived, because agricultural populations soon came to exert a debilitating effect on the environment. A more regular food supply allowed population to grow more rapidly, and population pressure soon became a serious problem once again. The solution was to intensify the agricultural system, but this adaptation soon led to difficulties that had to be counteracted. The whole process of the evolution of modes of subsistence technology is one in which people must run faster and faster just to try to stay in the same place, and yet for the most part they fall ever farther behind. The new adaptations they choose work for awhile, but soon people become hoist on their own petard.

It can also be argued that the high birth rates of peasants in contemporary Third World countries are adaptations to the economic circumstances in which they live – that many children are desired as farm workers. This may be adaptive for any particular peasant couple in the short run, but in the long run it is maladaptive for peasants in general because it produces high rates of population growth that eat up whatever economic gains are otherwise made and that contribute to the plight of Third World countries.

One of the most striking examples of a social phenomenon that is initially adaptive (at least for social elites) but that tends to become highly maladaptive over the long run is the emergence and continued evolution of social complexity. As was shown in chapter 4, highly complex agrarian states of the past several thousand years had a marked tendency to social collapse, and precisely because of their complexity. Complexity helps elites pursue various social, economic, and political objectives, but it is expensive, and over the long run it often becomes far too expensive and thus can no longer be maintained.

Another example concerns Randall Collins's demonstration of the role of credential inflation in educational expansion in the contemporary United States and other industrial societies. Individuals choose education as a means of economic success, but as more attain higher levels of schooling the value of diplomas and degrees is cheapened, leading to the need to stay in school even longer. A positive feedback spiral is set up that drives large segments of industrial societies to invest more money and more time in educational attainment. As in the case of the intensification of production, individuals begin running as fast as they can just to stay where they are, and thus a maladaptive and "irrational" element is introduced into behavior that was highly "rational" to begin with.

Finally, it is easy to see that the Industrial Revolution, though it has led to a dramatic increase in the material standard of living in the most developed societies, has produced a form of technology and economic life that is becoming more maladaptive with each passing year. This is simply a contemporary and especially glaring instance of how the intensification process is an adaptational one that produces ever greater degrees of maladaptation in the long run.

IV.4   *The extent to which adaptations lead to adaptedness varies greatly from one set of individuals and from one time and place to another.* In complex agrarian and industrial societies that are highly class divided, many features of social life derive from the needs and desires of dominant groups and work to their advantage. Caste rules regarding ritual purification, for example, benefit dominant castes at the expense of subordinate ones. In agrarian societies, which are normally intensively male dominated, elaborate ideologies of male supremacy benefit men and tremendously disadvantage women. (Examples like this can be multiplied endlessly.) Moreover, Mark Cohen has shown that throughout most of the last 10,000 years of human history the standard of living has been declining for the majority of human populations but improving for a minority, that is, for social, economic, and political elites. And let us not overlook the growth of social complexity. As we have seen, this seems to benefit elite groups, but it likely produces net disadvantages for the masses, who are made to pay the costs of the establishment of the basic features of complexity.

As to time, the ritual slaughter of cattle was before about AD 700 highly adaptive for Hindu priests, but after this time it gradually became maladaptive because of greater land scarcity and the need of cattle for plowing. As a result, Hindu priests gave up ritual slaughter of cattle and adopted a new practice of ritual protection of cattle now deemed to be sacred (Harris, 1977, 1985).

IV.5 *The individual is the basic unit of adaptation; any social pattern said to be adaptive for a group or society as a whole is so only as the result of the statistical aggregation of individual adaptations.* See section II.1, above.

IV.6 *Adaptations may arise in response to either the physical environment, the social environment, or both.* Most of the subsistence intensification process as we have discussed it in this book has been an adaptational process with respect to the physical environment. Most of the rest of social evolution as we have examined it, however, has been a matter of new adaptations arising with respect to particular social conditions. To a large extent, the increasing embracement of capitalist economic practices by feudal landlords was an adaptive response to their declining economic fortunes. The creation of mass educational systems was an adaptation to the need of state leaders for a responsible and enlightened citizenry. Mass democracy was an adaptation from the standpoint of the working class's desire for greater economic power and control over their work environment. The granting of huge amounts of aid and loans by the United States government to South Korea in the 1950s and 1960s was adaptive from the standpoint of the former's desire to keep the latter within the capitalist fold. Although we did not discuss it in this book, the skyrocketing divorce rate of recent decades can also be seen as a type of adaptational phenomenon. I would argue that the divorce rate soared in these decades primarily as a result of changes in the sexual division of labor. The movement of married women with children into the labor force in large numbers increased women's level of economic power, which gave women options previously unavailable. One of these options was to end unhappy marriages with greater and greater frequency (Cherlin, 1992). Readers can easily extract for themselves numerous other examples from the substantive discussions of the preceeding chapters.

IV.7   *When identifying a social trait as an adaptation it is necessary to specify the particular need or set of needs that are the basis for the origin of the trait.* This is a guiding premise not subject to empirical evaluation.

IV.8   *Adaptations developed by individuals are not necessarily the product of maximization or optimization strategies, but rather of "satisficing" strategies.* This is not really a proposition subject to empirical verification, but, again, a guiding premise. Like the concept of adaptation itself, this notion is a heuristic device.

IV.9   *The concept of adaptation implies no universal tendency toward human mastery that is the driving engine of social evolution.* It has become very clear in recent years that the drive for "mastery" is basically absent in many preindustrial societies. What we find in such societies among the bulk of the population is a conservative attachment to existing forms of technology and social life. There seems to be a tremendous "technological inertia" among hunter-gatherers, and in horticultural and agrarian societies as well. The drive for mastery is a socially conditioned motive that is most vigorously expressed in the age of modernity. This drive is best exemplified by the ceaseless accumulation of capital and the intensity of technological advancement that are the hallmarks of the modern world.

Where, though, does the drive for mastery come from if it is not innate? If it is socially learned, how is it acquired? My answer is that it is built up through a ratchet-like process. Something like the drive for mastery may be present in simple, small-scale societies – I am thinking of the Melanesian "big man" who is a political leader and economic organizer – but I do not think it becomes a strong human motive until the rise of chiefdoms, or perhaps until the evolution of civilization and the state. In modern capitalist and industrial society it is running rampant and is a large part of the Sensate cultural mentality of that type of society. I would say that the drive for mastery is built up gradually – ratcheted up – as the requirements for its expression evolve. Mastery takes a good deal of technological development, as well as a certain level of economic and political development. The potential for the drive for mastery is a fundamental part of the human psychobiological equipment, but the drive can gain expression and become highly developed only with a certain amount of social evolution. The greater the advancement of technological, economic, political, and military infrastructure, the greater the prominence of the drive for mastery. It has reached its peak so far in late Capitalist–Sensate society. It is what will probably destroy us, or at least produce devastating devolutionary consequences, in the near future.

IV.10 *Adaptedness is not a quality that necessarily increases or improves throughout social evolution.* In chapter 8 we reviewed recent anthropological and archaeological research which shows that prehistoric hunter-gatherer populations were better nourished than later agricultural populations. A very good empirical case can be made that the standard of living for a majority of the population actually declined with the shift from hunting and gathering to horticulture, and fell again with the transition from horticulture to intensive agriculture. A very good case can also be made for increases in the workload and in the alienating character of work, for a shift from highly egalitarian to highly stratified and tension-ridden societies, and for a movement from highly democratic arrangements to various forms of tyranny and despotism. Thus in some respects the level of adaptedness has actually declined during long-term social evolution.

Actually, history reveals a mixed bag with respect to adaptedness. Although social evolution has been largely regressive prior to the rise of capitalism and the Industrial Revolution, since that time considerable progress has been made in the standard of living and the overall quality of life, especially in the societies that are today's advanced industrial countries. The extent of progress in the less-developed part of the contemporary world is a much more contentious issue, but there is considerable evidence that a majority of the members of contemporary Third World nations are better off in several important respects from their predecessors in the old agrarian world. The point is, however, that it cannot automatically be assumed that later social forms will be associated with higher levels of human adaptedness than prevailed in earlier social forms, for in many ways this has not been the case.

V.1 *Humans are egoistic beings who are highly motivated to give priority to the satisfaction of their own needs and wants; individual self-interest is therefore the starting point for any evolutionary analysis.* Although many sociologists argue that selfishness is culturally conditioned, any careful and objective inspection of the world's societies through time and space shows that most human behavior is motivated by the pursuit of self-interest. That the individual organism is highly self-oriented should be obvious to any parent undertaking the socialization of a child, and it should also be obvious that even the most intensive forms of socialization cannot eliminate the desire to give priority to one's own interests.

Much behavior that is altruistic at the phenotypic level leads many social scientists to believe that the motives for the behavior are altruistic also. But this is seldom the case, and most cooperation is of the kind known as *antagonistic cooperation* or *enlightened self-interest*. A classic example involves hunter-gatherer reciprocity. The intensive cooperation among the members of hunter-gatherer bands is driven by their own self-interest, for they depend intimately on one another for survival, and phenotypically selfish behavior will be suicidal in the long run. Once we leave hunter-gatherer society, we find many more instances of phenotypic selfishness, and in direct proportion to the level of evolutionary development of a society. Cooperation and phenotypic altruism are still more prevalent than phenotypic selfishness in simple horticultural societies, but phenotypic selfishness begins to rear its (ugly) head. In more advanced horticultural societies this type of behavior is much more common, and is frequently associated with social stratification. By the time we get to agrarian societies, extreme forms of phenotypic selfishness are strongly associated with high levels of exploitation and oppression of the many by the few. Selfishness is not some sort of product of modern capitalism, as many sociologists would have it. Genotypic selfishness is universal and operates in the social evolutionary process just as it does in the process of biological evolution. It frequently leads to forms of cooperative behavior, and by no means produces only conflict, exploitation, and domination; but it is the fundamental assumption from which any evolutionary analysis must start. The phenomena of social evolution are inexplicable on any other assumption, as I hope the theoretical and substantive discussions of this book have demonstrated.

V.2 *Individuals acting in their own interests create social structures that are frequently – indeed, perhaps usually – constituted in ways that individuals never intended.* To illustrate this point, we can refer back to the examples of high birth rates among contemporary Third World peasants and the pursuit of higher and higher levels of schooling in modern industrial societies. Here we find classic instances of the sum of individual action producing structures and effects that are unintended and unwanted. Other examples are not difficult to find. The actions of modern capitalists led to the formation of a large working class, which they required in order to continue and enhance the process of capital accumulation. Yet the working classes of the major advanced capitalist societies struggled for, and eventually attained, mass suffrage as a means of promoting their economic interests. Capitalists never intended this, probably never expected it, and certainly did not want it. It was a byproduct of the very process of capitalist development, and has certainly required capitalists to make adjustments in their accumulation strategies. Also, consider the enormous effort engaged in by the United States after World War II to help rebuild Japan, and the enormous amount of loans and aid given to South Korea during the same period. These latter nations have benefited enormously from the United States's actions, and in fact probably far more than the United States ever intended, for they have become severe economic competitors of the United States. Social evolution continually leads to outcomes never expected or desired; as Anthony Giddens (1984) has so eloquently put it, society is the result of human intention but it is not an intended project.

V.3　*The social structures that individual action creates establish new constraints on the course of individual action. Social evolution involves the continuous interplay between structure and agency.* The Neolithic Revolution resulted from the agency of individuals who were trying to prevent further declines in living standards due to population growth. However, once the transition to fully agricultural societies had been achieved a situation was created in which individuals had committed themselves to a more intensive form of subsistence adaptation. There was no turning back, and now populations grew faster than they did previously, which led to new forms of environmental degradation that necessitated a new intensification of production. This new wave of intensification led to even more dramatic ecological and economic effects, which led to a new wave of intensification, and so on throughout the past 10,000 years. As we saw in chapter 9, humans created a modern industrial technology as an act of agency (the desire of capitalists for greater productivity and profits), and now this technology may spell the death of capitalism. Here we find humans constantly acting as agents in pursuit of their self-interest, yet constantly being constrained by the results of their previous actions or those of their ancestors. This should give the lie to the widespread social-scientific belief that social evolution is some sort of deterministic process having nothing to do with individual choice and action.

V.4   *Human agency is not something that occurs "freely"; all purposive human behavior is constrained at every moment.* This is really an ontological rather than an empirical proposition, and is used to orient analysis. It simply notes that all individual action occurs within a context that is constantly evolving and constantly constraining action.

VI.1   *Although individuals are the units of adaptation, they are not the units of actual evolution; the units of evolution are groups and societies at all levels of size and complexity.* As asserted previously, individuals are the basic units of adaptation; however, because individuals must live socially and interact with others to satisfy their individual needs, they create groups and societies of various types, and it is these groups and societies that do the actual evolving and that are the focus of evolutionary analysis. This proposition is essentially ontological rather than empirical.

VI.2   *Social evolution occurs through the action of both endogenous and exogenous forces, and priority cannot be given to either set of forces* on *a priori grounds. Determining the balance of endogenous and exogenous forces occurring at any time and place is an empirical matter to be pursued case by case.* Ever since the work of Immanuel Wallerstein it has become clear that much social evolution occurs as the result of the effects of large-scale intersocietal networks within which individual societies are located. This has especially been the case since the emergence of the modern capitalist world in the sixteenth century, as chapter 6 was at pains to point out. At earlier stages of social evolution endogenous forces may be of greater significance, but even here intersocietal forces are often important, as Carneiro's theory of the origin of the state shows. This proposition is simply a procedural one that asks social scientists to be sensitive to the existence of both endogenous and exogenous forces, and their interaction, in social evolution.

VII.1   *Both "gradualist" and "punctuationalist" forms of change characterize social evolution.* See section VII.2, below.

VII.2   *Social evolution at earlier stages and historical periods is slower and more gradual than evolution in more recent times and at later stages.* The notions of slow and fast are obviously relative, but as humans measure and perceive time most social evolution must be regarded as slow. The Neolithic Revolution affords an excellent example. The term "revolution" is actually misleading with respect to time, for the Neolithic was a very slow and gradual process. For several thousand years prior to the Neolithic we find all over the world hunter-gatherer societies gradually intensifying their foraging practices, and the move toward agriculture occurred in a very piece-meal way. Hunter-gatherers would begin practicing some agriculture while continuing to live mainly by foraging, and then over time they would gradually replace foraging with cultivation. The shift from complete reliance on hunting and gathering to complete reliance on agriculture usually took several thousand years in all of the regions of the Neolithic. The emergence of civilization and the state was also a relatively drawn-out process that occurred over thousands of years, and political evolution had to pass through a chiefdom stage before the level of the state was reached. During the long era between the rise of the first pristine states and the emergence of modern capitalism, little that can properly be called social evolution occurred, although there was quantitative social growth in such things as population, world commercialism, the size of political units, the scale and scope of warfare, and the level of technology. However, most change occurred slowly, and it took some 4,500 years for a qualitative shift to a new mode of social and economic life to come about.

What I have identified as the third great transformation in world history, the rise of modern capitalism, was, by contrast, a consider-ably more rapid evolutionary shift. Nevertheless, even it should be thought of as slow and gradual in the sense of human time percep-tion. It took several hundred years for the feudal societies of Europe and Japan to disintegrate and evolve into societies dominated by capitalism, and it took several hundred years more to get to the point where we are today. With respect to the industrialization process in the modern world, the more we have studied it the more it has become clear that it was not something that simply began in England after 1760. For two or three centuries before this time considerable protoindustrialization was occurring throughout west-ern Europe. What happened after 1760 was less dramatic than it has normally appeared, for the way had already been prepared.

However, it should be noted that the pace of social evolution has been increasing tremendously in the last 200 years, and especially in the twentieth century. The pace of social evolution is itself an evolving phenomenon.

VIII.1   *The comparative method is appropriate for the study of social evolution to the extent that it can be independently corroborated by historical and prehistorical data.* At the end of chapter 3 I showed in considerable detail how closely evolutionary schemes built by using the comparative method correspond to our understanding of social evolution derived from archaeological and historical data. The use of the comparative method as a device for the study of social evolution has clearly been vindicated.

VIII.2 *Diachronic data are preferred to synchronic data in the study of evolutionary processes.* For this reason, social evolutionists have relied increasingly in the past few decades on the use of prehistorical and historical data, and less on the comparative method. There is now a large mass of prehistorical and historical data suggesting that world history can certainly be intelligibly interpreted in evolutionary terms. A great many of these data have been discussed in this book.

VIII.3 *Evolutionary analysis is not separate and distinct from historical analysis, but is a form of historical analysis.* This is a methodological proposition not subject to empirical scrutiny in the usual sense. It simply states that the analysis of concrete historical events is not something to be left to historians with their idiographic outlook. The examination of particular historical events is an important part of evolutionary analysis. This book has engaged in many historical analyses of concrete events, such as the rise of modern capitalism, the creation of the modern state, the evolution of democracy in western Europe and North America, the creation of systems of mass education, the rise of science in seventeenth-century Europe, the rise and fall of British hegemony in the world-system, and the rapid ascent of South Korea in the world-system between 1950 and 1980.

VIII.4 *Proper evolutionary analysis requires data from ethnographic, archaeological, historical, and sociological sources.* By this point this proposition should be self-evident.

Afterword to the Expanded Edition
Biological Constraints on Social Evolution

FROM EVOLUTIONARY MATERIALISM
TO SYNTHETIC MATERIALISM

This book has tried to make clear the striking directionality of social evolution all over the world throughout prehistory and history. We observe certain definite trends rather than others. Everywhere we have seen the same directional patterns: from smaller and simpler societies to larger and more complex ones, from relatively egalitarian societies to highly stratified ones, from bands and tribes to centrally-coordinated chiefdoms to complex states, from low levels of commercialization (or no commercialization at all) to highly commercialized, capitalistic societies, and so on. These trends are quite striking from the Paleolithic era to the early modern world. Nowhere have things run in the opposite direction or even in a different direction. Only with the development of the modern world do we see any departures at all in these patterns, and even then on a very limited basis (e.g., the severity of stratification has been reduced in the transition from agrarian to modern industrial societies, but modern industrial societies are still far more stratified than anything found prior to the agrarian era). The ubiquity of these striking evolutionary trends suggests to me that there must be powerful biological constraints acting on the direction of social evolution. In this afterword I want to develop this idea and thus bring out an important dimension of human society and social change that was badly neglected in the first edition of this book.

Since formulating several years ago the theoretical approach that I call evolutionary materialism, I have come to see that it can be made a special case of an even more general theory. I have developed a preliminary version of this theory, which I call by the name of *synthetic materialism* (Sanderson, 1998a, 1998b). It is an extension of evolutionary materialism in a biological direction, incorporating into evolutionary materialism the theoretical approach known as sociobiology. Synthetic materialism is thus a synthesis of economic and ecological materialism with biological materialism, a kind of marriage of the materialism of Marx and Harris with that of Darwin. Synthetic materialism may be regarded as an attempt at a reasonably complete theory of human society, whereas evolutionary materialism is an application of synthetic materialism to the special case of social evolution.

Before we examine the biological constraints on social evolution a brief outline of sociobiology would seem to be in order.[1] Sociobiology is based on an explicit theory known as the *theory of inclusive fitness*, which is a specific dimension of Darwinian evolutionary biology. As is well known, the central concept in Darwin's theory is that of *natural selection*. Darwin argued that in every generation of every species more offspring are produced than have resources to be able to survive. There thus results a *struggle for survival* among organisms, and it is the fittest organisms that have the best chance of surviving. Organisms are fit to the extent that they have the genetic materials that are best suited to coping with the conditions of a particular environment. Fitness can actually be measured quantitatively in terms of *differential reproductive success*. Those organisms that survive to reproduce and to leave more offspring in the next generation than other organisms do are more fit.

Darwin assumed that the organism was the unit of selection and that every organism was selfish. The assumption of selfishness was the only assumption that made sense, because organisms are competing in a survival game. However, after Darwin scientists came increasingly to recognize that organisms also behaved altruistically, and such behavior seemed impossible to reconcile with the Darwinian view of the selfish organism. In the 1960s the introduction of the idea that the gene rather than the entire organism was the unit of selection solved this problem. Natural selection operates so as to preserve or eliminate genes rather than whole organisms. Organisms strive to promote not their own survival but the representation of their genes in future generations, or their *inclusive fitness*. Altruism toward other organisms, or at least related organisms, thus makes sense as a strategy of inclusive fitness maximization. Inclusive fitness is sometimes called *kin selection* by virtue of the assumption that organisms tend to favor kin, and favor close kin more than distant kin, because they share common genes.

The basic argument of sociobiology is that *many features of human social organization and behavior result from efforts made by individuals to maximize their inclusive fitness*. Let's look at the implications. The most fundamental implication of this argument is that men and women will have different ways of promoting their inclusive fitness and thus different *reproductive strategies*. Males can maximize their inclusive fitness by inseminating as many females as possible; thus we should expect men to have difficulty confining themselves to monogamous relationships. Instead, they should greatly desire a wide variety of sexual partners. Females, on the other hand, can have only a limited number of offspring in a lifetime, and it doesn't matter whether these offspring are produced by one man or several. Their inclusive fitness can best be served by choosing good mates— that is, mates who will stay around and provide for the offspring. Philandering can actually reduce a woman's reproductive fitness in that it can reduce a man's commitment to her.

But there is more to the story. If a man provides for offspring, he wants to be sure that these offspring are his. The worst thing for him is to provide for another man's offspring and thus promote that man's inclusive fitness at the cost of his own. Therefore, men should behave in ways so as to maximize their confidence that the offspring they are raising are their own. One way this can be done is by controlling their mates' sexual behavior, through the emotion of sexual jealousy or through such things as sequestering women (done throughout the Islamic world and in other places and times) or fitting them with chastity belts when the men are away. (These are called *anticuckoldry strategies*; a cuckolded man is one who has been deceived by his mate into believing that the offspring he is providing for are his own.)

Eyebrows will undoubtedly be raised with respect to any attempt to synthesize theoretical traditions that may seem, on the surface at least, utterly unsynthesizable. After all, Marxists are usually extremely critical of sociobiological arguments, on both theoretical and political grounds, and Harris and the cultural materialists have also been sharp critics of sociobiology. Indeed, it will probably be much more than just a single eyebrow that Harris will raise regarding the validity or even coherence of synthetic materialism. And yet I persist undaunted. Once one looks beyond the surface level, the cultural and biological materialisms are not only highly compatible with each other but in fact require each other. Harris's entire critique of sociobiology is not only misguided but is totally unnecessary. In fact, the principles of cultural materialism make sense only *in light of* sociobiology.

I am hardly the only one to see things this way. As Jerome Barkow (1989:310) has said, "Like Marxism, a sociobiological view of society yields conflict theory." This is exactly right, at least in terms of the kind of conflict theory constructed by Randall Collins (1974, 1975). Pierre van den Berghe, the leading proponent of sociobiology within the discipline of sociology, has for many years argued that Harris's rejection of sociobiology is entirely gratuitous (see especially van den Berghe, 1991). Richard Alexander (1987:29) has argued more forcefully than anyone that sociobiology and cultural materialism are complementary rather than competing approaches, noting that "the cost-benefit analyses of cultural materialism are necessarily subsumed under those which take into account the history of human strategies of reproductive success." This is my view exactly. Harris's material causes are proximate causes that can easily be linked to the ultimate reproductive causes of sociobiology. Consider in this regard Harris's so-called biopsychological constants. Harris proposes four such constants and claims that these are sufficient to give us a picture of basic human nature. That is an argument that cannot possibly succeed, but let us look at the content of the constants (Harris, 1979:63):

1 People need to eat and will generally opt for diets that offer more rather than fewer calories and proteins and other nutrients.
2 People cannot be totally inactive, but when confronted with a given task, they prefer to carry it out by expending less rather than more energy.
3 People are highly sexed and generally find reinforcing pleasure from sexual intercourse—more often from heterosexual intercourse.
4 People need love and affection in order to feel secure and happy, and other things being equal, they will act to increase the love and affection which others give them.

These proposed biopsychological constants are not only consistent with sociobiology, but are predicted by them and *only make sense in light of sociobiological principles.* Consider in particular the third constant. Why should people be highly sexed, and why should most be oriented toward heterosexual sex rather than toward any other? The answer can only be, because heterosexual sex, and lots of it, works to promote one's inclusive fitness. The general point is that these biopsychological constants need to be grounded in something deeper, and that is sociobiological theory. Harris's failure to engage in such grounding, and to expand the list of biopsychological constants appropriately, is entirely gratuitous and unnecessarily restrictive.

Synthetic materialism as I have formulated it thus far is far too lengthy and complex to present here (see Sanderson, 1998a, 1998b). However, an abbreviated version of it that emphasizes the more biological side looks approximately as follows:

1　Humans are organisms that have been built by millions of years of biological evolution, both in their anatomy/physiology and in their behavior. Humans have evolved a basic nature, or set of behavioral predispositions that facilitate survival and reproduction.
2　Like all other organisms, humans are caught up in an unceasing struggle for survival and reproduction with their conspecifics. Human social life is the complex product of this ceaseless struggle, and thus individuals pursuing their interests are the core of social life. The pursuit of interests—most fundamentally, reproductive interests—leads to both highly cooperative and highly conflictive social arrangements.
3　In this struggle for survival, humans give priority to kin as well as to self, and especially to close kin, because their most important and fundamental interests are their reproductive interests. Cooperative forms of interaction are found most extensively among individuals who share reproductive interests in common.
4　The various forms of cooperative behavior that exist outside of families and kinship groups exist because they are the relations that will best promote each individual's interests under particular circumstances, not because they promote the well-being of the group or society as a whole. Individuals have evolved to place great emphasis on the behavior known as reciprocity or reciprocal altruism, a strategy that is rooted in enlightened self-interest.
5　When conflictive behavior will more satisfactorily promote individual interests, cooperative relations decline in favor of conflictive relations.
6　Humans have evolved strong behavioral predispositions that facilitate their success in the evolutionary struggle. Because of its necessity in promoting their reproductive interests, humans are highly sexed and usually oriented toward heterosexual sex. Because humans must procure resources that promote their survival and well-being, they are naturally competitive and status-seeking, because more resources go to individuals with higher status. This means that humans are strongly economic animals. They are also strongly political animals

because politics—the struggle for power—is most importantly devoted to the aim of economic gain. However, at the experiential level, individuals do not necessarily have any conscious recognition that their behaviors are driven by these motives. At this level, people often experience economic and political behaviors as valuable in themselves and are often highly motivated to continue and elaborate such behaviors in their own right.

7   People are unequally endowed to compete in the social struggle (i.e., some are bigger, more intelligent, more aggressive or ambitious, more clever, more deceitful, etc.), and as a result social domination and subordination often appear as basic features of social life. The most important forms of social domination relate to human reproductive, economic, and political interests.

8   Although humans have a basic nature that evolved to promote their reproductive (and, secondarily, their economic and political) interests, this nature does not rigidly determine their behavior, but rather pushes behavior along certain lines rather than others. The actual forms of behavior that we observe are always the complex result of human nature interacting with many features of the sociocultural and natural environment.

Let us now see what new insights are gained by applying these basic principles to long-term social evolution, especially the evolution of economic and political systems.

THE EVOLUTION OF ECONOMIC SYSTEMS

Reciprocal altruism and cooperation

Many sociologists and other social scientists object to biomaterialist arguments because they see them as portraying humans in a very negative light, concentrating as they often do on human selfishness, dominance and status orders, the tendency toward aggression, and so on. However, a biomaterialist perspective recognizes that there is also a much more positive side to humans. They cooperate with each other extensively and frequently behave altruistically. It can even be said that cooperation and helping are just as fundamental a part of human nature and human society as selfishness and competition. However, what we need to see is how cooperation and helping have evolved as *selfish strategies*. For something to evolve by natural selection, it has to favor the survival and reproductive interests of the organisms behaving in that way.

In 1971 the biologist Robert Trivers introduced the concept of *reciprocal altruism* in order to understand cooperative and altruistic behavior that occurs between unrelated individuals rather than kin

(Trivers, 1971). Reciprocal altruism requires individuals to respond in kind if the behavior is to continue; it is based on the principle "You scratch my back and I'll scratch yours." It involves an organism's assisting another organism with the expectation that, in time, the favor will be repaid. This kind of cooperative behavior could evolve by natural selection, Trivers argued, because it served the selfish interests of the organisms displaying it. Both would be better off in the long run with the behavior than without it. For reciprocal altruism to work, organisms must interact frequently and be able to recognize each other. Fleeting relationships will not allow its development.

In his book *Social Evolution* (1985), Trivers provides a number of examples of reciprocal altruism in different animal species. Vampire bats feed on blood and cannot live for more than about two days without a meal. Bats missing a meal are usually able to get other bats with very full stomachs to regurgitate blood. However, once this happens, the bat that regurgitated blood expects to be fed at some future time by the other bat when it misses a meal. This kind of pattern does tend to hold up, and bats who are not reciprocated will themselves not reciprocate in the future. Dolphins and whales are legendary for their reciprocal altruism, and they even go so far as to extend their helping behavior to members of other species. They commonly give physical support to the sick, the injured, and the very young. They engage in three forms of help, which Trivers refers to as standing by, assisting, and supporting. Standing by occurs when an animal stays by another animal in distress without directly assisting it. Assisting involves such behaviors as approaching an injured conspecific and swimming between it and its attacker, biting the attacker, or pushing the injured individual away from its attacker. Supporting amounts to maintaining a distressed animal at the water's surface. Dolphins and whales commonly travel together in large groups, with species intermixed. Trivers believes that it is the threat of predation, especially by sharks, that has probably selected for this pattern. The altruistic behavior is adaptive under these conditions.

Moving phylogenetically closer to humans, we find that food sharing and cooperative hunting are common forms of behavior among chimpanzees. Frans de Waal (1996), a leading world expert on chimpanzee behavior, has shown that chimpanzees do not share plant foods but do engage in extensive sharing of meat. When they hunt for small monkeys or other prey, they show themselves to be very good cooperative hunters. They often work in pairs, trios, or sometimes even larger teams when they hunt arboreal monkeys. When a monkey is captured there is usually much celebration, with individuals gatherering into clusters and begging and handing meat to one another. De Waal's analysis of food sharing suggests that it is closely regulated by the principle of reciprocal altruism. He found that the number of transfers of food in one direction correlated with the number moving in the opposite direction. If chimpanzee A shared a lot with chimpanzee B, then B generally shared a lot with A; but if A shared little with C, then C also tended to share little with A. Unsurprisingly, the most extensive and highly developed systems of reciprocal altruism are found in humans. Much of human social life is based on this form of behavior. It is especially prominent in band and tribal societies, with the outstanding example being the sharing of meat among hunter-gatherers. We shall examine this form of reciprocal altruism shortly.

In recent years we have gained considerable insight into how reciprocal altruism may have evolved among highly social species, humans in particular. In game theory there is a famous game known as the Prisoner's Dilemma, which seems to underlie many of the behaviors of ordinary social life. In the Prisoner's Dilemma two people play a game in which neither player knows what the other is doing. If both players cooperate, each gets three points. If one refuses to cooperate (defects) and the other cooperates, the defector gets five points and the cooperator none (this is known as the sucker's payoff). If both defect, they each get one point. When people play this game, the rational thing for each player to do is to defect in order to avoid the sucker's payoff (no points), and that is what players usually do. However, something else happens when the players play the game more than once and no one knows when the game will end. Robert Axelrod (1984) held a computerized tournament in which he asked a number of game theorists to submit strategies for winning the Prisoner's Dilemma. They submitted a variety of strategies, some of them quite complicated, but the strategy that won was the simplest of all: Tit-for-Tat. In this strategy a player cooperates on the first move and then on each subsequent move does whatever his opponent did. Axelrod went on to conduct a second round of the tournament in which many more entries were submitted and in which the participants knew the results of the first round. Tit-for-Tat won again. What do these results mean? According to Axelrod (1984:20), they show that "under suitable conditions, cooperation can indeed emerge in a world of egoists without central authority."

It is important to realize that Tit-for-Tat did better as the tournaments wore on. It often fell behind nastier strategies early on, but gradually got better. The success of Tit-for-Tat has immense implications for evolutionary biology. John Maynard Smith (1974, 1978, 1982) has argued that natural selection should have designed species to behave, at least much of the time, according to the logic of Tit-for-Tat. As Axelrod has put it (1984:49):

Imagine that there are many animals of a single species which interact with each other quite often. Suppose the interactions take the form of a Prisoner's Dilemma. When two animals meet, they can cooperate with each other, not cooperate with each other, or one animal could exploit the other. Suppose further that each animal can recognize individuals it has already interacted with and can remember salient aspects of their interaction, such as whether the other has usually cooperated. A round of the tournament can then be regarded as a simulation of a single generation of such animals, with each decision rule being employed by large numbers of individuals.

Thus the assumption is that various forms of reciprocal altruism have evolved in various species, especially in humans, because reciprocal altruism is the strategy that has done the best job of maximizing benefits for each organism. Or at least reciprocal altruism has done the best for each individual under the kinds of conditions specified in the Prisoner's Dilemma game. Under different conditions, as we shall see, reciprocal altruism is likely to give way to very different strategies.

The big question now is: What does all of this have to do with economic behavior and the evolution of different types of economic systems? Reciprocal altruism underlies much of that kind of economic behavior we call exchange. More than two hundred years ago the famous political economist Adam Smith argued that humans have an innate tendency to "truck, barter, and exchange." This argument has been considered axiomatic by most Western economists, but many sociologists and anthropologists have strongly challenged it, arguing instead that economic behavior is socially constructed and culturally determined. They have considered Smith's argument tantamount to claiming that human nature is essentially "capitalistic." My view is that humans do indeed have a natural tendency to exchange, and to do so in a self-interested manner. However, this does not necessarily make all humans natural capitalists any more than it makes them all natural altruists. Humans are just as naturally one as the other, and the direction in which their behavior moves is determined by the interaction between their natural tendency to exchange and the range of environmental conditions they confront. Leda Cosmides and John Tooby (1992) have argued that the human brain is equipped with a highly specialized set of algorithms for social exchange that provides the biological basis for our economic and social institutions. However, this same set of algorithms leads to very different results in different circumstances.

Economic reciprocity in human society

Reciprocal altruism is found in all human societies and in all human economies, but in many respects it is the essence of economic life in most hunter-gatherer societies. Hunter-gatherer societies are famed for their extensive food sharing, and it is meat in particular that is shared. Hunters who give meat to others expect only that they will probably be repaid in some way at some time. A hunter may give to others time after time without any repayment taking place and without any mention being made of this fact. He understands that the chances are excellent that his acts will eventually be reciprocated. Where reciprocity is a crucial feature of economic life, sharing and individual humility become compulsory social habits (Lee, 1978).

What explains this enormous emphasis on cooperation and sharing? Probably the most common answer to that question is that it is a strategy of *variance reduction* (Wiessner, 1982; Cashdan, 1985; Winterhalder, 1986a, 1986b; cf. Kelly, 1995:168–72). The argument goes something like this. Hunter-gatherers normally live in very small groups, and those found in the modern era are usually located in less desirable environments. While resources might not be scarce in any absolute sense, they often vary markedly from region to region and from time to time. This is particularly the case for animal resources. Because of this, and because hunters differ in their skills and motivations, the success of individual hunters varies markedly as well. What to do? A rational response would be to place a great deal of emphasis on sharing because that will work in the self-interest of each individual over the long run, and quite often in the short run as well. If Morg kills a big animal now and only he and his immediate family eat it, he and his family will suffer, perhaps even starve, when Morg brings home nothing day after day and no one shares their game with them. But if Morg generously shares his kill with others, then those others will likely reciprocate by sharing their kills with him and his family in the future. Thus Morg's generous behavior helps to guarantee security for him and his family. Bruce Winterhalder (1986a, 1986b; discussed in Kelly, 1995) has shown that sharing is most likely to occur in hunter-gatherer societies when there is, in fact, a great deal of variation in the returns of foragers on any given day.

The main alternative to the variance reduction argument is that developed by Nicholas Blurton Jones (1984, 1987) and is known as *tolerated theft*. Blurton Jones argues that there is little difference between giving away a piece of food and allowing it to be taken by someone else. He reasons that among hunter-gatherers a common situation will occur in which one hunter will have killed a large animal while others have killed nothing. Since the successful hunter cannot eat the entire animal on the spot, nor would he benefit from trying to do so, it does not pay him to defend the kill against the unsuccessful hunters who happen upon it. By contrast, it would pay the unsuccessful hunters to fight for the remainder of the kill, and thus the most rational thing for the successful hunter to do if he wishes to avoid serious conflict is to allow others to take the rest of the kill. This situation will occur again and again, Blurton Jones notes, but with a different hunter likely to make the kill, and thus over time individuals will be repeatedly allowing others to take over the rest of their kills. As he puts it (1984:2), "In effect, each individual's 'donations' are sooner or later 'reciprocated.' Individuals who attempt not to reciprocate will suffer the losses of injuries in fights with more motivated opponents. Thus, if we suppose these individuals to meet often, we have exactly the conditions that Trivers proposed as necessary for the evolution of reciprocal altruism."

Which of these models, variance or tolerated theft, should be preferred? Blurton Jones (1987) claims that his model is the simpler of the two and that, moreover, tolerated theft actually leads to variance reduction. Robert Kelly (1995) suggests that both tolerated theft and variance reduction may explain food sharing. Either model is fully consistent with a synthetic materialist perspective, and it is difficult at this point to choose between them. More research is clearly needed.

When should sharing give way to hoarding? One major reason would appear to be a seasonal glut (Blurton Jones, 1987). Hunter-gatherer societies that experience a season of highly abundant resources combined with a season of scarcity, such as a cold and snowy winter, will be highly motivated to store large amounts of food. Indeed, Alain Testart (1982) has drawn an important distinction between hunter-gatherers who store and those who do not, and it seems that sharing is much less common among storers than among nonstorers. Sharing also declines as societies make the transition from hunting and gathering to agriculture, as we shall see shortly.

Three types of reciprocity

Marshall Sahlins (1965, 1972) has formulated a famous distinction between three types of reciprocity, which he calls *generalized, balanced*, and *negative* reciprocity. Generalized reciprocity is the most altruistic, and involves sharing, generosity, or pure gift. One of its hallmarks is the vagueness of reciprocation. Individuals to whom things have been given incur a debt and are obligated to repay it, but there is no specification of the time, quantity, or quality of the reciprocation. Under this type of reciprocity, it is considered inappropriate that there should be any overt calculation or discussion of the nature of the debt. The sharing of meat among hunter-gatherers is governed by this type of reciprocity. Balanced reciprocity is different in that overt calculation and discussion are not only permissible but expected. It is a more direct form of exchange in which the parties come to a clear understanding of the nature of the debt and the time and mode of its repayment. It is less "personal" and "more economic," and includes such things as gift exchange, trade, and buying and selling. Finally, negative reciprocity is the unsociable extreme, an attempt to get something for nothing. It is the most impersonal form of exchange and the "most economic," involving as it does such economic transactions as haggling, gambling, and theft. In its most extreme form it amounts to exploitation. The participants understand that their interests are opposed and that each will try to benefit at the expense of the other. In this sense, negative reciprocity is not really a form of reciprocity at all.

One of the most interesting aspects of Sahlins's analysis is the connection he draws between the form of reciprocity and the social circumstances under which each most frequently occurs. Generalized reciprocity is largely limited to the household or to the lineage and thus occurs primarily among kin. Within the larger village or within the tribe itself, generalized reciprocity normally gives way to balanced reciprocity. Negative reciprocity occurs largely outside the tribal sector and thus is mainly limited to interactions among strangers or at least among individuals who are barely acquainted. The remarkable thing about this formulation is that it fits the expectations of sociobiology almost perfectly, and yet Sahlins was one of the earliest and most dismissive critics of that approach (Alexander, 1975).

In thinking about generalized, balanced, and negative reciprocity ranging along a continuum from the most cooperative to the most competitive or conflictive forms of economic behavior, what now remains to be done is to show how these behavioral categories relate to the evolution of economic systems. Under what conditions will economic behavior be highly cooperative, and under what conditions will this kind of behavior break down and be replaced by much more competitive and exploitative behavior? People behave most cooperatively among kin, friends, and acquaintances, and they behave most competitively or exploitatively among strangers. The expectation is therefore that cooperation will gradually be replaced throughout social evolution by competition and exploitation. This is because one of the most important features of social evolution is an increase in the scale and complexity of social life. In more large-scale and complex societies most people cease to have either direct or sustained contact with most other people. Moreover, the economic evolution of human societies is closely tied up with technological advance and increases in economic productivity. In more evolutionarily advanced societies there are many more economic goods over which conflict can result. When there is more to be had, and when relationships become more impersonal and remote, people are much less likely to cooperate than to compete. It is a simple matter of people following their economic self-interest. As we will see, these expectations about economic evolution correspond closely to the actual record revealed by human history and prehistory.

From reciprocity to redistribution

As we have seen, in hunter-gatherer societies reciprocal altruism, often in the form of generalized reciprocity, is a fundamental form of economic behavior. This kind of economic behavior generally continues in the transition to horticultural societies, but a new form of behavior known as *redistribution* emerges. Redistribution is a process whereby goods, mostly in the form of food, are funneled from individual households to a central source and then returned to those households in some manner. Redistribution differs from reciprocity in that the former is a more formalized process involving the movement of goods into the hands of some person or group that serves as the focal point for their reallocation. Marvin Harris (1975) has identified two different forms of redistribution, which he calls *egalitarian* and *stratified*. These correspond to what Moseley and Wallerstein (1978) have called *pure* and *partial* redistribution. Pure redistribution is so called because the redistributive process is complete, i.e., the redistributive agent reallocates all goods and keeps no extra portion (or at most only a small extra portion) for himself. In partial redistribution the redistributive process is incomplete inasmuch as the redistributive agent, which in this case may be an organized group rather than a single individual, keeps a portion of goods, and sometimes a very large portion, for itself.

Pure redistributive economies are most commonly associated with small-scale horticulturalists. They work somewhat differently from one society to another. One version of a redistributive economy is found among simple horticultural groups in Melanesia and sometimes occurs in other parts of the world. These societies contain extremely ambitious men known as *big men*. Big men are individuals who seek renown through their roles as economic organizers. They spend a great deal of time cultivating their gardens and, if they have them, trying to increase the size of their pig herds. Ordinarily relatives are enlisted in this task. The aim of the big man is to accumulate enough goods to hold a feast, during which the various foodstuffs will be redistributed to other members of the village and perhaps to kin from other villages. One of the interesting things about the big man system is that, although any given village may have only one duly recognized big man, there may be several other ambitious individuals who are competing to attain this position of economic leadership. They too will be working harder in order to accumulate foodstuffs and hold their own feasts. One of the most striking features of this kind of redistributive economy is the competitiveness that is associated with it. Aspiring big men are men who are competing for attention and renown. They seek and often attain a kind of self-glorification that is considered abhorent in most hunter-gatherer societies. The role of big man arises in simple horticultural societies as the principal mechanism for the attainment of prestige, something that people in hunter-gatherer societies may secretly desire but that no person is permitted to seek openly. Cooperation is still a very fundamental part of simple horticultural societies, but a very significant dimension of competitiveness and rivalry has been added.

Marvin Harris (1974, 1977) stresses that a big man, despite seeking prestige, is still an egalitarian or pure redistributor. Big men are expected to redistribute in such a manner that everyone gets something, and he himself gets no more than anyone else. In the transition to more intensive or advanced horticultural societies, however, the redistributive agents become partial rather than pure redistributors: They redistribute to everyone, but they keep a portion, often a large portion, of what they accumulate for themselves. Advanced horticultural societies are in a position to produce an *economic surplus*, or a quantity of goods above and beyond what is necessary for daily subsistence. Much of this surplus remains in the hands of those who cause it to come into existence. In a brilliant article, Marshall Sahlins (1963) has highlighted the differences between pure and partial redistribution by comparing the redistributive systems of Melanesian and Polynesian societies. As he notes, most Melanesian societies have had small-scale horticulture and big-man systems, whereas most Polynesian societies have been characterized by more intensive horticulture and partial redistribution. Melanesian big men may have a great deal of prestige but they hold little or no real power over the rest of the society. By contrast, in many Polynesian societies big men had at some point been transformed into chiefs, political and economic leaders who hold considerable power and economic leverage over the population. Chiefs are able to produce an economic surplus by compelling the people to work harder and relinquish a portion of their harvests. A "public treasury" or "great storehouse" is thus created, from which chiefs support themselves and their families. They also use it for providing lavish entertainment for visiting dignitaries, initiating major public projects such as irrigation works, building temples, sponsoring military campaigns, and supporting a vast range of political functionaries and administrative officials. In addition, portions of the storehouse are redistributed to the people as the need arises, either during times of poor harvests or on special ceremonial occasions that require elaborate feasts.

From redistribution to expropriation

By the time the most advanced horticultural societies gave way to agrarian societies, partial redistribution had been replaced by what is often known as *surplus expropriation*. Surplus expropriation involves powerful landlords' compelling a large peasantry to work hard enough to produce and relinquish a large economic surplus. The surplus may be handed over in various ways, but this normally occurs in the form of rent, taxation, and labor services. Sometimes a fine line can exist between partial redistribution and surplus expropriation, but analytically the distinction is easy to make. Landlords have acquired much more economic power than chiefs, and as a result have been able to place greater economic burdens upon peasant producers than chiefs are capable of placing on their followers. The flow of goods and services between peasants and lords is by and large a one-way flow, there being little counterflow from lords to peasants.

This type of economic relationship has prevailed in virtually all agrarian societies. In medieval Europe, for example, peasants had to pay rent to their landlords, either in the form of cash or a percentage of the crop. Peasants also had to pay various kinds of taxes. For example, they had to pay a tax to grind their grain in the lord's mill, another tax to bake their bread in the lord's oven, and yet another to fish in the lord's fishpond. Peasants also owed their landlords labor services, being required to spend so many days each week working on the lord's demesne (home farm). In ancient Rome a vast system of surplus expropriation resting primarily on slave rather than peasant labor existed. It seems that slaves, who were acquired by political conquest of foreign lands, were much cheaper to employ than was peasant labor (Cameron, 1973). There were many huge Roman estates that were worked by large slave gangs. Slavery has also been found in many other agrarian societies. Many scholars have used the term *exploitation* to characterize the relationship between landlords and those who worked the land. This seems entirely appropriate. I would say that exploitation exists when one party is compelled to give to another party more than it receives in return. The notion of exploitation implies that one party is benefitting at the expense of another and that the disadvantaged party does not have the means to leave the relationship and enter another that would be less punitive. When exploitation exists there is always an element of compulson and unequal power. What then of the primary producers in advanced horticultural societies? Were they being exploited as well? Probably, and if so then we can mark the beginnings of true economic exploitation at the emergence of these types of societies. But the level of exploitation surely was much lower. There were definite limits on the abilities of horticultural chiefs to extract surplus production from the people. Indeed, in precontact Hawaii many a chief was killed who "ate the powers of government too much." That is a fate that almost never befell an agrarian landlord.

As has been suggested to some extent already, a major reason for the shift from reciprocity to redistribution to expropriation throughout the course of social evolution has involved who owned the means of production on which people have depended for a living. There is a clear evolutionary pattern in resource ownership away from more communal modes and toward increasingly privatized modes. In hunter-gatherer societies, especially those with low resource density and high resource unpredictability, there is little territoriality and little concept of ownership (Kelly, 1995). Under these conditions, which characterize the majority of contemporary hunter-gatherer societies, hunter-gatherers tend to share land to about the same extent that they share food (Kelly, 1995). In small-scale horticultural societies there is seldom any sort of privatized ownership, but a clear concept of ownership does exist. Land is usually owned and controlled by lineages or clans, and people only have the right to use the land that belongs to their kinship group. However, within these groups a strikingly egalitarian pattern of use prevails. In terms of the dichotomy communal vs. private, land is communally owned in this type of society. The shift to a more privatized form of landownership generally occurs with the shift to more intensive or advanced horticultural societies. Here, as might be suspected, land is often said to be formally owned by powerful chiefs who have the right to make use of the land as they see fit, including dispossessing commoners or requiring them to increase their rate of productivity and hand over a portion of their harvests. It is well known that in some advanced horticultural societies the claim to formal ownership of land by a chief is to some extent a fiction. For example, among the Kpelle of West Africa the ownership rights of chiefs were quite limited (Gibbs, 1965). Here every man in a lineage was entitled to the use of that lineage's land, and a chief was more like a steward than a true owner. In other advanced horticultural societies, such as precontact Hawaii, formal ownership of land by a chief, especially the paramount chief, was more reality than fiction.

Chiefly ownership marks a significant movement in the direction of private ownership, but because it often retains many of the characteristics of lineage ownership it is not a true mode of private ownership. True private ownership is reached with the emergence of what I have called *seigneurial ownership* (Sanderson, 1995). This involves ownership of the land by a powerful class of landlords and thus has been most characteristic of large-scale agrarian societies. Max Weber (1978[1923]; cf. Wolf, 1966) distinguished between two major types of seigneurial ownership. What he called *patrimonial* ownership was a type of ownership in which land is privately owned by a class of landlords who inherit it through family lines and who personally oversee its cultivation. This type of ownership was characteristic of medieval Europe. Weber's other type of seigneurial ownership, *prebendal* ownership, exists when land is owned by a powerful government that designates officials to supervise its cultivation and draw an income from it. This form of ownership was characteristic of such large centralized states as the Ottoman Empire, the Mogul Empire in India, and traditional China. In these societies the state attempted to override the claims to land made by private landlords and assert their own right to the land and the tribute received from it (Wolf, 1966).

As we can see, the evolution of modes of distribution has closely corresponded to the evolution of modes of ownership, and it seems to be the latter that has been driving the former. The evolution of property rights has been a steady movement away from communal rights toward private rights, from the right of everyone to use vital resources to the right of only a few to the full use of these resources.

And by and large, the more privatized the system of ownership has become, the more unequal has become the system of distribution. What, then, has been driving changing modes of property ownership? The answer, I think, is population pressure, which has been, as we have seen throughout this book, one of the great driving forces of all of social evolution. Population pressure has increased resource scarcity, especially the scarcity of land, and this has increased the fight over land with its consequent unbalanced outcomes. Once again we see human nature coming to the fore. When it is advantageous for them to do so, people share food and land, but they readily abandon the sharing of food and land when *that* is to their advantage. They begin adopting those modes of property ownership and resource distribution that are most suitable for them and their kin under the evolving conditions. The evolution of economic ownership and distribution has run in the same basic way all over the globe throughout history and prehistory, and that suggests the existence of the very kind of organism that the sociobiologists have described. Graeme Donald Snooks (1996) claims that humans have an innate desire to increase their wealth and power and will take advantage of available opportunities to do so. That might be overstating it a little, but I think Snooks is basically right. We seldom see such behavior among band and tribal societies because the conditions permitting the flourishing of wealth and power-seeking do not yet exist. But when those conditions have come into existence, the quest for wealth and power has been virtually omnipresent.

A NOTE ON THE BIOSOCIAL FOUNDATIONS OF POLITICS AND POLITICAL EVOLUTION

Politics is the struggle for power or control or, at the very least, for leadership. It is the struggle for dominance, and thus derives from the same basic part of the biogram as the struggle for status. Indeed, the two are inextricably intertwined. Lionel Tiger and Robin Fox (1971) describe political systems as "breeding systems" inasmuch as the struggle for dominance is, ultimately, the struggle for reproductive success. They go on to identify five basic principles of primate politics:

1   The males dominate the political system, and the older males dominate the younger ones.
2   Females often have great influence in promoting the dominance of particular males, and their long-term relationships to these males are critical for the stability of the system.
3   The dominant males keep order among and protect the females and juveniles.
4   Cooperation among males is a critical feature of primate politics inasmuch as coalitions of bonded males act as units in the dominance system.
5   The attractiveness of the dominants and the attention that is constantly paid to them by subordinates holds the whole structure together.

Tiger and Fox hold that all human political systems—aristocracies, oligarchies, plutocracies, tyrannies, despotisms, democracies, etc.— work according to these same basic processes despite their obvious differences.

In their book *Darwinism, Dominance, and Democracy* (1997), Albert Somit and Steven Peterson argue that humans have been built by biological evolution to favor authoritarian political systems. They note that throughout human history authoritarian political regimes of one type or another have been overwhelmingly the rule and democracy has been rare. From the beginnings of human history some 5,000 years ago until the middle of the nineteenth century, they argue, only ancient Athens and Rome had governments that could be described as at all democratic. They produce a "short list" of contemporary democracies containing only 28 countries (they limit themselves to what they call "macro-nations," or large states), or about 20 percent of the world's 148 macro-nations. They also point out that the ratio of democratic to nondemocatic nations has remained about the same for the past 75 years.

Somit and Peterson offer a great deal of evidence to support their major claim. First, of course, is simply the overwhelming presence of authoritarian states of one type or another throughout human history. Second, they suggest that the masses are easily indoctrinated into political beliefs that favor ruling elites and that they have a striking willingness to obey. In regard to this latter point they cite the famous experiments of Stanley Milgram (1974) showing the remarkable extent to which people will obey a person of authority even when it means causing serious pain to another individual. In addition to all this, they make much of the fact that the greatest philosophers throughout human history have rarely endorsed democratic modes of government.

Somit and Peterson limit themselves to state-organized societies, but our knowledge of the main lines of political evolution (see pp. 53–86) also seems to offer strong support for their argument. Bands and tribes are certainly not authoritarian forms of political order, but the overwhelming tendency in social evolution is for authoritarian systems to develop once the conditions necessary for their existence have come into play. As we have seen, these conditions have been primarily population pressure, warfare, environmental circumscription, and stratification. Once again it seems to be a matter of basic biological tendencies interacting with external conditions.

The existence of power elites in modern democratic societies is also strong confirmation of Somit and Peterson's major claim. Such social scientists as C. Wright Mills (1956), G. William Domhoff (1970, 1978, 1983, 1990), and Michael Useem (1984) have shown the extraordinary degree to which the most important decisions in modern American society are made by a very small number of very powerful people. Marxists (e.g., Miliband, 1977; Szymanski, 1978) have shown that the capitalist class, a tiny segment of the population, exerts an enormous influence over decision-making with respect to the economy. Indeed, C. Wright Mills argued in his famous book *The Power Elite* (1956) that the notion that the United States is a true democracy was actually so mythical that it was a fairy tale. This is not to say that the power elite theorists are right in everything they say, but simply that the reality of power elites is virtually undeniable.

Somit and Peterson argue that modern democracy became the major form of government in some societies in the modern world because of a variety of conditions. They list such things as a more egalitarian distribution of wealth, advanced education, urbanization, and a predisposing civic culture. Most of these are reasonable enough, although I would stress the first because it is the one most compatible with Rueschemeyer, Stephens, and Stephens's (1992) argument that it is the rise of a large and well-organized working class that is the key to democracy. But they go on to add that democracy has only become stable and long-lasting because of humans' extraordinary indoctrinability. Since humans are naturally predisposed toward authoritarianism, they have had to be indoctrinated against their nature to accept democracy. It is in this way that democracy has moved from the status of "ugly duckling" to that of "irresistible swan."

Somit and Peterson suggest that democracy may be only a fleeting phase that is destined to disappear in the near future—that authoritarian government is apt to be a persistent phenomenon rather than an archaic stage of political evolution. In this I fear they are correct. Indeed, many of the leaders of democratic nations seem to have the same fear. Repeatedly it is pointed out that democracy is fragile and requires the constant vigilance of the masses to maintain. We hear frequently of the need for democratic societies to have a well-educated citizenry because only by the presence of such a citizenry can democracy be preserved.

Although Somit and Peterson's major claim concerning the human inclination toward authoritarian politics rings true, at least in my view, there are some features of their analysis that are discomforting. In my view they overestimate considerably the human inclination to obey. It is true that humans do have a remarkable tendency to obey, but they also have virtually as strong a capacity to resist. Somit and Peterson say (1997:70), "For six millennia or more, rulers have commanded—and almost always their subjects have obeyed. Major collective acts of rebellion have been so relatively infrequent that almost any reasonably well educated person is familiar with most of them." Moreover (1997:70), "From the origin of organized political society, and over sixty some centuries of authoritarian and tyrannical rule by native and alien governors alike, the nearly (but fortunately not completely) invariable human response has been to obey. Taken in broad historical perspective, disobedience is a rarely encountered political phenomenon." I think the evidence will show that major acts of rebellion have been much more common than this, that disobedience is frequently rather than rarely encountered. Humans compete for dominance and power, but the losers frequently challenge the winners. In essence, that is what dominance hierarchies are all about. As I have noted at least once before, in precontact Hawaii paramount chiefs who "ate the powers of government too much" were frequently overthrown and killed. In state-level societies people were seldom successful when they rebelled, but they rebelled frequently nonetheless. Peasant revolts and slave rebellions have been commonplace in history, and attempted revolutions have occurred everywhere in the modern world. Indeed, how do we understand the rise of democracy in the modern world, especially in the sense of universal suffrage, but as an effort on the part of the masses to overthrow authoritarian rule?

The members of modern states have not accepted democracy simply because of indoctrination. The evidence is clear that they wanted it and struggled hard for it. Again, the very nature of a dominance order is that there is always some resistance from below to that which is imposed from above. In this sense, Somit and Peterson's conception of the human penchant for authoritarianism is incomplete because it is inaccurate (or at least highly exaggerated) in its conception of what the subordinates are doing.

NOTE

1. Some of the most important general treatments of sociobiology are Barash (1977), Daly and Wilson (1978), Dawkins (1976), Alexander (1979), Symons (1979), Lopreato (1984, 1989), Trivers (1985), Ruse (1985), Barkow (1989), Barkow, Cosmides, and Tooby (1992), Badcock (1991), Maxwell (1991), Tooby and Cosmides (1989, 1990), Nielsen (1994), and Crippen (1994a, 1994b). A collection by Betzig (1997) reprints many classic articles.

REFERENCES

Alexander, Richard D. 1975. "The search for a general theory of behavior." *Behavioral Science* 20:77–100.

———. 1979. *Darwinism and Human Affairs*. Seattle: University of Washington Press.

———. 1987. *The Biology of Moral Systems*. Hawthorne, NY: Aldine de Gruyter.

Axelrod, Robert. 1984. *The Evolution of Cooperation*. New York: Basic Books.

Badcock, Christopher. 1991. *Evolution and Individual Behavior: An Introduction to Sociobiology*. Oxford: Blackwell.

Barash, David P. 1977. *Sociobiology and Behavior*. New York: Elsevier.

Barkow, Jerome H. 1989. *Darwin, Sex, and Status*. Toronto: University of Toronto Press.

Barkow, Jerome H., Leda Cosmides, and John Tooby (eds.). 1992. *The Adapted Mind: Evolutionary Psychology and the Generation of Culture*. New York: Oxford University Press.

Betzig, Laura (ed.). 1997. *Human Nature: A Critical Reader*. New York: Oxford University Press.

Blurton Jones, Nicholas G. 1984. "A selfish origin for human food sharing: Tolerated theft." *Ethology and Sociobiology* 5:1–3.

———. 1987. "Tolerated theft: Suggestions about the ecology and evolution of sharing, hoarding, and scrounging." *Social Science Information* 26:31–54.

Cameron, Kenneth Neill. 1973. *Humanity and Society: A World History*. New York: Monthly Review Press.

Cashdan, Elizabeth A. 1985. "Coping with risk: Reciprocity among the Basarwa of northern Botswana." *Man* 20:454–74.

Collins, Randall. 1974. "Reassessments of sociological history: The empirical validity of the conflict tradition." *Theory and Society* 1:147–78.

———. 1975. *Conflict Sociology: Toward an Explanatory Science.* New York: Academic Press.

Cosmides, Leda, and John Tooby. 1992. "Cognitive adaptations for social exchange." In Jerome H. Barkow, Leda Cosmides, and John Tooby (eds.), *The Adapted Mind: Evolutionary Psychology and the Generation of Culture.* New York: Oxford University Press.

Crippen, Timothy. 1994a. "Toward a neo-Darwinian sociology: Its nomological principles and some illustrative applications." *Sociological Perspectives* 37:309–35.

———. 1994b. "Neo-Darwinian approaches in the social sciences: Unwarranted concerns and misconceptions." *Sociological Perspectives* 37:391–401.

Daly, Martin, and Margo Wilson. 1978. *Sex, Evolution, and Behavior.* North Scituate, MA: Duxbury Press.

Dawkins, Richard. 1976. *The Selfish Gene.* New York: Oxford University Press.

de Waal, Frans. 1996. *Good Natured: The Origins of Right and Wrong in Humans and Other Animals.* Cambridge, MA: Harvard University Press.

Domhoff, G. William. 1970. *The Higher Circles.* New York: Random House.

———. 1978. *The Powers That Be: Processes of Ruling Class Domination.* New York: Random House (Vintage Books).

———. 1983. *Who Rules America Now? A View for the '80s.* New York: Simon and Schuster (Touchstone).

———. 1990. *The Power Elite and the State: How Policy is Made in America.* Hawthorne, NY: Aldine de Gruyter.

Gibbs, James L., Jr. 1965. "The Kpelle of Liberia." In James L. Gibbs, Jr. (ed.), *Peoples of Africa.* New York: Holt, Rinehart, and Winston.

Harris, Marvin. 1974. *Cows, Pigs, Wars, and Witches: The Riddles of Culture.* New York: Random House.

———. 1975. *Culture, People, Nature: An Introduction to General Anthropology.* 2nd edition. New York: Crowell.

———. 1977. *Cannibals and Kings: The Origins of Cultures.* New York: Random House.

———. 1979. *Cultural Materialism: The Struggle for a Science of Culture.* New York: Random House.

Kelly, Robert L. 1995. *The Foraging Spectrum: Diversity in Hunter-Gatherer Lifeways.* Washington, DC: Smithsonian Institution Press.

Lee, Richard B. 1978. "Politics, sexual and nonsexual, in an egalitarian society." *Social Science Information* 17:871–95.

Lopreato, Joseph. 1984. *Human Nature and Biocultural Evolution.* Boston: Allyn & Unwin.

———. 1989. "The maximization principle: A cause in search of conditions." In Robert W. Bell and Nancy J. Bell (eds.), *Sociobiology and the Social Sciences.* Lubbock: Texas Tech University Press.

Maxwell, Mary (ed.). 1991. *The Sociobiological Imagination.* Albany: State University of New York Press.

Maynard Smith, John. 1974. "The theory of games and the evolution of animal conflict." *Journal of Theoretical Biology* 47:209–21.

———. 1978. "The evolution of behavior." *Scientific American* 239:176–92.

———. 1982. *Evolution and the Theory of Games*. Cambridge, UK: Cambridge University Press.

Milgram, Stanley. 1974. *Obedience to Authority: An Experimental View*. New York: Harper and Row.

Miliband, Ralph. 1977. *Marxism and Politics*. Oxford: Oxford University Press.

Mills, C. Wright. 1956. *The Power Elite*. New York: Oxford University Press.

Moseley, K.P., and Immanuel Wallerstein. 1978. "Precapitalist social structures." *Annual Review of Sociology* 4:259–90.

Nielsen, Francois. 1994. "Sociobiology and sociology." *Annual Review of Sociology* 20:267–303.

Rueschemeyer, Dietrich, Evelyne Huber Stephens, and John D. Stephens. 1992. *Capitalist Development and Democracy*. Chicago: University of Chicago Press.

Ruse, Michael. 1985. *Sociobiology: Sense or Nonsense?* Dordrecht: D. Riedel.

Sahlins, Marshall D. 1963. "Poor man, rich man, big man, chief: Political types in Melanesia and Polynesia." *Comparative Studies in Society and History* 5:285–303.

———. 1965. "On the sociology of primitive exchange." In Michael Banton (ed.),. *The Relevance of Models for Social Anthropology*. London: Tavistock.

———. 1972. *Stone Age Economics*. Chicago: Aldine.

Sanderson, Stephen K. 1995. *Macrosociology: An Introduction to Human Societies*. 3rd edition. New York: HarperCollins.

———. 1998a. "Expanding sociobiology's explanatory power: Synthetic materialism—an integrated theory of human society." Paper presented at the annual meetings of the European Sociobiological Society, Moscow, May 31-June 4, and at the annual meetings of the Human Behavior and Evolution Society, Davis, California, July 8–12.

———. 1998b. "Synthetic materialism: An integrated theory of human society." Paper presented at the annual meetings of the American Sociological Association, San Francisco, August 21–25.

Snooks, Graeme Donald. 1996. *The Dynamic Society: Exploring the Sources of Global Change*. London: Routledge.

Somit, Albert, and Steven A. Peterson. 1997. *Darwinism, Dominance, and Democracy: The Biological Bases of Authoritarianism*. Westport, CT: Praeger.

Symons, Donald. 1979. *The Evolution of Human Sexuality*. New York: Oxford University Press.

Szymanski, Albert. 1978. *The Capitalist State and the Politics of Class*. Cambridge, MA: Winthrop.

Testart, Alain. 1982. "The significance of food storage among hunter-gatherers: Residence patterns, population densities, and social inequalities." *Current Anthropology* 23:523–37.

Tiger, Lionel, and Robin Fox. 1971. *The Imperial Animal*. New York: Holt, Rinehart and Winston.

Tooby, John, and Leda Cosmides. 1989. "Evolutionary psychology and the generation of culture, part I: Theoretical considerations." *Ethology and Sociobiology* 10:29–49.

428   Afterword to the Expanded Edition

———. 1990. "The past explains the present: Emotional adaptations and the structure of ancestral environments." *Ethology and Sociobiology* 11:375–424.

Trivers, Robert L. 1971. "The evolution of reciprocal altruism." *Quarterly Review of Biology* 46:35–57.

———. 1985. *Social Evolution*. Menlo Park, CA: Benjamin/Cummings.

Useem, Michael. 1984. *The Inner Circle: Large Corporations and the Rise of Business Political Activity in the U.S. and the U.K.* New York: Oxford University Press.

van den Berghe, Pierre L. 1991. "Sociology." In Mary Maxwell (ed.), *The Sociobiological Imagination*. Albany: State University of New York Press.

Weber, Max. 1978[1923]. *Economy and Society*. Two volumes. Edited by Guenther Roth and Claus Wittich. Berkeley: University of California Press.

Wiessner, Polly. 1982. "Risk, reciprocity, and social influence in !Kung San economies." In Eleanor Leacock and Richard B. Lee (eds.), *Politics and History in Band Societies*. Cambridge, UK: Cambridge University Press.

Winterhalder, Bruce. 1986a. "Diet choice, risk, and food sharing in a stochastic environment." *Journal of Anthropological Archaeology* 5:369–92.

———. 1986b. "Optimal foraging: Simulation studies of diet choice in a stochastic environment." *Journal of Ethnobiology* 6:205–23.

Wolf, Eric B. 1966. *Peasants*. Englewood Cliffs, NJ: Prentice-Hall.

References

Abonyi, Arpad. 1982. "Eastern Europe's reintegration." In Christopher Chase-Dunn (ed.), *Socialist states in the world-system*. Beverly Hills, Calif.: Sage.

Abu-Lughod, Janet L. 1988. "The shape of the world system in the thirteenth century." *Studies in comparative international development* 22(4):3–24.

—— 1989. *Before European hegemony: the world system AD 1250–1350*. New York: Oxford University Press.

Adams, Richard E.W. 1991. *Prehistoric Mesoamerica*. Second edition. Norman: University of Oklahoma Press.

Adams, Robert M. 1966. *The evolution of urban society: early Mesopotamia and prehispanic Mexico*. Chicago: Aldine.

Aganbegyan, Abel. 1989. *Inside perestroika: the future of the Soviet economy*. Translated by Helen Szamuely. New York: Harper & Row.

Algaze, Guillermo. 1989. "The Uruk expansion: cross-cultural exchange in early Mesopotamian civilization." *Current anthropology* 30:571–608.

Allen, Mitchell. 1992. "The mechanisms of underdevelopment: an ancient Mesopotamian example." *Review* 15:453–76.

Amin, Samir. 1972. "Underdevelopment and dependence in black Africa: origins and contemporary forms." *Journal of modern African studies* 10: 503–24.

—— 1974. *Accumulation on a world scale*. New York: Monthly Review Press.

—— 1976. *Unequal development: an essay on the social formations of peripheral capitalism*. Translated by Brian Pearce. New York: Monthly Review Press.

—— 1991. "The ancient world-systems versus the modern capitalist world-system." *Review* 14:349–85.

Anderson, Perry. 1974a. *Passages from antiquity to feudalism*. London: New Left Books.

—— 1974b. *Lineages of the absolutist state*. London: New Left Books.

Angel, J. Lawrence. 1975. "Paleoecology, paleodemography, and health." In Steven Polgar (ed.), *Population, ecology, and social evolution*. The Hague: Mouton.

Apter, David E. 1987. *Rethinking development: modernization, dependency, and post-modern politics*. Beverly Hills, Calif.: Sage.

Arrighi, Giovanni. 1982. "A crisis of hegemony." In Samir Amin et al., *Dynamics of global crisis*. New York: Monthly Review Press.

Arrighi, Giovanni and Jessica Drangel. 1986. "The stratification of the world-economy: an exploration of the semiperipheral zone." *Review* 10: 9–74.

Athens, J. Stephen. 1977. "Theory building and the study of evolutionary process in complex societies." In Lewis R. Binford (ed.), *For theory building in archaeology*. New York: Academic Press.

Atwell, William S. 1986. "Some observations on the 'seventeenth-century crisis' in China and Japan." *Journal of Asian studies* 45: 223–44.

Bairoch, Paul. 1981. "The main trends in national economic disparities since the Industrial Revolution." In Paul Bairoch and Maurice Lévy-Leboyer (eds), *Disparities in economic development since the Industrial Revolution*. London: Macmillan Press.

—— 1988. *Cities and economic development: from the dawn of history to the present*. Translated by Christopher Braider. Chicago: University of Chicago Press.

Barfield, Thomas J. 1989. *The perilous frontier: nomadic empires and China*. Oxford: Basil Blackwell.

Barrett, Richard E. and Martin King Whyte. 1982. "Dependency theory and Taiwan: analysis of a deviant case." *American journal of sociology* 87: 1064–89.

Barrett, Ward. 1990. "World bullion flows, 1450–1800." In James D. Tracy (ed.), *The rise of merchant empires*. New York: Cambridge University Press.

Bartholomew, James R. 1989. *The formation of science in Japan*. New Haven: Yale University Press.

Becker, George. 1984. "Pietism and science: a critique of Robert K.

Merton's hypothesis." *American journal of sociology* 89:1065–90.

Bell, Daniel. 1973. *The coming of post-industrial society.* New York: Basic Books.

Bellah, Robert N. 1957. *Tokugawa religion.* Glencoe, Ill.: Free Press.

Bello, Walden and Stephanie Rosenfeld. 1993. "The rise and crisis of the dragon economies." In Mitchell A. Seligson and John T. Passé-Smith (eds), *Development and underdevelopment: the political economy of inequality.* Boulder, Colo.: Lynne Rienner.

Benavot, Aaron and Phyllis Riddle. 1988. "The expansion of primary education, 1870–1940: trends and issues." *Sociology of education* 61: 191–210.

Bender, Barbara. 1978. "Gatherer-farmer to hunter: a social perspective." *World archaeology* 10:204–22.

—— 1985. "Emergent tribal formations in the American midcontinent." *American antiquity* 50:52–62.

Berg, Ivar. 1971. *Education and jobs: the great training robbery.* Boston: Beacon Press.

Berger, Peter L. 1986. *The capitalist revolution: fifty propositions about prosperity, equality, and liberty.* New York: Basic Books.

Berger, Stephen D. 1974. "Review of Daniel Bell, *The coming of post-industrial society.*" *Contemporary sociology* 3:101–5.

Bergesen, Albert, Roberto M. Fernandez, and Chintamani Sahoo. 1987."America and the changing structure of hegemonic production." In Terry Boswell and Albert Bergesen (eds), *America's changing role in the world-system.* New York: Praeger.

Bernal, J.D. 1971. *Science in history.* Four volumes. Cambridge, Mass.: MIT Press.

Bienefeld, Manfred. 1981. "Dependency and the newly industrializing countries (NICs): towards a reappraisal." In Dudley Seers (ed.), *Dependency theory: a critical reassessment.* London: Frances Pinter.

Binford, Lewis R. 1983. *In pursuit of the past.* London: Thames & Hudson.

Blanton, Richard E. 1980. "Cultural ecology reconsidered." *American antiquity* 45:145–51.

Blanton, Richard E., Stephen A. Kowalewski, Gary Feinman, and Jill Appel. 1981. *Ancient Mesoamerica: a comparison of change in three regions.* New York: Cambridge University Press.

Blau, Peter and Otis Dudley Duncan. 1967. *The American occupational structure.* New York: Free Press.

Blauner, Robert. 1964. *Alienation and freedom*. Chicago: University of Chicago Press.

Bloch, Marc. 1961. *Feudal society*. 2 volumes. Translated by L.A. Manyon. Chicago: University of Chicago Press.

Blomstrom, Magnus and Bjorn Hettne. 1984. *Development theory in transition*. London: Zed Books.

Bluestone, Barry and Bennett Harrison. 1982. *The deindustrialization of America*. New York: Basic Books.

Boas, Franz. 1940. "The limitations of the comparative method of anthropology." In Franz Boas, *Race, language, and culture*. New York: Macmillan. (Originally published 1896.)

Boli, John, Francisco O. Ramirez, and John W. Meyer. 1985. "Explaining the origins and expansion of mass education." *Comparative education review* 29:145–70.

Boli-Bennett, John. 1980. "Global integration and the universal increase of state dominance, 1910–1970." In Albert Bergesen (ed.), *Studies of the modern world-system*. New York: Academic Press.

Bornschier, Volker and Christopher Chase-Dunn. 1985. *Transnational corporations and underdevelopment*. New York: Praeger.

Bornschier, Volker, Christopher Chase-Dunn, and Richard Rubinson. 1978."Cross-national evidence of the effects of foreign investment and aid on economic growth and inequality: a survey of findings and a reanalysis." *American journal of sociology* 84:651–83.

Boserup, Ester. 1965. *The conditions of agricultural growth*. Chicago: Aldine.

—— 1981. *Population and technological change*. Chicago: University of Chicago Press.

Bourdieu, Pierre and Jean-Claude Passeron. 1977. *Reproduction: in education, society and culture*. Beverly Hills, Calif.: Sage.

Bowles, Samuel and Herbert Gintis. 1976. *Schooling in capitalist America*. New York: Basic Books.

Boyd, Robert and Peter J. Richerson. 1985. *Culture and the evolutionary process*. Chicago: University of Chicago Press.

Braudel, Fernand. 1982. *The wheels of commerce*. (*Civilization and capitalism 15th–18th century, volume 2*.) Translated by Sian Reynolds. New York: Harper & Row.

—— 1984. *The perspective of the world*. (*Civilization and capitalism 15th–18th century, volume 3*.) Translated by Sian Reynolds. New York: Harper & Row.

Braverman, Harry. 1974. *Labor and monopoly capital: the degradation of work in the twentieth century.* New York: Monthly Review Press.

Brenner, Robert. 1976. "Agrarian class structure and economic development in pre-industrial Europe." *Past and present* 70:30–75.

—— 1977. "The origins of capitalist development: a critique of neo-Smithian Marxism." *New left review* 104:25–92.

Bronson, Bennet. 1972. "Farm labor and the evolution of food production." In Brian Spooner (ed.), *Population growth: anthropological implications.* Cambridge, Mass.: MIT Press.

—— 1975. "The earliest farming: demography as cause and consequence." In Steven Polgar (ed.), *Population, ecology, and social evolution.* The Hague: Mouton.

Butzer, Karl. 1976. *Early hydraulic civilization in Egypt.* Chicago: University of Chicago Press.

Cammack, Paul. 1986. "Resurgent democracy: threat and promise." *New left review* 157:121–8.

Cardoso, Fernando Henrique. 1982. "Dependency and development in Latin America." In Hamza Alavi and Teodor Shanin (eds), *Introduction to the sociology of "developing societies."* London: Macmillan Press.

—— 1986. "Democracy in Latin America." *Politics and society* 15:23–41.

Cardoso, Fernando Henrique and Enzo Faletto. 1979. *Dependency and development in Latin America.* Berkeley: University of California Press.

Carneiro, Robert L. 1970. "A theory of the origin of the state." *Science* 169:733–8.

—— 1972. "The devolution of evolution." *Social biology* 19:248–58.

—— 1978. "Political expansion as an expression of the principle of competitive exclusion." In Ronald Cohen and Elman R. Service (eds), *Origins of the state.* Philadelphia: Institute for the Study of Human Issues.

—— 1981. "The chiefdom: precursor of the state." In Grant D. Jones and Robert R. Kautz (eds), *The transition to statehood in the New World.* New York: Cambridge University Press.

—— 1987a. "Further reflections on resource concentration and its role in the rise of the state." In Linda Manzanilla (ed.), *Studies in the Neolithic and Urban Revolutions.* Oxford: British Archaeological Reports, International Series, No. 349.

—— 1987b. "Cross-currents in the theory of state formation." *American ethnologist* 14:756–70.

—— 1988. "The circumscription theory: challenge and response." *American behavioral scientist* 31:497–511.

—— 1991. *The nature of the chiefdom as revealed by evidence from the Cauca Valley of Colombia.* University of Michigan Museum of Anthropology Anthropological Papers, No. 85.

Chagnon, Napoleon A. 1983. *Yanomamö: the fierce people.* Third edition. New York: Holt, Rinehart & Winston.

Champion, Timothy, Clive Gamble, Stephen Shennan, and Alasdair Whittle. 1984. *Prehistoric Europe.* New York: Academic Press.

Chandler, Tertius. 1987. *Four thousand years of urban growth.* Lewiston, N.Y.: St. David's University Press.

Chang, Kwang-chih. 1986. *The archaeology of ancient China.* Fourth edition. New Haven: Yale University Press.

Chase-Dunn, Christopher. 1975. "The effects of international economic dependence on development and inequality: a cross-national study." *American sociological review* 40:720–38.

—— 1982. "Socialist states in the capitalist world-economy." In Christopher Chase-Dunn (ed.), *Socialist states in the world-system.* Beverly Hills, Calif.: Sage.

—— 1989. *Global formation: structures of the world-economy.* Oxford: Basil Blackwell.

—— 1990. "World-state formation: historical processes and emergent necessity." *Political geography quarterly* 9:108–30.

—— 1992. "The spiral of capitalism and socialism." In Louis Kriesberg (ed.), *Research in social movements, conflicts and change.* Volume 14. Greenwich, Conn.: JAI Press.

Chase-Dunn, Christopher and Thomas D. Hall. 1991. "Conceptualizing core/periphery hierarchies for comparative study." In Christopher Chase-Dunn and Thomas D. Hall (eds), *Core/periphery relations in precapitalist worlds.* Boulder, Colo.: Westview Press.

—— (eds). 1991. *Core/periphery relations in precapitalist worlds.* Boulder, Colo.: Westview Press.

—— 1993. "Comparing world-systems: concepts and working hypotheses." *Social forces* 71:851–86.

Chase-Dunn, Christopher and Kenneth O'Reilly. 1989. "Core wars of the future." In Robert K. Schaeffer (ed.), *War in the world-system.* Westport, Conn.: Greenwood Press.

Chaudhuri, K.N. 1985. *Trade and civilisation in the Indian Ocean.* Cambridge: Cambridge University Press.

Cheng, Tun-jen. 1990. "Political regimes and development strategies: South Korea and Taiwan." In Gary Gereffi and Donald L. Wyman (eds), *Manufacturing miracles: paths of industrialization in Latin America and East Asia.* Princeton: Princeton University Press.

Cherlin, Andrew J. 1992. *Marriage, divorce, remarriage.* Second edition. Cambridge: Harvard University Press.

Childe, V. Gordon. 1936. *Man makes himself.* London: Watts & Co.

—— 1951. *Social evolution.* London: Watts & Co.

—— 1954. *What happened in history.* Harmondsworth, UK: Penguin Books. (First edition 1942.)

Chirot, Daniel. 1977. *Social change in the twentieth century.* New York: Harcourt Brace Jovanovich.

—— 1985. "The rise of the West." *American sociological review* 50:181–95.

—— 1986. *Social change in the modern era.* San Diego: Harcourt Brace Jovanovich.

—— 1991. "What happened in Eastern Europe in 1989?" In Daniel Chirot (ed.), *The crisis of Leninism and the decline of the left.* Seattle: University of Washington Press.

Christenson, A. 1980. "Change in the human niche in response to population growth." In T. Earle and A. Christenson (eds), *Modeling change in prehistoric subsistence economies.* New York: Academic Press.

Cipolla, Carlo M. 1978. *The economic history of world population.* Seventh edition. Sussex, UK: Harvester Press.

Claessen, Henri J.M. and Peter Skalnik. 1978a. "The early state: theories and hypotheses." In Henri J.M. Claessen and Peter Skalnik (eds), *The early state.* The Hague: Mouton.

—— 1978b. "The early state: models and reality." In Henri J.M. Claessen and Peter Skalnik (eds), *The early state.* The Hague: Mouton.

—— 1978c. "Limits: beginning and end of the early state." In Henri J.M. Claessen and Peter Skalnik (eds), *The early state.* The Hague: Mouton.

Claessen, Henri J.M., and Pieter van de Velde. 1985. "Sociopolitical evolution as complex interaction." In Henri J.M. Claessen, Pieter van de Velde, and M. Estellie Smith (eds), *Development and decline: the evolution of sociopolitical organization.* South Hadley, Mass.: Bergin & Garvey.

Clark, Burton R. 1962. *Educating the expert society.* San Francisco: Chandler.

Coe, Michael D. 1981. "Religion and the rise of Mesoamerican states." In Grant D. Jones and Robert R. Kautz (eds), *The transition to statehood in the New World.* New York: Cambridge University Press.

Coghlan, H.H. 1954. "Metal implements and weapons." In Charles Singer, E.J. Holmyard, and A.R. Hall (eds), *A history of technology.* Volume 1. Oxford: Oxford University Press (Clarendon Press).

Cohen, Jere. 1980. "Rational capitalism in Renaissance Italy." *American journal of sociology* 85:1340–55.

Cohen, Mark Nathan. 1977. *The food crisis in prehistory: overpopulation and the origins of agriculture.* New Haven: Yale University Press.

—— 1981a. "Comment on Hayden." *Current anthropology* 22:532.

—— 1981b. "The ecological basis of New World state formation: general and local model building." In Grant D. Jones and Robert R. Kautz (eds), *The transition to statehood in the New World.* New York: Cambridge University Press.

—— 1985. "Prehistoric hunter-gatherers: the meaning of social complexity." In T. Douglas Price and James A. Brown (eds), *Prehistoric hunter-gatherers.* New York: Academic Press.

—— 1989. *Health and the rise of civilization.* New Haven: Yale University Press.

Cohen, Mark Nathan and George J. Armelagos (eds). 1984. *Paleopathology at the origins of agriculture.* New York: Academic Press.

Cohen, Ronald. 1978. "State origins: a reappraisal." In Henri J.M. Claessen and Peter Skalnik (eds), *The early state.* The Hague: Mouton.

Collins, Randall. 1975. *Conflict sociology: toward an explanatory science.* New York: Academic Press.

—— 1979. *The credential society: an historical sociology of education and stratification.* New York: Academic Press.

—— 1980. "Weber's last theory of capitalism: a systematization." *American sociological review* 45:925–42.

—— 1986a. *Max Weber: a skeleton key.* Beverly Hills, Calif.: Sage.

—— 1986b. *Weberian sociological theory.* New York: Cambridge University Press.

—— 1988. *Theoretical sociology*. San Diego: Harcourt Brace Jovanovich.

—— 1990. "Market dynamics as the engine of historial change." *Sociological theory* 8:111–35.

—— 1992. "The geopolitical and economic world-systems of kinship-based and agrarian-coercive societies" *Review* 15:373–88.

Collins, Randall and David Waller. 1992. "What theories predicted the state breakdowns and revolutions of the Soviet Bloc?" In Louis Kriesberg (ed.), *Research in social movements, conflicts and change*. Volume 14. Greenwich, Conn.: JAI Press.

Connah, Graham. 1987. *African civilizations*. Cambridge: Cambridge University Press.

Coulborn, Rushton (ed.). 1956. *Feudalism in history*. Princeton: Princeton University Press.

Cowgill, George L. 1975. "On causes and consequences of ancient and modern population changes." *American anthropologist* 77: 505–25.

Crane, George T. 1982. "The Taiwanese ascent: system, state, and movement in the world-economy." In Edward Friedman (ed.), *Ascent and decline in the world-system*. Beverly Hills, Calif.: Sage.

Crawford, Gary W. 1992. "Prehistoric plant domestication in East Asia." In C. Wesley Cowan and Patty Jo Watson (eds), *The origins of agriculture: an international perspective*. Washington: Smithsonian Institution Press.

Critchley, John. 1978. *Feudalism*. London: Allen & Unwin.

Crosby, Alfred W. 1986. *Ecological imperialism: the biological expansion of Europe, 900–1900*. New York: Cambridge University Press.

Culbert, T. Patrick. 1988. "The collapse of Classic Maya civilization." In Norman Yoffee and George L. Cowgill (eds), *The collapse of ancient states and civilizations*. Tucson: University of Arizona Press.

Cumings, Bruce. 1984. "The origins and development of the northeast Asian political economy: industrial sectors, product cycles, and political consequences." *International organization* 38:1–40.

Curtin, Philip D. 1984. *Cross-cultural trade in world history*. New York: Cambridge University Press.

Daumas, Maurice. 1969. *A history of technology and invention*. Volume 1. Translated by Eileen B. Hennessy. New York: Crown Publishers.

Delacroix, Jacques and Charles C. Ragin. 1981. "Structural blockage: a cross-national study of economic dependency, state efficacy, and underdevelopment." *American journal of sociology* 86:1311–47.

Derry, T.K. and Trevor I. Williams. 1961. *A short history of technology: from the earliest times to AD 1900.* New York: Oxford University Press.

Dobb, Maurice. 1963. *Studies in the development of capitalism.* Revised edition. New York: International Publishers. (First edition 1947.)

Dore, Ronald. 1976. *The diploma disease: education, qualification, and development.* Berkeley: University of California Press.

Dorn, Harold. 1991. *The geography of science.* Baltimore: Johns Hopkins University Press.

Dos Santos, Theotonio. 1970. "The structure of dependence." *American economic review* 60:231–6.

Dudley, Leonard M. 1991. *The word and the sword.* Oxford: Blackwell.

Dumond, Don E. 1972. "Population growth and political centralization." In Brian Spooner (ed.), *Population growth: anthropological implications.* Cambridge, Mass.: MIT Press.

Durham, William H. 1991. *Coevolution: genes, culture, and human diversity.* Stanford: Stanford University Press.

Durkheim, Emile. 1933. *The division of labor in society.* Translated by George Simpson. New York: Free Press. (Originally published 1893.)

Duus, Peter. 1969. *Feudalism in Japan.* New York: Alfred A. Knopf.

Earle, Timothy K. 1978. *Economic and social organization of a complex chiefdom: the Halelea district, Kaua'i, Hawaii.* University of Michigan Museum of Anthropology Anthropological Papers, No. 63.

—— 1987. "Chiefdoms in archaeological and ethnohistorical perspective." *Annual review of anthropology* 16:279–308.

Eckhardt, William. 1992. *Civilizations, empires and wars: a quantitative history of war.* Jefferson, NC: McFarland.

Eckstein, Susan. 1986. "The impact of the Cuban Revolution: a comparative perspective." *Comparative studies in society and history* 28:502–34.

Edens, Christopher. 1992. "Dynamics of trade in the ancient Mesopotamian 'world-system.'" *American anthropologist* 94:118–39.

Ehrensaft, Philip. 1985. "Phases in the development of South African capitalism: from settlement to crises." In Peter C.W. Gutkind and Immanuel Wallerstein (eds), *Political economy of contemporary*

Africa. Second edition. Beverly Hills, Calif.: Sage.

Eisenstadt, S.N. 1963. *The political systems of empires.* New York: Free Press.

Ekholm, Kajsa. 1981. "On the structure and dynamics of global systems." In Joel S. Kahn and Josep R. Llobera (eds), *The anthropology of pre-capitalist societies.* London: Macmillan.

Ekholm, Kajsa and Jonathan Friedman. 1982. " 'Capital' imperialism and exploitation in ancient world-systems." *Review* 4:87–109.

Eldredge, Niles and Stephen Jay Gould. 1972. "Punctuated equilibria: an alternative to phyletic gradualism." In Thomas J.M. Schopf (ed.), *Models in paleobiology.* San Francisco: Freeman, Cooper.

Ellison, Christopher and Gary Gereffi. 1990. "Explaining strategies and patterns of industrial development." In Gary Gereffi and Donald L. Wyman (eds), *Manufacturing miracles: paths of industrialization in Latin America and East Asia.* Princeton: Princeton University Press.

Elster, Jon. 1985. *Making sense of Marx.* Cambridge: Cambridge University Press.

Elvin, Mark. 1973. *The pattern of the Chinese past.* Stanford: Stanford University Press.

Engels, Friedrich. 1970. *The origin of the family, private property, and the state.* Edited by Eleanor Burke Leacock. New York: International Publishers. (Originally published 1884.)

Erickson, Robert and John H. Goldthorpe. 1993. *The constant flux: a study of class mobility in industrial societies.* Oxford: Oxford University Press (Clarendon Press).

Evans, Peter B. 1979. *Dependent development: the alliance of multinational, state, and local capital in Brazil.* Princeton: Princeton University Press.

—— 1987. "Class, state, and dependence in East Asia: lessons for Latin Americanists." In Frederic C. Deyo (ed.), *The political economy of the new Asian industrialism.* Ithaca, NY: Cornell University Press.

Fagan, Brian M. 1989. *People of the earth: an introduction to world prehistory.* Sixth edition. Glenview, Ill.: Scott, Foresman.

—— 1991. *Ancient North America: the archaeology of a continent.* New York: Thames & Hudson.

Feinman, Gary. 1991. "Demography, surplus, and inequality: early political formations in highland Mesoamerica." In Timothy Earle (ed.), *Chiefdoms: power, economy, and ideology.* New York: Cambridge University Press.

Fiedel, Stuart J. 1987. *Prehistory of the Americas.* New York: Cambridge University Press.

Fieldhouse, D.K. 1986. *Black Africa, 1945–1980: economic decolonization and arrested development.* Winchester, Mass.: Unwin Hyman.

Firebaugh, Glenn. 1992. "Growth effects of foreign and domestic investment." *American journal of sociology* 98:105–30.

Firebaugh, Glenn and Frank D. Beck. 1994. "Does economic growth benefit the masses? Growth, dependence, and welfare in the Third World." *American sociological review* 59:631–53.

Flora, Peter. 1983. *State, economy, and society in western Europe, 1815–1975.* Volume 1. Frankfurt: Campus Verlag.

Flynn, Dennis O. 1991. "Comparing the Tokugawa Shogunage with Hapsburg Spain: two silver-based empires in a global setting." In James D. Tracy (ed.), *The political economy of merchant empires.* New York: Cambridge University Press.

Forbes, R.J. 1954. "Extracting, smelting, and alloying." In Charles Singer, E.J. Holmyard, and A.R. Hall (eds), *A history of technology.* Volume 1. Oxford: Oxford University Press (Clarendon Press).

Fox, Edward Whiting. 1991. *The emergence of the modern European world.* Oxford: Blackwell.

Frame, J. Davidson. 1979. "National economic resources and the production of research in lesser developed countries." *Social studies of science* 9:233–46.

Frame, J. Davidson, Francis Narin, and Mark P. Carpenter. 1977. "The distribution of world science." *Social studies of science* 7:501–16.

Frank, Andre Gunder. 1966. "The development of underdevelopment." *Monthly review* 18(4):17–31.

—— 1967. "Sociology of development and underdevelopment of sociology." *Catalyst* 3:20–73.

—— 1969. *Capitalism and underdevelopment in Latin America.* New York: Monthly Review Press.

—— 1978. *World accumulation, 1492–1789.* New York: Monthly Review Press.

—— 1979. *Dependent accumulation and underdevelopment.* New York: Monthly Review Press.

—— 1980. *Crisis: in the world economy.* New York: Holmes & Meier.

—— 1987. "Political ironies in the world economy." In Terry Boswell and Albert Bergesen (eds), *America's changing role in the world-system*. New York: Praeger.

—— 1990. "A theoretical introduction to 5,000 years of world system history." *Review* 13:155–248.

—— 1991. "A plea for world system history." *Journal of world history* 2:1–28.

Freidel, David A. 1981. "Civilization as a state of mind: the cultural evolution of the lowland Maya." In Grant D. Jones and Robert R. Kautz (eds), *The transition to statehood in the New World*. New York: Cambridge University Press.

Fried, Morton. 1967. *The evolution of political society*. New York: Random House.

—— 1978. "The state, the chicken, and the egg: or, what came first?" In Ronald Cohen and Elman R. Service (eds), *Origins of the state: the anthropology of political evolution*. Philadelphia: Institute for the Study of Human Issues.

Friedman, Jonathan. 1982. "Catastrophe and continuity in social evolution." In Colin Renfrew, Michael J. Rowlands, and Barbara Abbott Segraves (eds), *Theory and explanation in archaeology*. New York: Academic Press.

Friedman, Jonathan and Michael Rowlands. 1978. "Notes toward an epigenetic model of the evolution of 'civilization.'" In Jonathan Friedman and Michael J. Rowlands (eds), *The evolution of social systems*. Pittsburgh: University of Pittsburgh Press.

Fröbel, Folker, Jürgen Heinrichs, and Otto Kreye. 1980. *The new international division of labour*. Cambridge: Cambridge University Press.

Galtung, Johan, Tore Heiestad, and Erik Rudeng. 1980. "On the decline and fall of empires: the Roman Empire and Western imperialism compared." *Review* 4:91–153.

Gardner, Peter M. 1991. "Foragers' pursuit of individual autonomy." *Current anthropology* 32:543–72.

Gerschenkron, Alexander. 1962. *Economic backwardness in historical perspective*. Cambridge: Harvard University Press.

Giddens, Anthony. 1981. *A contemporary critique of historical materialism*. Berkeley: University of California Press.

—— 1982. *Profiles and critiques in social theory*. Berkeley: University of California Press.

—— 1984. *The constitution of society.* Berkeley: University of California Press.

—— 1985. *The nation-state and violence.* Berkeley: University of California Press.

Gilbert, Alan. 1974. *Latin American development: a geographical perspective.* Harmondsworth, UK.: Penguin Books.

Gills, Barry K. and Andre Gunder Frank. 1991. "5,000 years of world system history: the cumulation of accumulation." In Christopher Chase-Dunn and Thomas D. Hall (eds), *Core/periphery relations in precapitalist worlds.* Boulder, Colo.: Westview Press.

Gilman, Antonio. 1981. "The development of social stratification in Bronze Age Europe." *Current anthropology* 22:1–23.

Gleick, James. 1987. *Chaos: making a new science.* New York: Penguin.

Goldfrank, Walter L. 1982. "The Soviet trajectory." In Christopher Chase-Dunn (ed.), *Socialist states in the world-system.* Beverly Hills, Calif.: Sage.

—— 1983. "The limits of analogy: hegemonic decline in Great Britain and the United States." In Albert Bergesen (ed.), *Crises in the world-system.* Beverly Hills, Calif.: Sage.

—— 1987. "Socialism or barbarism? The long-run fate of the capitalist world economy." In Terry Boswell and Albert Bergesen (eds), *America's changing role in the world-system.* New York: Praeger.

Goldsmith, Raymond W. 1987. *Premodern financial systems.* New York: Cambridge University Press.

Goldstein, Joshua S. 1988. *Long cycles: prosperity and war in the modern age.* New Haven: Yale University Press.

Goldstone, Jack A. 1991. *Revolution and rebellion in the early modern world.* Berkeley: University of California Press.

Gordon, David M. 1988. "The global economy: new edifice or crumbling foundations?" *New left review* 168:24–64.

Goudsblom, Johan, E.L. Jones, and Stephen Mennell. 1989. *Human history and social process.* Exeter, UK: University of Exeter Press.

Gould, Stephen Jay. 1989. *Wonderful life: the Burgess shale and the nature of history.* New York: Norton.

Gould, Stephen Jay and Niles Eldredge. 1977. "Punctuated equilibria: the tempo and mode of evolution reconsidered." *Paleobiology* 3:115–51.

Greaves, Richard L. 1969. "Puritanism and science: the anatomy of a controversy." *Journal of the history of ideas* 30:345–68.

Gunst, Péter. 1989. "Agrarian systems of central and eastern Europe." In Daniel Chirot (ed.), *The origins of backwardness in eastern Europe*. Berkeley: University of California Press.

Haas, Jonathan. 1982. *The evolution of the prehistoric state*. New York: Columbia University Press.

Haggard, Stephan. 1990. "Pathways from the periphery: the politics of growth in the newly industrializing countries." Ithaca, NY: Cornell University Press.

Hall, John A. 1985. *Powers and liberties: the causes and consequences of the rise of the West*. Berkeley: University of California Press.

Hall, John Whitney. 1970. *Japan: from prehistory to modern times*. New York: Delacorte Press.

Hall, Thomas D. and Christopher Chase-Dunn. 1992. "World-systems in prehistory." Paper presented at the annual meetings of the Society for American Archaeology, Pittsburgh.

Hammer, Heather-Jo and John W. Gartrell. 1986. "American penetration and Canadian development: a case study of mature dependency." *American sociological review* 51:201–13.

Hane, Mikiso. 1992. *Modern Japan: a historical survey*. Second edition. Boulder, Colo.: Westview.

Hanley, Susan B. 1972. "Population trends and economic development in Tokugawa Japan: the case of Bizen province in Okayama." In D.V. Glass and Roger Revelle (eds), *Population and social change*. London: Edward Arnold.

Hanley, Susan B. and Kozo Yamamura. 1972. "Population trends and economic growth in pre-industrial Japan." In D.V. Glass and Roger Revelle (eds), *Population and social change*. London: Edward Arnold.

Harlan, Jack R., J.M.J. de Wet, and Ann Stemler. 1976. "Plant domestication and indigenous African agriculture." In Jack R. Harlan, J.M.J. de Wet, and Ann Stemler (eds), *Origins of African plant domestication*. The Hague: Mouton.

Harris, David R. 1977. "Alternative pathways toward agriculture." In Charles A. Reed (ed.), *Origins of agriculture*. The Hague: Mouton.

Harris, Marvin. 1968. *The rise of anthropological theory*. New York: Crowell.

—— 1974. *Cows, pigs, wars, and witches: the riddles of culture*. New York: Random House.

444   *References*

—— 1977. *Cannibals and kings: the origins of cultures.* New York: Random House.

—— 1979. *Cultural materialism: the struggle for a science of culture.* New York: Random House.

—— 1985. *Good to eat: riddles of food and culture.* New York: Simon & Schuster.

Harris, Marvin and Eric B. Ross. 1987. *Death, sex, and fertility: population regulation in preindustrial and developing societies.* New York: Columbia University Press.

Harvey, David. 1989. *The condition of postmodernity.* Oxford: Basil Blackwell.

Hassan, Fekri A. 1981. *Demographic archaeology.* New York: Academic Press.

Hayden, Brian. 1981. "Research and development in the Stone Age: technological transitions among hunter-gatherers." *Current anthropology* 22:519–48.

—— 1990. "Nimrods, piscators, pluckers, and planters: the emergence of food production." *Journal of anthropological archaeology* 9:31–69.

Hechter, Michael and William Brustein. 1980. "Regional modes of production and patterns of state formation in western Europe." *American journal of sociology* 85:1061–94.

Heilbroner, Robert L. 1980. *An inquiry into the human prospect.* New York: Norton.

Helms, Mary W. 1979. *Ancient Panama: chiefs in search of power.* Austin: University of Texas Press.

Henry, Donald O. 1989. *From foraging to agriculture: the Levant at the end of the Ice Age.* Philadelphia: University of Pennsylvania Press.

Herman, Edward and James Petras. 1985. "Resurgent democracy: rhetoric and reality." *New left review* 154:83–98.

Hill, Christopher. 1953. "The transition from feudalism to capitalism." *Science and society* 17:348–51.

Hill, Kim, Hillard Kaplan, Kristen Hawkes, and Ana Magdelena Hurtado. 1985. "Men's time allocation to subsistence work among the Aché of eastern Paraguay." *Human ecology* 13:29–47.

Hobsbawm, Eric J. 1991. "Out of the ashes." In Robin Blackburn (ed.), *After the fall: the failure of communism and the future of socialism.* London: Verso.

Hodges, Henry. 1970. *Technology in the ancient world*. New York: Alfred A. Knopf.

Hogbin, H. Ian. 1964. *A Guadalcanal society: the Kaoka Speakers*. New York: Holt, Rinehart & Winston.

Holton, Robert J. 1981. "Marxist theories of social change and the transition from feudalism to capitalism." *Theory and society* 10: 833–67.

——— 1985. *The transition from feudalism to capitalism*. New York: St Martin's Press.

Hoogvelt, Ankie M.M. 1982. *The third world in global development*. London: Macmillan Press.

Hopkins, Terence K., Immanuel Wallerstein, and associates. 1982."Patterns of development of the modern world-system." In Terence K. Hopkins, Immanuel Wallerstein, and associates (eds), *World-systems analysis: theory and methodology*. Beverly Hills, Calif.: Sage.

Hoselitz, Bert F. 1960. *Sociological aspects of economic growth*. New York: Free Press.

Hoston, Germaine A. 1986. *Marxism and the crisis of development in prewar Japan*. Princeton: Princeton University Press.

Howell, David L. 1992. "Proto-industrial origins of Japanese capitalism." *Journal of Asian studies* 51:269–86.

Huff, Toby E. 1993. *The rise of early modern science: Islam, China, and the West*. New York: Cambridge University Press.

Hugill, Peter J. 1993. *World trade since 1431*. Baltimore: Johns Hopkins University Press.

Isbell, William H. and Katharina J. Schreiber. 1978. "Was Huari a state?" *American antiquity* 43:372–89.

Ishida, Takeshi and Ellis S. Krauss. 1989. "Democracy in Japan: issues and questions." In Takeshi Ishida and Ellis S. Krauss (eds), *Democracy in Japan*. Pittsburgh: University of Pittsburgh Press.

Israel, Jonathan I. 1989. *Dutch primacy in world trade, 1585–1740*. Oxford: Oxford University Press (Clarendon Press).

Jacobs, Norman. 1958. *The origin of modern capitalism and Eastern Asia*. Hong Kong: Hong Kong University Press.

Jannetta, Ann Bowman. 1987. *Epidemics and mortality in early modern Japan*. Princeton: Princeton University Press.

Jansen, Marius B. 1992. *China in the Tokugawa world*. Cambridge: Harvard University Press.

Janssen, Jac. J. 1978. "The early state in ancient Egypt." In Henri J.M.Claessen and Peter Skalnik (eds), *The early state*. The Hague: Mouton.

Johansen, J.H., H.W. Collins and J.A. Johnson. 1986. *American education*. Fifth edition. Dubuque, Iowa: Wm. C. Brown.

Johnson, Allen W. and Timothy Earle. 1987. *The evolution of human societies*. Stanford: Stanford University Press.

Jones, E.L. 1987. *The European miracle: environments, economies and geopolitics in the history of Europe and Asia*. Second edition. Cambridge: Cambridge University Press

—— 1988. *Growth recurring: economic change in world history*. Oxford: Oxford University Press (Clarendon Press).

Jowitt, Kenneth. 1978. *The Leninist response to national dependency*. Berkeley: University of California Institute of International Studies.

Kahn, Herman. 1993. "The Confucian ethic and economic growth." In Mitchell A. Seligson and John T. Passé-Smith (eds), *Development and underdevelopment: the political economy of inequality*. Boulder, Colo.: Lynne Rienner.

Kaneda, Tatsuo. 1988. "Gorbachev's economic reforms." In P. Juviler and H. Kimura (eds), *Gorbachev's reforms*. Hawthorne, NY: Aldine de Gruyter.

Kautsky, John H. 1982. *The politics of aristocratic empires*. Chapel Hill: University of North Carolina Press.

Kennedy, Paul. 1993. *Preparing for the twenty-first century*. New York: Random House.

Kerr, Clark, J.T. Dunlop, F.H. Harbison, and C.A. Myers. 1960. *Industrialism and industrial man*. Cambridge, Mass.: Harvard University Press.

Kiernan, V. G. 1965. "State and nation in western Europe." *Past and present* 31:20–38.

—— 1980. *State and society in Europe, 1550–1650*. New York: St Martin's Press.

Kirch, Patrick V. 1984. *The evolution of the Polynesian chiefdoms*. New York: Cambridge University Press.

—— 1988. "Circumscription theory and sociopolitical evolution in Polynesia." *American behavioral scientist* 31:416–27.

Kochanowicz, Jacek. 1989. "The Polish economy and the evolution of dependency." In Daniel Chirot (ed.), *The origins of backwardness in eastern Europe*. Berkeley: University of California Press.

References 447

Kohl, Philip 1987. "The ancient economy, transferable technologies and the Bronze Age world-system: a view from the northeastern frontier of the ancient Near East." In Michael Rowlands, Mogens Larsen, and Kristian Kristiansen (eds), *Centre and periphery in the ancient world*. Cambridge: Cambridge University Press.

Kohlberg, Lawrence. 1981. *The philosophy of moral development*. New York: Harper & Row.

Kolko, Gabriel. 1962. *Wealth and power in America*. New York: Praeger.

Kondratieff, Nikolai. 1984. *The long wave cycle*. New York: Richardson & Snyder. (Originally published 1928.)

Koo, Hagen. 1987. "The interplay of state, social class, and world system in East Asian development: the cases of South Korea and Taiwan." In Frederic C. Deyo (ed.), *The political economy of the new Asian industrialism*. Ithaca, NY: Cornell University Press.

Kornai, János. 1992. *The socialist system: the political economy of Communism*. Princeton: Princeton University Press.

Kranzberg, Melvin and Carroll W. Pursell, Jr. 1967. *Technology in Western civilization*. Volume 1. New York: Oxford University Press.

Kriedte, Peter, Hans Medick, and Jürgen Schlumbohm. 1981. *Industrialization before industrialization*. Cambridge: Cambridge University Press.

Kuhn, Thomas S. 1970. *The structure of scientific revolutions*. Second edition. Chicago: University of Chicago Press.

Kumar, Krishan. 1978. *Prophecy and progress: the sociology of industrial and post-industrial society*. Harmondsworth, UK: Penguin Books.

—— 1992. "The revolutions of 1989: socialism, capitalism, and democracy." *Theory and society* 21:309–56.

Kushnirsky, F. I. 1988. "Soviet economic reform: an analysis and a model." In S. Linz and W. Moskoff (eds), *Reorganization and reform in the Soviet economy*. Armonk, NY: Sharpe.

Lamberg-Karlovsky, C.C. and Jeremy A. Sabloff. 1979. *Ancient civilizations*. Prospect Heights, Ill.: Waveland Press.

Landes, David S. 1969. *The unbound Prometheus: technological change and industrial development in western Europe from 1750 to the present*. New York: Cambridge University Press.

Landsberg, Martin. 1979. "Export-led industrialization in the third world: manufacturing imperialism." *Review of radical political economics* 11:50–63.

Lane, David. 1984. "The structure of Soviet socialism: recent Western theoretical approaches." *Insurgent sociologist* 12:101–12.

Lane, Jan-Erik, David McKay, and Kenneth Newton. 1991. *Political data handbook: OECD countries*. New York: Oxford University Press.

Lapidus, Gail Warshofsky. 1988. "Gorbachev's agenda: domestic reforms and foreign policy reassessments." In P. Juviler and H. Kimura (eds), *Gorbachev's reforms*. Hawthorne, NY: Aldine de Gruyter.

Larrain, Jorge. 1989. *Theories of development*. Cambridge, UK: Polity Press.

Lash, Scott and John Urry. 1987. *The end of organized capitalism*. Madison: University of Wisconsin Press.

Laudan, Larry. 1977. *Progress and its problems: towards a theory of scientific growth*. Berkeley: University of California Press.

Lee, Richard B. 1968. "What hunters do for a living, or, how to make out on scarce resources." In Richard B. Lee and Irven DeVore (eds), *Man the hunter*. Chicago: Aldine.

——— 1972. "The !Kung bushmen of Botswana." In M. G. Bicchieri (ed.), *Hunters and gatherers today*. New York: Holt, Rinehart & Winston.

——— 1978. "Politics, sexual and nonsexual, in an egalitarian society." *Social science information* 17:871–95.

——— 1979. *The !Kung San: men, women, and work in a foraging society*. New York: Cambridge University Press.

——— 1984. *The Dobe !Kung*. New York: Holt, Rinehart & Winston.

——— 1990. "Primitive communism and the origin of social inequality." In Steadman Upham (ed.), *The evolution of political systems*. New York: Cambridge University Press.

Leggett, Robert E. 1988. "Gorbachev's reform program: 'radical' or more of the same?" In S. Linz and W. Moskoff (eds), *Reorganization and reform in the Soviet economy*. Armonk, NY: Sharpe.

Lenski, Gerhard. 1966. *Power and privilege: a theory of social stratification*. New York: McGraw-Hill.

——— 1970. *Human societies: a macro-level introduction to sociology*. New York: McGraw-Hill.

Lenski, Gerhard and Patrick D. Nolan. 1984. "Trajectories of development: a test of ecological–evolutionary theory." *Social forces* 63:1–23.

Le Roy Ladurie, Emmanuel. 1974. *The peasants of Languedoc.* Translated by J. Day. Champaign: University of Illinois Press.

Leupp, Gary P. 1992. *Servants, shophands, and laborers in the cities of Tokugawa Japan.* Princeton: Princeton University Press.

Lévy-Bruhl, Lucien. 1923. *Primitive mentality.* Translated by Lilian A. Clare. London: George Allen & Unwin.

Leys, Colin. 1982. "African economic development in theory and practice." *Daedalus* 111(2):99–124.

Liepitz, Alain. 1992. *Towards a new economic order: postfordism, ecology, and democracy.* Translated by Malcolm Slater. New York: Oxford University Press.

Lipset, Seymour Martin and Reinhard Bendix. 1959. *Social mobility in industrial society.* Berkeley: University of California Press.

Livi-Bacci, Massimo. 1992. *A concise history of world population.* Translated by Carl Ipsen. Oxford: Blackwell.

Lopez, Robert. 1971. *The commercial revolution of the middle ages, 950–1350.* Englewood Cliffs, NJ: Prentice-Hall.

Lukes, Steven. 1972. *Emile Durkheim: his life and work.* New York: Harper & Row.

McClelland, David C. 1961. *The achieving society.* Princeton: Van Nostrand.

McClelland, David C. and David G. Winter. 1969. *Motivating economic achievement.* New York: Free Press.

McCorriston, Joy and Frank Hole. 1991. "The ecology of seasonal stress and the origins of agriculture in the Near East." *American anthropologist* 93:46–69.

MacDonald, Peter. 1988. "Historical school reform and the correspondence principle." In M. Cole (ed.), *Bowles and Gintis revisited.* London: Falmer Press.

McIntosh, Susan Keech and Roderick J. McIntosh. 1988. "From stone to metal: new perspectives on the later prehistory of West Africa." *Journal of world prehistory* 2:89–133.

McNeill, William H. 1976. *Plagues and peoples.* Garden City, NY: Doubleday (Anchor Books).

—— 1982. *The pursuit of power: technology, armed force, and society since AD 1000.* Chicago: University of Chicago Press.

MacNeish, Richard (ed.). 1970. *The prehistory of the Tehuacán Valley.* Austin: University of Texas Press.

—— 1978. *The science of archaeology.* North Scituate, Mass.: Duxbury Press.

Mandel, Ernest. 1989. *Beyond perestroika: the future of Gorbachev's USSR.* Translated by Gus Fagan. London: Verso.

Mandelbaum, Maurice. 1971. *History, man, and reason: a study in nineteenth-century thought.* Baltimore: Johns Hopkins University Press.

Mann, Michael. 1986. *The sources of social power: Volume 1. A history of power from the beginning to AD 1760.* Cambridge: Cambridge University Press.

—— 1988. *States, war, and capitalism.* Oxford: Basil Blackwell.

—— 1993. *The sources of social power: Volume 2. The rise of classes and nation-states, 1760–1914.* New York: Cambridge University Press.

Marcus, Joyce. 1975. "The rise of the Classic Maya state." Paper presented at the annual meetings of the American Anthropological Association, San Francisco.

Marshall, T.H. 1964. *Class, citizenship, and social development.* Garden City, NY: Doubleday.

Marx, Karl. 1963. *Early writings.* Translated and edited by T.B. Bottomore. New York: McGraw-Hill. (Originally written 1844.)

—— 1967. *Capital.* Volume 1. New York: International Publishers. (Originally published 1867.)

Marx, Karl and Frederick Engels. 1959. *On colonialism.* Moscow: Progress Publishers. (Originally written 1850–94.)

Maryanski, Alexandra and Jonathan H. Turner. 1992. *The social cage: human nature and the evolution of society.* Stanford: Stanford University Press.

Maslow, Abraham H. 1971. *The farther reaches of human nature.* New York: Viking Press.

Meadows, Donella, Dennis L. Meadows, and Jørgen Randers. 1992. *Beyond the limits: confronting global collapse, envisioning a sustainable future.* Post Mills, Vt.: Chelsea Green.

Meadows, Donella, Dennis L. Meadows, Jørgen Randers, and William H. Behrens III. 1974. *The limits to growth.* Second edition. New York: Universe Books.

Mellars, Paul A. 1985. "The ecological basis of social complexity in the Upper Paleolithic of southwestern France." In T. Douglas Price and James A. Brown (eds), *Prehistoric hunter-gatherers.* New York: Academic Press.

Mendels, Franklin F. 1972. "Proto-industrialization: the first phase of the industrialization process." *Journal of economic history* 32: 241–61.

Merton, Robert K. 1957. *Social theory and social structure.* New York: Free Press.

—— 1970. *Science, technology, and society in seventeenth century England.* New York: Howard Fertig. (Originally published 1938.)

Meyer, John W., Francisco O. Ramirez, Richard Rubinson, and John Boli-Bennett. 1977. "The world educational revolution, 1950–1970." *Sociology of education* 50:242–58.

Meyer, John W., David Tyack, Joane Nagel, and Audri Gordon. 1979. "Public education as nation-building in America: enrollments and bureaucratization in the American states, 1870–1930." *American journal of sociology* 85:591–613.

Milisauskas, Sarunas. 1978. *European prehistory.* New York: Academic Press.

Miller, Daniel. 1985. "Ideology and the Harappan civilization." *Journal of anthropological archaeology* 4:34–71.

Minge-Klevana, Wanda. 1980. "Does labor time decrease with industrialization? A survey of time-allocation studies." *Current anthropology* 21:279–98.

Mitchell, B.R. 1992. *International historical statistics, Europe, 1750–1988.* Third edition. London: Macmillan Press.

—— 1993. *International historical statistics, the Americas, 1750–1988.* Second edition. London: Macmillan Press.

Modelski, George. 1978. "The long cycle of global politics and the nation-state." *Comparative studies in society and history* 20:214–35.

Mooers, Colin. 1991. *The making of bourgeois Europe.* London: Verso.

Moore, A.M.T. 1989. "The transition from foraging to farming in southwest Asia: present problems and future directions." In D.R. Harris and G.C. Hillman (eds), *Foraging and farming: the evolution of plant exploitation.* London: Unwin Hyman.

Moore, Barrington, Jr. 1966. *Social origins of dictatorship and democracy.* Boston: Beacon Press.

Morgan, Lewis Henry. 1974. *Ancient society, or researches in the lines of human progress from savagery through barbarism to civilization.* Gloucester, Mass.: Peter Smith. (Originally published 1877.)

Moseley, K.P. and Immanuel Wallerstein. 1978. "Precapitalist social structures." *Annual review of sociology* 4:259–90.

Moulder, Frances V. 1977. *Japan, China and the modern world economy*. New York: Cambridge University Press.

Mulligan, Lotte. 1973. "Civil War politics, religion, and the Royal Society." *Past and present* 59:92–116.

Nakamura, Satoru. 1990. "The development of rural industry." (Translated by J. Victor Koschmann). In Chie Nakane and Shinzaburo Oishi (eds), *Tokugawa Japan: the social and economic antecedents of modern Japan*. Translation edited by Conrad Totman. Tokyo: University of Tokyo Press.

Naroll, Raoul. 1967. "Imperial cycles and world order." *Peace research society papers* 7:83–101.

Ndabezitha, Siyabonga W. and Stephen K. Sanderson. 1988. "Racial antagonism and the origins of apartheid in the South African gold mining industry, 1886–1924: a split labor market analysis." In Cora Bagley Marrett and Cheryl Leggon (eds), *Research in race and ethnic relations*. Volume 5. Greenwich, Conn.: JAI Press.

Needham, Joseph. 1954–86. *Science and civilisation in China*. 6 volumes. Cambridge: Cambridge University Press.

Nisbet, Robert A. 1969. *Social change and history: aspects of the Western theory of development*. New York: Oxford University Press.

Nolan, Patrick D. and Gerhard Lenski. 1985. "Technoeconomic heritage, patterns of development, and the advantage of backwardness." *Social forces* 64:341–58.

Nove, Alec. 1989. *Glasnost in action: cultural renaissance in Russia*. London: Unwin Hyman.

Ogilvie, Sheilagh C. 1993. "Proto-industrialization in Europe." *Continuity and change* 8(2):159–79.

O'Donnell, Guillermo. 1973. *Modernization and bureaucratic authoritarianism*. Berkeley: University of California Institute of International Studies.

Oliver, Douglas. 1955. *A Solomon Island society: kinship and leadership among the Siuai of Bougainville*. Cambridge, Mass: Harvard University Press.

Pacey, Arnold. 1990. *Technology in world civilization*. Cambridge, Mass.: MIT Press.

Palat, Ravi, Kenneth Barr, James Matson, Vinay Bahl, and Nesar Ahmad. 1986. "The incorporation and peripheralization of south Asia, 1600–1950." *Review* 10:171–208.

Parkin, Frank. 1979. *Marxism and class theory: a bourgeois critique.* New York: Columbia University Press.

Parsons, Talcott. 1951. *The social system.* New York: Free Press.

—— 1960. *Structure and process in modern societies.* Glencoe, Ill.: Free Press.

—— 1966. *Societies: evolutionary and comparative perspectives.* Englewood Cliffs, NJ: Prentice-Hall.

—— 1967. *Sociological theory and modern society.* New York: Free Press.

—— 1971. *The system of modern societies.* Englewood Cliffs, NJ: Prentice-Hall.

Pearson, M.N. 1991. "Merchants and states." In James D. Tracy (ed.), *The political economy of merchant empires.* New York: Cambridge University Press.

Peaslee, Amos Jenkins. 1966–70. *Constitutions of nations.* Third edition. Volumes III and IV. The Hague: Martinus Nijhoff.

Petras, James. 1987. "The anatomy of state terror: Chile, El Salvador and Brazil." *Science and society* 51:314–38.

Phillips, Kevin. 1990. *The politics of rich and poor.* New York: Random House.

Phillipson, David W. 1985. *African archaeology.* Cambridge: Cambridge University Press.

Pollard, Sidney. 1981. *Peaceful conquest: the industrialization of Europe, 1760–1970.* New York: Oxford University Press.

Porter, Kirk H. 1918. *A history of suffrage in the United States.* Chicago: University of Chicago Press.

Possehl, Gregory L. 1990. "Revolution in the Urban Revolution: the emergence of Indus urbanization." *Annual review of anthropology* 19: 261–82.

Postan, M.M. 1972. *The medieval economy and society.* Berkeley: University of California Press.

Price, Derek de Solla. 1963. *Little science, big science.* New York: Columbia University Press.

Price, T. Douglas and James A. Brown. 1985. "Aspects of hunter-gatherer complexity." In T. Douglas Price and James A. Brown (eds), *Prehistoric hunter-gatherers.* New York: Academic Press.

Prigogene, Ilya and Isabelle Stengers. 1984. *Order out of chaos: man's new dialogue with nature.* New York: Bantam Books.

Pryor, Frederic L. 1983. "Causal theories about the origins of agriculture." In P. Uselding (ed.), *Research in economic history.* Volume 8. Greenwich, Conn.: JAI Press.

—— 1986. "The adoption of agriculture: some theoretical and empirical evidence." *American anthropologist* 88:879–97.

Rabb, Theodore K. 1965. "Religion and the rise of modern science." *Past and present* 31:111–26.

Ramirez, Francisco O. and John Boli. 1987. "The political construction of mass schooling: European origins and worldwide institutionalization." *Sociology of education* 60:2–17.

Ramirez, Francisco O. and Gili S. Drori. 1992. "The globalization of science: an institutionalist perspective." Paper presented at the annual meetings of the American Sociological Association, Pittsburgh.

Rathje, William L. 1971. "The origin and development of lowland Maya Classic civilization." *Amerian antiquity* 36:275–85.

—— 1972. "Praise the gods and pass the metates: a hypothesis of the development of lowland rainforest civilizations in Mesoamerica." In Mark P. Leone (ed.), *Contemporary archaeology.* Carbondale: Southern Illinois University Press.

Rawls, John. 1971. *A theory of justice.* Cambridge, Mass.: Harvard University Press.

Redding, Richard W. 1988. "A general explanation of subsistence change: from hunting and gathering to food production." *Journal of anthropological archaeology* 7:56–97.

Reischauer, Edwin O. 1956. "Japanese feudalism." In Rushton Coulborn (ed.), *Feudalism in history.* Princeton: Princeton University Press.

Rindos, David. 1980. "Symbiosis, instability, and the origins and spread of agriculture: a new model." *Current anthropology* 21: 751–72.

—— 1984. *The origins of agriculture: an evolutionary perspective.* New York: Academic Press.

—— 1989. "Darwinism and its role in the explanation of domestication." In D.R. Harris and G.C. Hillman (eds), *Foraging and farming: the evolution of plant exploitation.* Winchester, Mass.: Unwin Hyman.

Ronan, Colin A. and Joseph Needham. 1978–81. *The shorter science and civilisation in China.* 2 volumes. Cambridge: Cambridge University Press.

Rosenberg, Michael. 1990. "The mother of invention: evolutionary theory, territoriality, and the origins of agriculture." *American anthropologist* 92:399–415.

Ross, Robert J.S. and Kent C. Trachte. 1990. *Global capitalism: the new Leviathan.* Albany: State University of New York Press.

Rossides, Daniel. 1976. *The American class system.* Boston: Houghton Mifflin.

Rostow, W.W. 1960. *The stages of economic growth: a non-communist manifesto.* New York: Cambridge University Press.

Rowlands, Michael, Mogens Larsen, and Kristian Kristiansen (eds). 1987. *Centre and periphery in the ancient world.* Cambridge: Cambridge University Press.

Roxborough, Ian. 1979. *Theories of underdevelopment.* London: Macmillan Press.

Rozman, Gilbert. 1974. "Edo's importance in the changing Tokugawa society." *Journal of Japanese studies* 1:91–112.

Rubinson, Richard. 1986. "Class formation, politics, and institutions: schooling in the United States." *American journal of sociology* 92: 519–48.

Rueschemeyer, Dietrich. 1986. *Power and the division of labour.* Stanford: Stanford University Press.

Rueschemeyer, Dietrich, Evelyne Huber Stephens, and John D. Stephens. 1992. *Capitalist development and democracy.* Chicago: University of Chicago Press.

Runciman, W.G. 1989. *A treatise on social theory. Volume II: Substantive social theory.* Cambridge: Cambridge University Press.

Sahlins, Marshall D. 1958. *Social stratification in Polynesia.* Seattle: University of Washington Press.

—— 1960. "Evolution: specific and general." In Marshall D. Sahlins and Elman R. Service (eds), *Evolution and culture.* Ann Arbor: University of Michigan Press.

—— 1963. "Poor man, rich man, big man, chief: political types in Melanesia and Polynesia." *Comparative studies in society and history* 5:285–303.

—— 1972. *Stone Age economics.* Chicago: Aldine.

Sakudo, Yotaro. 1990. "The management practices of family business." (Translated by William B. Hauser). In Chie Nakane and Shinzaburo Oishi (eds), *Tokugawa Japan: the social and economic antecedents of modern Japan.* Translation edited by Conrad Totman. Tokyo: University of Tokyo Press.

Sanders, William T. 1972. "Population, agricultural history, and societal evolution in Mesoamerica." In Brian Spooner (ed.), *Population growth: anthropological implications.* Cambridge, Mass.: MIT Press.

—— 1984. "Pre-industrial demography and social evolution." In Timothy Earle (ed.), *On the evolution of complex societies.* Malibu, Calif.: Undena Publications.

Sanders, William T. and Deborah L. Nichols. 1988. "Ecological theory and cultural evolution in the Valley of Oaxaca." *Current anthropology* 29:33–80.

Sanders, William T. and Barbara J. Price. 1968. *Mesoamerica: the evolution of a civilization.* New York: Random House.

Sanders, William T. and David Webster. 1978. "Unilinealism, multilinealism, and the evolution of complex societies." In Charles L. Redman et al. (eds), *Social archaeology: beyond subsistence and dating.* New York: Academic Press.

Sanders, William T., Jeffrey R. Parsons, and Robert S. Santley. 1979. *The Basin of Mexico: ecological processes in the evolution of a civilization.* New York: Academic Press.

Sanderson, Stephen K. 1987. "Eclecticism and its alternatives." In John Wilson (ed.), *Current perspectives in social theory.* Volume 8. Greenwich, Conn.: JAI Press.

—— 1990. *Social evolutionism: a critical history.* Oxford: Basil Blackwell.

—— 1991a. *Macrosociology: an introduction to human societies.* Second edition. New York: HarperCollins.

—— 1991b. "The evolution of societies and world-systems." In Christopher Chase-Dunn and Thomas D. Hall (eds), *Core/periphery relations in precapitalist worlds.* Boulder, Colo.: Westview Press.

—— 1995. *Macrosociology: an introduction to human societies.* Third edition. New York: HarperCollins.

Sansom, George. 1961. *A history of Japan, 1334–1615.* Stanford: Stanford University Press.

Santley, Robert S. 1980. "Disembedded capitals reconsidered." *American antiquity* 45:132–45.

Schacht, Robert M. 1988. "Circumscription theory: a critical review." *American behavioral scientist* 31:438–48.

Schneider, Jane. 1977. "Was there a pre-capitalist world-system?" *Peasant studies* 6:20–9.

Schott, Thomas. 1991. "The world scientific community: globality and globalisation." *Minerva* 29:440–62.

—— 1993. "World science: globalization of institutions and partici-pation." *Science, technology, and human values* 18:196–208.
Service, Elman R. 1962. *Primitive social organization: an evolutionary perspective.* New York: Random House.
—— 1971. *Primitive social organization: an evolutionary perspective.* Second edition. New York: Random House.
—— 1975. *Origins of the state and civilization.* New York: Norton.
—— 1978. "Classical and modern theories of the origins of govern-ment." In Ronald Cohen and Elman R. Service (eds), *Origins of the state.* Philadelphia: Institute for the Study of Human Issues.
Sheldon, Charles David. 1958. *The rise of the merchant class in Tokugawa Japan, 1600–1868.* (Monographs of the Association for Asian Studies, V.) Locust Valley, NY: J.J. Augustin.
Singer, Charles, E.J. Holmyard, and A.R. Hall (eds). 1954. *A history of technology.* Volume I. Oxford: Oxford University Press (Clarendon Press).
Singer, Charles, E. J. Holmyard, A. R. Hall, and Trevor I. Williams (eds). 1956. *A history of technology.* Volume II. Oxford: Oxford University Press (Clarendon Press).
Skidmore, Thomas E. and Peter J. Smith. 1989. *Modern Latin America.* Second edition. New York: Oxford University Press.
Skocpol, Theda. 1977. "Wallerstein's world capitalist system: a theoretical and historical critique." *American journal of sociology* 82:1075–90.
Smith, Adam. 1776. *The wealth of nations.* Volume 1. New Rochelle, NY: Arlington House.
Smith, Philip E.L. and T. Cuyler Young, Jr. 1972. "The evolution of early agriculture and culture in Greater Mesopotamia: a trial model." In Brian Spooner (ed.), *Population growth: anthropological implications.* Cambridge, Mass.: MIT Press.
Smith, Thomas C. 1959. *The agrarian origins of modern Japan.* Stanford: Stanford University Press.
—— 1988. *Native sources of Japanese industrialization, 1750–1920.* Berkeley: University of California Press.
Smout, T.C. 1980. "Scotland and England: is dependency a symp-tom or a cause of underdevelopment?" *Review* 3:601–30.
So, Alvin Y. 1984. "The process of incorporation into the world-system: the case of China in the nineteenth century." *Review* 8:91–116.

—— 1990. *Social change and development: modernization, dependency, and world-system theories.* Newbury Park, Calif.: Sage.

Sorokin, Pitirim A. 1927. *Social mobility.* New York: Harper & Brothers.

—— 1957. *Social and cultural dynamics.* Revised and abridged edition. Boston: Porter Sargent.

Soysal, Yasemin Nuhoglu and David Strang. 1989. "Construction of the first mass education systems in nineteenth-century Europe." *Sociology of education* 62:277–88.

Spencer, Charles S. 1990. "On the tempo and mode of state formation: neoevolutionism reconsidered." *Journal of anthropological archaeology* 9:1–30.

Spencer, Daniel Lloyd. 1958. "Japan's pre-Perry preparation for economic growth." *American journal of economics and sociology* 17:195–216.

Spencer, Herbert. 1972. *Herbert Spencer on social evolution.* Edited with an introduction by J.D.Y. Peel. Chicago: University of Chicago Press.

Stanley, Steven M. 1979. *Macroevolution: pattern and process.* San Francisco: Freeman.

Stark, Barbara L. 1986. "Origins of food production in the New World." In David J. Meltzer, Don D. Fowler, and Jeremy A. Sabloff (eds), *American archaeology past and future.* Washington, DC: Smithsonian Institution Press.

Stearns, Peter N. 1993. *The industrial revolution in world history.* Boulder, Colo.: Westview Press.

Stephens, Evelyne Huber. 1989. "Capitalist development and democracy in South America." *Politics and society* 17:281–352.

Steward, Julian H. 1949. "Cultural causality and law: a trial formulation of the development of early civilizations." *American anthropologist* 51:1–27.

—— 1955. *Theory of culture change: the methodology of multilinear evolution.* Urbana: University of Illinois Press.

Stewart, Ian. 1989. *Does God play dice? The mathematics of chaos.* Oxford: Basil Blackwell.

Sugimoto, Masayoshi and David L. Swain. 1978. *Science and culture in traditional Japan, AD 600–1854.* Cambridge, Mass.: MIT Press.

Sweezy, Paul. 1976. "A critique." In Rodney Hilton (ed.), *The transition from feudalism to capitalism.* London: Verso. (Originally published 1950.)

Szelenyi, Ivan and Balazs Szelenyi. 1992. "Why socialism failed: causes of the disintegration of East European state socialism." Paper presented at the annual meetings of the American Sociological Association, Pittsburgh.

Szymanski, Albert. 1978. *The capitalist state and the politics of class.* Cambridge, Mass.: Winthrop.

—— 1979. *Is the red flag flying? The political economy of the USSR today.* London: Zed Press.

—— 1981. *The logic of imperialism.* New York: Praeger.

—— 1982. "The socialist world-system." In Christopher Chase-Dunn (ed.), *Socialist states in the world-system.* Beverly Hills, Calif.: Sage.

Taagepera, Rein. 1978. "Size and duration of empires: systematics of size." *Social science research* 7:108–27.

—— 1990. "Patterns of empire growth and decline." Unpublished paper, University of California, Irvine.

Taeuber, Irene B. 1958. *The population of Japan.* Princeton: Princeton University Press.

Tainter, Joseph A. 1988. *The collapse of complex societies.* New York: Cambridge University Press.

Takahashi, H.K. 1952. "The transition from feudalism to capitalism: a contribution to the Sweezy–Dobb controversy." *Science and society* 16: 313–45.

Testart, Alain. 1982. "The significance of food storage among hunter-gatherers: residence patterns, population densities, and social inequalities." *Current anthropology* 23:523–37.

—— 1988. "Some major problems in the social anthropology of hunter-gatherers." *Current anthropology* 29:1–32.

Thomas, Keith. 1964. "Work and leisure in pre-industrial society." *Past and present* 29:50–66.

Tilly, Charles. 1983. "Flows of capital and forms of industry in Europe, 1500–1900." *Theory and society* 12:123–42.

—— 1990. *Coercion, capital, and European states, AD 990–1990.* Oxford: Basil Blackwell.

Toby, Ronald P. 1984. *State and diplomacy in early modern Japan.* Princeton: Princeton University Press.

Trigger, Bruce. 1982. "The rise of civilization in Egypt." In J.D.

Clark (ed.), *The Cambridge history of Africa*. Volume 1. Cambridge: Cambridge University Press.

Trow, Martin. 1966. "The second transformation of American secondary education." In Reinhard Bendix and Seymour Martin Lipset (eds), *Class, status, and power*. Second edition. New York: Free Press.

Turnbull, Colin M. 1961. *The forest people: a study of the pygmies of the Congo*. New York: Simon & Schuster (Touchstone).

Tylecote, Andrew B. 1982. "German ascent and British decline, 1870–1980: the role of upper-class structure and values." In Edward Friedman (ed.), *Ascent and decline in the world-system*. Beverly Hills, Calif.: Sage.

Tylor, Edward Burnett. 1871. *Primitive culture: researches into the development of mythology, philosophy, religion, language, art, and custom*. 2 volumes. London: John Murray.

—— 1916. *Anthropology: an introduction to the study of man and civilization*. New York: D. Appleton. (First edition 1881.)

United Nations. 1948. *Statistical yearbook*. New York: United Nations.

—— 1992a. *Human development report*. New York: United Nations.

—— 1992b. *Statistical yearbook*. New York: United Nations.

US Bureau of the Census. 1992. *Statistical abstract of the United States*. Washington, DC: US Government Printing Office.

van den Berghe, Pierre L. and Peter Frost. 1986. "Skin color preference, sexual dimorphism, and sexual selection: a case of gene–culture coevolution?" *Ethnic and racial studies* 9:87–113.

Villarreal, René. 1990. "The Latin American strategy of import substitution: failure or paradigm for the region?" In Gary Gereffi and Donald L. Wyman (eds), *Manufacturing miracles: paths of industrialization in Latin America and East Asia*. Princeton: Princeton University Press.

Vlastos, Stephen. 1986. *Peasant protests and uprisings in Tokugawa Japan*. Berkeley: University of California Press.

Wagar, W. Warren. 1992. *A short history of the future*. Second edition. Chicago: University of Chicago Press.

Wallerstein, Immanuel. 1974a. "The rise and future demise of the world capitalist system: concepts for comparative analysis." *Comparative studies in society and history* 16:387–415.

—— 1974b. *The modern world-system: capitalist agriculture and the origins of the European world-economy in the sixteenth century.* New York: Academic Press.

—— 1979. *The capitalist world-economy.* New York: Cambridge University Press.

—— 1980a. *The modern world-system II: mercantilism and the consolidation of the European world-economy, 1600–1750.* New York: Academic Press.

—— 1980b. "One man's meat: the Scottish great leap forward." *Review* 3:631–40.

—— 1982. "Crisis as transition." In Samir Amin et al., *Dynamics of global crisis.* New York: Monthly Review Press.

—— 1983. *Historical capitalism.* London: Verso.

—— 1984. *The politics of the world-economy.* New York: Cambridge University Press.

—— 1985. "The three stages of African involvement in the world-economy." In Peter C.W. Gutkind and Immanuel Wallerstein (eds), *Political economy of contemporary Africa.* Second edition. Beverly Hills, Calif.: Sage.

—— 1987. "The United States and the world 'crisis.' " In Terry Boswell and Albert Bergesen (eds.), *America's changing role in the world-system.* New York: Praeger.

—— 1989. *The modern world-system III: the second era of great expansion of the capitalist world-economy, 1730–1840s.* San Diego: Academic Press.

—— 1992. "The West, capitalism, and the modern world-system." *Review* 15:561–619.

Warren, Bill. 1973. "Imperialism and capitalist industrialization." *New left review* 81:3–44.

—— 1980. *Imperialism: pioneer of capitalism.* London: Verso.

Watson, Patty Jo. 1989. "Early plant cultivation in the eastern woodlands of North America." In D.R. Harris and G.C. Hillman (eds), *Foraging and farming: the evolution of plant exploitation.* London: Unwin Hyman.

Webb, Malcolm C. 1973. "The Petén Maya decline viewed in the perspective of state formation." In T. Patrick Culbert (ed.), *The Classic Maya collapse.* Albuquerque: University of New Mexico Press.

—— 1975. "The flag follows trade: an essay on the necessary interaction of military and commercial factors in state formation." In C.C. Lamberg-Karlovsky and Jeremy A. Sabloff (eds), *Ancient civilization and trade*. Albuquerque: University of New Mexico Press.

Webber, Carolyn and Aaron Wildavsky. 1986. *A history of taxation and expenditure in the Western world*. New York: Simon & Schuster.

Weber, Max. 1958. *The Protestant ethic and the spirit of capitalism*. New York: Charles Scribner's Sons. (Originally published 1904.)

—— 1976. *The agrarian sociology of ancient civilisations*. Translated by R.I. Frank. London: New Left Books. (Originally published 1896/1909.)

—— 1981. *General economic history*. Translated by Frank H. Knight. With an introduction by Ira J. Cohen. New Brunswick, NJ: Transaction Books. (Originally published 1927.)

Wenke, Robert J. 1990. *Patterns in prehistory: humankind's first three million years*. Third edition. New York: Oxford University Press.

White, Benjamin. 1982. "Child labour and population growth in rural Asia." *Development and change* 13:587–610.

White, James W. 1988. "State growth and popular protest in Tokugawa Japan." *Journal of Japanese studies* 14:1–25.

White, Leslie A. 1943. "Energy and the evolution of culture." *American anthropologist* 45:335–56.

—— 1959. *The evolution of culture*. New York: McGraw-Hill.

White, Lynn, Jr. 1962. *Medieval technology and social change*. New York: Oxford University Press.

Wilkinson, David. 1992. "Cities, civilizations, and oikumenes: I." *Comparative civilizations review* 27:51–87.

—— 1993. "Cities, civilizations, and oikumenes: II." *Comparative civilizations review* 28:41–72.

Wilkinson, Richard G. 1973. *Poverty and progress: an ecological perspective on economic development*. New York: Praeger.

Wittfogel, Karl A. 1957. *Oriental despotism: a comparative study of total power*. New Haven: Yale University Press.

Wolf, Eric R. 1982. *Europe and the people without history*. Berkeley: University of California Press.

Woodburn, James. 1968. "An introduction to Hadza ecology." In Richard B. Lee and Irven DeVore (eds), *Man the hunter*. Chicago: Aldine.

World Bank. 1992. *World development report*. New York: Oxford University Press.

Wright, Erik Olin. 1979. *Class structure and income determination.* New York: Academic Press.
—— 1985. *Classes.* London: Verso.
Wright, Henry T. 1986. "The evolution of civilizations." In David J. Meltzer, Don D. Fowler, and Jeremy A. Sabloff (eds), *American archaeology past and future.* Washington, DC: Smithsonian Institution Press.
Wright, Henry T. and Gregory A. Johnson. 1975. "Population, exchange, and early state formation in southwestern Iran." *American anthropologist* 77: 267–89.
Wuthnow, Robert. 1980. "The world-economy and the institutionalization of science in seventeenth-century Europe." In Albert Bergesen (ed.), *Studies of the modern world-system.* New York: Academic Press.
Yamamura, Kozo. 1980. "The agricultural and commercial revolution in Japan, 1550–1650." In Paul Uselding (ed.), *Research in economic history.* Volume 5. Greenwich, Conn.: JAI Press.
Yellen, J. E. 1977. *Archaeological approaches to the present: models for reconstructing the past.* New York: Academic Press.
Yoffee, Norman. 1988. "Orienting collapse." In Norman Yoffee and George L. Cowgill (eds), *The collapse of ancient states and civilizations.* Tucson: University of Arizona Press.
Yoshihara, Kunio. 1986. *Japanese economic development.* Second edition. Tokyo: Oxford University Press.
Zeitlin, Irving M. 1973. *Rethinking sociology: a critique of contemporary theory.* Englewood Cliffs, NJ: Prentice-Hall.
Zemtsov, Ilya and John Farrar. 1989. *Gorbachev: the man and the system.* New Brunswick, NJ: Transaction Books.
Zhimin, An. 1989. "Prehistoric agriculture in China." In D.R. Harris and G.C. Hillman (eds), *Foraging and farming: the evolution of plant exploitation.* London: Unwin Hyman.
Zipf, George Kingsley. 1965. *Human behavior and the principle of least effort.* New York: Hafner. (Originally published 1949.)
Zolberg, Aristide R. 1981. "Origins of the modern world system: a missing link." *World politics* 33:253–81.
Zvelebil, Marek. 1986. "Mesolithic societies and the transition to farming: problems of time, scale, and organisation." In Marek Zvelebil (ed.), *Hunters in transition.* Cambridge: Cambridge University Press.

Index

Abonyi, Arpad   260, 261
absolutism   285–7
Abu Hureyra   24
Abu-Lughod, Janet   110, 121,
   123, 160, 162–4, 328
Aché (of Paraguay)   338, 342
Adams, Richard E.W.   65, 66, 78
Adams, Robert M.   59, 69
adaptation   9–12, 13, 392–7
Africa   61–2, 69, 72, 85, 193;
   agriculture in   27–8;
   civilization and the state in
   60–2; and world-system
   theory   227–30
Aganbegyan, Abel   266
agency   12–13, 400
agrarian states   352, 382;
   dynastic cycles   101–2;
   evolutionary dynamics   96–8,
   132–3; forms of social
   growth   103–13; growth
   versus evolution   98–103; old
   and new   229–30; as
   precapitalist world-systems
   113, 120–5; social change in
   98–113; social devolution and
   collapse of   125–32
agriculture, and cultural
   selectionist theory   46–8, 49;
   explanation of worldwide
   transition to   34–8; origin

of   383; origin of, as automatic
   technological growth   35–6,
   52; and population pressure
   theories   36–42, 49; and
   resource stress theories   44–6,
   49; and theories emphasizing
   climate changes   42–4, 49;
   true   23; worldwide
   transition to   23–4, 50, 51
Algaze, Guillermo   121
Ali Kosh   24
alienation   353, 378, 397
Allen, Mitchell   121
Amazon Basin   30
Amin, Samir   96, 122, 169, 207,
   208, 227
Anasazi (of American
   Southwest)   31
Anatolia   24
Anderson, Perry   129–30,
   136–8, 165, 167, 172, 173, 176,
   285–6, 287, 288
Angel, J. Lawrence   340
Apter, David E.   212
Arab world   326–7, 391
Arrighi, Giovanni   368; and
   Drangel, Jessica   182, 241
Asia   25, 121, 192, 221–7; and
   world-system theory 221–7,
   228–30
Asiatic mode of production   135

About the Author

STEPHEN K. SANDERSON is professor of sociology at Indiana University of Pennsylvania, where he has taught for the past 24 years. He is the author of numerous articles and the author or editor of four other books: *Macrosociology: An Introduction to Human Societies* (4th ed., Longman 1999), *Social Evolutionism: A Critical History* (Blackwell 1990), *Civilizations and World Systems: Studying World-Historical Change* (AltaMira Press 1995), and *Sociological Worlds: Comparative and Historical Readings on Society* (Roxbury Press 1995). He is currently at work on a book entitled *Synthetic Materialism: An Integrated Theory of Human Society,* to be published by Rowman and Littlefield.